Humanae Vitae

A GENERATION LATER

Humanae Vitae

A GENERATION LATER

Janet E. Smith

The Catholic University of America Press

Washington, D.C.

The paper used in this publication meets the minimum
requirements of American National Standards for Information
Science—Permanence of Paper for Printed Library materials,
ANSI Z39.48-1984.
∞

Library of Congress Cataloging-in-Publication Data
Smith, Janet E., 1950–
    Humanae Vitae: a generation later / by Janet E. Smith
        p.   cm.
    Includes bibliographical references and index.
    ISBN 0-8132-0739-8 (alk. paper). — ISBN 0-8132-0740-1 (pbk. :
alk. paper)
        1. Birth control—Religious aspects—Catholic Church.   2. Catholic
Church. Pope (1963–1978 : Paul VI). Humanae Vitae.   1. Title.
HQ766.3.S57   1991
241'.66—DC20   90-39456

Contents

Contents

Preface

It is to say nothing controversial to say that *Humanae Vitae* is a document that has met with much criticism both on its promulgation and still today. Many think it failed to meet the challenge given to Vatican II to bring the Church into the modern world; some critics argue that it contradicts the view of marriage articulated in *Gaudium et Spes*. Many, even those who respect the wisdom of *Humanae Vitae*, lament that the document does not provide sufficient or convincing argumentation for the teaching that it sets forth. It has also been said that the document provides no new insight into why the Church condemns contraception: it just reiterates the tired and unconvincing arguments rooted in a moral theology grounded in an antiquated theory of natural law.

The Church's teaching on contraception was virtually unchallenged within the Church until the middle decades of this century. The reasons for the challenge were many and are forthrightly acknowledged in *Humanae Vitae;* the perceived population explosion and the discovery of the anovulant pill are generally mentioned among the most notable of these reasons. Many argued that a change in Church teaching would simply be a legitimate and even inevitable doctrinal development of moral norms for sexual intercourse within marriage. They argued that the Church had slightly modified its teaching on marital sexuality several times in its history and that the permission to use contraception would simply be another appropriate modification necessitated by a deeper appreciation of the values of conjugal love. They maintained that the Church had not fully realized the personalist values of conjugal love and thus had not seen that they could, for serious reasons, supersede the procreative values, as long as these values were preserved in the whole of the marriage.

Humanae Vitae was written to reassert the Church's unbroken condemnation of the use of contraception. *Humanae Vitae* is terse and compact; clearly it is not designed to present a full-scale defense of Church teaching on the proper means of regulating family size and related matters. Although there is more argumentation or justification provided than is customarily conceded, much of the document relies on argumentation or principles established elsewhere within the Catholic tradition of moral theology. It is not intended to stand alone. This book strives to expand some of the compressed arguments of the document and to explain some of the principles of Catholic moral thought that justify some of the claims made.

As the debate about contraception has developed, it has become clear that a change in the Church's teaching on contraception would not be only a slight modification, a logical development of traditionally honored teachings, but would have radical implications for other fundamental claims of the Church. Consequently, one aim of this book is to show that the differences between opponents and supporters of contraception are far greater and more unbridgeable than might be supposed. Yet, most ardent advocates of each side are, almost without exception, Catholics, whom most would expect to share a basic view of reality. A constant question, then, will be, What accounts for the different assessments of contraception between those who seem to have so much in common? This will lead to the question, Is the controversy a result of a disagreement over the application of principles or is it over more fundamental principles?

The earlier stages of the debate would lead one to expect that those who maintained that contraception is morally permissible would seek to clarify the importance of the personalist values of conjugal love and show how the use of contraception preserves or promotes these. But, for the most part, this is not the direction that their arguments have taken. Rather, those who approved of contraception began to revise their understanding of traditional natural law theory. In the light of the assault on traditional natural law theory, one would also have expected a defense of natural law by those who defended *Humanae Vitae* and its condemnation of contraception. But, again, although there has been vigorous support for the document from those who argue from natural law principles, often it is a revised version of natural law from which they argue.

What is especially significant, though, is the very energetic defense of *Humanae Vitae* made by those who argue from a perspective of "personalist values." They agree that it is important to develop a deeper appreciation of the personalist values of conjugal love and that as we do, we will come to understand better why contraception is intrinsically wrong. Tracing the development of the arguments of the opposing positions will be one of the subthemes of this book. We shall see that the challenge to the Church's teaching on contraception provoked a refinement and broadening of arguments by moral theologians of both persuasions. Eventually the opponents came to differ radically on such fundamental questions as Man's relation to nature, God's relation to nature, and the very nature of reality itself. And perhaps an even more fundamental difference has emerged in their anthropology or their understanding of Man. Of great concern to Catholics are the most fundamental differences that have emerged about the proper role of conscience and of the authority and nature of the Catholic Church itself. This book will discuss all the differences but focus on those that bear most directly on the kinds of arguments that can be provided for or that challenge the central teaching of the document, the condemnation of contraception.

Chapter 1 attempts to define the dimensions of the debate through a comparison of the reports that came out of the Papal Commission that advised Paul VI. The seeds of the later arguments against *Humanae Vitae* are present in these reports.

The discussion of these works and much of the analysis of *Humanae Vitae* are often embroiled in a detailed philosophical analysis of points that many will regard as quibbles. Although it is the view of this author that these seemingly minute distinctions are of the utmost importance, there is a danger that the grand and ennobling view of human destiny and the role of marriage in that destiny that ultimately informs *Humanae Vitae* might be lost in philosophical and theological clarifications. Chapter 2, in particular, attempts to convey some of the grandeur of the Catholic view of marriage and childbearing as it reviews the teachings of *Casti Connubii* and *Gaudium et Spes*.

Chapters 3 and 4 provide an analysis of *Humanae Vitae* itself and thus constitute the heart of the book. Chapter 3 reviews how the encyclical deals with arguments that had been advanced in favor of contraception, especially those based on the principle of totality. It also explains the concept of natural law employed by the encyclical and argues that most have misunderstood the type of natural law argument that the encyclical offers. Chapter 4 concentrates on four arguments against contraception based on natural law principles and found in the text of *Humanae Vitae*.

Chapter 5 takes up some of the theological considerations that bear on the teaching of the encyclical. It briefly reviews the scriptural support for the teaching and provides an extensive discussion of the word *munus* (a word that has many meanings, among them, "gift," "reward," "duty," "task," and "mission"). This word and concept play a predominant role in the documents of Vatican II; its presence in the first line of *Humanae Vitae* suggests that this concept is one of the key links between *Humanae Vitae* and the teachings of Vatican II. Chapter 5 closes with a discussion of the questions of conscience and the infallibility of the teaching of *Humanae Vitae*.

Chapter 6 begins the consideration of the aftermath of *Humanae Vitae*. The early arguments of those who dissented from *Humanae Vitae*, particularly the works of Rev. Charles E. Curran and Bernard Haering, C.SS.R., are considered. These initial attempts at dissent have developed into a very focused challenge to the traditional means of evaluating moral action. This challenge, examined in Chapter 7, rejects the claim that any kind of action is intrinsically immoral. Rather, revisionists argue that some actions may involve premoral or ontic evil but that no kind of action can be judged before a consideration of the circumstances in which an action takes place.

Chapter 8, the final chapter, provides an exposition of the views of John Paul II, the most energetic theological defender of *Humanae Vitae*. He pursues a unique path of justification for the teaching of the document, a path based on interpretations of a few key texts from Scripture and based on an understanding of the meaning of human sexuality thoroughly shaped by personalist values.

Appendix 1 is a new translation of *Humanae Vitae*. Providing a new translation is not a condemnation of those currently available. The meaning of *Humanae Vitae* is sufficiently problematic to make it desirable that there be several translations available; consulting the several translations should assist those who cannot read Latin and Italian in puzzling out the meaning of the text. All of the currently available translations are based not on the official Latin text (though they occasionally make some selective reference to it) but on the Italian, which reportedly is the language in which *Humanae Vitae* was written. Thus the translation offered here has the distinction of being the only one based primarily on the Latin text. Surely it is important to have a translation based on the official text, but there are other virtues to translating from the Latin. As the analysis of the word *munus* in Chapter 5 establishes, the Latin displays the encyclical's links with previous Church teaching, with the philosophical and theological language of the Church, that modern languages simply cannot have.

Appendix 2 is a commentary on the text of *Humanae Vitae* that consists primarily of a review of the content of the relevant passages from the documents cited in the footnotes to *Humanae Vitae*. Several other appendices deal with special topics.

One important distinction of vocabulary must be noted. The text frequently refers to "birth control," "artificial birth control," and "contraception." As used in the following text *birth control* refers to any effort made to limit family size, which would include all forms of natural family planning requiring some period of abstinence and all contraceptives, that is, all devices and drugs used to prevent conception, all actions taken to impede the union of egg and sperm, before, during, or after intercourse. The terms *artificial birth control* and *contraceptives* are used synonymously. These distinctions are not meant to prejudge the question of the moral equivalency of natural forms of family planning and contraceptives; they are meant to preserve an important distinction about how they work, which may or may not have implications for the moral evaluations of these actions. Whether there is any moral difference between using a thermometer and chart to gauge a woman's period of fertility and using a condom, pill, or other contraceptive device is a question directly addressed at several points in the chapters that follow.

Let me explain a typographical oddity used in this book. I believe that we abandon the generic *man* and *he* at the peril of rendering more inaccessible many great works of literature. For if we train young people to understand that *man* and *he* always refer to the male, they will be sorely misled in reading literature of the past. And the inelegant *he/she, he or she* configurations have made many a text unreadable and will be used only on the rare occasion here. Nonetheless, I do not wish to offend the sensitivities of those who think relentless reference to *man* and *he* tends to give the impression that more than half of the human species is excluded. A compromise practice has been adopted of capitalizing *Man* whenever the reference is to the genus man, that is, whenever the reference is meant to be inclusive of both male and female. Forms of the pronoun *he* will not be capitalized, a dignity accorded to God and His Son alone. Thus, a sentence that reads, "Since Man is a social animal, it is good for him to structure harmonious societies" refers to all human beings of both sexes and all races and all religions. Citations from other texts remain unaltered.

Few comprehensive works on contraception from a philosophical or theological point of view have been written. Germain Grisez's *Contraception and the Natural Law* and John Noonan's *Contraception* were both published before *Humanae Vitae* was issued. More than two decades have passed since *Humanae Vitae* was promulgated. This is, perhaps, a good vantage point from which to assess the status of a document, especially one that had such a traumatic entry into the world. *Humanae Vitae* has unquestionably received more opposition than support. Some argue that it is permissible, if not obligatory, for Catholics to dissent from the teachings of such Church documents as encyclicals when they disagree with these teachings. They also maintain that before such dissent is legitimate, Catholics must first give the document an intelligent, open, and respectful reading. Yet how many Catholics have given this sort of reading to *Humanae Vitae*? This book grew out of the desire to assist Catholics in reading *Humanae Vitae* intelligently, openly, and respectfully. It will explain many fundamentals of Catholic moral reasoning, not because it is meant to be an elementary introduction to Catholic moral reasoning, but because it has been losing sight of the fundamentals that has led many, even prominent and influential theologians, to misunderstand some of the teachings of *Humanae Vitae*.

There is a whole generation of adult Catholics who were born after *Humanae Vitae*; they may be interested in learning of the turmoil out of which this document grew and that it fomented. Indeed, some sense that there has been a veritable revolution in moral theology since, and in part because of, its issuance. It seems the proper time to assess the nature of the challenge to the Church's teaching and to evaluate the strength of the response to this challenge. The views of both dissenters and defenders receive considerable attention in the pages that follow.

The half-attentive reader will soon realize that the author finds the teaching of *Humanae Vitae* to be true, wise, and authentically Christian, in part because she finds the arguments of the defenders to be stronger and more persuasive. This book owes a great deal to the work of many theologians who have worked zealously to convey the wisdom of the moral principles informing *Humanae Vitae*. Unfortunately much of their work has appeared in rather out-of-the-way journals; it would be much to the purpose of this work if it should draw attention to these articles. This book also owes a great deal to the work of those who have challenged Church teaching. Indeed, all those who have attempted to meet the challenge of the dissenters acknowledge that the exercise has forced them to clarify and deepen their understanding of the principles of Catholic moral thought. This book seeks to represent the strengths of both the opposition and the defense faithfully and to assess them judiciously.

The Catholic condemnation of contraception has become a source of mystery for very many Catholics and non-Catholics alike, in an age that thinks no more of using contraception than of taking aspirin. It is hoped that the explanations here will, together with the work of others, help those who are interested in and who wish to understand better the unswerving opposition of the teaching magisterium of the Catholic Church to all forms of contraception.

The study of the ethical issue of contraception necessarily involves the study of the documents of the Church, here, obviously, especially *Humanae Vitae*. One particular grace is asked of the reader: not to understand all sentences that begin with "The Church teaches" or with "Pope X states" as appeals to authority. My reference to such documents is to them as sources of information and argumentation. This book attempts to provide philosophical defenses for the Church's teaching and to expand upon its argumentation. A theological defense, on the other hand, would begin with a call to

Christian discipleship and a statement of the nature of the Church. Since it has been largely theologians who have addressed the ethical issue of contraception and since the Church naturally provides both theological and philosophical defenses of its own position, it has not been possible to remain entirely free from a theological context. Still, the arguments advanced against contraception in *Humanae Vitae* and in this book are centered on natural law principles, not theological ones. As a part of a full consideration of *Humanae Vitae*, the authoritative status of *Humanae Vitae* is discussed in Chapter 5, but, again, this is done for informational purposes, not to justify appeals to the document as authoritative.

Finally, many thanks must be given to the supporters of *Humanae Vitae* who have cheered and helped this book along the way. I would first like to thank my parents and my many married friends and acquaintances who live by the Church's teaching and have greatly edified and inspired me by their deep faith, their generous spirits, their happy marriages, and their exemplary family life. In fear that I may omit the names of any of those who offered their assistance, in a more direct way let me take this opportunity to thank (in no particular order) Ron Tacelli, S.J., Marc Calegari, S.J., Ralph McInerny, Fred Everett and Lisa Everett, Steve Brock, Dave Twetten, Peter Finnigan, Germain Grisez, William May, Joseph Boyle, James Lehrberger, O.Cist., the Costanzo Foundation, Monsignor Richard Malone, John Kippley, William Frank, John Crosby, Mark Lowery, Lance Simmons, Ger Wegemer, Fred Freddoso, Barry Jones, Suzie Andres, and John Finnis. Few if any of the above would agree with all the claims I defend, but without their help this book would be much the worse. I do not doubt that my arguments will meet with much criticism both from those who oppose and those who support the Church's teachings, but if it serves in some way to advance the debate, and better yet, to convince some to teach more fervently and live more truly by the Church's teaching, I will consider my labor successful.

Humanae Vitae

A GENERATION LATER

ONE

Beginnings of the Debate

WHAT ARE THE main points of disagreement about the morality of contraception? Why is it that so many think the use of contraception is morally justifiable and a sign of responsibility, whereas others count it among the grave sins against marriage? It is striking that the most ardent voices on each side are Catholics who, one would think, share fundamental values. But we find Catholics disagreeing about the purpose of marriage, about the place of children within marriage, about how one comes to discern God's will about marriage as well as about the morality of contraception. Moreover, in the last two decades Catholic moral theologians have experienced a veritable division in their ranks and have found that they have very serious disagreements about the principles that ought to inform moral decision making. What could account for the sharp disagreement among them on these matters? It would be strange to say that the encyclical *Humanae Vitae* was the cause of these disagreements, but it is probably true to say that *Humanae Vitae* disclosed the initial stirrings of these disagreements and that the dissent against the encyclical has sharpened them.

For whom was *Humanae Vitae* written? First, it seems fair to say that it was not written to convince skeptical non-Christians. This is not to say that Pope Paul VI thought the arguments of *Humanae Vitae* would be unpersuasive to non-Catholics—indeed, it is addressed to "men of good will" as well as Christians. Insofar as anyone accepts the principles of natural law and has an authentic understanding of the nature of marriage, he or she, in the understanding of the Church, should also object to contraception. *Humanae Vitae* was written, though, primarily as a teaching document for Catholics, that is, to instruct Catholics, who were expected to have identifiable fundamental beliefs in common; it therefore drew on principles that have had a revered place in the Catholic philosophical and theological tradition. Nor is this to say that the teaching of the document could be expected to be unproblematic for those who share these beliefs and know how to apply these principles; the arguments are complicated enough that questions can be raised about links in the arguments even by those predisposed to accept them. But what is most certainly the case is that there should be no expectation that those who do not share the principles traditionally employed by the Church in moral teaching will find the arguments convincing or satisfactory.

It should also be kept in mind that *Humanae Vitae* was not designed to defend the principles informing its teaching. Rather, it relied on principles developed throughout the history of the Church. Portions of this chapter and later chapters of this book will examine and to some extent explain these principles and the contemporary challenge to them. But what this chapter hopes to establish is the grounds of disagreement for the dispute surrounding *Humanae Vitae*: it will show that although the early advocates for a change in Church teaching did not think they were promoting a radical change in the Church's thinking on moral matters, the principles informing their advocacy, in fact, were precursors to radical change. The first portion provides a very brief history of the Church's opposition to contraception with the primary intent of showing the constancy of that opposition. The second portion involves an analysis of the reports written by the special commission set up to advise Pope Paul VI in his writing of the encyclical. These reports serve to show the status of the debate on contraception before *Humanae Vitae*. They also suggest the kind of arguments used both by those who sought to challenge the Church's teaching and also by those who worked to defend its teaching.

A Brief History of the Church's Condemnation of Contraception

Among Christian churches there was nearly undivided opposition to contraception until the early part of this century. The reasons for the Catholic condemnation can be found in the writing of Catholic theologians, answers from the Holy See in regard to questions about penitentials, and statements of national hierarchies of bishops.[1] The most extensive history of the Church's condemnation of contraception is to be found in John T. Noonan's *Contraception*.[2] In his introduction, in an overview of the Church's teaching on contraception, he concludes:

Since the first clear mention of contraception by a Christian theologian, when a harsh third-century moralist accused a pope of encouraging it, the articulated judgment has been the same. In the world of the late Empire known to St. Jerome and St. Augustine, in the Ostrogothic Arles of Bishop Caesarius and the Suevian Braga of Bishop Martin, in the Paris of St. Albert and St. Thomas, in the Renaissance Rome of Sixtus V and the Renaissance Milan of St. Charles Borromeo, in the Naples of St. Alphonsus Liguori and the Liège of Charles Billuart, in the Philadelphia of Bishop Kenrick and in the Bombay of Cardinal Gracias, the teachers of the Church have taught without hesitation or variation that certain acts preventing procreation are gravely sinful. No Catholic theologian has ever taught, "Contraception is a good act." The teaching on contraception is clear and apparently fixed forever.[3]

In spite of this strong statement about its likely immutability, Noonan's treatment of the history of the Church's teaching subtly supports the hope that it may change.[4] Indeed, the last sentence of Noonan's introduction seems to undercut the force of the paragraph cited. There he suggests that developments in the doctrine may be forthcoming and observes, "[my] study may provide grounds for prophecy." As special consultant to the commission that eventually advised Pope Paul VI that a change in Church teaching was warranted, Noonan reportedly played an instrumental role in leading the commission to this conclusion. Thus, because of his conviction that a change would and should be forthcoming, Noonan's witness to the unbroken opposition to contraception in Church teaching is particularly forceful. Here, then, let us (largely following Noonan) briefly trace the major contours of this unbroken tradition before we consider in much greater detail the break that took place in the middle decades of this century.

In the early centuries of the Church there was a strong emphasis on the procreative power of sexual intercourse. Christians in these centuries were noted for their reverence for life, in particular their reverence for new life, both the infant and the fetus. Their condemnation of contraception was part of their overall interest in not interfering in the life-giving processes that they believed were the domain of God.[5] In the fourth century, Augustine wrote extensively about sex and marriage,[6] largely in the context of the controversy with the Manichees, who opposed marriage, heterosexual union, and procreation.[7] Augustine, who spoke of the three ends of marriage as offspring, fidelity, and sacrament, insisted that spouses must respect the procreative purpose of sex. He is understood to condemn artificial contraceptives explicitly in a passage where he condemns the use of "poisons of sterility" (*sterilitatis venena*) by husband and wife.[8]

Noonan considers the next period in the history of the Church's opposition to contraception to be the age of the monks from 500 to 1100 and notes that there was repeated and constant opposition to contraception in this period. In the sixth century Saint Martin included condemnation of "steps taken that a woman not conceive" in a list of canons intended to instruct Christians in out-of-the-way corners of Christendom.[9] Penitentials of the period regularly condemned potions that seemed to have contraceptive powers, and penalties were severe.[10] One of the most important texts from the penitentials reads: "If someone [*si aliquis*] to satisfy his lust or in deliberate hatred does something to a man or woman so that no children be born of him or her, or gives them to drink, so that he cannot generate or she conceive, let it be held as homicide."[11] This text became a part of the law of the Catholic Church until 1917.[12] What are we to make of the statement that contraception is to be treated as homicide? Noonan earlier in his history noted that the practice of calling contraception "homicide" was not a "biological" or "legal" description, but a moral one.[13] That is, the authors of these texts did not think that contraception killed an actual human being but that it prevented a human being from being conceived, from coming to life; they assessed this prevention to be the moral equivalent of homicide.[14]

Thomas Aquinas spoke of contraception as wrong, not because it was equivalent to homicide but because it was an act against nature; his became the more common justification for the condemnation of contraception. His view rested on the premise that God was the author of nature and that respecting the order of nature was respecting God's will.[15]

During the following centuries (1450–1750), greater numbers of authors attempted to determine more precisely the role of pleasure in sexual intercourse and the extent to which seeking pleasure alone could justify having sexual intercourse. This analysis never served to justify tampering with the procreative power of intercourse, although it did allow the deliberate subjective intention to have sexual intercourse when one did not wish there to be a conception. Noonan thinks that a change in the teaching on contraception might have been expected to have followed the development of understandings of what are moral intentions for intercourse. Yet, as he notes, "The prohibition against contraception resisted modification. It was, indeed, not merely passively retained and transmitted, but actively maintained and defended by arguments. The repetition, variations, and patterns of argumentation are the best internal index to the doctrine's strength."[16]

Toward the end of the eighteenth century, concerns about growing population (Malthus published his *Essay on the Principle of Population* in 1798) were first expressed. Contraception was cautiously proposed by some (not Malthus) as a possible solution. In the next century the use of contraceptives became widespread to the point that many European states legislated against contraceptive propaganda and there were laws in the United States against such practices as sending contraceptives through the mail, importing contraceptives, and in general distributing contraception. Nonetheless public opinion and medical opinion were changing and in the Anglican church this led to a change in church teaching.

In 1930 Anglicans broke ranks with nearly the whole of the traditional Christian opposition to contraception with a declaration at the Lambeth Conference that permitted use of contraception by married couples, for grave reasons. Shortly after this event Pius XI, on December 31, 1931, issued *Casti Connubii*. There he reiterated Catholic opposition to contraception, applauded elevated notions of conjugal love and parenthood, and explained that confining conjugal acts to known infertile periods, for right reasons, was morally permissible. *Casti Connubii* is widely considered as a good instance of a true development in the Church's teaching on marriage. That is, it remains within the framework of accepted principles, accepts legitimate development of those principles, and shows the proper implications and applications of those principles. Pius XI's encyclical indicated that the recent greater appreciation of conjugal love developed by several moral theologians was a legitimate deepening of the traditional evaluation of love between the spouses; he also explained that use of the infertile period in a woman's cycle (relatively recently acquired knowledge[17]) was not contraceptive and was not opposed to the Church's understanding of natural law.

The condemnation of contraception in *Casti Connubii* was nonetheless unequivocal. *Casti Connubii* reiterated the constant teaching of the Church that "the sacred partnership of true marriage is constituted both by the will of God and the will of man. From God comes the very institution of marriage, the ends for which it was instituted, the laws that govern it, the blessings that flow from it; while man, through generous surrender of his own person made to another for the whole span of life, becomes, with the help and cooperation of God, the author of each particular marriage, with the duties and blessings annexed thereto from divine institution."[18] *Casti Connubii* also states, "Amongst the blessings of marriage, the child holds the first place" and notes, "The Creator of the human race Himself . . . in His goodness wished to use men as His helpers in the propagation of life. . . ."[19] The condemnation of contraception is listed first because contraception is an "evil opposed to the benefits of matrimony":

First consideration is due to the offspring, which many have the boldness to call the disagreeable burden of matrimony and which they say is to be carefully avoided by married people not through virtuous continence (which Christian law permits in matrimony when both parties consent) but by frustrating the marriage act. Some justify this criminal abuse on the ground that they are weary of children and wish to gratify their desires without their consequent burden. Others say that they cannot on the one hand remain continent nor on the other can they have children because of the difficulties whether on the part of the mother or on the part of family circumstances.

But no reason, however grave may be put forward by which anything intrinsically against nature may become conformable to nature and morally good. Since, therefore, the conjugal act is destined primarily by nature for the begetting of children, those who in exercising it deliberately frustrate its natural power and purpose sin against nature and commit a deed which is shameful and intrinsically vicious.[20]

Pius XII in several of his addresses reiterated and clarified this teaching in the following decades; in particular he explicitly acknowledged the licitness of the use of the infertile period to regulate births.[21] Within the Catholic Church the position of *Casti Connubii* was virtually unchallenged until the middle decades of this century.

First Stirrings of Dissent

In 1962 John J. Lynch, S.J., writer of notes on moral theology for *Theological Studies*, stated, "Since theological discussion of the anovulant drugs began some four or more years ago, moralists have never been less than unanimous in their assertion that natural law cannot countenance the use of these progestational steroids for the purpose of contraception as that term is properly understood in the light of papal teaching."[22] They were also agreed that anovulant pills had certain licit therapeutic uses. Both of these views were confirmed by Pius XII in his September 12, 1958, speech to a congress of hematologists.[23] Lynch took notice in this year of an article published by Dr. John Rock, a Boston physician, who described himself as a Catholic and who had been instrumental in the development of the progesterone pill and was highly energetic in his promotion of the pill and his advocacy of a change in Church teaching.[24] Lynch describes Rock's work, *The Time Has Come*, as "illustrat[ing] the sort of specious reasoning, unreasoning emotionalism, half-truths and fallacies to which the faithful are being exposed on this elemental question of the oral contraceptives."[25] Noting that an abundance of theological literature had been published over the last four years to counter these "adverse influences," he declared that the problem of the moral status of the pill was a "theologically closed issue."

Two years later in his 1965 notes Lynch continued to maintain that among "established theologians" there is no indication of any "concerted movement" breaking from the traditional teaching of the Church.[26] Yet, he noted that there have been some proponents of a contrary view. He dated the beginning of the disagreement among theologians to mid-1963 which "found moral theologians generally agreed" that anovulant pills were contraceptive and therefore illicit.[27] During this year articles defending oral contraceptives written by three theologians, Rev. L. Janssens, Rev. W. van der Marck, O. P., and Bishop J. M. Reuss, appeared simultaneously in European journals.[28] Lynch maintained that the weakness of their views had been exposed by their fellow theologian Gerald Kelly, S.J.,[29] but believed that in the interim "the real issues involved had been so obscured in the secular and religious press that confusion at the popular level reached monumental proportions."[30] Indeed, Rock's book was followed by a flood of popular and theological literature arguing for the morality of contraception.[31] Lynch believed that these developments led Paul VI to make his famous speech to a group of cardinals in which he stated that there was "no adequate reason for considering the relevant norms of Pius XII to be superseded and therefore no longer obligatory; they should, therefore, be regarded as valid, as long as We do not consider Ourselves in conscience obliged to modify them."[32] The reference here to Pius XII may indicate that Paul VI intended the study he proposed not to be about the larger issue of all forms of contraception but to be simply about the pill, for what is peculiar about Pius XII's contribution to the teaching about contraception concerns the pill. Lynch cites only one sentence of Paul VI's talk. The rest of the paragraph may be of some interest here. Paul VI went on to say: "In a matter of such importance it seems right that Catholics desire to follow one single law propounded authoritatively by the Church. So it seems advisable to recommend that for the present no one should arrogate to himself the right to take a stand differing from the norm now in force."[33] In spite of Paul VI's admonitions to the cardinals, in speeches directed towards the sections of *Gaudium et Spes* that concerned the family, several council fathers urged—in quite circumspect terms—that it was time for the Church to revise its teaching about what are morally permissible means of family planning.[34]

The question of the morality of contraception soon broke wide open—to the point that in the next year, 1966, the author of the "Notes on Moral Theology" in *Theological Studies*, Richard McCormick, S.J., wrote, "Contraception continues to be . . . the major moral issue troubling the Church."[35] He noted that the literature on contraception in the previous six months was "voluminous." At that time, he himself placed his allegiances with those who would uphold the Church's teaching. But two years later, he observed, "The documents of the Papal Commission represent a rather full summary of two points of view. They incorporate most of the important things that have been said on the subject of contraception over the past three or four years, plus a few very interesting and important nuances. The majority report, particularly the analysis in its 'rebuttal,' strikes this reader as much the more satisfactory statement."[36] (It is these documents that will become our focus shortly.) Whereas two years earlier he had maintained, "The effect of repeated authoritative Church pronouncements on a matter of this importance is a presumptive certitude of their correctness,"[37] he now believes that the matter of contraception is in a state of "practical doubt."[38]

Few deny that it was largely social indications—not philosophical deliberations—that prompted the reconsideration of the Church's teaching on contraception. Nearly every article and document dealing with the issue tells about the fear of overpopulation, the new role of women in society, and the increased financial strains in raising a family well. The recent discovery and more widespread availability of anovulant pills were among the foremost reasons for the investigation into the morality of contraception. Initially, this investigation was assumed to proceed upon the lines of an inquiry among those who shared the same principles; they were opposed to contraception but were not decided on the question of the anovulant pill as a contraceptive. There was some question whether the pill violated the Church's prohibition against contraception because it did not violate the integrity of the sexual act and served only to delay ovulation, a process also effected by nature.[39] Several also raised the question "The anovulant pill seems to have some legitimate therapeutic purposes. What are these? Are there times when fertility (e.g., during lactation) may be considered a defect of nature?"[40] But soon those who were involved in deliberating about this matter moved away from the specific concern about the morality of the pill and asked a more fundamental question: Is the Church's prohibition of contraception justifiable?

Here we find the first stirrings of what came to be a major controversy in Catholic moral theology. Not only did theologians come to question the prohibition of contraception in terms of the traditional principles of moral theology; they also came to question these very principles. No longer was the central question, Is the Church's prohibition of contraception justifiable in terms of the traditional principles of moral reasoning? Rather the question came to be, Are the traditional principles of moral reasoning that the Church has used to condemn contraception true? Again, the debate was no longer simply about the single issue of contraception or about the proper application of agreed-on principles. The debate now was about the fundamental principles to be used in moral reasoning.[41] Moreover, since the Church has historically claimed to be a reliable interpreter of moral principles, calling into question these principles also entailed calling into question the reliability of the Church as teacher on moral issues. This major controversy, however, took some time to develop; at the time of *Humanae Vitae* the issue was very narrowly circumscribed to the issue of the morality of contraception, and, at first, to the even narrower question of the morality of one form of contraception, the pill.

Let us expand momentarily on the nature of the debate about moral principles that was largely spawned by the controversy over the morality of contraception. There are basically three kinds of grounds for agreement or disagreement among ethicists. (1) They may agree or disagree on what principles ought to govern their reasoning; (2) they may agree or disagree on the justification or foundation for these principles; and (3) they may agree or disagree on the application of principles. For instance, ethicists may or may not agree with the principle that "it is always immoral to take an innocent human life." Even those who agree on this principle may disagree on its justification; for instance, some may claim that it is intuitively obvious; others may claim that it is a necessary foundation for civil society; others may claim that God has revealed this "law" to mankind. And, again, those who agree on this principle may disagree on its proper application. For instance, some may argue that capital punishment is not a violation of this principle since they would argue that some criminals are guilty of crimes deserving of the death penalty. Others may argue that capital punishment does violate this principle since criminals are not an immediate threat to life and they are "innocent" in this sense.

The debate about contraception involves all these types of disagreement. Most Catholic moral theologians would agree on a principle stated in this way: The procreative good of sexual intercourse ought to be protected. But they might disagree intensely on the reasons that justify this principle; for instance, some would invoke natural law principles; some would invoke scriptural support (such as "Be fruitful and multiply"); others would cite the coherence of this principle with personalist values. The most serious disagreement would, though, be on the absoluteness of this principle. Some claim that the procreative good of sexual intercourse is an absolute good, never to be violated. They would argue that contraception is an intrinsic moral wrong and thus could never be morally justified as a direct and deliberate moral choice. Others argue that procreation is not an absolute good and that thus it may be necessary to weigh other goods against the good of procreation. For instance, some may argue that the good of the spontaneous union of the spouses, or the good of prevention of pregnancy out of wedlock, might supersede the good of procreation and that thus, at times, this good could be sacrificed to other goods.

When the debate on contraception began there was considerable agreement among moral theologians on the principles that ought to govern moral decision making about sexual matters, about the justification for these principles, and about the application of these principles to specific sexual acts. Again, this disagreement began to unravel in the early sixties; a close analysis of the reports that came out of Paul VI's special commission indicates that the elements of a revolution in moral thinking were present in those documents.

Papal Commission

Three documents were published out of Paul VI's Papal Commission for the Study of Problems of the Family, Population, and Birth Rate.[42] This commission was initially established by John XXIII and was continued by Paul VI to advise him on the issues named in the title of the commission. The proceedings of this commission were to be confidential. The report of the proceedings was to be strictly advisory: it was not to be definitive or authoritative in any way. Written in 1966, portions were leaked to the press and published in the *Tablet* and the *National Catholic Reporter* in spring 1967.

The commission, enlarged several times, eventually was composed of over sixty individuals: cardinals, bishops, experts on such matters as population, doctors, and married couples. The commission was reconstituted in early 1966 when several bishops and cardinals were added; at that time they became the voting members. Three documents were leaked, only one was a part of the body of the report voted on by the members; the others were added to the report as appendices. The one portion of the final report that was leaked was entitled *Schema Documenti de Responsabili Paternitate* (Draft of a Document concerning Responsible Parenthood), which was accompanied by a pastoral introduction written (in French) by Monsignor Dupuy. This document was meant to be a draft of a statement on the subject and to be sent to Pope Paul VI; this is the most widely known report of the commission and it is often referred to as "The Majority Report." Here it will be referred to as "The Schema." The names of Rev. Alfons Auer, Raymond Sigmond, O.P., Rev. Paul Anciaux, Michel Labourdette, O.P., Joseph Fuchs, S.J., and Rev. Pierre de Locht were attached to it. Those voting in favor of the full report were Cardinals Doepfner (Munich), Suenens (Malines-Brussels), Shehan (Baltimore), and Lefebre (Bourges) and Archbishops Dearden (Detroit), Dupuy (Albi), Mendez (Venezuela), Reuss (Meinz), and Zoa (Cameroons). Three were reported as opposing the report: Cardinal Ottaviani (Holy Office), Bishop Colombo (Milan), and Archbishop Morris (Cashel, Ireland); three abstained: Cardinal Heenan (Westminster), Cardinal Gracias (Bombay), and Archbishop Binz (St. Paul, Minnesota). Archbishop Karol Wojtyla from Poland was unavoidably absent, though he may have had some influence on the pope's thinking through written communications. In 1969 he convened a group of theologians to study the norms governing conjugal life; the paper they wrote reads like a response, a very critical response, to the report of the Papal Commission.[43]

Two of the appendices that were leaked are generally and mistakenly believed to be the primary documents of the commission though they were more accurately simply working papers of the commission; again, they were included with the report as appendices. *Documentum Syntheticum de Moralitate Regulationis Nativitatum (Synthetic Document Concerning the Morality of Birth Regulation)* was attached to the report as Appendix V. This paper reads like a rebuttal to the Minority Report and will be referred to here as the "Majority Rebuttal"; it was signed by three theologians: Joseph Fuchs, S.J., Rev. Philippe Delhaye, and Raymond Sigmond, O.P.[44] Appendix VI was entitled *Status Quaestionis Doctrina Ecclesiae Eiusque Auctoritas (The Status of the Question, the Teaching of the Church, and Its Authority;* often known and here referred to as "The Minority Report"). The Minority Report was signed by four moral theologians: John Ford, S.J., Jan Visser, C.SS.R., Marcelino Zalba, S.J., and Stanislaus de Lestapis, S.J.

It is not possible to find a published statement that makes clear the purpose of this commission. It is certainly not clear that it was convened with the purpose of discerning whether the Church's prohibition of contraception was justifiable. Its original purpose seemed to have been a rather broad study of the Church's teaching on marriage but came to focus on the question of contraception. It seems possible that Paul VI never really questioned the prohibition against contraception[45] but that he did have doubts about the status of the pill and wanted a more updated defense of the Church's teaching in light of contemporary problems, such as population.[46] His public statements are not very illuminating. In 1965, in a speech to the commission he stated:

These are, dear Sons, the levels on which your researches are situated: on the one hand, a better knowledge of physiological laws, psychological and medical data, population shifts and social upheavals; on the other hand, and above all, the level of the higher light cast upon these facts by the data of Faith and the traditional teaching of the Church. Like an attentive mother, the Church has at all times had an interest and concern about supplying an answer that is adapted to the great problems posed by men. In keeping with the counsel of the Lord, and with this aim in mind, she welcomes *nova et vetera* [new things and old], in order to provide the divine leaven of the Gospel with all its richness and to obtain for men an abundance of the supernatural life.

In the present case, the problem posed can be summed up like this: in what form and according to what norms ought married couples, in exercising their love for each other, to fulfill this life-giving function to which their vocation calls them?[47]

A statement by Bernard Haering, C.SS.R., indicates what he had been told were the limitations of the commission when he was invited to join it as consultant: "I received from officials on all levels of the Holy Office unequivocal instructions and warnings that I was to keep precisely within the framework of *Casti Connubii*. However, efforts to restrain freedom of speech were only partially successful."[48] The commission itself reportedly raised and voted on whether the Church's teaching was "reformable" and, obviously, voted that it was.[49] The majority reports that came out of the commission were clearly concerned to advance the Church's understanding of marriage but did so largely with a view to justifying contraception.

These documents deserve careful attention because, as McCormick noted previously, they serve to summarize the status of the debate on contraception before *Humanae Vitae*. Moreover, they were among the documents provided to Paul VI to guide him in his deliberations about the morality of contraception.[50] It must be remembered that these were only working papers and summary statements. This may account for the lack of argumentation justifying the positions taken.[51] It becomes readily apparent that the documents provided more assertions than arguments. Part of the purpose of the following analysis will be to suggest that these reports were only the beginning of a debate and that much of the work on contraception that followed *Humanae Vitae* involved finding support for assertions that preceded *Humanae Vitae*.

The analysis of the Minority Report and Majority Rebuttal shows that investigation into the issue of contraception had moved beyond an inquiry among those who shared fundamental principles. These documents exhibit at least four primary areas of disagreement: (1) they differ on the meaning of the constancy of the Church's opposition to contraception; (2) they differ on the effect that a change in Church teaching would have on Church authority; (3) they exhibit a different understanding on how contraception violates natural law; (4) they have a different assessment of the impact that a change in the Church's teaching on contraception would have on her teaching on other sexual acts. Let us take up each of these topics separately and see how each of the reports responds.

*Does the Church Have a Constant Teaching
against Contraception?*

Both documents raise the question, Does the Catholic Church have a constant history of condemnation of contraception? Is this of sufficient clarity and solemnity to constitute an infallible and irreformable teaching? To some, this question itself might seem a curious one to be part of a debate about a moral issue. But as indicated, Catholic moral theologians, because of their understanding of the nature of the Church, ask several questions about moral matters that are not of interest to strictly philosophical ethicists. This question is of interest to Catholic moral theologians since, if it were to be determined that the teaching were a constant part of Church heritage, this would justify a strong predisposition in its favor, because the Church understands itself to have the guidance of the Holy Spirit in its moral teachings. Furthermore, the kind of constancy that it has may give it the marks of infallible teaching and then, obviously, there would be no possibility that this teaching could change.

The Minority Report claims:

One can find no period of history, no document of the church, no theological school, scarcely one Catholic theologian, who ever denied that contraception was always seriously evil. The teaching of the Church in this matter is absolutely constant. Until the present century this teaching was peacefully possessed by all other Christians, whether Orthodox or Anglican or Protestant.[52]

The Majority Rebuttal does not counter by citing Church documents or fathers of the Church who have approved of contraception; indeed it grants, "In this [the Catholic] tradition contraceptive intercourse is never approved, but when the question arises it is condemned. This has occurred many times in the last few centuries." But it further observes, "However, this is by no means an apostolic tradition or an attestation of faith but merely the tradition of a teaching formulated in diverse ways at diverse times."[53] This last line seems to suggest that the teaching does not represent a reliable or authoritative teaching *simply* because it has been routinely reiterated. What calls this reiterated teaching into doubt for the theologians of the Majority Rebuttal is that they do not find the *reasons*

given for it convincing. They find the scriptural evidence for condemnation of contraception slim and find the natural law arguments
"vague and unconvincing" (more about this later). They suggest
that the core of the constant teaching is directed more toward
protecting the good of procreation than condemning contraception
(this argument is essentially that advanced by Noonan). They tend
to understand the Church's constant teaching against contraception
not as a sign of its infallibility but as a teaching that has supported
the great good of procreation, a support that could take different
forms at different times.

In spite of this important disagreement, the reports seem to share
an important principle. That is, whereas they disagree on the proper
interpretation of Church teaching, they seem to agree where one
looks to find Church teaching; one looks to the councils, to papal
encyclicals, to constant teachings of theologians, especially Church
Fathers, to teachings of the bishops, and to pronouncements by
various offices at the Vatican as an extension of the popes' teaching.
Later, this agreement vanished. Many theologians came to disagree
about what the Church is and what the source of Church teaching
is. Some came to argue that the "people are the Church" and that
since most Catholic spouses admit to using some form of contraception, "Church" teaching has changed, although the change has just
not yet been appropriated into the "official" documents.[54] Others
came to argue that the Church has *never* taught infallibly about
moral matters.[55]

Would a Change Discredit the Teaching Authority of the Church?

The second area of disagreement is related to the first: Would a
recognition of the morality of contraception be a reversal of Church
teaching or would this be a legitimate development of Church
teaching? What sort of implications would this have for the Church
as an authoritative teacher in matters of morals? This question is
important, for one understanding of the Church maintains that it
can *develop* its teaching on fundamental truths in accord, for instance, with an advance in human knowledge but not *change* its
teaching fundamentally (here, seemingly *reverse* it). If permission
to use contraception could be shown to be a development of Church
doctrine—and a legitimate one at that—this would pose no difficulty

for the Church as an authoritative teacher. But if judging contraception to be moral is a fundamental change in Church teaching, this would have serious implications for the Catholic understanding of the authority of the Church.

The Minority Report believes a change in the Church's teaching on contraception would amount to a repudiation of its moral authority, indeed, a denial that it is the authoritative guide established by Christ:

> The Church cannot substantially err in teaching doctrine which is most serious in its import for faith and morals, throughout all centuries or even one century, if it has been constantly and forcefully proposed as necessarily to be followed in order to obtain eternal salvation. The Church could not have erred through so many centuries, even through one century, by imposing under serious obligation very grave burdens in the name of Jesus Christ, if Jesus Christ did not actually impose these burdens. The Catholic Church could not have furnished in the name of Jesus Christ to so many of the faithful everywhere in the world, through so many centuries, the occasion for formal sin and spiritual ruin, because of a false doctrine promulgated in the name of Jesus Christ.[56]

The argument here, clearly, is that if the Church could err in such a way, the authority of the ordinary magisterium in moral matters would be thrown into question. The faithful could not put their trust in the magisterium's presentation of moral teaching, especially in sexual matters.

The Majority Rebuttal begins by denying that the condemnation of contraception in *Casti Connubii* constitutes true doctrinal definition. It claims that *Casti Connubii* was doing "nothing other than reaffirm[ing] the common teaching at the time."[57] It allows only that *Casti Connubii* was confirming the "constant concern [of the tradition] for protecting the goodness of procreation."[58] The Rebuttal argues that there has been an evolution in Church teaching on marriage. It understands the Church to be freeing itself from an inadequate concept of nature and of the natural law as it increasingly saw the importance of conjugal love in marriage.

To the concern that a change in the official teaching of the Church on contraception could damage the confidence of Catholics in the teaching authority of the Church, the Majority Rebuttal answers, "In point of fact, we know that there have been errors in the teaching of the magisterium and of tradition." It further makes the point that there is the tendency in many to "consider the authentic non-infallible magisterium infallible in practice." Finally, it states, "Such a change is to be seen rather as a step toward a more mature comprehension of the whole doctrine of the Church. For doubt and reconsideration are quite reasonable when proper reasons for doubt and reconsideration occur with regard to some specific question."[59]

Let us note that the Minority Report does not argue that the Church should not change *because* it would lose credibility but holds that it would be right that the Church lose credibility if it were to change its teaching on contraception, for changing on this matter would invalidate other claims the Church makes about itself. The Majority Rebuttal is less troubled by this prospect because it holds that the Church may have been wrong about its teaching on moral matters and since these have not been proclaimed infallibly, to change them would not be to undermine the authority of the Church. Ten years later Charles Curran chided those who spoke of "legitimate development" and proclaimed what many seemed hesitant to state at the time:

> Once *Humanae Vitae* was issued and the older teaching reaffirmed, those opposed to it could no longer call upon a theory of historical development. However, there were ways in which the encyclical's condemnation of artificial contraception could be interpreted so that one could mitigate its teaching without at the same time accusing the pope of being in error. From my perspective it was imperative then to take the more radical approach. The teaching condemning artificial contraception is wrong; the pope is in error; Catholics in good conscience can dissent in theory and in practice from such a teaching.[60]

Why/How Does Contraception Violate the Natural Law?

The third area of disagreement is the validity of natural law reasoning on which the condemnation of contraception is based. To explore this area of disagreement fully would in itself require an enormous tome. Yet, in some ways this is the crux of the resistance to and rejection of *Humanae Vitae* and thus it deserves special consideration. The importance of natural law claims to the teaching of *Humanae Vitae* is treated more extensively in chapters 3 and 4, and chapter 6 provides a detailed consideration of the primary arguments of two of the foremost opponents of traditional natural law reasoning and its influence on *Humanae Vitae*, Charles Curran and Bernard Haering. The chief controversy centers on how determinative of the moral evaluation of contraception the biological ordination of the sexual organs to the generation of new life ought to be. Some of those who support the Church's teaching on contraception, most notably Germain Grisez, also reject the claim that the ordination of the sexual organs is relevant to the moral evaluation of sexual intercourse. Grisez finds this claim an application characteristic of the manualist tradition of moral theologians of fairly recent times and not necessarily a part of the tradition. He denies that the biological ordination of the generative organs is determinative in any degree of the morality of sexual behavior.[61]

Theologians disagreeing about the morality of contraception nonetheless exhibit a fair amount of apparent agreement on related matters, even those that have customarily been justified through natural law principles. It is rarely contested, at least not by theologians concerned with contraception, that it is fair to say that generation of new life is a defining characteristic of sex and deserves at least some measure of respect; that is, the sexual organs are ordained to procreation at least analogously to the eye's being ordained to sight. The use of sex for hedonistic or egotistical purposes, although not disdained by much of modern society, remains a matter of disapproval by Catholic moral theologians (often on grounds of natural law), both those who oppose contraception and those who approve of it. Furthermore, both groups of theologians believe that a Christian marriage should welcome children and that spouses who marry and who are completely closed to the prospect of having children are, in fact, not validly married.

But when it comes to contraception, they disagree. One group argues that spouses cannot deliberately render their sexual acts infertile, though they may use periodic abstinence to limit their family size. The other group claims that the good of the love between the spouses and the good of responsible parenthood serve to justify the use of contraceptives on occasion. Their grounds of disagreement would, then, seem to most to be relatively narrow and almost insignificant quibbling over means of limiting family size that differ very little. Yet these two groups sense a radical divergence between themselves. A look at their understanding of nature and Man's proper relationship to nature will ratify this perception. The claims made in this regard by the Minority Report and the Majority Rebuttal disclose a radical divergence, or at least an incipient radical divergence, that becomes clearer as the debate developed after the issuance of *Humanae Vitae*. Both the reports were "position papers" and not intended to give an exhaustive defense of their position; the following discussion will point out some areas in each report that required further elaboration.

The Minority Report and Natural Law

The Minority Report identifies what it considers to be two false claims against the Church's opposition to contraception as a violation of natural law. It notes that some claim that the teaching of the Church "was founded on the false supposition that all conjugal acts are procreative by their very nature, whereas the facts of physiology show that very few of them are actually fertile or productive of new life."[62] That is, some moderns claim that if the Church had known that some sexual acts are by nature infertile, the Church would not have thought contraception to be a violation of nature: they would have understood it to be in accord with nature. The Minority Report notes, however, "Older thinkers knew that many conjugal acts are actually sterile, e.g., during pregnancy and old age."[63]

The Minority Report also contests the claim "that the teaching of the Church is based on an obsolete medieval notion of 'nature.'" This claim maintains that the view of nature employed by the Church holds that it is always wrong to violate the laws of nature. It holds that the Church's opposition to contraception is based on the understanding that sexual intercourse has as its natural end procreation and, because this is a "law" of nature, it is wrong to thwart this natural end. The Minority Report makes several responses to this claim: (1) It notes that the Church's opposition to contraception predates the Middle Ages; (2) it denies that the Church's teaching "derives from any philosophy of nature . . . in which the natural physical order is inviolable with respect to being 'natural' "; and (3) it insists that theology (as well as philosophy) is not guilty of making nature determinative of morality. The Minority Report notes, however, that the Church has taught that there is a special inviolability to the generative processes "precisely because they are generative of new *human life*, and life is not under man's dominion."[64]

In the section of the Minority Report entitled "Why Does the Church Teach That Contraception Is Always Seriously Evil?" the primary explanation given is the following: "The fathers, theologians, and the Church herself has always taught that certain acts and the generative processes are in some way specially inviolable precisely because they are generative. This inviolability is always attributed to the act and to the processes, which are biological; not inasmuch as they are biological, but inasmuch as they are human, namely inasmuch as they are the object of *human acts* and are destined by their nature to the good of the human species."[65] Two points, in particular, need elaboration. One is the denial that the view of the inviolability of the purpose of the generative acts articulated here is (solely) based on their biological ordination. The other is the claim that their defining feature is their destination to the *good of the human species*. The Minority Report, in the passage cited, states that what makes the generative processes different from other biological processes is that they are "destined by their nature to the good of the human species." The Report, though, provides only the most minimal explanation of why this should render the generative acts inviolable. In truth, it gestures toward three explanations, one given by the Fathers of the Church, one by a school of modern Thomists (Grisez et alii), and one that suggests that "revealed truths" may provide further illumination about this point.[66]

The Fathers (and theologians and canon law) argued that the prohibition of contraception was part of the general inviolability of human life itself. The Minority Report gives some slight elaboration of this position: "Human life already existing (*in facto esse*) is inviolable. Likewise, it is also in some sense inviolable in its proximate causes (*vita in fieri*). To put it another way: just as already existing human life is removed from the dominion of man, so also in some similar way is human life as it comes to be; that is, the act and the generative process, inasmuch as they are generative, are removed from his dominion."[67] The Report goes on to give a helpful "substratum" to this teaching, that is, that God is the author of life and that therefore human life has a kind of sacredness about it; therefore, the processes that generate human life have a special status of much greater importance than other biological processes. Further elaboration of this position would require justification of the claim that the respect due to life is also due to the generative processes and that God has a special interest in the generative process.[68]

The Minority Report notes that various philosophical arguments have been provided in defense of the Church's condemnation of contraception. The philosophical reason mentioned in the Minority Report is the following: "Some see the malice [evil] [of contraception] principally in the fact that procreation itself (that is, the act and the generative process) is a certain fundamental human good (as truth, as life itself is such a good). To destroy it voluntarily is therefore evidently evil. For to have an intention, directly and actively contrary to a fundamental human good, is something intrinsically evil."[69]

This argument is suggestive of the work of Germain Grisez, and such is not surprising since he worked closely with John Ford, one of the authors of the Minority Report. An element of considerable importance here is the focus on the voluntary intention of the agent to act against a basic human good, a focus that Grisez maintains in his most recent work on contraception.[70]

Finally, the Minority Report claims that the Church's opposition to contraception is not based principally on philosophical arguments. Rather, "It depends on the nature of human life and human sexuality, as understood theologically by the Church."[71] This is a very important point, for whereas it is commonly claimed that the Church's opposition is based on natural law arguments, and whereas this is commonly taken to mean that the arguments then are based on philosophical rather than theological grounds, the Minority Report does not make precisely this claim. Surely it holds that the Church's condemnation of contraception is based on natural law but that "based on" does not necessarily mean that natural law arguments are confined strictly to the realm of philosophical justification. Rather, the Church's understanding of the nature of Man, an understanding shaped by revelation, informs its understanding of natural law. This statement does not necessarily suggest that the theologians who wrote the Minority Report thought that philosophical arguments do not suffice to indicate the immorality of contraception; however, it does indicate that "the question"—here, Why does the *Church* teach that contraception is always seriously evil?—is to be understood in the light of revealed truths about the "nature of human life and sexuality" as well as in light of philosophical truths.

The Majority Rebuttal and Natural Law

The Majority Rebuttal speaks of the natural law in this way: "The reference in the encyclical [*Casti Connubii*] to the argument from reason or natural law is vague and imprecise, especially since this argument does not consider sufficiently man, God's creature, as the prudent administrator and steward of the gifts of nature."[72]

The Rebuttal speaks of "the responsibility of man for humanizing the gifts of nature and using them to bring the life of man to greater perfection."[73] Then in a section entitled "A Systematic Examination of the Arguments from the Law of Nature" it immediately asserts: "The arguments based on the law of nature are not persuasive. The principal argument is founded on the inviolability of the sources of life; like human life itself, it is said, they do not fall under the dominion of man but pertain to the dominion of God."[74] It goes on to reject an "unconditional respect for nature as it is in itself (as if nature in its physical existence were the expression of the will of God)" and claims that this view has nourished fears that "any human intervention tends to destroy rather than perfect this very nature" and that this view has prohibited "many interventions of the art of medicine." (No examples of such prohibition are given.) These passages do not really provide arguments supporting the claims made but simply present the conclusions the Rebuttal hopes to support.

The Rebuttal first attempts to support its rejection of the claim that life is solely under the dominion of God. It argues that this is a dominion that God has shared with Man: "To take his own or another's life is a sin not because life is under the exclusive dominion of God but because it is contrary to right reason unless there is question of a good or a higher order."[75] The strength of this claim is supported by giving instances in which Man is permitted to take life (for example, capital punishment). The suggestion here is that Man shares in God's dominion and that his criteria for his proper use of this share should not be God's will as discerned through the physical structures of nature but that it should be the demands of "right reason." The Majority Rebuttal makes a division here between the "dominion of God and God's will and nature" and "right reason." This division needs further elucidation since this way of speaking suggests a greater division between God and nature and gives greater power to Man than has traditionally been accorded. Most of Catholic moral theology has argued that God's will and right reason (and acting in accord with nature) are in fact identical; for instance, Man can defend himself against an unjust attacker, because this is in accord with both right reason and God's will (and with natural law). Moreover, as argued previously, natural law theory is not rooted strictly in discernment of the workings of biological processes; for instance, it considers the state to be a natural institution and the rights of the state to be in accord with nature: for example, use of capital punishment is not considered to be a "justifiable" violation of the laws of nature but to be in accord with the natural law. The objections that are raised here by the Majority Rebuttal hint at certain assumptions about the relations among biological processes, God's will, and right reason that need to be spelled out.

The use of the example of Man's dominion over human life raises some other interesting questions. The suggestion is that because there are times when Man may exercise sovereignty over life, there must also be times when he may exercise sovereignty over that which is related to life, that is, the generative organs. What the argument fails to acknowledge is that the reasons for taking human life are narrowly circumscribed; these involve such reasons as self-defense, defense of the innocent, and defense of the state. The moral tradition of the Church has carefully delineated and justified these; it seems right to assume that the reasons for the use of contraception must be serious and must be justified; the argument of the Rebuttal suggests the need to work out similar justifications for contraception.

The Rebuttal builds upon the claim "the dominion of God is exercised through man, who can use nature for his own perfection according to the dictates of right reason"[76] to justify contraception in this way: "In the matter at hand [contraception], then, there is a certain change in the mind of contemporary man. He feels that he is more conformed to his rational nature, created by God with liberty and responsibility, when he uses his skill to intervene in the biological processes of nature so that he can achieve the ends of the institution of matrimony in the conditions of actual life, than if he would abandon himself to chance."[77] The basic argument, here, is that Man is master over nature, even over the nature of his generative organs. That the "generative" power or nature of the generative organs is defining of their purpose is not contested; indeed, surprisingly, this document retains the designation of procreation as the "essential end of sexuality and of conjugal life,"[78] a designation that is repudiated by later advocates of contraception. The argument here is that Man may use technology to perfect nature, and the claim is that the use of contraception would perfect certain goods of marriage. The argument depends on the assumption that Man is more "free and responsible" about childbearing when he takes control over it than when he lets "nature takes its course." The Rebuttal makes the claim that the nonuse of contraception amounts to "abandon[ment] . . . to chance, rather than abandonment to God's will." Yet, traditionally, the creation of new life has not been seen to be the product of chance but a product of God's intervention in the workings of nature. This departure from tradition is not acknowledged.

After citing the passage from *Gaudium et Spes* that allows that parents have the right to determine how many children they have, the Rebuttal gives its key argument:

It is more and more evident today that in man sexual relations in marriage are raised to the expression of a mutual personal giving (herein lies the change of object). Intercourse materially considered carries with it some orientation toward fecundation, but this finality must be rationally directed by man according to the measure and conditions of human love, size of the family, educational need, etc. The mutual giving of self perdures throughout the entire life: biological fecundity is not continuous and is subject to many irregularities and therefore ought to be assumed into the human sphere and be regulated within it. Finalisation towards fecundity can formally come only from man, though this finality is found materially in the organs. Fecundation must be a personal human act (deliberate, responsible for its effects, etc.). With the progress of knowledge, man can exercise this dominion and ought to exercise it with responsibility.[79]

The argument of this passage is based on several assumptions; the most fundamental is that material nature must not dictate to Man what are the proper uses of that matter. The ends of Man must supersede whatever "value" matter might have. Since the biological fecundity in Man (here primarily woman!) is irregular, it is a humanizing and perfecting act to regularize it. The larger argument is that the requirements of mutual self-giving, of size of the family, and so on, may warrant this regularization.

Implicit here and in the next section is the premise that Man may not interfere with the processes of nature without sufficient reason. Certainly, the Church has always taught that Man may interfere with nature in order to "perfect" nature. It fully accepts procedures that restore diseased organs to their healthy or natural state. Since fertility is a healthy (and natural) condition, reasons need to be given why contraception could be considered perfective of nature. But the Rebuttal does not address this problem. It does, though, ask, "What are the limits of the dominion of man with regard to the rational determination of his fecundity?" Its general answer is "It is the duty of man to perfect (or to order it to the human good expressed in matrimony) but not to destroy it. Even if the absolute untouchability of the fertile period cannot be maintained, neither can complete dominion be affirmed."[80] This question and this response indicate that some measure of respect is due to material nature, or physical processes. It is not clear what justification the document could provide for demanding this respect or for saying that "complete dominion" cannot be affirmed unless it is prepared to grant some moral determinacy to biological processes and some inviolability to matter or physical processes. Both reports, then, claim that the natural ordination of biological processes is not irrelevant to morality. Both must strive to explain what relevance they do have and what proper dominion Man has over them.

The Rebuttal also asserts, "When man intervenes in the procreative process, he does this with the intention of regulating and not excluding fertility."[81] (Again, no explanation is given why, if matter is at the disposal of Man, it is not at his absolute disposal, in accord with right reason, or why *excluding* fertility would be wrong.) There is some sense that fertility is among the goods of marriage and that thus to regulate it would be proper but to exclude it would be wrong. (This distinction raises a question about the illicitness of sterilization, for if a couple believed they had reached the right regulation of children for themselves, why could they not choose to be sterilized and to preclude any further fertility?) The following description of conjugal acts is given: "Conjugal acts which by intention are infertile (or which are rendered infertile) are ordered to the expression of the union of love; that love, however, reaches its culmination in fertility responsibly accepted. For that reason other acts of union in a certain sense are incomplete and they receive their full moral quality with ordination toward the fertile act. . . . Infertile conjugal acts constitute a totality with fertile acts and have a single moral specification."[82] The report later states, "The procreative end is substantially and really preserved even when here and now a fertile act is excluded; for infecundity is ordered to a new life well and humanly possessed."[83] Again, the Majority Rebuttal does retain the claim "The 'procreative end' [is] the essential end of sexuality and of conjugal life." But it allows this end to be circumvented, for instance, "when parents already have children to educate or they are not prepared to have a child." It speaks of "an obligation of conscience" and the "rights" of already existing children and of future children.[84] The claim that conjugal acts are a totality that has a single moral specification remains a constant objection to *Humanae Vitae* and came to be known as "the argument from the principle of totality."[85] Since it is a claim that is specifically addressed in *Humanae Vitae* it will be discussed at some length in Chapter 3.

Both reports rely heavily on natural law but they interpret that law differently; there are the stirrings here of major disagreements to come.

Would a Change in the Teaching on Contraception Change the Church's Teaching on Other Sexual Acts?

There is a fourth and final area of disagreement manifest in these documents that needs to be noted, however briefly.[86] The Minority Report fears that the arguments used to justify contraception also logically lead to the justification of other sexual acts that have traditionally been considered morally impermissible, such as extra-marital sex, masturbation, and oral and anal sex. It argues that the Church has condemned such actions because they are a violation of the intrinsic ordination of sexual acts to procreation.[87] The Majority Rebuttal takes up these acts one by one and offers some explanation why each would still be considered immoral.

Let us take one issue, the issue of masturbation, for the sake of comparison. The Church has always taught that masturbation is intrinsically immoral. A likely explanation for this condemnation would not be unlike the reasons for the condemnation of contraception. One might argue that masturbation involves a violation of the purpose of the generative organs. These organs are meant to bring forth new life and to foster unity between members of the opposite sex, the only unity that will lead to generation of new life. To masturbate is to engage in a solitary and sterile way in activity that is meant to be unitive and procreative. The Minority Report argues that on the grounds offered by the Majority—that intervention in the generative process is permissible if it can be shown to be directed toward the good of marriage—masturbation could be justified by some. These might claim that it can be "a remote preparation for realizing a harmonious sexual life in marriage. Many psychologists judge this to be a normal phase in adolescence for sound sexual formation and maintain that its forced suppression could cause much wrong in such formation."[88] The logic here would be if the sex act need not be in any immediate way procreative, why must it be in an immediate way unitive? If the act can be seen as a part of a whole, why may not each separate act gain its moral specification from the ordination of the whole, in regard to both fertility and unity?

The Majority Rebuttal counters, "Masturbation . . . negates . . . intersubjectivity. Masturbation, in as much as it turns the individual on himself and seeks mere egocentric satisfaction, totally perverts the essential intentionality of sexuality whereby man is directed out of himself towards another. For intercourse even with intervention [of contraception] is self-offering and heterosexual."[89] The Majority Rebuttal, then, understands masturbation to be immoral and incapable of justification by appeal to greater goods because it is *egocentric*.

Its reason for deeming masturbation to be egocentric seems to be simply that it does not involve another. The Minority would agree, of course, that masturbation is egocentric and that sexual intercourse needs to involve another. The authors of both documents would agree that the "other" who should be involved needs to be a member of the opposite sex and one to whom one is married, for both of these stipulations protect the procreative good of marriage (though many theologians have come to question these moral parameters as well). But the Minority would argue that every such union should protect the procreative good. It argues that the Majority understanding of the principle of totality would justify masturbation as long as the act contributes to a totality of acts that may foster conjugal love.

The Majority Rebuttal's steadfast argument that what have been called deviant sex acts by the Church would still be considered deviant by its criteria depends on an understanding of what kind of acts contribute to conjugal love; evidently, in their eyes, sexual acts that are naturally fertile, naturally infertile, and deliberately rendered infertile can all contribute to conjugal love and thus are morally permissible. Clearly, what is needed here (and in the Minority Report as well) is a definition of conjugal love and of the kinds of acts that promote conjugal love. Evidently the Majority Rebuttal thinks that masturbation is not the kind of act that fosters conjugal love, but until a definition of conjugal love is given and until an analysis of the kind of causation involved between certain acts and conjugal love is provided, this claim remains unsubstantiated.[90]

Certainly it is not out of place to mention that the predictions of the Minority Report that changing the Church's moral evaluation of contraception would lead to change in the moral evaluation of other sexual behavior seem to have been prophetic. Here is not the place to spell out a causal connection, but it is true that after many theologians broke with the Church's teaching on contraception, they came rather quickly to break with the Church's teaching on many other matters of sexual morality. As Charles Curran observed less than ten years later:

Catholic theologians frequently deny the existing teaching of the hierarchical magisterium on such issues as contraception, sterilization, artificial insemination, masturbation, the generic gravity of sexual sins. Newer

approaches have recently been taken to the question of homosexuality.
. . . All these questions in the area of medical and sexual morality are
being questioned today because some theologians believe that the absolute
prohibitions define the forbidden action in terms of the physical structure
of the act seen in itself apart from the context, the existing relationships
or the consequences.[91]

Catholic moral theology was clearly breaking with its past and
needed to find new definitions and explanations to justify the positions taken, whether old or new.

The Final Report, The Schema

As stated, the Minority Report and Majority Rebuttal were meant
to be strictly working documents of the commission and were sent
as appendices to the final report issued by the commission. The
complete final report of the commission has never been published.
The Doctrinal Schema (also known as the Majority Report) with a
Pastoral Introduction (in French) are the only two portions that
have been published. The Pastoral Introduction was written after
the Doctrinal Schema because many considered the Schema to be
technical and not readily accessible. The remarks on contraception
in the Pastoral Introduction are guarded and somewhat vague—
there is no acknowledgment that it is breaking with centuries of
Church teaching—but nonetheless they convey the message that it
understands some forms of contraception to be morally acceptable:

If an arbitrarily contraceptive mentality is to be condemned, as has
always been the church's view, an intervention to regulate conception in
a spirit of true, reasonable and generous charity (cf. Matt. 7:12, John
13:34–5; 15:12–7; Rom. 13:8–10) does not deserve to be, because if it
were, other goods of marriage might be endangered. So what is always to
be condemned is not the regulation of conception, but an egotistic married
life, refusing a creative opening-out of the family circle, and so refusing a
truly human—and therefore truly Christian—married love. This is the
anti-conception that is against the Christian ideal of marriage.

As for the means that husband and wife can legitimately employ, it is
their task to decide these together, without drifting into arbitrary decisions,
but always taking account of the objective criteria of morality. These
criteria are in the first place those that relate to the totality of married life
and sexuality.[92]

The first section of the Schema takes some pains to situate its remarks within the context of the documents of Vatican II. A few remarks are of special interest here. It maintains, "A couple (*unio conjugum*) ought to be considered above all a community of persons which has in itself the beginning of new human life. Therefore those things which strengthen and make more profound the union of persons within this community must never be separated from the procreative finality that specifies the conjugal community."[93] The first indication that a change in Church teaching will be counseled can be detected in the statement "Conjugal love and fecundity are in no way opposed, but complement one another in such a way that they constitute an almost indivisible unity."[94] The key word here is *almost*; it opens the door for separation of the unitive and procreative meanings of intercourse. (*Humanae Vitae* 12 constitutes a response to this claim when it notes that there is an "inseparable connection" between the unitive and procreative meanings of the conjugal act.)

In the next section the Schema defines responsible parenthood as "generous and prudent" parenthood. It states, "Genuine love, rooted in faith, hope and charity, ought to inform the whole life and every action of a couple. By the strength of this chastity the couple tend to the actuation of that true love precisely inasmuch as it is conjugal and fruitful."[95] It tells us, "The regulation of conception appears necessary for many couples who wish to achieve a responsible, open and reasonable parenthood in today's circumstances."[96] It calls for "decent and human" means of regulation of conception, for means "agreeable and worthy of man." The Schema does not explicitly acknowledge that it is counseling that the Church permit means heretofore prohibited, but such is the sense of the document. Nor is a full justification given for counseling change. There are, though, indications of what the building blocks for a justification would be.

In the first place, the document states, "It is proper to man, created to the image of God, to use what is given in physical nature in a way that he may develop it to its full significance with a view to the good of the whole person."[97] The document, it seems, understands Man to have greater freedom to manipulate nature than the Church has hitherto understood Man to have. It notes that human and decent regulation of contraception will require "intervention . . . into physiological processes" and notes that in a separate section criteria for judging the morality of such intervention will be presented. The document also places great weight on a principle of central importance to the Majority Rebuttal, the principle of totality. It states: "The morality of sexual acts between married people takes its meaning first of all and specifically from the ordering of their actions in a fruitful married life, that is one which is practiced with responsible, generous and prudent parenthood. It does not then depend upon the direct fecundity of each and every particular act."[98] This statement is a direct break with *Casti Connubii*, which states: "Any use whatsoever of matrimony exercised in such a way that the act is deliberately frustrated in its natural power to general life is an offense against the law of God and of nature, and those who indulge in such are branded with the guilt of a grave sin" (DSP 29). *Humanae Vitae* 11 reiterates this principle in the famous statement "Each and every marital act must remain ordained to procreation."

The Schema closes this section by rejecting "a mentality and way of married life which in its totality is egoistically and irrationally opposed to fruitfulness." Noting that the Church has traditionally condemned both contraceptive practice and mentality as gravely sinful, the Schema approves of the practice of contraception while continuing to maintain that the contraceptive mentality is to be considered gravely sinful.

Chapter 3 of the Schema attempts to show how its understanding of what makes for moral practice of regulation of conception is a true continuation of Church teaching and one that deepens but does not break with Church teaching. It notes that the same values have been "again and again reaffirmed." Its reading of the tradition leads it to conclude, "Consequently an egotistical, hedonistic and contraceptive way which turns the practice of married life in an arbitrary fashion from its ordination to a human, generous and prudent fecundity is always against the nature of man and can never be justified."[99]

In defense of its own advocacy of contraception it goes on to say: "The large amount of knowledge and facts which throw light on today's world suggest that it is not to contradict the genuine sense of this tradition and the purpose of the previous doctrinal condemnations if we speak of the regulation of conception by using means, human and decent, ordered to favoring fecundity in the totality of married life and toward the realization of the authentic values of a fruitful matrimonial community."[100] The Schema briefly states what facts and knowledge have led it to these conclusions. These include various changes in society such as changes in the role of women and concerns with population. It also maintains that its position is based on a "better, deeper, and more correct understanding of conjugal life."[101] Again, it insists, "The doctrine on marriage and its essential values remains the same and whole, but it is now applied differently out of a deeper understanding."[102]

The fourth section states four criteria whereby one should judge the morality of various means of contraception. Again, without defining what it means by natural law, this section invokes natural law and reason illuminated by Christian faith as the source of the objective criteria that will lead to the right ordering of the human act. Very little if any justification or explanation of these criteria is given. Let us review these criteria.

Four Criteria for Moral Use of Contraception

The first criterion is right out of *Gaudium et Spes:* "The action must correspond to the nature of the person and his acts so that the whole meaning of the mutual giving and of human procreation is kept in a context of true love."[103] It seems that the Schema understands *Gaudium et Spes* to have given the criterion of personalist values a priority over the good of procreation. It seems to claim that with a greater appreciation of the unitive power of sexual intercourse comes a diminishment of the centrality of procreation to the marital act, to the point that the procreative power of sexual intercourse may be deliberately excluded in order to advance the unitive aspect.

The second criterion is "The means which are chosen should have an effectiveness proportionate to the degree of right or necessity of averting a new conception temporarily or permanently."[104] This criterion seems to mean that if the spouses are very determined not to have a child, they should use the most effective means possible.

The third criterion asserts, "The means to be chosen, where several are possible, is that which carries with it the least possible negative element, according to the concrete situation of the couple."[105] This criterion is the only one receiving some explanation.

It is based on the principle "Every method of preventing conception—not excluding either periodic or absolute abstinence—carries with it some negative element or physical evil which the couple more or less seriously feels."[106] This statement seems to be the precursor to later claims that contraception is an evil, but a physical or premoral evil, not a moral evil. These terms are not explained here.[107]

The fourth criterion, stated without elaboration, is "In choosing concretely among means, much depends on what means may be available in a certain region or at a certain time or for a certain couple; this may depend on the economic situation."[108] This criterion seems to mean that the couple ought not to pay more than they can afford for contraception or more than the market requires.

The Schema is notably lacking in arguments and justifications for the positions that it takes. It certainly does not confront the arguments that have traditionally been given in opposition to contraception. Several prominent theologians, both those who argue for change in Church teaching and those who do not, have observed that the reports coming out of the commission were hardly of a quality to effect a change in centuries of Church teaching.[109] it was only after *Humanae Vitae* was issued that more extensive justifications were given for the moral permissibility of contraception.

Given the status of the debate at the time and the brevity of the documents, it is not surprising that these reports left many assumptions unstated and unjustified. There are many agreements and disagreements between them, but the major ones may be stated in this way; they agree that Man has some but not complete liberty over the use of his biological processes. The Minority Report sees God as the author of nature and of life and claims that by respecting the nature of the generative organs, which is directed toward life, Man is respecting the life that God creates through these organs. The Majority Rebuttal sees Man as having greater freedom over nature and as having been directed by God to direct nature to the goods of Man; use of contraception will assist Man in pursuing the goods of marriage, and therefore is permissible. The divergence between these two perspectives is not as sharp as it comes to be in the writings of later opponents. But perhaps this review of the arguments of the two sides is sufficient to show that the difference between them is not a quibble but verges on being a radical difference in what kinds of principles are proper guides for moral decision making. This divergence widened as the advocates of each side reflected more on the assumptions governing their positions and the implications of their positions. Later chapters will attempt to sketch out how these arguments developed.

The preceding analysis has sought to show that disagreements about ethical matters entail a host of assumptions that shape the argument. It was also meant to justify the claim that *Humanae Vitae* cannot be held accountable for addressing all the kinds of disputes that its teaching has spawned. *Humanae Vitae* is a document that rests in a tradition. It speaks to those who share the principles of that tradition and attempts to answer any questions raised about its teaching in terms of that tradition. It uses the principles of the tradition to deal with questions that might be raised even by those who are sympathetic to its tradition. Chapters 3 and 4 comment further on the natural law claims of *Humanae Vitae* and explain some of the more essential moral principles guiding the teaching. This chapter has considered the deliberations that immediately preceded *Humanae Vitae*. What needs to be done next is to look at the other immediate context—or tradition—from which *Humanae Vitae* came, the context of the Church's teaching on marriage, most particularly that expounded in Vatican II.

TWO

Christian Marriage

Humanae Vitae depends on a Christian understanding of the nature or meaning of marriage and in particular on a Christian understanding of the importance of the marital gift of having children. Although the condemnation of contraception fundamentally depends on natural law principles, the Church draws on specifically Christian understandings when it calls on Christian disciples to live a moral life. In this chapter, *Humanae Vitae* will be placed primarily within the context of the teaching on marriage conveyed through *Casti Connubii* (1930) and *Gaudium et Spes* (1965). These documents, of course, are not the only place to look for the Church's teaching on marriage. The teaching comes through a variety of sources, notably Scripture, the writings of theologians, and speeches by the popes; decrees and decisions by various Vatican offices are, for instance, other sources of Church teaching. Here there is not space to investigate all these sources; fortunately others have done so.[1] Our task here is to test the compatibility of *Humanae Vitae* with the Church's teaching on marriage, to mark its continuity with the tradition, and to explore any advances made on it.

To focus our inquiry, we shall first review the basics of the Church's teaching on the nature of marriage. Second, we shall turn to our first area of particular concern, the meaning and the status of the claim that procreation is the primary end of marriage. There is some risk in focusing on this question for to do so may give the unfortunate impression that this claim is the kingpin to the teaching of *Humanae Vitae* and that the argument against contraception is completely dependent on it. The arguments against contraception are many and varied; the Church gives no single or "official" argu-

36

+ CONSENT

ment against contraception. Certainly, the claim that procreation is the primary end of marriage has a long and honored history in the teaching of the Church. Yet, those who think that if the Church were to abandon its claim that procreation is the primary end of marriage it would be without resources to condemn contraception may be surprised at the wide variety of arguments advanced against contraception. As subsequent chapters of this book will show, the arguments currently advanced against contraception are not based exclusively on the claim that procreation is the primary end of marriage but draw on a very full understanding of the meaning of marital relationships. Nonetheless, an examination of the meaning of this claim should help to demonstrate the importance of childbearing to the meaning of marriage, an importance the modern age is particularly likely to underestimate.

The third section of this chapter attempts to define conjugal love, provides a consideration of personalist values, and examines the teaching of *Gaudium et Spes* on conjugal love. We shall be keeping in mind that some theologians have charged that in its teaching on marriage, the Church has paid insufficient attention to the value of conjugal love. They claim that the Church has focused too exclusively on the value of procreation in marriage, on the biological purposes of sex. Our review of the Majority Report or Schema indicated that many believed (and many still believe) that a due evaluation of conjugal love and of personalist values would serve to justify the use of contraception. The following analysis seeks to trace the emergence of the interest in the place of conjugal love in marriage and its relation to the importance of childbearing within marriage. Subsequent chapters argue that the emphasis on conjugal love has not served to diminish opposition to contraception by many theologians, but it has given them another ground on which to build a case against contraception; they argue that contraception violates the good of conjugal love, as well as the good of procreation.

Christian Marriage

The Catholic Church teaches that monogamous, indissoluble marriage is not just one of many possible and equally legitimate arrangements concocted by Man to serve his needs for a sensible family arrangement, for securing a clear line of inheritance, for stabilizing his sexual life, and so forth. Rather, the Church teaches that there is a proper relationship between spouses that is properly safeguarded and nourished in monogamous and indissoluble marriage. This relationship is somewhat like the relationship of parent to child in that it is rooted in nature and thus conducive to the good of the parties involved. Like the relation of parent to child, the relation of spouses has an objective reality; that is, it has a nature that can be studied and known, and that must be respected in order for the goods of such a relationship to come to be. *Casti Connubii* states, "From God comes the very institution of marriage, the ends for which it was instituted, the laws that govern it, the blessings that flow from it."[2] *Gaudium et Spes* makes a similar claim:

The intimate partnership [*communitas*] of life and love which constitutes the married state has been established by the creator and endowed by him with its own proper laws: it is rooted in the contract [*foedere*] of its partners, that is, in their irrevocable personal consent. It is an institution confirmed by the divine law and receiving its stability, even in the eyes of society, from the human act by which the partners mutually surrender themselves to each other; for the good of the partners, of the children, and of society this sacred bond [*vinculum sacrum*] no longer depends on human decision alone. For God himself is the author of marriage and has endowed it with various benefits and various ends in view [*bonis ac finibus*]. . . . (GS 48)[3]

And we find *Humanae Vitae* repeating this claim: "It is false to think, then, that marriage results from chance or from the blind course of natural forces. Rather, God the Creator wisely and providently established marriage with the intent that He might achieve His own design of love through Men" (HV 8).[4] Again, the Church teaches that marriage is not an arrangement invented by Man for his own convenience and thus open to whatever revisions or forms he may prefer. Rather, it is a relationship instituted by God for Man's well-being and it has a form, function, or essence that corresponds to Man's nature and thus is not open to radical redefinition; to a large extent for spouses to succeed at marriage they must submit themselves to this reality. Many claim that marriages so often fail in our modern age because spouses expect and want marriage to be something it simply is not and cannot be. Just as it benefits Man to learn the nature of whatever he deals with, so too does it benefit

Man to learn and live in accord with the nature of marriage. Just as parents can expect to do a better job of parenting the more they know about the natural and right relationship of parent to child, so too the better spouses might expect to be at being spouses, the more they know about the nature and dynamics of marriage.

The Church teaches that marriage, though designed by God, is not an institution whose proper form is known only to Christians. Christian marriages differ in certain important respects from "natural" marriages, but Christian marriage in many respects shares the characteristics of these "natural" marriages or marriages constituted outside the Church.[5] The Church teaches that the goodness of marriage is known to Man through natural law: that is, Man needs no special revelation to realize that marriage is an institution that is conducive to what is good for Man. Marriage, of course, existed long before Christianity arrived and exists in cultures that are not Christian. The Church for the most part respects the validity of these marriages since they generally share the characteristics necessary for a true marriage: that is, most societies expect marriages to be freely undertaken, faithful and indissoluble, and open to children, all, according to the Church, characteristics of true marriages. It has long been the understanding of the Church that mankind in general has recognized that marriage is by nature a relationship of unity and stability, that is, that marriage is a relationship that serves to unite the spouses and is designed to be lasting—for the well-being of the spouses, of the children they may have, and of society as a whole. Church documents have asserted that natural law teaches Man such precepts as "extra-marital intercourse is morally evil."[6] It teaches that marriage by its nature is monogamous.[7] It teaches that marriage is perpetual and indissoluble; for instance, Pius XI quotes Pius VI about the indissolubility of marriage: "Hence it is clear that marriage even in the state of nature, and certainly long before it was raised to the dignity of a sacrament, was divinely instituted in such a way that it should carry with it a perpetual and indissoluble bond which cannot therefore be dissolved by any civil law."[8]

A Christian marriage certainly shares the characteristics of a natural marriage but has a deeper meaning. For instance, like a natural marriage, it is by its nature perpetual and indissoluble. But, as Canon 1134 of the new Code of Canon Law states, "In a valid marriage, there is formed between the spouses a bond which is by its nature perpetual and indissoluble; in a Christian marriage spouses are strengthened by a special sacrament and, as it were, consecrated for the duties and dignity of their state in life."[9] The sacramental nature of Christian marriage is what largely sets it apart from "natural" marriage. The expectations, thus, for a Christian marriage are higher than those for a "natural" marriage, for the graces of the sacrament are available to help spouses live up to the promises of marriage. In fact, despite the fact the marriage is by nature indissoluble, divorce was permitted in the Old Testament largely because the graces won by Christ were not available in the same ready way. Marriage as a sacrament also means that marriage has a special role to play in the pursuit of salvation. It has a role to play in the sanctifying of the spouses and in the bringing of Christ's message into the world.

The sacrament of marriage is also a vocation. That is, it is a state in life to which individuals are called and through which they are to make a contribution to advancing God's intent for this world, to transforming this world in accord with the love of Christ. Like those who are called to other vocations, spouses must be prepared to accept the full demands of their vocation. A priest could not become a priest and choose not to perform some of the sacraments; it is of the very nature of his calling that he is to be willing to perform the sacraments when called on to do so. Priests have a wide variety of "careers" and are certainly not all clones of each other, but there is a set of core responsibilities that is theirs by virtue of their being priests. When they freely and knowingly answer the call to be priests they are answering the call to accept these responsibilities. Similarly, marital relationships need not all be exactly the same, but neither are spouses free to make marriage be whatever they wish it to be. Let us now try to explain somewhat more precisely the nature of marriage to which spouses are expected to conform.

We have already learned that marriages are to be freely undertaken, faithful, and indissoluble, but we have not yet stated explicitly what marriage fundamentally is. A wide variety of terms have been used in Church documents to describe marriage. For instance, it has been called a bond, a contract, a covenant, a partnership, a friendship, a communion of persons.[10] Some argue that a shift in the terms used to define marriage manifests a shift in the Church's understanding of marriage.[11] For instance, some claim that it is highly significant that *covenant* appears more prominently in the documents of Vatican II than *contract*, which was used more commonly before Vatican II. Undoubtedly these terms serve to disclose different aspects of marriage, but it is unlikely that they signal a radical shift in the Church's understanding of marriage. Different contexts for treating marriage require different terms. *Contract* has its source primarily in canon law, which is concerned to determine the juridical status of marriages; and *covenant*, a term widely used even before Vatican II, is more appropriate in contexts where the theological understanding of marriage is of concern. Briefly stated, marriage is a *contract* in that it is a freely chosen and legally binding agreement between male and female to be responsible to one another, to their children, and to society; it is a *covenant* in that it reflects the love that Christ has for His Church and thus obliges the couple to unconditional and faithful love for each other. Indeed, the word *covenant* recalls the relationship that Yahweh had with his people Israel in the Old Testament. The Israelites learned a great deal about their relationship with God and about marriage through the prophets' nearly constant use of marital imagery. The notion of marriage as a covenant is a singularly rich concept and is a source of some of the other descriptions of marriage given previously, such as the notion that it is a "communion of persons." Such descriptions of marriage serve to highlight certain features of the desired relationship between the spouses.

Though the words *contract* and *covenant* for marriage are eminently suitable to and revealing of the nature of marriage, the essence of marriage is most likely best captured by the word *bond*. The Latin word for marriage is *conjugium*, from which we derive our *conjugal*, and it means "yoked together." This image is compatible with the word *vinculum*, or "bond," the Latin word most often used to define marriage and a word that embraces all the terms suggested. The marriage bond is a special bond that confers on the spouses certain duties and rights. The Church has always taught that this bond must be freely and deliberately undertaken by individuals who intend to seek the good of the other and who are prepared to embrace the responsibility of parenthood. The Church teaches that neither obligation can be properly fulfilled unless the relationship or bond is faithful and indissoluble. It teaches further that marriage as a sacrament provides graces to assist spouses in meeting their obligations.

The Church also speaks of the "ends," "benefits," or "purposes" of marriage. Before *Humanae Vitae* many theologians, following Augustine, taught that marriage had three ends or blessings or goods (*bona*): offspring, fidelity, and sacrament.[12] *Casti Connubii* provides considerable discussion of these and cites Saint Augustine on this point: "These are all the blessings of matrimony on account of which matrimony itself is a blessing; offspring, conjugal faith and the sacrament" (8).[13]

In the debate about contraception, the claim that has created the most controversy is that procreation is the primary end of marriage. Again, some have argued that this claim grows out of an undue focus on the biological or physiological understanding of sexuality. Much of the objection to speaking of "procreation" as the primary end of marriage seems to be rooted in the sense that this designation places human sexual intercourse on a plane with the sexual intercourse between animals. Since many argue that sexual union between animals has as its primary—and sole—purpose the perpetuation of the species, they balk at having human sexual intercourse described in a way that suggests that such is its sole purpose. The following analysis attempts to show that this is a false understanding of the claim that procreation is the primary end of marriage.

Marriage and Procreation

Some have also claimed that the failure of *Gaudium et Spes* to repeat the designation of procreation as the primary end of marriage indicates a repudiation by the Church of this understanding and suggests that such a repudiation opens the door to legitimizing contraception.[14] Let us here attempt to understand what the Church means by stating that "procreation is the primary end of marriage" and to determine whether there has been a repudiation of this way of speaking.

Casti Connubii states, "Amongst the blessings of marriage, the child holds the first place" (8). *Gaudium et Spes* speaks of children as the "supreme gift of marriage" (50) and *Humanae Vitae* 9 repeats this claim. If past ages have been somewhat reticent to expound upon the personalist goods of marriage, perhaps our age is somewhat less aware of and enthusiastic about the goods of procreation. Certainly the prevalence of abortion, the popularity of contraception, and the reluctance to have large families all point to a perspective that children are more of a burden than a blessing. Children seem to be seen more as a strain on the resources of a couple than a "means" by which couples may increase their love for each other and assist each other in growing in maturity and generosity. Moreover, modern couples place a very high value on the ability to control with precision the number and spacing of the children that they have. Indeed, many theologians and married couples hailed contraception as a great benefit that would enable spouses to exercise rational control over their fertility, that would allow them to enjoy the "unitive" or "personalist" goods of marriage while remaining free from anxiety about a possible, undesired pregnancy. To many, the insistence that procreation is the primary end of marriage represents a devaluation of the personalist values of marital union; it suggests to some that humans are being viewed as mere animals who are to be unreasonably submissive to their physiology. Humans, in their view, should employ rationality to enable them to have the fullest possible control of their fertility; they should not have children by *chance* but by *planning*. Contraception should be seen as a good, then, because it allows spouses the opportunity to express their love sexually and to be responsible about being parents. The Church's insistence that each act of marital union remain ordained to children seems to many to be irrational and subhuman, if not punitive.

This way of thinking, though, may betray an insufficient appreciation of the procreative meaning of the conjugal act. When the Church claims that procreation is the primary end of marriage, it is, in the first place, assuming that children are a great good of marriage. The objection to speaking of procreation as the primary end of marriage generally not only bespeaks a misunderstanding of what is meant by the claim that procreation is the primary end of marriage but also suggests an inadequate understanding of the good that offspring are to a marriage, of the good that parents experience precisely through being parents. Few recognize that the procreative values of sexuality do not oppose personalist values but in fact may be vital to the full realization of personalist values.

The first step in understanding the procreative meaning of marital union is to recognize the undeniable physiological and biological reality that unimpeded sexual intercourse occasionally results in the creation of a new life.[15] That is, the union of the sexes is the way in which new life is engendered. Yet, of course, no one would argue that this is a sufficient description of the whole meaning of human spousal love. Whereas it is adequate to describe the purpose of sexual intercourse in the animal kingdom as being the propagation of the species, it is not adequate to describe the purpose of human sexual intercourse in this way. First, it must be noted that in human "reproduction," the parents of the new life are much more than simply its source. In *Casti Connubii* the emphasis throughout the section on the blessing of children is on the role that parents play in "raising up fellow-citizens of the Saints, and members of God's household" (9). This responsibility clearly requires of parents that they be not only the source of physical life for their offspring but also their educators, especially in regard to matters of faith. This is a distinctive *human* responsibility, for only humans have responsibilities of this nature.

The sexual union of animals seems to do little to unite the sexes or to foster union by drawing together different families or to promote the other goods achieved by spousal sexual union. The fact that we find it awkward if not ridiculous to speak of *spousal* love in the animal kingdom indicates how radically human sex differs from animal sex. It shows how limited is the practice of drawing parallels between the purpose of sexual union in the animal kingdom and the purpose of marital union between human spouses.[16] A passage from *Casti Connubii* speaks very much to this point: "By matrimony . . . the souls of the contracting parties are joined and knit together more directly and more intimately than are their bodies, and that not by any passing affection of sense or spirit, but by a deliberate and firm act of the will; and from this union of souls by God's decree, a sacred and inviolable bond arises. Hence the nature of this contract, which is proper and peculiar to it alone, makes it *entirely different* both from the union of animals entered into by the blind instinct of nature alone in which neither reason nor free will plays a part . . ." (my emphasis, 6). Not only does the relation between human "mates" differ radically from the union of animals but so too does the relation that parents have with their offspring differ radically from the relations of animal parents and offspring. Evidently some animals show particular care for their offspring, but the care and concern that human parents regularly show for their children seem again to be so radically different as to make the usefulness of the comparison quite slim.

Human sexual intercourse and human child rearing, then, are radically different from strictly animal sexual intercourse and animal care of offspring. The comparison with the sexual intercourse of animals is perhaps most useful for highlighting what is distinctive about human sexual union. Dogs and cats have *reproductive* sexual intercourse, sexual intercourse that brings another member of their species into existence. Humans have *procreative* sexual intercourse, intercourse wherein they cooperate with God to bring into existence a new immortal being, whose growth in love and understanding of God they undertake to guide. The importance of the new human person is not confined or even rooted in the role he or she plays in sustaining the existence of the species. As a creature with an immortal soul and thus as a potential sharer in the beatific vision, the individual person has an infinite worth in his or her own right. Some of the significance of the radical difference between the generating of new animal life and the generating of new human life is reflected in the difference of the terms *reproductive* and *procreative*. [17] *Reproduction* means to bring forth something from preexisting materials. *Procreation* is rooted in the term *create*, an act that, properly speaking, only God can perform since "to create" means to bring something out of nothing. Moderns find it strange to speak of plants and animals as having souls, but the ancients and medievals argued that any living thing has a soul; and souls have many powers, the powers of keeping something alive (the nutritive powers of the soul), of responding affectively to one's environment (the sensate powers of soul), and of reasoning about reality (the rational powers of the soul). Not all souls are immortal: only rational souls are immortal; nutritive and sensate souls are not. Those beings that are material only or those with only mortal souls share in existence only temporally, whereas humans, being immortal, have a share in God's eternal being. Whereas animal souls come into existence through the uniting of certain kinds of matter, the coming to be of human life requires a special act of creation by God: a human soul is not "reproduced" out of preexisting materials but is "procreated" through a unique act of divine creation bringing a new, special, and unique being out of nothing.

Furthermore, *pro-create* means to create *for:* in this case spouses create "for" God; that is, they help God create new life. Spouses are privileged to share in the "transmitting" of human life; God initiates this new life; spouses "transmit" it. The first line of *Humanae Vitae* speaks of the "very important mission of *transmitting life*, entrusted by God to spouses. . ." (my emphasis). *Casti Connubii* speaks of God using men as His helpers in the propagation of human life (8) and of husband and wife "receiving children with joy and gratitude from the hand of God," to be regarded as "a talent committed to their charge by God. . ." (10). Yet, the role of spouses in the transmitting of life is not strictly instrumental. It is not that God "uses" the spouses as passive instruments to bring forth new human life. Rather, spouses freely and willingly enter into actions the nature of which they are capable of understanding. Humans, unlike creatures in the animal kingdom, are capable of taking responsibility for their sexual acts, of knowing that they may bring forth new life and of knowing the value and dignity of the life that they bring forth. They are capable of knowing the responsibilities that bringing forth new life entails. Made in God's image, they, too, act freely, responsibly, and *lovingly*. For we must remember that God creates out of love; He wishes to share the goods of existence with others. God is a trinity, a community of lovers whose goodness overflows into the creation of new being. Spouses, too, are a community of lovers, whose loving acts, joined with the creative power of God, may pour forth into the (pro)creation of a new human life. Their responsibility for this life is enormous. And here we find one connection between the procreative end and personalist values, for spouses must strive for "mutual perfection" so that they might assist each other in growing in maturity and virtue, so that together they might create an environment wherein their children might also grow in virtue. By being good parents, they become better persons.

Children, then, are a multifold source of goods for a marriage, goods that far supersede the simple perpetuation of the species. But, still, why does the Church claim that they are the *primary* end of marriage?

Casti Connubii briefly states the scriptural grounding for the claim that children are the primary end of marriage:

Amongst the blessings of marriage, the child holds the first place. And indeed the Creator of the human race Himself, Who in His goodness wished to use men as His helpers in the propagation of life, taught this when, instituting marriage in Paradise, He said to our first parents, and through them to all future spouses; "Increase and multiply, and fill the earth." As St. Augustine admirably deduces from the words of the holy Apostle Saint Paul to Timothy when he says: "The Apostle himself is therefore witness that marriage is for the sake of generation: 'I wish,' he says, 'young girls to marry.' And, as if some one said to him 'Why?,' he immediately adds: "To bear children, to be mothers of families." (8)

And later *Casti Connubii* notes that the Code of Canon Law states, "The primary end of marriage is the procreation and the education of children."

In 1944, a decree of the Holy Office reaffirmed procreation as the primary end of marriage when it responded in the negative to a question about the legitimacy of denying that the primary end of marriage is procreation and the validity of the claim that the secondary ends were not subordinate to the primary end but were equally primary and independent.[18] Pius XII clearly reiterated the hierarchy of ends in his speech of October 29, 1951, to the Union of Italian Catholic Midwives.[19]

In spite of these strong affirmations, the fact that neither *Gaudium et Spes* nor *Humanae Vitae* speaks explicitly of procreation as the primary end of marriage has led some to insist that the Church has in recent years repudiated this understanding of marriage.[20] Indeed, *Gaudium et Spes* seems to "sidestep" the question: "Without intending to underestimate the other ends of marriage, it must be said that true married love and the whole structure of family life which results from it is directed to disposing the spouses to cooperate valiantly with the love of the Creator and Saviour, who through them will increase and enrich his family from day to day" (50). But it also states, "By its very nature the institution of marriage and married love is ordered to the procreation and education of the offspring and it is in them that it finds its crowning glory" (48). And "Marriage and married love are by nature ordered to the procreation and education of children" (50). Furthermore, of great importance is a footnote[21] attached to the passage cited previously from section 48, which refers to God as the author of marriage who has endowed it with various ends. This note makes reference to passages in Augustine and in Aquinas, to several papal statements, and to *Casti Connubii*; the passages referred to are the very ones that make the claim that procreation is the primary end of marriage. The footnote reference, then, would seem to indicate that there has been no repudiation of this understanding.

The reason that *Gaudium et Spes* did not reiterate this understanding explicitly in the text can, perhaps, be found in a response to 190 fathers of the council who requested that the traditional ordering of the ends of marriage be included in the text. The response stated, "In a pastoral text intended to initiate dialogue with the world such legal language (*elementa illa iuridica*) is not required." Another portion of the response noted that the hierarchy of the goods of marriage is able to be considered according to different aspects.[22] Thus it would seem that the fathers of the council did not choose to repudiate the understanding of a hierarchy of ends within marriage but, rather, chose not to use such technical language in a pastoral document. Moreover, the remark about the different ways of understanding the language of hierarchy of goods suggests the care that must be taken in explaining what is meant by the claim that procreation is the primary end of marriage.

The first fundamental distinction that must be made is that between the *finis operantis* and the *finis operis*, that is, the difference between the end or intention of the agent, in this case the spouses, and the end or intention of the act, in this case marital intercourse. When the Church claims that marital intercourse has procreation as its end, it is not saying that spouses marry primarily for the sake of having children or that they must intend in an immediate and direct way to have children when choosing to have sexual intercourse. The Catechism of the Council of Trent (1564) gives the following description of the reasons for marriage: "The reasons for marriage as a natural institution should be explained. The first reason is the instinctive mutual attraction of the two sexes to form a stable companionship of the two persons, as a basis for mutual happiness and help amid the trials of life extending even to sickness and old age. The second reason is another instinctive desire: to have offspring. This desire should be not so much to have heirs for one's property, as rather to provide new recipients for the gift of faith and new heirs for heaven."[23] Spouses, then, may have many reasons for undertaking marriage, but this does not invalidate the claim that marriage has an end independent of their reasons for seeking marriage. The claim that procreation is the primary end of marriage seems to be based on the observation that the conjugal act itself has a primary ordination to the begetting of children and that marriage embraces the purpose of the act of sexual intercourse.

A distinction that Aristotle makes may also help us in our deliberations about these matters. In his *Categories* (section 12) he explains that the word *prior* (or *primary*) has four different senses. First, it has a temporal sense, that one thing comes to be in time before another. Second, A is said to be prior to B if B's existence requires A's but A's does not require B's. For instance, if two exists, there must also be one. Third, one thing is prior to another according to some order; for instance, in grammar the letters are prior to the syllables. In a fourth sense, one thing is thought to be better or more honorable than another; a lover may refer to his beloved as "number one." It would seem that some theologians, especially those rejecting the claim that procreation is the primary end of marriage, believe the Church to be using *primary* in the fourth sense, as an end that is better and more honorable than other ends. Obviously, that need not be the case. The primacy of procreation as an end could be meant in the second sense described: it could mean if marriage is truly ordained to union, it must also embrace the good of procreation. Or it could be meant in the third sense, that the good of procreation helps explain the other goods; that the good of procreation is a "part of" the goods of indissolubility and faithfulness (which, indeed, protect the good of procreation). Indeed, several scholars have done careful work on the meaning of the language of the ends of marriage. Here we will be relying primarily on the work of John Ford and Germain Grisez.[24]

Ford makes a distinction between the ends of marriage and the goods of marriage. Following the Code of Canon Law of 1917, he maintains that the three essential ends of marriage are procreation and education of offspring, remedy for concupiscence, and mutual help. He understands indissolubility and unity to be properties of marriage, not ends, and sacrament to be a good of marriage. In spite of the difference in terminology, his analysis of how these different ends are related to each other is relevant to our concerns here. He provides these important cautions:

First, they are not three entirely distinct ends, although we separate them for purposes of analysis. They are bound up together and partially overlap in many respects. For instance, the same acts which bring about the procreation of children result in the remedy of concupiscence. Not the least important element of mutual help is the fact that by it the partners form an adequate principle for the education of the children God may send them. The acts by which they educate the child are acts of mutual help. The sexual act, too, when lovingly performed, as the partners are obliged to perform it, is an act of mutual help as well as a procreative act. And in cases where conception is impossible there is only a limited sense in which it can be called procreative—it is principally an act of mutual help. It is a mistake, therefore, to take the division into three purposes too literally. The institution of marriage is aimed at all these ends together, and they are inextricably intertwined with one another.

Secondly, though marriage aims at all these ends, the actual realization of none of them is essential to any given marriage. This is obvious upon a moment's reflection. A marriage which produces no children is still a marriage. A marriage which is never sexually consummated is a real marriage. A marriage in which lust is not remedied, but reigns, is still a marriage. Even a marriage in which there is no mutual help, no life in common, hatred instead of love, and complete separation, both bodily and spiritually, remains a true marriage in the sense that the essence of marriage is still there; that is, the partners are still married, and in virtue of the essential marriage bond they are still bound to one another.

Nevertheless, though the actual attainment of the ends of marriage is not essential to any marriage, theologians do state generally that the three ends of marriage are *all essential* ends. I believe that it is common teaching to say that all three ends are essential to marriage, so that *de facto*, in the present order of things, marriage cannot exist without being related to these three ends. The partners may, of course, have any number of ends in view in making the contract. But marriage itself, the thing they consent to, cannot exist without being objectively ordered to the three essential ends —procreation and education, remedy for concupiscence, and mutual help.[25]

Further on, Ford notes that saying that procreation is the primary end of marriage does not suggest that it is more essential than the other ends or more important than the other ends. He understands procreation to be more fundamental in the sense that "procreation and education of children implies and includes mutual help to a certain extent." And second he states, "Procreation is of more importance to the species" and "One can, therefore, for valid philosophical reasons call procreation primary (i.e., more important, more fundamental) by saying that since the good of the species is more important to nature than the good of individuals, procreation is a more important aim of marriage than mutual help."[26] Ford's reasoning seems cogent but seems to place the natural end of marriage, the good of the species, ahead of the supernatural end of marriage, the sanctification of the spouses. It would seem that the ends of marriage can be ordered differently when looked at from either the natural or the supernatural perspective.

In an article written after *Gaudium et Spes* but before *Humanae Vitae*, Grisez explains this different ordering through a careful analysis of the various meanings of *primary*. He turns to Aquinas for assistance in understanding the claim that procreation is the primary end of marriage and concludes, "We do not receive a simple answer. The reason is that primacy is determined in different ways, for sometimes we consider to be first what is more basic, and sometimes we consider to be first what is more valuable in itself."[27] He cites a lengthy passage from Aquinas that makes the proper distinctions; it would serve us well to repeat it here:

If we are considering the question from the point of view of intrinsic value, then by every way of comparing the three goods, the sacrament takes primacy, for it belongs to matrimony as a sign of grace, while the other goods belong to it as a natural institution, and the perfection of grace is intrinsically superior to the perfection of nature. But if what is more basic is called primary, a distinction is needed, because fidelity and offspring can be considered in two ways. In one way in their actual attainment, and so they belong to the actions of married life, by which offspring are procreated and the commitment of the marital vow is fulfilled. Indissoluble unity, which the sacrament connotes, belongs to the state of matrimony in itself, for by the very fact that the spouses mutually and permanently give themselves over to one another by their marital vows it follows that they can never be separated. This is why marriage never occurs without inseparability, but it does occur without fidelity and offspring, because the existence of an institution does not depend on the action that fulfills it. And so in this way the sacrament is more basic than fidelity and offspring. In another way, fidelity and offspring can be considered as they exist in principle, so that by "offspring" one means the intention of offspring and by "fidelity" one means the obligation of serving fidelity and then marriage cannot exist without these goods too, for they flow into marriage directly from the conjugal vows themselves. Hence if anything incompatible with these goods is included in the commitment required to constitute marriage, no true marriage exists. And so in this way of understanding fidelity and offspring, offspring is most fundamental, fidelity is second, and sacrament comes third, just as natural reality is more basic to man than the life of grace, although the latter is of greater intrinsic value (*In 4 Sent.*, d. 31, q. 1, art. 3).[28]

From this Grisez concludes: "Here we find Aquinas saying, in other words, that the procreation and raising of children is the primary end of marriage only in a certain qualified sense—that is, that the intention of offspring is the most basic principle of marriage, providing as it does the content of the commitment to which the partners avow themselves, a commitment which itself establishes the good of fidelity and the permanent bond whose indissoluble unity is a sign of grace."[29] (Here, let it be clear that *intention* in this passage does not refer to the subjective intention of the spouses but to the natural ordination of marriage.) Grisez goes on to mention one further sense in which procreation can be said to be the primary end of marriage. He informs us, "In another passage, Aquinas explains that human marriage has offspring as an end in virtue of man's generic nature, for man shares with all animals the goal of continuing himself, while marriage has fidelity as an end in virtue of man's specifically personal nature, and it has the sacramental function as its end in virtue of believing man's participation in divine life through the grace of Christ" (*In 4 Sent.* d. 33, q. 1, art. 1).[30] The claim that procreation is the primary end of marriage, then, does not mean that it is the most important end of marriage. Rather, it is primary in several different senses: (1) Because man does have an animal nature, and clearly in nature, "reproduction" is the end of sexual activity, this would be the initial, first, or "primary" observation that one makes about sexual intercourse; it would be curious to speak about sexual intercourse without noting that it has procreation as an end. It is not a wild speculation to note that this, in most ages, would be the first observation most would make about the purpose of sexual intercourse. Looking at marriage and sexual intercourse from different perspectives, of course, discloses other purposes and ends of sexual intercourse. (2) And more in keeping with the rational nature of Man, procreation, or responsibility toward children, is primary in another sense. It sets one of the foundations (and is thus, "primary") for the requirement that marriage be faithful and indissoluble. Since sexual intercourse may result in children, those who engage in sexual intercourse must have this "primarily" in mind so that they might be responsible for any children begotten. That is, first, before they engage in sexual intercourse, they must be prepared to provide for any children begotten. The Church has always taught that marriage is the proper relationship that begins to provide the right atmosphere for bringing up children. And marriage must be such as to provide for the well-being of those children. Thus, for this reason (as well as for others) marriages should be faithful and indissoluble, for only such relationships are truly conducive to the well-being of children. Marriage, then, has as a primary end procreation, because marriage, in a sense, primarily protects the children that are a product of sexual intercourse.

To speak of procreation as the primary end of marriage, then, does not mean that the Church puts the highest value in simple biological reproduction. Rather procreation as an end includes the education of the children as well as their coming-to-be. Nor does procreation as the primary end of marriage serve to diminish the importance of the other ends or goods of marriage. Indeed, these are also essential and in some senses more important and more excellent. But the admission that calling procreation the primary end of marriage does not necessarily mean that it is the end of the most worth will most likely not satisfy many modern theologians who contest this claim. It seems that they are not interested in elevating the other ends of marriage to the same level as procreation or even in succeeding in having them supersede the importance of procreation. Their radical break with tradition rests not so much in a reordering of the ends of marriage as in their claim that the ends or goods of marriage could on occasion be in conflict with each other, that is, for instance, that at times it would be impossible to pursue the goods of conjugal love while also being open to procreation. And in this era of in vitro fertilization and surrogate motherhood, they are also willing to allow pursuit of the good of offspring while sacrificing some of the traditional safeguards of conjugal love.

What might be concluded here is that the terms *primary* and *secondary* are technical and that it is easy to misinterpret them. Furthermore, it is important to note that the Church's teaching against contraception may not depend on this terminology; that, as *Humanae Vitae* teaches, an understanding of procreation as one of the *inseparable* meanings of marriage may suffice to indicate the wrongness of contraception. Later chapters will take up this point.

Let us now turn to a consideration of this other good of marriage so valued in our times, the good of conjugal love, and attempt to discern whether in fact it is in tension with the good of procreation.

Conjugal Love and Personalist Values

In spite of the constancy of the teaching about the "ends" or "blessings" of marriage throughout the documents of the Church, there is a notable shift of terminology in more modern sources that may also indicate a shift in focus or emphasis. Many have claimed that earlier times stressed the procreative and societal values of marriage to the detriment of a full appreciation of the personalist values of marriage. They claim that only in more modern times have men come to appreciate the value of conjugal love.[31] Many have seen a development in the emphasis put on the personalist value of conjugal love in modern theological considerations of marriage and occasionally argue that such an emphasis might warrant a change in the Church's condemnation of contraception.[32] This is a central claim of John Noonan's *Contraception*. Noonan finds that the Church's teaching has been greatly dominated by the teaching of St. Augustine, who, Noonan argues, did not approve of sexual intercourse engaged in strictly for pleasure and without a procreative intent. Although this view of Augustine seems to be widely accepted, Noonan's claim has not been uncontested.[33] Here is not the place to attempt to mediate this controversy, but it is to our purpose to provide at least a sketchy account of the history of the role of conjugal love in the Church's teaching on marriage.

But first let us note that in the literature on this topic there is much looseness and imprecision in the use of the terms *conjugal love* and *personalist values.* On occasion, conjugal love is seen as the sole personalist value; on others it is seen as one of many personalist values to be fostered through marriage. And the understandings of conjugal love vary greatly. Conjugal love is variously said to be the meaning of marriage, the end of marriage, and the reason for or source of marriage.[34] Occasionally it seems to be closely equated with romantic love, and on other occasions it seems to refer very narrowly to the sexual attraction felt by the spouses, or to the act of sexual intercourse within marriage, or to the pleasure consequent on that act. Here the term will be used to specify the love that is especially appropriate to spouses, the unconditional, exclusive, and faithful love of marriage that expresses itself, among other ways, through the act of sexual union.[35] (See *Humanae Vitae* 9 for a listing of characteristics of conjugal love.)

Let us note more emphatically that the term *conjugal love* as used here is not equivalent to the sense of "romantic" love that so dominates modern consciousness; conjugal love is not incompatible with romantic love and may certainly help foster it, but it is decidedly not identical to it. Having conjugal love for another, or more accurately, being committed to living in accord with the demands of conjugal love with another, does not mean that one must see one's spouse as perfect, or as one's only beloved soul mate; it does not mean that one cannot imagine happiness or a life worth living without being married to this particular spouse or that one must yearn for the presence of the beloved at all times. These are all attitudes that seem to be characteristic of romantic love. Conjugal love is quite different. In fact, it is possible that one could be true to conjugal love for a spouse whom one did not much like. This would mean that in spite of annoyance with one's spouse, or disappointment with one's spouse, or even positive dislike for one's spouse, one is willing to try to live with, help, care for, and be faithful to one's spouse. These are the characteristics of conjugal love. This love may not be as exhilarating as romantic love, but when accompanied by affection for one's spouse, it can be the source of deep joys, of complete trust in another, and of great appreciation for another. Of course, conjugal love may be enhanced if accompanied by a feeling of romantic love for one's spouse, although often romantic lovers do not treat one another well; romantic love is by its nature quite ephemeral and not the stuff of which permanent relationships are made. Those who seek to find an appreciation for romantic love in Church teaching on marriage will find little that will satisfy them. But those who seek to find an appreciation for the kind of committed love that leads spouses to live with, help, care for, and be faithful to each other will find beautiful testimonies to this love from the earliest documents of the Church.

Conjugal love in the sense of a devoted commitment to pursuing the goods of marriage with one's spouse is very much a part of, very much a necessity for, the goal of marriage that is the mutual sanctification or perfection of the spouses. A passage from *Casti Connubii* speaks of the centrality to marriage of this seeking of "mutual perfection" by the spouses: "This mutual interior formation of the spouses, this earnest desire of perfecting one another, can be said in a certain very true sense, as the *Roman Catechism* teaches, to be the primary cause and reason of marriage—if only marriage is taken not strictly as an institution for the proper procreation and rearing of children, but in a broader sense as a sharing, a community, a union of their whole life [*totius vitae communio, consuetudo, societas*]."[36] A later section of *Casti Connubii* elaborates on these concepts:

> Conjugal faith . . . which is most aptly called by St. Augustine the "faith of chastity" blooms more freely, more beautifully and more nobly, when it is rooted in that more excellent soil, the love of husband and wife which pervades all the duties of married life and holds pride of place in Christian marriage. For matrimonial faith demands that husband and wife be joined in an especially holy and pure love, not as adulterers love each other, but as Christ loved the Church. This precept the Apostle laid down when he said: "Husbands, love your wives as Christ also loved the Church," that Church which of a truth He embraced with a boundless love not for the sake of His own advantage, but seeking only the good of His Spouse. The love, then, of which We are speaking is not that based on the passing lust of the moment nor does it consist in pleasing words only, but in the deep attachment of the heart which is expressed in action, since love is proved by deeds. This outward expression of love in the home demands not only mutual help but must go further; it must have as its primary purpose that man and wife help each other day by day in forming and perfecting themselves in the interior life, so that through their partnership in life they may advance ever more and more in virtue, and above all that they may grow in true love towards God and their neighbor. . . . (13–14)

Conjugal love, then, should be a source of growth in virtue for spouses, a source of perfection. This seeking of perfection is at the very root of personalist values.

Personalist Values of Marriage

The term *personalist values* in a general way refers to goods that benefit the human person as distinct from values that protect other goods, such as goods that benefit society at large or goods that respect the laws of nature. *Personalism* focuses on the innate dignity of each individual, and Christian personalism sees this dignity rooted in Man's having been created in the image and likeness of God. Thus all human actions must be in accord with this dignity. Judging actions in accord with personalist values is distinct, in certain senses, from judging actions in accord with law, for law seems external to the person and imposed on him. But although the judgments may have apparently different criteria, for Christians there should be no conflict between the values of law (here the laws of God) and the values of the person, for the same God created both and gave Man law for the sake of his person. Laws, though, generally more directly protect the common good, whereas personalist values more directly benefit the individual. Yet, again, in the Christian scheme individuals who act in violation of the common good do not achieve true personal benefit and, thus, there is no true contradiction between the common good and personalist goods. Indeed, the same value may be conducive to and protective of more than one good. For instance, "truth telling" can be seen both as a societal value, insofar as it promotes trust between members of society, and as a personalist value, insofar as it protects the integrity and authenticity of the human person and perfects the human person. Marriage, too, has both societal and personalist value. It, for instance, protects the societal good of the family with all the goods that it provides society (such as education of the young, care of the sick, clear lines of inheritance). Its personalist values are also considerable: through their love for each other spouses become more responsible and generous, more self-assured and more fulfilled.[37]

No list of "personalist values" is readily to be found. To some extent these values have been defined in opposition to the claim that the primary purpose of marriage is procreation. As we have noted several times, in the eyes of some the claim that sex is for procreation has seemed to devalue the importance of the love relationship of the spouses as a good in its own right. In their eyes personalist values are those goods fostered by the marital relationship that are not directed specifically toward procreation. These goods are said to be those that foster love between the spouses and that are expressed through the act of sexual intercourse. But it begs the question to define "personalist values" as those that are *not* procreative. If, in a larger—and truer—sense the "personalist values" of marriage are those that foster the "mutual perfection" of the spouses, there need not necessarily be a conflict between the value of procreation and personalist values.

Mutual perfection most certainly refers to the growth of the spouses in maturity, responsibility, generosity, selflessness, ability to trust and be intimate, and undoubtedly a multitude of other qualities and virtues perfective of the human person. Ultimately, the perfection they seek is the perfection that all Christians are to seek, a perfection that makes them worthy of eternal union with God. Those who have the vocation of marriage are called to behave in such a way that their behavior particularly assists both them and their spouses in growing in virtue. Their acts of sexual intimacy must foster their perfection, the perfection they seek together, as must all the acts of their marriage.

Is this, as some would allege, a new value in the Church? Is there not powerful evidence that, although early Church writings did not give the modern emphasis to these values, it certainly recognized and appreciated these values?

First, it is important to note that the term *personalist values* and terminology associated with this term (for example, *communion of persons, self-giving*) are relatively new; they are not regularly found in documents written before the middle decades of this century. (Pius XII seems to have been very instrumental in introducing personalist "language" into discussions of marriage.)[38] Thus we must be sensitive to the fact that failure to use these terms does not mean that earlier authors have not understood and appreciated the concept of personalist values. If we are looking not for terms but for an expression of the importance of a committed love between the spouses, we may find rather abundant evidence for it. The book Song of Songs in Scripture, the book of Tobit, and the story of Jacob and Rachel depict beautifully the role that love and deep personal intimacy played in marriage for the Hebrews. These texts have regularly been a part of the meditations on marriage for the Fathers of the Church and for theologians. And consider this famous passage (c. 200) from Tertullian, one of the earliest Fathers:

Where shall we find eloquence to describe the joys of that marriage which is approved by the Church, sustained by the Eucharist, sealed by blessing, witnessed by angels, confirmed by the Father. It rightly asks the heavenly Father's approval for no good child even on earth will marry without his earthly father's approval. What a union is that of two Christians, who share one single hope, one law, one obedience. Both are brothers together, both slaves of Christ together; there is no division of soul or body between them. They are indeed two in one flesh; where there is one flesh, there must be one soul. Together they pray, together they do penance and fast; they teach one another, inspire one another, encourage one another. They are inseparable in the Church of God, inseparable at the Communion table, indivisible in trial and hardship, inseparable in consolation. Neither has any secrets from the other, neither avoids the other, neither would cause the other any pain. . . . Christ rejoices to see and hear their love, and sends down on them His peace. Where they two are, there He is too; and where He is, there is no room for the Evil One.[39]

This passage is among the reasons that several historians and theologians have challenged the claim that the ancients and medievals neglected the importance of love in marriage. They express the caution noted earlier that it is not right to expect them to have used the language and terms to which we have become accustomed; rather, if we look more deeply at their descriptions of marriage, we find that love was considered of the essence of marriage. John Connery, for instance, notes: "In general, it is under the heading of sacramentality that the Fathers deal with marital love. While the term does not have the technical meaning of a later date, it clearly refers to the symbolic meaning of marriage in reference to Christ and his church. The basis for this meaning is the love of the spouses for each other. The Fathers clearly assume that this love is present. It is only because of this love that marriage has the symbolic meaning they attribute to it."[40] Fabian Parmisano wrote two articles refuting Noonan's charge that conjugal love has been largely undervalued in theological considerations about marriage.[41] In the first he reviews the works of several medieval theologians, particularly those of Nicole Oresme, who studied theology at the University of Paris around 1348. After reviewing extensive passages from Nicole's writings, Parmisano concludes:

It would be difficult to conceive a more integrated doctrine of marriage than that set forth in Oresme's commentary. Marriage, love, and sex are all of a piece, and all is good. The union between man and woman in marriage is fully natural. It is meant to spring from love and to be grounded upon love—a love that is both physical and spiritual, that is productive of an intensity of joy and pleasure, that makes equals of a man and woman and makes each to be supreme in the other's affections. The marriage act is good if decently and lovingly engaged in. It has purposes beyond generation: it preserves fidelity and deepens and intensifies the love between husband and wife. Sin may enter into the union, but if the union is of reason and is basically good, there is no need to worry about it. It is only when love becomes "bestial"—when one is intent only upon his isolated pleasure—that there is cause for concern. Marriage is for children, but it is first and foremost for husband and wife and their mutual fullness of love and lasting fidelity.[42]

In his second article, Parmisano objects to Noonan's presentation of Aquinas as one who "failed to incorporate love into the purposes of marriage."[43] Parmisano claims in his article to demonstrate that Aquinas "did indeed teach that love and marriage go together, and did also teach that love—human, passionate, pleasurable love—not only entered into the purposes of the marriage act but was also the root and source of the act's ultimate beneficial value for the spouses."[44] He goes on to note: "There can be no doubt, however, that to the Scholastics, as well as to St. Augustine, married people were to love each other as Christ loved the church. This love must be extended to and expressed in every aspect of their married lives, not excluding their sexual relations. Although these relations were to be aimed explicitly at the *bonum prolis* [the good of offspring] or the *bonum fidei* [the good of fidelity], they must ultimately spring from this love, since it was basic to the relationship."[45] These theologians argue that earlier theologians did not neglect the importance of love in marriage and that there is much more explicit discussion of the role of love in marriage than is generally allowed. They also claim that the importance of love is assumed in many of the discussions of marriage and is included under some of the traditional goods of marriage.[46] They acknowledge that there is an increased explicit emphasis on these values in modern times, but they do not find this to be a radical change; they find it to be simply a continuation of earlier treatments of love. Indeed, it could be argued that there is a greater concentration on these values now and that they have been newly discovered because they are more threatened in our time. For instance, the phenomenon of nuptial contracts that provide for a possible divorce settlement may suggest that indissolubility and trust are no longer assumed to be a part of marriage. Men in earlier periods may not have seen marriage as a union for which love was the primary motive, but they may have expected husband and wife to come to love each other. Christian love, rather than romantic love, was considered the proper foundation for marriage. Certainly they would have thought that a marriage in which love ruled was truly a more perfect marriage. Yet, whatever the awareness or appreciation of the personalist values of conjugal love among spouses in any period, or among savants in any period, it seems true to say that our age focuses on these values in a way that earlier ages did not. It is widely believed that we can see these personalist values assuming a new importance in Church teaching through their prominence in *Gaudium et Spes*.

Gaudium et Spes

Many would argue that *Gaudium et Spes* is the most modern of the documents of Vatican II. It explicitly addressed itself to the task of "reading the signs of the times and of interpreting them in the light of the gospel" (GS 4) and was addressed not only to the Church but to the "whole of humanity" (GS 2). It has a well-earned reputation as a document permeated with personalist values. Indeed, it states, "It is man . . . who is the key to this discussion, man considered whole and entire, with body and soul, heart and conscience, mind and will" (GS 3). Furthermore, it sought "In language intelligible to each generation . . . [to] be able to answer the ever recurring questions which men ask about the meaning of this present life and of the life to come, and how one is related to the other" (GS 40). The document is concerned both to make an evaluation

of the conditions of modern society and to restate some of the
fundamentals of the Christian faith that those living in modern
times most need to hear. Among the topics that it takes up are the
advances in social communications that have brought peoples closer
together, the rapidly changing technology that has so transformed
social life, the increasing abandonment of religious belief and practice, and the importance of structuring society to preserve fundamental human rights. Among the Christian truths it seeks to promulgate
are those of the fundamental dignity of man, the importance of
living by a true conscience and in accord with authentic freedom,
Man's need for community, and the effects of original sin on his
soul and his endeavors (the passages GS 10–14 are of particular and
unsung importance).

Here, of course, the passages of most interest to us are those on
marriage. *Gaudium et Spes* tells us: "The man and woman, who 'are
no longer two but one' (Mt. 19:6), help and serve each other by
their marriage partnership [*foedere*]; they become conscious of their
unity and experience it more deeply from day to day. The intimate
union of marriage, as a mutual giving of two persons, and the good
of the children demand total fidelity from the spouses and require
an unbreakable unity between them" (GS 48). *Gaudium et Spes*
speaks of conjugal love as being "eminently human" and involving
the whole good of the person: "It can enrich the sentiments of the
spirit and their physical expression with a unique dignity and enno-
ble them as the special elements and signs of the friendship proper
to marriage. The Lord, wishing to bestow special gifts of grace and
divine love on it, has restored, perfected, and elevated it. A love
like that, bringing together the human and the divine, leads the
partners to a free and mutual giving of self, experienced in tenderness
and action, and permeates their whole lives; besides, this love is
actually developed and increased by the exercise of it" (GS 49).
Speaking of conjugal love as fostering the dignity of the spouses,
Gaudium et Spes maintains that the spouses "increasingly further
their own perfection and their mutual sanctification, and together
they render glory to God" (GS 48).

How then does *Gaudium et Spes* differ from *Casti Connubii?* Largely
in language and emphasis. The first portion of *Gaudium et Spes* had
made much mention of the concepts of "communion of persons"

and of "self-giving," concepts and terms that permeate the sections on marriage. One of the central passages of the first part of this document reads: "The dignity of man rests above all on the fact that he is called to *communion with God*. The invitation to converse with God is addressed to man as soon as he comes into being. For if man exists it is because God has created him through love, and through love continues to hold him in existence. He cannot live fully according to truth unless he freely acknowledges that love and entrusts himself to his creator" (my emphasis, GS 19). The communion that Man is to cultivate with God is also the source of his ability to join in true communion with his fellow Man. Section 24 notes: "The Lord Jesus, when praying to the Father, 'that they all may be one . . . even as we are one' (Jn. 17:21–22) has opened up new horizons closed to human reason by implying that there is a certain parallel between the union existing among the divine persons and the union of the sons of God in truth and love. It follows, then, that if man is the only creature on earth that God has wanted for its own sake, *man can fully discover his true self only in a sincere giving of himself*" (my emphasis). This communion with God and "self-giving" are accomplished by a devotion to Christ, by conforming oneself to the example that Christ gave; this is Man's "most high calling" (GS 22) for Christ is "the image of the invisible God" (Col. 1:15), "himself the perfect man" (GS 22).

Section 48 reflects these emphases in many ways; indeed, it begins by calling marriage an "intimate community [*communitas*]." It uses forms of the word *mutual* five times, for instance, in references to the "mutual gift of two persons" [*mutua duarum personarum donatio*] and "mutual self-bestowal" [*mutua deditione*]. It speaks of marriage as fostering "personal development"; it speaks of the spouses as "advancing in their own perfection" as well as "mutual perfection"; it speaks of parents as helping their children to find the path of human maturity, of salvation, and of holiness and of children as contributing in their own way to making their parents holy. The concepts and values expressed here are certainly coherent with those of *Casti Connubii*, but the language in which they are expressed is somewhat distinctive of this document.

These emphases are continued throughout the rest of the section on marriage. In section 50, which is devoted to defining conjugal love, we read that (1) conjugal love is "eminently human," that is, involving the whole person, soul and body; and that (2) conjugal love leads spouses to "a free and mutual gift of themselves, a gift proving itself by gentle affection and by deed." It states that through this "mutual self-giving . . . spouses enrich each other with a joyful and thankful will"; and (3) "mutual faithfulness" ensures a unity that "will radiate with the equal personal dignity of wife and husband, a dignity acknowledged by mutual and total love."

The sexual act itself is seen as a source of personal perfection: "Married love is uniquely expressed and perfected by the exercise of the acts proper to marriage. Hence the acts in marriage by which the intimate and chaste union of the spouses takes place are noble and honorable; the truly human performance of these acts fosters the self-giving they signify and enriches the spouses in joy and gratitude" (GS 49). And true to its "personalist" emphasis, its emphasis on the goods the person is to obtain from his acts, it states, "Outstanding courage is required for the constant fulfillment of the duties of this Christian calling: spouses, therefore, will need grace for leading a holy life: they will eagerly practice a love that is firm, generous, and prompt to sacrifice and will ask for it in their prayers." (These claims are echoed very clearly in HV 9.)

Part of the generosity of spouses in their married life is to be their generous acceptance of the blessing of children: "It is the married couple themselves who must in the last analysis arrive at these judgments before God. Married people should realize that in their behavior they may not simply follow their own fancy but must be ruled by conscience—and conscience ought to be conformed to the law of God in the light of the teaching authority of the Church, which is the authentic interpreter of divine law" (GS 50). Spouses, then, are the ones entrusted with the judgment of what constitutes generosity to God in respect to their childbearing. But this passage asserts an important caution: the spouses should form their consciences in accord with the law of God as interpreted by the Church.

Gaudium et Spes only briefly addresses the question of moral means of regulation of family size and in a rather circumspect way.[47] There are, though, several important references in this section of *Gaudium et Spes* to forms of birth control. (These references were somewhat sharpened through quite extraordinary interventions by Paul VI in the drafting of the final form of these sections of *Gaudium et Spes;* see Appendix 3 for a discussion of these interventions.[48]) The first reference appears in section 47, which mentions the attitudes and actions that profane married love; "illicit practices against human generation" are listed along with "excessive self-love" and "the worship of pleasure." Section 51 to some extent takes up this point. It begins by acknowledging:

The Council realizes that married people are often hindered by certain situations in modern life from working out their married love harmoniously and that they can sometimes find themselves in a position where the number of children cannot be increased, at least for the time being: in cases like these it is quite difficult to preserve the practice of faithful love and the complete intimacy of their lives. But where the intimacy of married life is broken, it often happens that faithfulness is imperiled and the good of the children suffers: then the education of the children as well as the courage to accept more children are both endangered.

Some read this passage as an acknowledgment that means of family regulation that require periodic abstinence are unworkable and thus thought that this passage may nod in the direction of approving other forms of family regulation. (Great advances in methods of natural family planning have occurred since this was written and strongly indicate that the abstinence required is not unworkable and that benefits to the marriage are the more common result.) The document rules out "shameful" solutions but mentions only the "taking of life" and later explicitly refers to abortion and perhaps to infanticide as well (GS 51). It would seem very peculiar not to count contraception among these shameful solutions, especially because the same section states, "In questions of birth regulation the sons of the Church, faithful to these principles, are forbidden to use methods disapproved of by the teaching authority of the Church in its inter-pretation of the divine law." Still, in spite of these passages and the references in footnote 14 to documents that condemned contracep-tion, some argued that *Gaudium et Spes* took no position on the morality of contraception, that the question was left to the Papal Commission to decide. *Gaudium et Spes* seems, to some extent, to have sent mixed signals, for the footnote states: "By the order of the Holy Father, certain questions requiring further and more careful investigation have been given over to a commission for the study of population, the family, and births, in order that the Holy Father may pass judgment when its task is completed. With the teaching of the magisterium standing as it is, the Council has no intention of proposing concrete solutions at this moment."

Nonetheless, it seems that passages in *Gaudium et Spes* can very plausibly be read to support the position that contraception is portrayed as a violation not solely of the procreative good of marriage but also of the values of conjugal love. *Gaudium et Spes* states this point more explicitly than *Casti Connubii*, but we find an intimation of it in this statement from *Casti Connubii*: "Every sin committed as regards the offspring becomes in some way a sin against conjugal faith, since both these blessings are essentially connected" (36). (This seems to anticipate the claim of *Humanae Vitae* 12 that the unitive and procreative meanings of conjugal love are inseparable.) But in *Gaudium et Spes* we find this strong statement: "The Church wishes to emphasize that there can be no conflict between the divine laws governing the transmission of life and the fostering of authentic married love" (GS 51). There are other indications that the violation of the procreative meaning of marriage may also be a violation of conjugal love. The most extensive statement referring to the moral question of limiting family size also stresses personalist values as well as the good of procreation:

When it is a question of harmonizing married love with the responsible transmission of life, it is not enough to take only the good intention and the evaluation of motives into account; the objective criteria must be used, criteria drawn from the nature of the human person and human action, criteria which respect the total meaning of mutual self-giving and human procreation in the context of true love; all this is possible only if the virtue of married chastity is seriously practiced. In questions of birth regulation the sons of the Church, faithful to these principles, are forbidden to use methods disapproved of by the teaching authority of the Church in its interpretation of the divine law. (GS 51)

The mention here of "mutual self-giving" and of "human procreation" as allied values again underlines the interconnection between the two meanings of the sexual act. The interconnection between these values is worth exploring since so many theologians believe there can be a conflict between them. Chapter 4 extensively discusses an argument in behalf of the teaching of *Humanae Vitae* rooted in the inseparability of the procreative and unitive meanings of sexual intercourse.

The Church's teaching on marriage is a rich and complicated one; the surface of that teaching has only been skimmed here. A fuller treatment would certainly require much reference to Scripture and also to other papal pronouncements, perhaps particularly those of Pius XII.[49] *Humanae Vitae* focuses on a fairly narrow concern of marriage, the moral exercise of sexual intercourse. But, again, to understand this narrow concern, it is necessary to understand the larger context of the meaning of Christian marriage. The preceding exposition has attempted to provide a sketch of that meaning sufficient at least to prepare us for the claims of *Humanae Vitae*; let us now turn to the document itself.

THREE

Humanae Vitae:
Preliminary Philosophical Considerations

O N JULY 29, 1968, Pope Paul VI issued his long-awaited encyclical on the question of moral means for limiting family size.[1] Humanae Vitae is a succinct text that does not offer much elaboration of the claims that it makes. Such elaboration is the work of this chapter and the next. This chapter will establish some of the foundational perspectives of natural law theory; it will consider the claim of the Church to be a teacher on moral matters and will provide an explanation of the claim that organs and their related acts have purposes. We will clear the way for sound natural law arguments by eliminating some of the arguments that have wrongly been identified as those used by the Church against contraception. This will also give us an opportunity to see how the principle of totality and the principle of toleration of the lesser evil have been utilized incorrectly by those attempting to justify contraception. The text of Humanae Vitae mentions both arguments. Chapter 4 presents the arguments, based on natural law ethics, for the immorality of contraception.

Humanae Vitae is more than a condemnation of contraception; it is a carefully fashioned response to problems of the times. A brief commentary on the complete encyclical, section by section, can be found in Appendix 2. The commentary summarizes the content of the footnote references given by the encyclical, references that often clarify the moral principles used in the document.

Natural Law

The principles of Catholic moral teaching are based both on natural law and divine revelation. Natural law provides a foundation for those moral precepts that Man is capable of discerning through the power of his reason, that is, apart from any special divine revelation. Shortly we shall describe natural law more fully and sketch out several possible natural law arguments against contraception. Yet first let us note (as does *Humanae Vitae*) that the Church teaches that Man need not rely on his intellect alone to determine what is moral and what is not. God has given Man the gift of divine revelation, available through Scripture and through the tradition of the Church. Divine revelation reveals to us moral truths that we cannot grasp by the power of reason and also affirms truths that are accessible through natural law. It is customarily taught that most of the Ten Commandments represent moral truths that Man can know apart from revelation. The commandment "Keep holy the sabbath" is an example of a moral truth that is solely based on revelation,[2] but prohibitions against adultery, lying, and stealing, for instance, are considered accessible to Man through his reason.

Furthermore, it must be noted that the Church constantly speaks of "interpreting" and "guarding" the natural law, not of inventing it. Section 18 of *Humanae Vitae* states: "Since the Church did not make either of these laws [the natural law and the law of the Gospel], she cannot change them. Nonetheless, she is, as it were, their guardian and interpreter; thus it would never be right for her to declare as morally permissible that which is truly not so. For what is immoral is by its very nature always opposed to the true good of Man."[3] Section 4 of *Humanae Vitae* explains that it is within the competence of the Church to interpret the moral law and thus to answer the questions raised in this document. Christ imparted this power to the apostles, and through apostolic succession this power has been preserved in the Church. No demonstration of this claim is offered, not even in any of the references given in the footnotes. In fact, only a few of these references give any justification for the claim to apostolic succession; they speak primarily rather of the nature of Man and Christianity and of the nature of faith and reason;

they seek to show that there can be no true conflict between these (a summary of these references can be found in the commentary in Appendix 2).

Obviously, no philosophic demonstration could ever be given for the claim that the Church is competent to interpret natural law, for the Church is a supernatural reality, whose "nature" is not within the competence of philosophy to determine. But, nonetheless, a kind of evidence for the truth of this claim is offered through the footnote references. When in her consideration throughout different ages and in different contexts the Church returns to the same teaching, this repetition counts as a kind of evidence for the truth of a claim, for the Church claims guidance by the Holy Spirit and teaches that what has been constantly proclaimed by the Church throughout its history is true by tradition, if not by demonstration.

Humanae Vitae *and Natural Law*

Humanae Vitae 4 clearly states that its teachings are based on natural law; it states that the teaching concerning marriage is one "rooted in natural law, illuminated and made richer by divine revelation" and claims that the Church is an "authentic guardian and interpreter of the whole moral law, that is, not only of the law of the Gospel, but also of natural law. For natural law [as well as revealed law], declares the will of God; [thus] faithful compliance to natural law is necessary for eternal salvation."

Admittedly because there are several different natural law theories or perspectives and many different meanings possible for the word *nature* it is challenging to discern the precise meaning of references to "natural law" in Church documents. Nonetheless, this complexity does not render the endeavor impossible; careful reading of the texts in which the phrase occurs, and due attention to the history of the Church's teaching on specific points, are, for the most part, sufficient to disclose the meaning of "natural law" in any given context.

If any author is a reliable guide to the Church's teaching regarding natural law, it is surely Thomas Aquinas. Indeed, *Humanae Vitae* does refer (in footnote 9) to question 94, article 2, of the *Summa Theologiae* I–II. This article is his famous succinct statement of natural law, and so it would seem that whatever claims are made about the natural law theory on which *Humanae Vitae* is based ought to cohere with the teachings of Aquinas. A very simple summary of that teaching would be the following three foundational truths:[4]

1. Man, by the power of his reason, is capable of discerning some moral truths. "Natural law" refers both to Man's inherent desire to seek the good and avoid what is evil and to his ability to discern what is good and thus to be sought, what is evil, and thus to be avoided.

2. The workings of nature, the "laws" of nature, are not the same as the natural law—for natural law includes Man's ability to reason as well as his natural inclinations. But the laws of nature are, nonetheless, important guides in Man's process of discernment. Included in the category of "nature" is the nature of Man in all his physical, psychological, and spiritual dimensions. The better Man knows his natural inclinations, the better he can act, and ultimately such action should promote human well-being and happiness.

3. Nature is an important guide to truth because God is the author of nature, and, thus, in some sense respect for nature manifests a respect for God. Moreover, nature is designed in accord with reason, for God governs the universe. Thus to act in accord with nature is to act in accord with reason and to act in accord with reason is to act in accord with nature. Most understandings of natural law, however, do not require that the recognition that God is the author of the natural law be a conscious element in reasoning well about moral matters.

The Church teaches that Man by the power of his reason, if he reasons correctly, is capable of knowing such moral truths as that murder is immoral and that rape is immoral. The moral truth about murder is based on an understanding of the intrinsic worth of human life and also on an understanding of justice. The moral truth about rape is based on an understanding of the human person as a free individual and of the proper realm for sexual activity. All claims that an act is immoral are ultimately claims based on natural law; murder, rape, stealing, lying, and so on—all violate natural law. Some moral truths are easier than others to discern on the basis of natural law; certainly to claim that something is based on natural law is not to say that it is immediately evident to Man. Rather it is evident only to those who understand human nature well and reason intelligently about it.[5]

The Church also teaches that after the fall, Man's desires can be inordinate and in conflict with his reason and that these desires can befog the clear light of reason. Thus, for instance, because of selfishness or sexual desire, Man may desire to do what he knows to be evil; for instance, he may know that adultery is immoral but commit it anyway. And at times because of his ignorance Man may have difficulty discerning that certain actions are immoral, even though such discernment is per se accessible to his reason. (For instance, there was initially much confusion about the morality of the intentional bombing of civilian sites, but there is now a consensus that this is immoral.)

There may also be a fourth foundational claim of some versions of natural law. This is the claim that the coming of Christ, in a sense, has reconstituted the natural law.[6] That is, Christ has revealed Man to himself and also restored Man to himself. Through Christ, Man has a better knowledge of himself, and through the graces made available by Christ, Man can attain a higher standard of behavior. This position is not the strict natural law position outlined previously, for it draws on revelation rather than relying strictly on reason, but it does not rely on revelation so much as a source of explicit moral norms, as a source of a sort of insight—insight that completes and perfects what Man can know about himself through reason. Some argue that it is impossible for philosophers any longer to distinguish between what they know of Man from the Christian view that predominated for so many centuries and what they know from their philosophical reflections; that is, some think that nearly everyone's thought has now been greatly influenced by a Christian view of Man. Thus, although philosophers may not make explicit reference to revelation they may, in fact, be drawing on revelation in some remote way. Yet a careful distinction must be made here. Although there are certain truths about Man that have entered the philosophical tradition largely through the influence of Christianity, this is not to say that these truths are not fundamentally rational. That is, it is possible that some few Men could have come to have realized these truths through reason, as, for instance, some of the ancient philosophers seem to have come to an appreciation for brotherly love, an appreciation not shared widely by their cultures. Nonetheless, some suspect that some of these insights would never have become common knowledge without the spread of Christianity. Centuries after Christ, it becomes increasingly difficult to determine what truths we are able to discern independently of Christianity and what truths we grasp under the influence of Christianity, an influence we are no longer able to identify. For instance, the great progress made in the recognition of civil rights of minorities could, it seems, be justified simply on the basis of a view of the equality of Man. But it is difficult to argue that mankind would have come to see this natural law truth without the prompting of Christianity.

Most of the natural law arguments given against contraception make use of natural law in their understanding of the nature and purpose of the sexual act and of the moral importance of respecting this nature and purpose. But they also draw on a vision of the dignity of the human person, on the value of human life and on the nature of marital relations that it seems mankind has rarely appreciated apart from Christian revelation. The words cited from HV 4 are then very apt. There the claim is made that the Church's teaching on marriage is "a teaching that is rooted in natural law, illuminated and made richer by divine revelation." There are certain claims fundamental to the condemnation of contraception, such as that conjugal love is a love that requires total self-giving and that a human life has intrinsic worth, which are easily supported through Christian principles but less easily recognized by unaided reason. Thus, natural law arguments against contraception draw on some truths fairly readily accessible to Man through the power of his reason and other truths that are considered somewhat distinctive of the Christian tradition but that may be per se accessible to reason.

The Purpose of the Sexual Organs

What is common to natural law arguments against contraception (with the exception of Grisez's formulations, to be discussed later) is the claim that physical organs have certain purposes and that honoring these purposes is good, at least for the most part.[7]

Section 4 of *Humanae Vitae*, which speaks about the Church's commitment to natural law, refers in the footnote to a speech given by Pius XII to the Italian Medico-Biological Union of St. Luke (1944). There he teaches physicians that "God, the Creator, has given its proper function to each of the body's organs" and that they must respect these functions in all of their work.[8] He maintains that neither Man nor the state has unlimited power over the human body. Applying these principles to questions surrounding marriage, he speaks of sexual intercourse as having the primary purpose of procreation and education of children and states, "Marriage alone, regulated by God Himself in its essence and in its properties, realizes this purpose in accordance with the dignity and well-being of the child and of the parents." He says nothing directly about contraception but states, "We must conform ourselves [to the above norm] in all concrete cases, in all particular questions." He warns that physical, psychic, and societal harm will result if this norm is ignored. Acknowledging that there is much pressure on doctors to compromise these principles, he counsels them not only to conduct their practice in these terms but also to advise their patients in accord with them; they, he says, "will credit him [the physician] more readily than the theologian."[9]

Reference is made elsewhere in *Humanae Vitae* to the importance of acknowledging and respecting the physiological end of the sexual organs and acts. Section 10 on responsible parenthood states: "If we consider biological processes first, responsible parenthood means that one has an awareness of and respect for the responsibilities involved in these processes. Human reason has discovered that there are biological laws in the power of procreating life that pertain to the human person." Several times reference is made to an objective order of reality and to laws of nature established by God that must be respected; section 10 further speaks of the "intrinsic foundation" (*intimam rationem*) of responsible parenthood, which is "rooted in an objective moral order established by God"; section 11 speaks of "God wisely arrang[ing] the natural laws and times of fertility"; section 12 of the inseparable connection of the procreative and unitive meanings established by God and of "laws" written into the very natures of male and female; section 13 of the "laws of generation" established by God; section 16 of an order of reality established by God. In the comparison of contraception to periodic abstinence in section 16, contracepting couples are spoken of as "imped[ing] the order of generation from completing its own natural processes." The concluding paragraph of section 17 is quite strong: "Therefore, if we do not want the mission of procreating human life to be conceded to the arbitrary decisions of Men, we need to recognize that there are some limits to the power of Man over his own body and over the natural operations of the body, that ought not to be transgressed. No one, neither a private individual nor a public authority, ought to violate these limits. For these limits are derived from the reverence owed to the whole human body and its natural operations. . . ." Clearly, claims that organs have natural functions that deserve to be respected and that respecting these functions amounts to respecting an order established by God are central to the teaching of *Humanae Vitae*.

Many have challenged *Humanae Vitae* on this very point of understanding bodily organs to have natural functions; some claim that this principle is based on an antiquated view of nature. The precise deficiency of this principle is rarely articulated, though the criticism is often asserted that an antiquated view saw nature as static, whereas modern science understands that "nature" is evolving.[10] The tradition has argued that the primary way of discerning the purpose of an organ is to observe what purpose in fact it accomplishes when healthy and functioning properly. By this principle, the purpose of an eye is to see; the purpose of the heart is to pump blood; and so forth. Of course, organs may have more than one purpose: for instance, our tongues are used for both speaking and eating. It clearly is one of the purposes of genital organs to produce offspring (more is said on this point in the commentary on HV 11). Adult human beings who are infertile are considered to be suffering a defect of the body; their organs do not fulfill their natural purpose. The fact that few acts of genital intercourse result in conception does not militate against procreation as a description of the purpose of these organs, for throughout the natural world nature squanders more seed than it fertilizes and brings to adulthood.

Leon Kass in his *Toward a More Natural Science* argues that medicine cannot function without notions of nature, purpose, goal, end, or *telos*.[11] In a chapter entitled "Teleology, Darwinism, and the Place of Man," he argues that the theory of evolution in certain respects supports rather than repudiates the claim that organs have functions. He defines function as "a kind of teleological notion; function is not a material or a mechanism, nor does it have extension; rather it is the end of the extended material structure and its mechanism." Further on he states, "The parts of an organism have specific functions, which define their nature as parts: the bone marrow for making red blood cells; the lungs for exchange of oxygen and carbon dioxide; the heart for pumping the blood."[12] In this sense, it is legitimate to describe organs as having natural functions. Granting this does not, of course, necessarily entail any ethical norms, but it must be noted that the Church's teaching depends on such a description.

It also should be noted that the understanding that organs have purposes or natures is rarely directly challenged. That is, it is difficult—if not impossible—to find argumentation that explains why it is incorrect to describe reproduction as a purpose of sexual intercourse (though recall the distinction that was made earlier between the words *reproduction* and *procreation*). Although this understanding of nature is frequently rejected, little effort is made to confront this claim and dismiss it on its own terms. Sweeping statements are made about talk of nature and ends as being characteristic of an outmoded Aristotelian biology, but a specific explanation of why it is inappropriate to speak of procreation as a purpose, goal, or end of sexual intercourse is not provided. The argument usually begins elsewhere with related but separate questions. One separate issue is the question of the legitimacy of claiming that any one purpose of sexual intercourse ought to limit the moral use of sexual intercourse. Other separate questions are whether the nature that something has is evolving or constant; whether the purpose of sexual organs has indeed evolved to the point that their purpose is different from what it was in the past; whether the purpose of an organ is the result of evolutionary development of God's design, or of God's working through evolution.

It is best to keep in mind that the word *natural* when used in the context of the natural law does not refer solely to the functional integrity of bodily organs. It refers to whatever facilitates the well-being of anything, both in its parts and as a whole. Since the human being is more than his physiology, we can speak of the nature of his emotional and intellectual condition as well. Again, what is "natural" is in accord with the very being of a thing, with the natural inclinations of a thing, and tends to promote what is good for that thing. Since Man is a rational animal it is natural for him to act in accord with his reason. For Man, then, whatever violates right reason is unnatural. It is reasonable and natural for humans to feed and educate their children; it is natural for them to worship God. Moral laws, then, seek to promote and protect what is natural. Thus it is immoral, that is, not in accord with the natural law, to withhold education from one's children, and it is immoral, that is, not in accord with natural law, to forbid Men the freedom of worship. Those actions that tend to destroy marriage, an institution that promotes the well-being of Man, are immoral. The nature of one's organs and physiology is just one of the pertinent elements of natural law. But it *is* pertinent and is one of the controlling principles of *Humanae Vitae.*

The Position of Humanae Vitae on Contraception and on the Purpose of the Sexual Organs

Humanae Vitae does consider contraception to violate the purpose of the sexual organs, though this consideration does not constitute the whole of its condemnation of contraception.

Let us first clarify what is meant by contraception. HV 14 refers to "all acts that attempt to impede procreation, both those chosen as a means to an end and those chosen as ends. This includes acts that precede intercourse, acts that accompany intercourse, and acts that are directed to the natural consequences of intercourse." *Humanae Vitae* 14 is directed against acts that use chemicals and devices to prohibit procreation from taking place, and here *contraception* will be used to designate these chemicals and devices used to prohibit procreation. Several popular forms of "contraception" are not truly contraceptive; that is, they do not work by preventing the fertilization of an egg. Rather they work as abortifacients: that is, they work after an egg has been fertilized and after there exists a new human life.[13] The anovulant pill occasionally works this way; the IUD seems always to work this way, as does the new RU 486 pill. These are not truly contraceptives, then, and thus should more properly be included in the condemnation of abortion since they take a life that has already begun.[14]

HV 11 clearly states that its teaching against contraception is based on natural law. The core of the teaching of the document is to be found in the last sentence of this section: "The Church, which interprets natural law through its unchanging doctrine, reminds men and women that the teachings based on natural law must be obeyed, and teaches that it is necessary that each and every conjugal act [*matrimonii usus*] remain ordered in itself [*per se destinatus*] to the procreating of human life." There is a brief elaboration of this dictum in HV 14: "There must be a rejection of all acts that attempt to impede procreation, both those chosen as means to an end and those chosen as ends. This includes acts that precede intercourse, acts that accompany intercourse, and acts that are directed to the natural consequences of intercourse."

The statement in HV 11 is the most precise prohibition against contraception and will provide the focus of our discussion here. A note about translation is needed, so that we might understand precisely what the text is saying.[15] The Italian (the language in which *Humanae Vitae* was written) reads, "che qualsiasi atto matrimoniale deve rimanere aperto alla trasmissione della vita." The Latin (the official language of the Church) substitutes the words *per se destinatus* (in itself ordered) for the Italian *aperto* (open) although the Latin *apertus* would easily have worked here.[16] The phrase *per se destinatus*, though, is philosophically more precise and more in keeping with the context. One version of the Catholic Truth Society translation reads: "[It is] absolutely required that any use whatever of marriage must *retain its natural potential* to procreate human life."[17] Another version renders this phrase rather freely but faithfully: "In any use whatever of marriage there must be *no impairment of its natural capacity* to procreate human life" (my emphasis in both translations).[18] (For further comparison of translations of this sentence, see my notes to HV 11 in Appendix 1).

Although the translations cited are more precise, the common translation of this line that is based on the Italian and speaks of "each and every act [remaining] . . . open to procreation" gives rise to some misunderstandings. Some erroneously argue that this line means that when engaging in sexual intercourse, the spouses must be desiring to have a child. Thus, they claim that the document is inconsistent in permitting sexual intercourse during infertile times since couples choosing periodic abstinence are not "open" to another child.

Is there an inconsistency in permitting sexual intercourse during a woman's infertile period and also insisting that "each and every marital act must remain ordered to procreation"? Are not couples who confine their acts of sexual intercourse to the infertile periods "closed" to procreation? To be sure, they may be as determined not to have children at a given time as are couples who are contracepting; thus, it must be granted that in the subjective sense, they may be no more "open" to having children. But it is important to understand that the document is not speaking of the subjective "openness" of the spouses; it is speaking of the ordination of their objective *acts* of sexual intercourse. One source of misunderstanding is that the word *open* in English tends to have an association with a subjective state of mind rather than with objective reality; again, to some it suggests that the spouses must be actively desiring or at least be quite receptive of a pregnancy. But the document is not referring to the subjective desires of the spouses; the Latin *per se destinatus* is directed toward the marital *acts* of the spouses. It is these *acts* that must remain "open" or *per se destinatus*. The spouses may do nothing to deprive the *act* of its ordination or destination to procreation. They may do nothing to "close off" the possibility of the act's achieving its natural ordination. And here is the point. At certain times, procreation is simply not available to spouses for reasons beyond their control. Although their marital acts will be no more fertile than those of a couple practicing contraception, the acts have not by the couple's own will been deprived of their proper ordination. As HV 11 states, "Marital *acts* do not cease being legitimate if they are foreseen to be infertile because of reasons independent of the spouses . . ." (my emphasis).

Still, in spite of this important distinction between subjective desire and objective act, perhaps all is not yet clear. Another question must be raised. What can it mean to say the *acts* of sexual intercourse during the infertile periods are "legitimate"? Can it mean that they are in some sense "open to" or *per se destinatus* to procreation (as they must be if they are to be moral)? And if these "naturally" infertile acts are still ordered to procreation, why is this not also true of acts deliberately made infertile—of contracepted acts? The distinctions to be made here are at times subtle but they are nonetheless real and important.

First, it must be understood that the sexual *organs* are naturally ordered to procreation and nothing can render them not ordered to procreation. This ordination, whether capable of being actualized or not, is inherent. This is equivalent to saying that eyes that are being used to see, eyes that are closed, and blind eyes are still ordered to seeing; eyes blind at birth and eyes blinded by some deliberate act are still ordered to seeing. "Being ordered to seeing" means that the eye, even the eye that cannot perform its function, has a natural function and specific work. Only eyes can be "given" or restored to the power of seeing because only eyes do that kind of work; ears and noses do not. The same is true of sexual organs; sexual organs, whether fertile or infertile, temporarily or permanently, by the choice of the individual or not, are ordered to procreation. They are organs of the reproductive *kind*; thus, they are often called reproductive organs; the word *genitals* has Latin roots with the word *birth*.

Still, although organs always in some sense retain their natural ordination, is there not a difference between the situation in which an organ cannot perform its function because of some defect and one in which some agent deliberately deprives the organ of its ability to perform its function? Does not being blind through a birth defect differ greatly from being blind through a deliberate act of one's own will? There is no shame in having an organ that cannot perform its functions, but there may be shame and immorality involved if one deliberately deprives an organ of the ability to perform its proper function. Being blind "independently of one's will" is not to have done something immoral. But to blind oneself deliberately would be to strike a blow at the proper ordination of the eye. A deliberately blinded eye remains an eye. It is still the organ of sight and thus still ordered to seeing, but the act of deliberately depriving it of this ability is an act against its natural ordination. One has not allowed the eye to retain its ability of *achieving* its per se destination.

Let us use another analogy to clarify what is suspect about tampering with the ordination of organs. The act of eating is by nature ordered to nutrition. Consider a woman whose digestive system is working well. This woman eats and achieves the end of supplying her system with nutritious vitamins, and so on. Consider another woman whose system is not working well, who also eats nutritious food but, because of a defect in her system, is not nourished by this food. The systems of both are equally digestive systems; both are equally ordered to the specific work of digestion; both of their acts are equally ordered to supplying nutrition for the body. But one woman is able to achieve nutrition and the other is not. Now suppose the healthy woman deliberately tampers with her digestive system so that she might enjoy the sensation of eating without achieving the end of nutrition. She thwarts the natural ordination of her digestive system; she attempts to prevent it from achieving the end toward which it is naturally ordered. Her action does not retain its ability to achieve its per se destination. Her system does not change in kind; it remains a digestive system, naturally ordered to a specific work: digestion. Although through some equivocation she might be said to be "eating," it seems that she has not performed a true act of eating. She has deprived her action of achieving the very end to which her digestive system is naturally ordered, its per se ordination.

The parallel with sexual intercourse is clear; the sexual organs of both the fertile and the infertile are ordered to procreation. In the case of those who are infertile, the inability to achieve the ordered end is independent of the will of the spouses; in the case of the fertile but contracepting couple, they are deliberately tampering with their fertility; they do not allow it to remain capable of achieving the end to which it is ordered.

Let us probe this analogy even further. The digestive organs are ordered to providing nutrition for the body. There are occasions when the digestive organs may not be working correctly and thus one's act of eating will not achieve its end of nourishing the body. So, too, if one is infertile, one's act of sexual intercourse will not achieve its procreative end. In neither of these cases has one thwarted the natural ordination of the act; the organs retain their per se ordination. Or one may eat a completely non-nutritious substance, and thus, although one is performing an act of eating, one is not performing an act that assists the digestive system in achieving its ordination to nutrition. Such acts seem innocent enough. But if one hoped to gain nutrition and did not, one could then suffer some harm from eating "junk" food. One may eat food that positively does one harm, and thus one is actually violating the purpose of the digestive system; one is not seeking nutrition or even harmless pleasures, but one is misusing the digestive system. Contraceptive sex may be likened to "junk" food. One argument against contraception (version F, laid out in Chapter 4) maintains that when contraception is used, the sexual act not only loses its ordination to procreation but also violates the unitive meaning. Spouses participate in actions that should be fraught with meaning and that are deprived of that meaning. Such "non-nourishing" sexual activity may ultimately harm a marriage.

The preceding analysis should help us understand what *Humanae Vitae* means by stating that every marital *act* must remain *per se destinatus* to procreation. It means that couples must not tamper with the natural ordination of their marital acts. It does not mean that couples must be desiring children with each and every act of intercourse. Nor does it rule out sexual intercourse during a woman's infertile period, for sexual intercourse during these periods, as we have seen, does meet the criterion of being ordered to procreation.

A caveat must be stated here. The intent of this initial portion of the discussion is not to assess the morality of tampering with the natural ordination of organs, but to clarify what it means to speak of respecting the natural ordination of an organ or act. Indeed, although much of the analysis carries the clear implication that tampering with the natural ordination of organs may be immoral and perhaps is immoral for the most part, it is also certainly true that not all tampering is immoral. For instance, there is little controversy about the moral permissibility of medical procedures necessary for the health of an individual that may result in blindness or sterility. The point of the discussion, again, is to clarify, by use of analogy, what it means to say that an organ has a per se destination and what it means to say that that destination has been thwarted. The moral evaluation of this tampering is a separate issue.

But perhaps it is appropriate to mention here that some moralists have argued that if contraception is morally permissible, if it is permissible to engage in sexual activity deprived of procreative meaning, there would then be little grounds for condemning other forms of sexual activity. Elizabeth Anscombe argues:

If contraceptive intercourse is permissible, then what objection could there be after all to mutual masturbation, or copulation *in vase indebito*, sodomy, buggery, when normal copulation is impossible or inadvisable (or in any case, according to taste)? It can't be the mere pattern of bodily behaviour in which the stimulation is procured that makes all the difference! But if such things are all right, it becomes perfectly impossible to see anything wrong with homosexual intercourse, for example. I am not saying: if you think contraception all right you will do these other things; not at all. The habit of respectability persists and old prejudices die hard. But I am saying: you will have no solid reason against these things. You will have no answer to someone who proclaims as many do that they are good too.[19]

Again, this is not to say that contraception and homosexuality, for example, are morally equivalent, but it is to suggest that the principles used to justify contraception, principles that find the procreative meaning of the sexual act dispensable, can with justice be used to justify other sexual actions such as homosexuality.

Shortly we shall begin the work of explaining what precisely the procreative meaning of sexual intercourse is and why it is so important to respect that meaning. But let us first note that although there are few who argue that the knowledge of the physiological ordination of the sexual organs is sufficient to explain the condemnation of contraception, this information is considered by nearly all to be an essential component of fuller arguments against contraception.[20] This information also seems to suggest that contraception does have some element of evil in it simply as a violation of physiological organs and processes (for we do not cavalierly violate the ordinations of other organs). We may be able to see that often and even for the most part it is unwise and perhaps immoral to violate the natural purposes of organs. But the Church's condemnation of contraception is not simply that its use is often or even usually wrong but that its use is always wrong. Before we embark on the long-awaited attempt to explain what further evils inherent in contraception make it the kind of action that ought never to be chosen by human beings, let us note the strength of the Church's condemnation of contraception.

Contraception: An Intrinsic Evil

The footnote to the final sentence of HV 11 cites two texts that condemn contraception in strong terms: The first, from *Casti Connubii* (1930), states, "Any use whatever of matrimony exercised in such a way that the act is deliberately frustrated in its natural power to generate life is an offense against the law of God and of nature, and those who indulge in such are branded with the guilt of a grave sin."[21] The second reference is to Pius XII's "Speech to the Congress of the Italian Catholic Association of Midwives" (1951),[22] which refers to another passage from *Casti Connubii*. Reference of this kind, through one papal document to another, serves to rein-force the authority of the teaching since it shows constancy in the tradition. The passage from *Casti Connubii* reads: "But no reason, however grave may be put forward by which anything intrinsically against nature may become conformable to nature and morally good. Since, therefore, the conjugal act is destined primarily by nature [*suapte natura . . . destinatus*] for the begetting of children, those who in exercising it deliberately frustrate its natural power and purpose sin against nature and commit a deed which is shameful and intrinsically vicious [*intrinsece inhonestum*]" (DSP 28).

The debate about the morality of contraception has become a part of a larger debate in moral theology about whether or not there are kinds of actions that can be deemed intrinsically wrong. This debate will be discussed at some length in Chapter 7. Here let us note that *Casti Connubii* is quite firm on this point and *Humanae Vitae* reiterates this claim. Let us also note that these documents are not being cited as authorities as a means of "settling an argument": they are cited simply to inform the reader that the Church considers contraception to be intrinsically immoral. We will continue to proceed to offer arguments, largely of a philosophic nature, to show why contraception is intrinsically immoral.

Contraception is intrinsically immoral not because it violates the purpose of the reproductive organs but because it violates the procreative meaning of sexual acts; because it violates the nature of the conjugal act. Again, it is important to note that *Casti Connubii* does not say that it is wrong to use contraception because of the nature of the *sexual organs*, but because of the nature of the *conjugal act*. That is, whereas there is a prima facie plausibility to the claim that for the most part there should be no direct violation of natural processes and the function of natural organs, it may be going too far to say that it is intrinsically wrong to tamper with these organs simply because such tampering is a violation of their nature. Thus, an argument from natural ordination of organs is not the whole of the argument against contraception. And still again, what needs to be stressed is that it is not just the purpose or the nature of the generative organs that is violated through contraception; rather, it is the purpose of the conjugal act that is violated.[23] Anscombe is very strong on this point: "Contraceptive intercourse within marriage is a graver offence against chastity than is straightforward fornication or adultery. For it is not even a proper act of intercourse, and *therefore* is not a true marriage act."[24]

What then is this procreative meaning of sexual intercourse that transcends the mere physiological ordination of the organs? What are the natural law arguments against the use of contraception?

Unnatural Acts

A paradigm argument against contraception on the basis of nature can be constructed in syllogistic form in this fashion:

1. Unnatural acts are wrong.
2. Contraception is unnatural.
3. Therefore, contraception is wrong.

Wrong in this syllogism means "ought never to be freely chosen." *Immoral, evil, wrong,* and *sinful* all suffice in this context; all are proper translations of the Latin *malum,* but they carry widely different connotations in English (Chapter 7 more fully explains the relation of these words). Although I would prefer *immoral* since it is more idiomatic, it is problematic since *immoral* seems to refer only to an evaluation of the act in terms of its impact on the agent (that is, it seems to suggest that the agent has sinned) and not to the status of the act itself, to its coherence or lack thereof with right reason. I have chosen to use *wrong* since I think it conveys that one has done something that one ought not to do but does not necessarily imply that one has sinned. It is only if an agent has freely and knowingly chosen to do something wrong that he has sinned. It is possible to do something wrong without sinning; for instance, one could act out of ignorance.

Unnatural in this syllogism means "violates natural law."[25] Since for Man to violate the natural law is to do what is immoral, to call an action "unnatural" is to say that it is wrong. For Man to act against right reason, for him to do something that is not in accord with the dictates of reason, is to violate the natural law; thus, to say that an action violates right reason is to say that it violates the natural law and is wrong.[26] The preceding syllogism has been explained and justified in many different ways and rejected for many different reasons, largely depending on the reasons given for stating that contraception is unnatural, for claiming that it violates the natural law. In this chapter two faulty versions, often portrayed as the sole natural law arguments against contraception, are considered; four sounder versions are considered in Chapter 4.

Contraception Is Artificial (Version A)

The claim that contraception is wrong because it is artificial is commonly attributed to supporters of *Humanae Vitae*, but is one that no one in fact has seriously made.[27] The argument is said to proceed in this fashion:

1. What is artificial is unnatural and wrong.
2. Contraception is artificial.
3. Therefore, contraception is unnatural and wrong.

Again, let us note that neither *Humanae Vitae* nor any of its supporters make this argument, insofar as *unnatural* means here not natural. No one condemns contraception simply because it is the product of human technology. As many of the critics of *Humanae Vitae* observe, the Church has long accepted artificial interventions into the working of natural organs and processes and, in fact, considers some of them "natural" insofar as they assist nature and are in accord with the dictates of reason. None of the supporters of *Humanae Vitae* denies this. The Church most readily accepts those interventions that perfect and work in accord with nature, such as most medicines and such devices as eyeglasses and braces for one's teeth. *Donum Vitae*, the Vatican Instruction on Bioethics, states, "Interventions are not to be rejected on the grounds that they are artificial. As such, they bear witness to the possibilities of the art of medicine."[28] Nevertheless, some artificial things work against nature and harm nature and thus may be immoral to use. The spraying on foods of cancer-causing pesticides is perhaps a good example. When

Humanae Vitae speaks against artificial birth control (HV 16), it is using the word *artificial* in a narrow and specific sense; that is, it speaks against forms of birth control that work against and violate nature, rather than those that work in accord with and honor nature. Thus, it is not the *artificiality* of contraception that makes it immoral; it is its *unnaturalness* that makes it immoral. The following arguments will attempt to explain why contraception is properly understood as an act that is unnatural, that is, why it is understood as an act that *violates* nature.

The Physiological Argument against Contraception (Version B)

The claim that organs have purposes and that the purpose of the sexual organs is procreation has led some to argue that this knowledge of the natural physiological ordination of the sexual organs and the sexual act is sufficient to show that contraception is immoral. That is, they think that an argument of the following type is sufficient to demonstrate the immorality of contraception:

1. It is wrong to interfere with the natural purposes of organs and acts.

2. The purpose of sexual intercourse is reproduction (of the species).

3. Therefore, since contraception interferes with the purpose of sexual intercourse, contraception is wrong.

Few theologians have ever made use of such an argument.[29] This is often called the "perverted faculty" argument. Many think that it was the favored argument of the Church until the reconsideration of the issue prompted by *Humanae Vitae*, though, in fact, several articles preceding *Casti Connubii* indicate that theologians struggled with this argument for many reasons.[30] Although it has few proponents today, a fairly pure and sophisticated form of this argument can be found in an article by Richard Connell written in 1971. The summary Connell gives of his argument seems to be a summary of the physiological argument as stated previously:

The immediate goal toward which coitus—as a part of the generative process—is oriented is the depositing of sperm in some proximity to the ovum, a proximity sufficient to make fertilization somewhat indeterminate but possible. The evidence which shows that this is the term for which the act exists is the same as for any natural operation: the activity of coitus terminates once the sperm is deposited. Therefore, the use of devices or chemicals to prevent the achievement of the end-state toward which the natural power is directed before it ever exercises its activity is to interfere with a relation of a function to the goal that is determinative of it.[31]

This is the argument that I believe most dissenters identify as the argument on which the Church bases its teaching. Connell provides an excellent justification for the claim that organs and acts have ends and that it is good and right to respect these ends. Nonetheless, there are difficulties with determining how his principles could require an absolute condemnation of contraception; that is, it seems correct to say, that *for the most part*, since contraception violates the natural end of the sexual organs and of sexual intercourse, it is thus not a moral good. The following discussion attempts to show that the physiological argument is not sufficient in itself to warrant an *absolute* condemnation of contraception. It will also argue that the physiological argument is, nonetheless, a part of any argument that contraception is intrinsically wrong (again, with the exception of that by Grisez et alii).

The early dissenters were much given to charging the Church with what was called "biologism" and "physicalism." As Charles Curran stated: "The primary objection of most dissenting theologians centers on the papal insistence that the biological structure of the marital act is normative, and human beings must always respect its God-given finality and structure. This approach has been called physicalism."[32] Elsewhere he noted: "The natural law theory employed in the encyclical thus identifies the moral and human action with the physical structure of the conjugal act itself."[33] What Curran and his fellow dissenters often claim is that Man interferes with nature all the time; he uses medicines and such devices as earplugs and crutches. To some extent this objection misses the point made previously: medicines, earplugs, and crutches work to protect what is natural and to restore what is natural to its proper functioning. These interventions are permissible because they work in accord with nature. It is, rather, interventions that go against the workings of nature that are considered to be possibly immoral. And it is certainly true that many contraceptives do pose considerable threats to the health and well-being of the woman who uses them.[34] Furthermore, although some forms of contraception are not threats to health, it can be argued that they, in a sense, render a healthy organism nonfunctional, for fertility is a healthy and wholesome condition in an adult person and contraception serves to negate that condition. Such realities may serve to make many hesitant to use contraception for the same reason that many are hesitant to use medicines or foods that have some harmful effect on the body. The question remains, however: Is it not morally permissible to interfere with the workings of one's organs if some greater good could be obtained by doing so?

Let us observe that humans have little hesitation in tampering with the natural functioning of the organs and processes of animals; we will sterilize them and breed them and quite readily violate the natural workings of their organs when it is to our benefit to do so. So we seem to think that a higher good may supersede the good of respecting the nature or purposes of organs and processes. Why would contraception be intrinsically wrong? Why would it not be permissible to violate the procreative purpose of sexual intercourse if some greater good could be attained? And need it necessarily be a greater good? Why could not just another good be obtained, one that is more important at the time? These are the questions generally raised in reference to what is known as the "principle of totality."

The Principle of Totality

Although *Humanae Vitae* makes little acknowledgment of possible arguments advanced in behalf of contraception, it does allude several times to the principle of totality. The attempts in *Humanae Vitae* to respond to the justification for contraception based on the "principle of totality" are minimal. (This is another indication that *Humanae Vitae* was not written with the purpose of providing arguments, but that it largely relies on arguments to be provided elsewhere). Yet material given in the footnote references to HV 17 provide the principles by which one can construct an argument against the use of the principle of totality to justify contraception.[35]

Sections 3 and 14 of *Humanae Vitae* set up the problem. Section

3 specifically asks whether the principle of totality might not justify "acts causing sterility," or, in other words, contraception. The principle of totality, simply stated, holds that under certain circumstances it is morally permissible to sacrifice the good of a part for the sake of the whole; for instance, one may amputate a gangrened foot for the sake of the whole body. The implication of this principle for the question of contraception is suggested in the question posed in HV 3: "Would it not clearly be right to consider the goal [finem] of having children to pertain more to the whole of married life than to each and every act of [sexual intercourse]?" The final sentence of HV 14 speaks of the serious error of "think[ing] that a conjugal act, deprived deliberately of its fertility, and which consequently is intrinsically wrong, can be justified by being grouped together with the fertile acts of the whole of the marriage." Although not explicitly identified as such, this is clearly a reference to attempts to justify contraception by reason of the principle of totality.

Many contend that if a marriage in a general way is open to children, this need not be true of each marital act. They argue that sexual intercourse is directed toward the totality of the marriage. Thus, if the good of the marriage, which requires the bonding achieved through sexual intercourse, would be damaged by having children at a given time, on occasion the good of procreation could be sacrificed to the total good of the marriage, much in the same way that the good of one organ of the body might be sacrificed for the good of the whole. That is, it is argued that as long as the "totality" of the sexual acts of a marriage are ordered to procreation, it is not necessary for each act to be so ordered. Or, in other words, it is argued that it is all right to sacrifice the good of the part (that is, the procreative power of one act of sexual intercourse) for the sake of the whole of the marriage. This argument was made in the Schema and has been made by many dissenting theologians.[36]

The references in the footnote to HV 17 are to papal documents that were issued to clarify the meaning and applicability of the principle of totality to other medical-moral problems submitted to the Vatican. In his "Speech to the Twenty-Sixth Congress of the Italian Association of Urology" (1953),[37] Pius XII refers to the possible need to amputate an organ to eliminate an evil that threatens another organ. To address this question, he clearly articulates the rationale for the principle of totality: "Each particular organ [of the body] is subordinate to the whole of the body and ought therefore to yield to it, in case of conflict." His rejection of an application of this principle in his talk "Speech to Leaders and Members of the Italian Association of Cornea Donors and Italian Association for the Blind" may assist us in understanding why this principle does not justify contraception.[38] The pope was addressing those who argued that the principle of totality justified the removal of vital organs from dying [and thus still *living*] human beings for transplanting into the bodies of those who have a better chance of survival. He states their argument in this way: "If it is permitted, when necessary, to sacrifice a particular member (hand, foot, eye, ear, kidney, sexual gland) to the organism of 'the man,' it should likewise be permitted to sacrifice a particular member to the organism 'humanity' (in the person of one of its members who is sick and suffering)."[39] Although he praises the desire to alleviate suffering, he rejects this argument as erroneous. He notes, "The essential difference between a physical organism and a moral organism is neglected. . . ."[40] That is, he notes that the organs of a body exist for the sake of the body and have no independent end. But each human being does not exist for the sake of the whole of humanity. Each human being has an independent value and thus cannot be sacrificed for the sake of the "whole." To cause the death of one innocent person in order to save the life of another would suggest that the value of humans is not independent of their being a part of some whole and that they can therefore be sacrificed for that whole (or, here, more precisely, another part of that whole).

Those who argue that on the principle of totality it is permissible to sacrifice the good of procreation to the good of union of the marriage would have to demonstrate that each act of intercourse is a part of the whole of the marriage in the way that organs are a part of a body. This seems quite impossible to do for it seems that each act of intercourse has an independent value as well as a possible value for the "whole" of the marriage. There is certainly no "organic" relationship between acts of intercourse; there is nothing other than a very abstract sense in which the sum of acts of intercourse can be considered a whole. That is, a marriage is not a sum of acts of intercourse or even the sum of acts of intercourse and other goods.

It is a reality of a very different nature. Marriage is not a composite of different elements; it is a freely chosen, exclusive, and indissoluble bond that renders two individuals spouses.

Even if marriage were some kind of whole of the sort that the various parts contribute to its well-being, it would be a whole more on the order of the state or the Mystical Body of Christ than on the order of a physical body. Pius XII alludes to this possibility in his discussion; as mentioned, he asserts that one must distinguish between physical and moral organisms. In a physical organism, the parts are clearly subordinate to the whole. In a moral organism, each part has a value independent of the whole. For instance, though an argument could be made that the state or the common good would be better off were a certain portion of the population to be eliminated, this argument could not be made on the basis of the principle of totality, for no group or individual exists for the sake of the whole. Indeed, such action is counterproductive. The state and the common good are both harmed when members of these "wholes" are treated unjustly, for justice is of the essence of the state and of the common good. So, too, as stated, every act of spousal intercourse has a value and is not solely a part of a whole that has a value.

To state the problem another way: how do we know what kinds of acts receive their moral specification individually and which ones receive their moral specification as a part of a totality? The following counterexample may assist us in making the necessary distinctions. Restaurant owners may be open on occasion to serving blacks, but on occasion not. Could they argue that the "totality" of their acts are open to integration? They may also argue that the good of the restaurant requires such occasional discrimination, otherwise they would not get enough business to stay open. Moreover, staying open is in the best interests of the blacks whom they would like to integrate into the clientele of the restaurant. Some would argue that each act of discrimination is wrong, but the principle of totality, as understood by many theologians, would seem to justify acts of discrimination designed to serve the purpose of integration. To put this question even more squarely in the context of marriage, why do all the acts of intercourse between spouses need to be loving? If the totality of these acts are loving, why would it not be permissible that some of them be the product of force? The Church teaches that acts of sexual intercourse must be with one's spouse. Do spouses need always to be faithful? Could not someone use the principle of totality to argue that an occasional affair might help the whole of the marriage? How do conjugal acts stand, especially in their ontic relation and moral evaluation, relative to the totality of the marriage in which they take place?

The Principle of Tolerating the Lesser Evil

Section 14 mentions another principle that is used to justify contraception, "the principle of tolerating the lesser evil." This principle allows that on occasion it is morally permissible to tolerate evil, a lesser evil, so that some good may come from it. This principle is used occasionally to justify contraception, for instance, in circumstances in which a couple believed their marriage was endangered because their lovemaking was marred by anxiety about having another child or the woman's health was seriously threatened by another pregnancy. Divorce and endangering of the health of the woman are considered to be greater evils than contraception, and therefore contraception is considered to be tolerable as the lesser evil.

The principle of the toleration of the lesser evil has been used in a multitude of ways.[41] Let us review here some of the possibly legitimate uses of this principle in reference to the use of contraception.

It is appropriate to begin with the citation given by *Humanae Vitae*. A passage from Pius XII's "Speech to the Fifth National Congress of the Union of Catholic Jurists" (1953)[42] is cited to explain the practice of tolerating the lesser evil. Pius XII addresses the question of religious toleration and asks whether it is permissible to tolerate error. He discusses the "principle of *non impedire*," or "principle of toleration," and asks whether God Himself does not practice this principle in regard to sin and error in certain circumstances. Pius XII answers: "Reality shows that error and sin are in the world in great measure. God reprobates them, but He permits them to exist. Hence the affirmation: religious and moral error must always be impeded when it is possible, because toleration of them is in itself immoral, is not valid *absolutely and unconditionally*." Pius

XII goes on to note that in Scripture we are told the parable of the cockle that advises, "Let the cockle grow in the field of the world together with the good seed in view of the harvest (cf. Matthew 13, 24–30)." He draws the following lesson from this parable: "The duty of repressing moral and religious error cannot therefore be an ultimate norm of action. It must be subordinate to *higher and more general* norms, which *in some circumstances* permit, and even perhaps seem to indicate as the better policy toleration of error in order to promote *a greater good.*"[43] This principle does not refer to *doing* evil so that good may come of it, but to *tolerating* evil, in order to promote a greater good. It is difficult to see how the direct choice to use contraception could be counted as "tolerating" evil in any kind of analogous sense to what Pius XII allows.

Humanae Vitae notes that although it is sometimes permissible to tolerate evil, it is never permissible to choose evil. The footnote citation on this claim leads us to Scripture. In Romans 3:8 St. Paul mocks the notion that one can do evil for the sake of good. In the previous verse he asked, "If my falsehood brings to light God's truth and thus promotes his glory, why must I be condemned as a sinner?" Verse 8 states, "Or why may we not do evil that good may come of it? This is the very thing that some slanderously accuse us of teaching; but they will get what they deserve."

Let us stress, as does *Humanae Vitae*, that the principle of tolerating the lesser evil does not mean that it is permissible deliberately to choose to do what is intrinsically immoral. Often this principle is used, for instance, to justify taking an innocent person as a hostage in order to gain what one believes are greater goods for a greater number; one chooses the lesser evil of torture to gain a greater good. But this is an improper application of the principle. Tolerating the lesser evil is more properly stated as "choosing the means that result in less evil." The principle of tolerating the lesser evil properly applies when one is going to choose to do a good action that has some bad consequences; one must determine whether it is proportionate to the good gained to tolerate the evil suffered. On occasion one is faced with a situation in which one has a choice of two moral means to a good end, each of them having some good consequences and some bad consequences. Clearly one should choose the means that has fewer bad consequences, that results in the lesser evil. Also, if one is faced with a situation in which one is inevitably going to perform an act that results in some evil, one attempts to minimize the evil done. For instance, if one were driving a car and sensed that the brakes were not working and realized that one was very likely going to hit either one pedestrian on the right or five pedestrians on the left, clearly one should make the choice that results in the "lesser evil" of risking the life of the one pedestrian rather than risking the life of the five. But obviously, no moral evil has been done; one is not choosing to kill the one pedestrian; one is choosing to avoid killing the five. Nor is one choosing the death of the one pedestrian as a means to saving the life of the five, for the death of the one is a consequence of one's choice to avoid killing the five, not a means to one's end. To risk the life of one, for the sure saving of the lives of five, is, in this case, a proper calculation of goods.

Classical moral theology holds that it is never right to choose deliberately to do something that is intrinsically wrong; no end, however good, justifies deliberately choosing what is intrinsically immoral. Those acts are intrinsically immoral that strike at or negate a basic or absolute good. For instance, the deliberate, direct taking of an innocent human life is an intrinsically immoral action; nothing justifies it. If one were faced with the choice of deliberately and directly choosing to take an innocent human life or allowing a great evil to occur, one would not be justified in the choice to take the innocent life. If possible, other means must be found to prevent the impending great evil; if these are not found one must suffer the evil rather than do something evil. Consider a common example illustrating this claim. A lynch mob threatens a sheriff that they will riot and kill many blacks if he will not release to them a suspect he is holding, a suspect who has not yet been tried. It would not be moral for the sheriff to render this "innocent until proven guilty" suspect to the crowd in order to prevent the death of many others. He may reason that releasing the suspect and having him killed by the mob is a lesser evil than allowing a lynch mob to kill many others. Yet, the sheriff would be reasoning incorrectly for he must not sacrifice the innocent to achieve what is good. He must find other ways to pacify the mob. It may complicate matters if the sheriff believes he is certain of the suspect's guilt or innocence, but ultimately such a judgment is not his to make; it is properly made by the courts.

It is important to clarify some terms here. The sheriff, if he were to turn over the suspect, would be doing a moral evil since it is his responsibility to see that justice is done to the suspect. The mob, clearly, would be doing moral evil were they to kill the suspect or other blacks at random both because it is not their responsibility to be judge, jury, and hangman and because they will undoubtedly kill innocent human beings. The sheriff must take responsibility for his action, and the mob must take responsibility for theirs. The sheriff has not done moral evil by refusing to do the moral evil of releasing the prisoner and thereby "allowing" the mob to riot. Their rioting is not caused by his refusal; it is caused by their free choice. The sheriff is not responsible for the evil that they do if he has used what moral means are available to him to prevent their evil action. Here it is not appropriate for him to make a calculation of the goods and evils that will result from his action. He must stand by the principle that a man cannot be killed without a trial.

Classical moral theology justifies the principle that one should never deliberately choose to do evil by pointing to the example of Christ Himself. Christ came to give witness to the truth that one should never deny the truth or good that one knows because of fear of evil; one should be willing to endure evil to give witness to the truth, to preserve what is intrinsically good. To save His life, He could not deny that He was the Son of God.

The Church teaches that natural law shows that contraception is an intrinsically wrong action. It is an action that denies a truth, that destroys a fundamental good. (The natural law arguments given in Chapter 4 attempt to identify this fundamental good.) Therefore, it is not morally permissible to contracept even if one might thereby prevent some evil, such as an untimely pregnancy or estrangement from one's spouse. Other means must be found to avoid the anticipated evil.

The Principle of Double Effect

The principle of tolerating the lesser evil is often considered a part of the "principle of double effect." This principle justifies choices that have two effects, one good and one evil. The evil effect must be a side effect of the good choice and cannot be a means to bring about the good choice and must be proportionate to that good.[44] This principle does indeed justify the use of medication or procedures that may have a sterilizing or contraceptive effect. For instance, a woman may take medication for the purpose of correcting some health condition such as dysmenorrhea and this medication may prevent ovulation. She is justified in taking this medication because she is not seeking the contraceptive effect but is seeking relief from dysmenorrhea. (If such medication were to be the sort that might work by destroying a zygote, that is, a very young human life, she should refrain from intercourse since the side effect of the death of a young human life would not be proportionate to the good of relief from dysmenorrhea.) This is not a case of allowing contraception for the greater good of relief from dysmenorrhea; rather it is the case of taking a medication designed to relieve one condition that has the unfortunate side effect of causing another. (See Chapter 7 for a fuller discussion of this principle and the role it has played in the effort to justify contraception.)

This chapter has sought to sketch out several of the fundamental *philosophical* moral principles necessary for a defense of the Church's condemnation of contraception. It has attempted to explain the reasons for the natural law claim that organs and acts have natural purposes or ends. While suggesting that this claim is necessary for any arguments condemning contraception, the argument here has held that it does not suffice to demonstrate the immorality of contraception, thus the rejection of the "physiological argument" against contraception. Furthermore, it has argued that contraception is not considered immoral simply because it is artificial. Finally, it has attempted to explain various principles—the principle of totality, the principle of tolerating the lesser evil, and the principle of double effect—which have often been used (and according to this chapter, misused) to defend contraception as morally permissible.

Now that we have eliminated a series of misrepresentations of arguments against contraception and have dealt with some of the justifications for contraception mentioned and rejected by *Humanae Vitae*, let us now turn to Chapter 4, which considers several arguments, all based on natural law principles, that strive to demonstrate that contraception is intrinsically wrong.

FOUR

Natural Law Arguments against Contraception

THE TEXT OF *Humanae Vitae* provides the foundations for several arguments against contraception constructed along the lines of a natural law analysis.[1] Most of them (with the exception of version E) depend on a recognition that organs have purposes and one purpose of the genital organs is reproduction. None of the arguments considers this feature sufficient to render contraception intrinsically wrong; all develop an understanding of the conjugal act that transcends defining it as ordained simply to reproduction. The final argument given here, version F, draws greatly on what have come to be known as "personalist" values; it nonetheless remains fundamentally a natural law argument. A final section of this chapter explains the differences between the use of contraception and methods of natural family planning.

Chapter 3 gave two versions of natural law arguments against contraception. We list them here with four additional arguments:[2]

VERSION A

1. What is artificial is unnatural and wrong.
2. Contraception is artificial.
3. Therefore, contraception is unnatural and wrong.

VERSION B

1. It is wrong to interfere with the natural purposes of organs and acts.

2. The purpose of sexual intercourse is reproduction (of the species).

3. Therefore, since contraception interferes with the purpose of sexual intercourse, contraception is wrong.

VERSION C

1. It is wrong to impede the procreative power of actions that are ordained by their nature to the generation of new human life.

2. Contraception impedes the procreative power of actions that are ordained by their nature to the generation of new human life.

3. Therefore, contraception is wrong.

VERSION D

1. It is wrong to impede the procreative power of actions that are ordained by their nature to assist God in performing His creative act that brings forth a new human life.

2. Contraception impedes the procreative power of actions that are ordained by their nature to assist God in performing His creative act that brings forth a new human life.

3. Therefore, contraception is wrong.

VERSION E

1. It is always wrong to have a contralife will.

2. The use of contraception entails a contralife will.

3. Therefore, contraception is wrong.

VERSION F

1. It is wrong to destroy the power of human sexual intercourse to represent objectively the mutual, total self-giving of spouses.

2. Contraception destroys the power of human sexual intercourse to represent objectively the mutual, total self-giving of spouses.

3. Therefore, contraception is wrong.

The following analysis assesses the soundness of versions C, D, E, and F. It finds C, D, and F to be sound; E essentially true but inadequate. Again, the foundations for the arguments supporting versions C, D, and F are all found in *Humanae Vitae* itself.[3]

The "Intrinsic Worth of Human Life" Argument against Contraception (Version C)

Again, almost no one who presently argues in support of the Church's teaching on contraception depends solely on the argument identified earlier as the "physiological" argument, though there is widespread belief among the dissenters that this is the whole of the

Church's teaching. Most supporters of that teaching argue that the physiological argument is not sufficient. They think that contraception is wrong not simply because an act of sexual intercourse has its natural physiological end violated but because it is a *human* act of sexual intercourse and thus a violation of Man not only in his physiological dimension but in his psychological and spiritual dimensions as well. This observation was made before *Humanae Vitae* by Cahal Daly: "The traditional doctrine never was that the physical integrity of the sexual act was *enough* to ensure its personal and spiritual completeness, but only that deliberate interference with its physical integrity deprived it of its personal and spiritual integrity."[4] Section 7 of *Humanae Vitae* seems to be making this claim: "The question of having children, like other questions regarding human life, cannot be addressed adequately by examining it in a piecemeal way, that is, *by looking at it through the perspectives of biology, psychology, demography and sociology. Rather, [the question] must be addressed in such a way that the whole Man and the whole mission to which he has been called* will be taken into account, for this [mission] pertains not only to his natural and earthly existence but also to his supernatural and eternal existence" (my emphasis). This passage suggests that although the physiological argument may not be sufficient to demonstrate that contraception is intrinsically wrong, it might, in combination with other arguments, provide such a demonstration.

The first argument to be considered, here called the "intrinsic worth of human life argument," holds that what is wrong about contraception is not that it impedes the coming to be of a member of just any species, but that it impedes the coming to be of a *human* life. This is version C:

1. It is wrong to impede the procreative power of actions that are ordained by their nature to the generation of new human life.

2. Contraception impedes the procreative power of actions that are ordained by their nature to the generation of new human life.

3. Therefore, contraception is wrong.

This argument depends on the claim that human life is such a great good, that the actions that result in the coming to be of such a good have a special status. *Humanae Vitae* does not explicitly speak of respecting only life but also the processes that lead to life. It does, however, repeatedly mention "transmitting human life," indicating that it sees the reproductive processes aligned closely with human life.

The major premise here is the one that needs justification. Generally human life is considered to be a great good. The greatness of human life derives from the exalted nature of the human being. Only human beings are rational and free and thus are capable of noble and creative actions and of loving relationships far beyond those of which other animals are capable. It is commonly acknowledged that humans, simply because they are human, deserve a certain kind of treatment; the whole theory of natural rights is based on this concept. Charters for human rights generally speak of an inherent or inalienable set of rights, such as the right to life, liberty, and the pursuit of happiness. What this argument claims is that human life is such a great good that not only should life itself be respected but so too should the actions that lead to the coming to be of human life. This transference of respect for one thing to something else that is not identical to it is not uncommon. For instance, we often extend the respect that we have for an individual to members of his or her family. We tend to value highly objects that belong to or have belonged to our loved ones. In fact, the respectful treatment accorded corpses of human beings derives not from the status of their current state of being but from our respect for what they once were.

Perhaps the argument about the intrinsic worth of life can be stated even more strongly. Human life is such a great good that it is considered to be an intrinsic good (as opposed to an instrumental good). Thus the direct taking of an innocent human life is generally considered to be a great and intrinsic evil. Contraception clearly does not take a human life, yet it is a kind of vote or strike against life, again not just remotely but directly in the thwarting of actions that may lead to new life. The individuals involved want to participate in an action that is ordained to new life but do not want the action to come to its full perfection or completion. Thwarting the procreative processes seems to share in the intrinsic immorality of treating human life cavalierly. This is the argument that was very much behind the early categorization of contraception as a sin against the Fifth Commandment, the commandment not to kill.[5] Contraception was not considered identical to homicide nor equivalent in gravity, but it was considered a related sin, a sin against life.[6] According to this analysis, contraception is unnatural and thus immoral because it does not acknowledge the great good that life is to Man; it does not allow the sexual act to achieve its natural and possible end of resulting in the conception of a new human life. This argument indicates why it is permissible to tamper with and thwart the reproductive processes of other animals and not to do so for Man. The natural end of animal intercourse is another animal of the same species, which has no intrinsic worth; the natural end of human intercourse is another human being, who does have intrinsic worth.

The "Special Act of Creation" Argument (Version D)

Section 13 of *Humanae Vitae* provides the principles for another argument against contraception, closely related to the argument articulated previously:

An act of mutual love which impairs the capacity of bringing forth life contradicts both the divine plan which established the nature [*normam*] of the conjugal bond and also the will of the first Author of human life. For this capacity of bringing forth life was designed by God the Creator of All according to specific laws.

Thus, anyone who uses God's gift [of conjugal love] and cancels, if only in part, the significance and the purpose [*finem*] of this gift, is rebelling against either the male or female nature and against their most intimate relationship, and for this reason, then, he is defying the plan and holy will of God. On the other hand, the one who uses the gift of conjugal love in accord with the laws of generation, acknowledges that he is not the lord of the sources of life, but rather the minister of a plan initiated by the Creator.

This passage is based on the claim that God is the source of human life. But that is to understate the case, for God is the source of all life. What is pertinent here is the understanding that God is the creator of every human life; that a special act of creation is required for the coming to be of each human soul. Thomas Aquinas explains why this is so:

The rational soul is a subsistent form, as was explained [Q. 75, a. 2], and so it is competent to be and to be made. And since it cannot be made of pre-existing matter,—whether corporeal, which would render it a corporeal being,—or spiritual, which would involve the transmutation of one spiritual substance into another, we must conclude that it cannot come to be except by creation.[7]

Creation is the act of bringing something into being from nothing, an act that can only be performed by God.[8] Aquinas argues that the human soul comes to be through creation rather than through an act of generation, because it is not corporeal (and thus could not be made of preexisting materials). If it were made from a preexisting spiritual substance, this would require that one spiritual substance be changed into another, which is an impossibility since spiritual substances are incorruptible and cannot pass out of existence or undergo an essential change in the nature of their substance.[9]

This fairly technical language essentially means that since human beings generate other human beings by means of the body they cannot be the source of a soul, which is a purely spiritual substance. Spouses do, however, have a role to play in the coming to be of a new human life: they "transmit" human life. God has chosen to employ the services of spouses in bringing forth this life (see HV 1). HV 8 reflects the view that conjugal love is in service of life, and thus in service of God the Creator: "Truly, conjugal love most clearly manifests to us its true nature and nobility when we recognize that it has its origin in the highest source, as it were, in God, Who 'is Love' and Who is the Father, 'from Whom all fatherhood in heaven and earth receives its name.' "

An argument based on this understanding of human life would object to contraception as an act that serves to shut God out of an arena designated by Him as the special locus for His creative action. Man does not act in accord with reason (that is, he violates the natural law; he does what is immoral) when he opposes the design of God. Again, the syllogism form of this argument would be:

1. It is wrong to impede the procreative power of actions that are ordained by their nature to assist God in performing His creative act, which brings forth a new human life.

2. Contraception impedes the procreative power of actions that are ordained by their nature to assist God in performing His creative act, which brings forth a new human life.

3. Therefore, contraception is wrong.

A recent statement of this argument has been made by Monsignor Carlo Caffarra.[10] He argues that human life can come to be through three sources only: chance, necessity, or a free, creative act of God. Further, recognition of the truth that human life is the result of the free and creative act of God befits the freedom and dignity of Man. Finally, the use of contraception is inconsistent with this truth. He succinctly states his position:

The exercise of conjugal sexuality, when it is fertile, constitutes the mysterious tangential point between the created universe of being *and* God's creative love; it is even the point at which this creative love comes *within* the created universe of being, with a view to the *new* term of its potency. At that moment—the moment when a fertile conjugal act is completed—a *new* created person becomes *really* and *proximately* possible. The man and the woman have the responsibility of respecting this possibility *or* of rejecting it, destroying it through contraception. The fertility inherent in the conjugal act is not merely a biological fact. It brings the spouses, objectively, into a real relationship with God the Creator, whether or not they are conscious of the fact.

Earlier he writes: "As Dante writes at the beginning of the third canto, the Glory of God *"per l'universo penetra e risplende / in una parte più e meno altrove"* (penetrates in splendour through the universe / in one part more and in another less). There are places in the created universe of being in which the Glory of God shines forth and lets itself be seen with particular splendour. One of these is the *fertile* conjugal act. In this and through this, indeed, a space is opened up in the created universe for a creative act of God; a holy place in which God shows his creative love."

An expansion on this argument includes the understanding that God wants many human beings to share eternal bliss with Him. He uses spouses as transmitters of this life—they aid Him through their act of procreation—but He is directly the source of the creation of a new human soul. A suggestion of this position is found in the opening lines of *Humanae Vitae*: "God has entrusted spouses with the extremely important mission [*munus*] of transmitting life. In fulfilling this mission spouses freely and deliberately render a service to God, the Creator." Couples who contracept would then, in a sense, be refusing to perform a service that God has asked of them. This argument, clearly, transcends natural law arguments, but this is not a violation of the enterprise of *Humanae Vitae* that purports to offer natural law arguments "illuminated and made richer by revelation" (HV4).

The "Contraception Is Contralife" Argument
(Version E)

Grisez, Boyle, Finnis, and May[11] make an argument (here, version E) similar to version D. Indeed they claim their argument is consistent with the pre-1917 Code of Canon Law statement that held contraception to be like homicide. The chief difference here is that although these ethicists consider their argument to be a natural law argument, the argument departs from traditional natural law theory in a few very significant ways. The chief departure is in the denial that their argument depends on a recognition of the natural end of organs and acts. They hold that to argue from natural fact to a moral norm is to commit what is called the "is/ought" fallacy or the "fact/value" fallacy. That is, some claim it is incorrect to reason that the fact that sexual intercourse is naturally ordained to procreation does not imply any "ought," does not imply any value. In short, there is a denial that the natural ordination of a thing, organ, or act has any necessary moral implications. Grisez and company do not argue that one must respect not only life itself but the processes that bring forth life; rather, they locate the evil of contraception in the contralife will of the contraceptors. They argue from a position that posits certain basic human goods that are naturally known to Man. They argue that human life is such a good and that to contracept is to set one's will against this good.

They begin by giving their interpretation of the last sentence of HV 11: "We think that the only plausible interpretation of 'Every marital act ought to be open to new life' is the following: It is wrong for those who engage in marital intercourse to attempt to impede the transmission of life, which they think their act otherwise might bring about. For if they do try to impede that to which their act of itself might lead, they choose to close it to new life."[12] They describe the will of those who contracept in this fashion: "They look ahead and think about the baby whose life they might initiate. Perhaps for some further good reason, perhaps not, they find the prospect

repugnant: 'We do not want that possible baby to begin to live.'
As the very definition of contraception makes clear, that will is
contralife; it is a practical (though not necessarily an emotional)
hatred of the possible baby they project and reject, just as the will
to accept the coming to be of a baby is a practical love of that
possible person."[13]

And further: "In short, contraception is similar to deliberate
homicide, despite their important differences, precisely inasmuch
as both involve a contralife *will*. Our thesis is that the contralife will
that contraception involves also is morally evil, although we do not
claim that it is usually as evil as a homicidal will."[14] Stated in
syllogistic form, their argument reads:

1. It is always immoral to have a contralife will.
2. The use of contraception entails a contralife will.
3. Therefore, contraception is immoral.

Although they argue that the chief evil of contraception is in the
will, they do identify two injustices that the choice to contracept
causes. They do not think there is an injustice against the possible
child that the contraceptors choose against (for it is not possible to
do an injustice to someone who does not exist). They argue, rather,
that the injustices done are to babies who come to be as the result
of failed contraception, for they come into the world unwanted.
And some forms of contraception work after conception takes place
and thus contraceptors are participating in an act that takes a human
life.[15]

Few who accept the teaching of the Church against contraception
would disagree with their formulation of *Humanae Vitae* and with
the description of the contraceptive will's being, at least in some
sense, contralife.[16] Yet, some may have many difficulties with the
philosophical underpinnings of the argumentation offered in behalf
of version E, with its implicit understanding that the biological
purpose of sexual intercourse and actions is not determinative, even
in part, of the morality of sexual acts,[17] with its description of the
will of most contraceptors as being most accurately described as
contralife, and finally with its view that the only injustice done by
true contraception is against any unwanted children that may come
to be.[18] A limited response to this position is given in Appendix 4.

Let it stand here as one of the arguments offered in behalf of the Church's teaching.

The "Violation of the Unitive Meaning of the Conjugal Act" Argument (Version F)

As has been mentioned, most of the arguments for contraception by advocates of the importance of personalist values over biological ordinations have claimed that the use of contraception helps to foster conjugal love. Defenders of *Humanae Vitae*, however, have met this challenge by arguing that contraception violates personalist values. They maintain that the very good that couples hope to achieve through the use of contraception—the good of greater love for each other—is a good that is diminished rather than enhanced by contraception. These defenders argue that contraception violates the nature of sexual intercourse not only insofar as it is an act destined by nature for procreation but also insofar as it is an act destined by nature for the fostering of conjugal love.[19] The foundations for this claim are to be found in *Humanae Vitae* itself, as well as in *Casti Connubii* and *Gaudium et Spes*.

As mentioned in Chapter 2, there is often much confusion about what conjugal love really is. In modern times, romantic love tends to be valued so highly that conjugal love is often identified with romantic love. The discussion in Chapter 2 concentrates on conjugal love as a committed union of spouses that prospers through their willingness to make a gift of themselves to each other as elaborated in *Gaudium et Spes*. As was noted, humans enter into many different kinds of loving relationships, but conjugal love is a special kind, proper only to spouses. Conjugal love is a friendship, but unlike other friendships that involve some limitations on the extent of the sharing and giving and union, the friendship of spouses is total; it has no limitations of the usual kind and requires a sharing that is most extraordinary, for this sharing goes far beyond the sharing of possessions, as it requires a commitment to share one's life with another, for better or worse. In the documents of the Church this commitment is often spoken of as making a "gift" of oneself to one's spouse. Talk of marriage requiring making a gift of oneself becomes a central element in the argument against contraception based on the understanding of the inseparability of the procreative and unitive meanings of sexual intercourse.

Conjugal Love as Mutual Self-Giving

The concept of making a gift of oneself to another or to others is central to Christianity and pervades *Gaudium et Spes,* where early on we find the claim "Man can fully discover his true self only in a sincere giving of himself" (GS 24).[20] The phrase itself is a kind of modern restatement of a key passage in Scripture: "Whoever tries to preserve his life will lose it; whoever loses it will keep it" (Luke 17:33). This phrase, in a sense, defines the Christian calling and thus the vocation of marriage as well. Christians are to live a life of self-giving; within marriage Christians are to live a life of *mutual* self-giving. Two paragraphs of *Gaudium et Spes* 49 describe marriage precisely as a union based on mutual self-giving:

[Married love], bringing together the human and the divine, leads the partners to a free and mutual giving of self, experienced in tenderness and action, and permeates their whole lives; besides, this love is actually developed and increased by the exercise of it. This is a far cry from mere erotic attraction, which is pursued in selfishness and soon fades away in wretchedness.

Married love is uniquely expressed and perfected by the exercise of the acts proper to marriage. Hence the acts in marriage by which the intimate and chaste union of the spouses takes place are noble and honorable; the truly human performance of these acts fosters the self-giving they signify and enriches the spouses in joy and gratitude.

Humanae Vitae 9 is clearly an expansion on *Gaudium et Spes* and a more precise definition of the characteristics of conjugal love.[21] The greater precision is necessitated by the need to draw out the characteristics of conjugal love that are likely to be threatened by the use of contraception. Section 9 lists four "characteristics and requirements" of conjugal love; it is human, total, faithful and exclusive, and fruitful. The way in which *Humanae Vitae* 9 treats of the characteristic of conjugal love labeled "fruitfulness" is illuminating. The fact that "fruitfulness" is included as a characteristic of conjugal love indicates that "offspring" are not considered as a separate good of marriage, a procreative good of marriage distinct from a personalist good of marriage, but as one of the personalist values of marriage. Just as God's love overflows into His creation of new beings, so too does the love of spouses extend beyond themselves into the creation of new life. *Humanae Vitae* 9 closes by citing a portion of *Gaudium et Spes* that brings together the theme of marriage and conjugal love "being *ordained* by their very nature" to children and the theme of spouses making a gift of themselves to each other. This "gift" leads to the perfection of spouses, which, in turn, leads them to share the gift of life with children. The circle is complete insofar as having children further promotes the good of the parents.

These passages are preparatory for *Humanae Vitae* 12, which states: "There is an unbreakable connection between the unitive meaning and the procreative meaning [of the conjugal act] and both are inherent in the conjugal act. This connection was established by God, and Man is not permitted to break it through his own volition." We find a version of this claim in *Casti Connubii:* "Every sin committed as regards the offspring becomes in some way a sin against conjugal faith, since both these blessings are essentially connected."[22] This insight, that contraception violates the unitive as well as the procreative meaning of conjugal intercourse, has come to the fore as one of the primary arguments against contraception only in the later part of this century. It is developed primarily by Catholic thinkers who, of course, often rely on scriptural passages to support their claims. It should be noted, though, that the understanding of marital love undergirding this argument is not necessarily distinctively Christian. The understanding that the spousal relationship is one of a lifetime bond between two individuals who hope to grow in trust and concern for one another is not exclusively Christian. The caveat should also be made that in this line of reasoning the phrase "total self-giving" does not have the excessively romantic connotation it may quite readily have for modern ears.[23] Total self-giving means living one's life in a way that joins one's life to one's spouse's in an intimate way, respecting the autonomy of the spouse, and seeking the happiness of the spouse. Innate selfishness may hinder most from achieving this completely successfully, but it is the kind of relationship appropriate for marriage and one that spouses true to the meaning of marriage seek to have. Let us see how this argument is developed.

Contraceptive Sex as a Lie

Presently, Pope John Paul II is the most articulate spokesman for
the argument that contraception violates the unitive as well as the
procreative meaning of sexual intercourse,[24] followed closely by
Rev. Cormac Burke, a student of John Paul's views.[25] John Paul's
arguments, those that are more properly philosophical, provide the
primary basis for the arguments advanced in this chapter; Chapter 8
gives a fuller presentation of John Paul's commentaries on *Humanae
Vitae*. The argument that is defended here has been designated
version F:

   1. Acts that destroy the power of human sexual intercourse to represent
objectively the mutual, total self-giving of spouses are wrong.
   2. Contraception destroys the power of human sexual intercourse to
represent objectively the mutual, total self-giving of spouses.
   3. Therefore, contraception is wrong.[26]

Let us note that this argument is also an argument based on natural
law, for natural law embraces the spiritual and psychological dimensions of the human person as well as the physiological dimensions.[27]

John Paul makes central to his argument the claim that sexual
intercourse is an action that is meant to express total self-giving
between the spouses. He develops a concept of a "language of the
body" to explain his position. A crucial premise of his argument is
that contracepted sex does not express an act of total self-giving,
for it is an act that withholds from one's spouse one's fertility and
all that it means. Indeed, in *Familiaris Consortio* he goes so far as to
call a contracepted act of sexual intercourse a lie:

> When couples, by means of recourse to contraception, separate these
> two meanings that God the Creator has inscribed in the being of man and
> woman and in the dynamism of their sexual communion, they act as
> "arbiters" of the divine plan and they "manipulate" and degrade human
> sexuality—and with it themselves and their married partner—by altering
> its value of "total" self-giving. Thus the innate language that expresses
> the total reciprocal self-giving of husband and wife is overlaid, through
> contraception, by an objectively contradictory language, namely, that of
> not giving oneself totally to the other. This leads not only to a positive
> refusal to be open to life but also to a falsification of the inner truth of
> conjugal love, which is called upon to give itself in personal totality.[28]

John Paul claims that certain of our bodily actions have an inherent meaning that we must respect; sexual intercourse is one of those actions that have an objective truth to which we must conform our behavior. This claim is fully supported by passages from both *Gaudium et Spes* and *Humanae Vitae*. *Gaudium et Spes* 51 states: "When it is a question of harmonizing married love with the responsible transmission of life, it is not enough to take only the good intention and the evaluation of motives into account; the objective criteria must be used, criteria drawn from the nature of the human person and human action, criteria which respect the total meaning of mutual self-giving and human procreation in the context of true love. . . ." *Humanae Vitae* 10 cites the preceding passage in a footnote reference. It makes a similar claim in several different ways; it speaks of "human reason needing to be aware of and respect the functions inherent in the biological structures of the sexual act"; it speaks of an "objective moral order established by God" and states that "in regard to the mission [*munus*] of transmitting human life, it is not right for spouses to act in accord with a private judgment, as if it were permissible for them to define subjectively and willfully what is right for them to do." A paragraph from HV 12 is also relevant here: "Because of its intrinsic nature, the conjugal act, which unites husband and wife with the closest of bonds, also makes them capable of bringing forth new life according to the laws written into their very natures as male and female. And if both essential meanings are preserved, that of union and procreation, the conjugal act fully maintains its capacity for [fostering] true mutual love and its ordination to the highest mission of parenthood, to which Man has been called."

John Paul insists that spouses must conform their actions to the meaning of the sexual act, to its intrinsic nature. Part of this meaning is that the act is to be an act of total self-giving; and, again, he claims that to use contraception is not to engage in an act of total self-giving.[29]

He maintains that spouses wish to give of themselves totally through sexual intercourse, that they desire the most complete union possible with each other. He attempts to show that it is not against Man's desires, not against the dynamics of a love that desires complete union with another, to conform to the meaning that sexual intercourse has of both procreation and union. To deny our procreative powers, to withhold deliberately this power from sexual union is to make the union less than what it ought to be; it is to offer only a part of ourselves, not the whole, to the beloved. And this reduced offering is particularly serious in that it robs the act of sexual intercourse of what makes it ultimately most unitive; it robs it of the ability for two to become one flesh through the new life they could create. That is, John Paul is saying that the act of sexual intercourse that is not open to procreation is not truly unitive, and since union is what we seek through spousal intercourse, we are working against our own desires when we use contraception.

He uses the phrase and concept of "language of the body" to clarify his claim and explains the evil of contraception in this way:

The conjugal act "signifies" not only love, but also potential fecundity, and therefore it cannot be deprived of its full and adequate significance by artificial means. In the conjugal act it is not licit to separate the unitive aspect from the procreative aspect, because both the one and the other pertain to the intimate truth of the conjugal act: the one is activated together with the other and in a certain sense the one by means of the other. This is what the encyclical teaches (cf. HV 12). Therefore, in such a case the conjugal act deprived of its interior truth, because artificially deprived of its procreative capacity, ceases also to be an act of love.

It can be said that in the case of an artificial separation of these two aspects, there is carried out in the conjugal act a real bodily union, but it does not correspond to the interior truth and to the dignity of personal communion: communion of persons. This communion demands in fact that the "language of the body" be expressed reciprocally in the integral truth of its meaning. If this truth be lacking, one cannot speak either of the truth of self-mastery, or of the truth of the reciprocal gift and of the reciprocal acceptance of self on the part of the person. Such a violation of the interior order of conjugal union which is rooted in the very order of the person, *constitutes the essential evil of the contraceptive act.* (my emphasis)[30]

The evil of contraception, then, is that it belies the truth that the "language of our bodies" should be expressing: the truth that we are seeking complete union with the beloved.

Let us explore the richness of this phrase "language of the body" further. It is not so very different from the phrase "body language." This phrase grows out of the observation that our bodies convey messages in the way we move and position them. John Paul goes perhaps a bit further in claiming that certain acts of the body have an inherent meaning that should not be violated. An example from verbal language should help to clarify this claim. Certain words have fairly unambiguous meanings and carry with them certain obligations. Almost everyone has felt betrayed by someone who has said "I love you." Most take this to mean "I will care for you," "I will treat you kindly," "I will not hurt you." Many have learned that some use these words to seduce them into serving others in differing ways, perhaps into giving them gifts and into having sexual inter-course with them. When they later learn that the words did not carry the meanings they believed them to have, they feel betrayed, they feel used, they feel deceived.

Is it right to say that certain actions, like certain words, carry inherent meaning? The best example of this, I think, can be found in Scripture, when Judas kisses Christ. Is not a kiss a sign of affection, of friendly feeling? But Judas uses a kiss to do an unfriendly thing: to betray Christ. With his kiss he has lied to Christ: he is not expressing affection with his kiss.

John Paul is saying that the act of sexual intercourse carries with it an inherent meaning: it says among other things, "I find you attractive" and "I marvel and rejoice in your existence." But perhaps most distinctively it means, "I am grateful for the gift of yourself and wish to make a gift of myself to you"; that is, "I thank you for wanting to share yourself (and life) with me and I wish to share myself (and life) with you." The sexual act means these things because it is the kind of act that befits a union of those who wish to live together and to develop the fully trusting and loving relationship appropriate for spouses. The possibility of procreation also demands that those partaking in the act of sexual intercourse be prepared to accept the responsibility of parenthood, a lifetime commitment. Thus John Paul maintains that the act of sexual intercourse says, "I wish to become wholly one with you and to accept the possibility of having children with you." One must accept and mean what sexual intercourse itself means; since the act is by its very nature ordained to the possibility of the conception of a child, those who engage in it honestly should mean all that the act itself means. To have sexual intercourse without being open to procreation diminishes the union one is having with one's beloved;

the individual treats his partner like one with whom he does not wish to have children. An individual demeans his love, he demeans his beloved, by not expressing desire for union of this depth.

For this reason, John Paul calls contracepted sexual intercourse a lie. On the one hand, if the spouses truly do mean that they wish to give of themselves totally, the meaning of their contracepted act of sexual intercourse does not make that statement. Their hearts say, "I want to unite completely with you," but their bodies with their impaired fertility say, "I do not want to give myself completely to you." The bodies during sexual intercourse are going through an action that signifies total self-giving, but through contraception it has been robbed of the ability to be an actual act of self-giving. The act of sexual intercourse is an act of union in appearance only, not in reality; it is a lie.[31]

The act of sexual intercourse signifies union quite unlike any other action. By participating in almost any action with another, we experience some sense of union. If we go to a sporting event with a friend, we may feel that we have "bonded" somewhat more closely with that friend. But the bond is hardly significant of anything more than sharing a mutual pleasure with another. Certainly holding hands, kissing, and caressing create bonds and "mean something." They mean that one is attracted to another, feels some affection for another, to some extent one trusts another and is open to sharing something privileged and precious with another. But one makes no pledges through these acts; one does not "mean" the intent to form lifetime bonds with these actions. The act of sexual intercourse, though, responsibly engaged in, means all that and almost unimaginably more. One may wish to enjoy sexual pleasure with many individuals, but the prospect of the bond that is inherently entailed in having sexual intercourse with another, which is the bond of having children with another, requires that those who are responsible and who know what actions mean not casually engage in sexual intercourse. They realize the vast difference between the meaning "I find you attractive and wish to engage in a wonderfully pleasurable act with you" and the meaning "I am willing to be a parent with you," a meaning that is inherent in the act of sexual intercourse. For it is only through sexual intercourse that one can have the unfathomable bond of creating new life with another, of joining one's very genetic makeup, one's unique incarnational identity, with another. Again, to do so responsibly means that one is making a lifetime commitment to share with another the concern for the physiological, psychological, and spiritual well-being of another. It is rare (surrogate motherhood notwithstanding) for one to wish to have children by one for whom one does not have the intensity of love that is properly spousal; that is, a sign that one loves another as a spouse is one's willingness to have and raise children with this individual, the willingness to interlock one's life together with another's.

Sexual intercourse certainly is an act of sharing in pleasure with another. It is an act that could be shared with many. And contracepted sexual intercourse often is. Sexual intercourse of this sort does not bespeak—does not "mean"—that one desires to have a lasting union with another. It is simply the sharing of a temporary, ephemeral pleasure. Sexual intercourse that is meant to express the depth of love of spouses, however, is not properly expressed through such an ephemeral act. Spouses desire to have a committed, lifelong, exclusive union with each other. "Uncontracepted" sexual intercourse expresses this desire, this intention, in a most profound and appropriate fashion. The willingness to have a child with another bespeaks a willingness to share a lifetime bond with another. Cormac Burke has a particularly apt way of explaining how sexual intercourse open to procreation most fully expresses the desire of spouses to give themselves totally to one another:

The greatest expression of a person's desire to give himself is to give the seed of himself. Giving one's seed is much more significant, and in particular is much more real, than giving one's heart. "I am yours, I give you my heart; here, take it" remains mere poetry, to which no physical gesture can give true body. But "I am yours; I give you my seed; here, take it" is no poetry; it is love. It is conjugal love embodied in a unique and privileged physical action whereby intimacy is expressed ("I give you what I give no one else") and union is achieved. "Take what I have to give. This will be a new me. United to you, to what you have to give, to your seed, this will be a new you-and-me, fruit of our mutual knowledge and love." In human terms, this is the closest one can get to giving oneself conjugally and to accepting the conjugal self-gift of another, and so achieving spousal union.[32]

He goes on to say:

Other physical expressions of affection do not go beyond the level of a mere gesture; they remain a symbol of the union desired. But the conjugal act is not a mere symbol. In true marital intercourse, something real has been exchanged; and there remains, as witness to their conjugal relationship and the intimacy of their conjugal union, the husband's seed in the wife's body.[33]

To rob that seed of its procreative power is to rob it of its unique power, of its future-oriented binding power. It reduces the act of sexual intercourse to a mere sharing of a physical pleasure; it robs it of the implicit promise of the procreative act, of sharing a future together.[34]

Yet, too, it should be noted that spouses note that many of their sexual acts, even those that are not contracepted, are not always or even often fraught with the kind of deep meaning described. They state that acts of sexual intercourse even in the most loving of marriages are on occasion frivolous, urgent, perfunctory. But these claims do not invalidate the description of the "meaning" of sexual intercourse given. One may not have consciously in mind all that one's acts (or even words) mean, but if one undertakes them responsibly, one does nonetheless "mean" at some level what one's acts and words entail. Many parents nightly tell their children they love them without having fully in mind at that instance what they mean and their words mean, a meaning they accept and to which they are committed. They are not being hypocritical or false; they are repeating in a rather routine and unthinking way what has a much deeper meaning for them. Surely between spouses there are often such exchanges. For instance, one may enter into an anniversary celebration while not particularly pleased with one's spouse on this given day. Or one may participate in the celebration rather absentmindedly, without renewing one's commitment in the fullest and most profound way. But if one were to think about it, one would mean all that an anniversary celebration can and should mean: a recommitment of one another to each other. The act of celebration carries a meaning that one does not reject, though this meaning may not fully be in the forefront of one's mind at the moment. Acts of sexual intercourse that are less than perfect efforts to express the complete extent of one's love for one's spouse can nonetheless on a deeper level still express that love. In fact, keeping the procreative meaning of sexual intercourse intact is a key element in ensuring that one's acts of conjugal intercourse retain, in a certain sense, in spite of the intentions of the spouses, the full meaning that conjugal intercourse truly bears. One's actions "mean" more than one feels, in a sense, and this meaning is appropriate for such an intimate communication with one's spouse.

When an act of sexual intercourse successfully results in a child, the spouses have achieved an actual bond of the sort that is appropriate for spouses. Children are an incarnational manifestation of the bond desired by spouses; children are flesh of their flesh, made up of their very bodily matter, constituted by their shared genetic makeups. Moveover, children, to be raised well, require parents with a lifetime commitment to them and to each other. And raising a child has the potential of creating more and more bonds with one's spouse, of fostering greater and greater mutual love. Acts of sexual intercourse that are not robbed of their procreative meaning through contraception express a desire for all the goods that might accompany the good of having a child together.[35]

The preceding argument does not, of course, imply that couples who use contraception do not love each other, do not desire a bond with each other, do not desire to be parents with one another. What it does maintain is that contracepting couples in using contraception are engaging in actions that are designed to and are appropriate to express this desire but that have been robbed of the power that makes them appropriate for expressing such a desire. They are the opposite of couples not using contraception who have intercourse in a rather routine way; the sexual acts of the noncontracepting couple carry all the meaning these acts have by nature, whether or not their feelings correspond. No amount of feeling can provide the meaning that contracepting couples seek to express.

Humanae Vitae 13 further explains the claim that both the unitive and procreative significances of the conjugal act must be respected. The argument here moves from what is more obvious to what is less obvious. The point is first made that we understand that those conjugal acts that are imposed by one spouse upon the other violate the moral order. Such actions violate the unitive significance of the conjugal act. The conjugal act is meant to be an act of love, an act of two willing individuals who freely give of themselves to each other for the purposes of intimate union. If we understand that it is wrong to violate one meaning, we should be able to understand that it is wrong to violate the other meaning.

The argument, to this point, is free of distinctively Christian views. Perhaps it is distinctively Christian to understand that God is the author of nature and that to violate nature is to violate God's will. If so, Christians would have even further motivation for respecting the inherent meanings of sexual intercourse. To be consistent, we should be able to see that those who attempt to deprive the conjugal act of its procreative meaning are violating what is expected of marriage and are attempting to thwart the will of God. In brief, God is a loving God and to act unlovingly (to force one's spouse to have sex) is to violate God's will; God is also a life-creating God; to act against the power of creating life is also to act against God.

It may shed further light on this section to consider this following possibility. One spouse may impose his/her will on the other and have "imposed sex" for the purpose of conceiving a child. Or couples may resort to in vitro fertilization to produce a child. Both actions may result in a child but neither respects the unitive meaning of sexual intercourse.[36] And although a child may result from both actions, it is not true to say that a "procreative" action has been accomplished. Procreation requires a free and loving act of both individuals; an act of imposition will not serve, nor will an action undertaken by lab technicians.

A key argument against contraception, then, is that it violates not only the procreative good of sexual intercourse but also the unitive meaning of sexual intercourse. As explained in this chapter, the argument has not drawn on the theological sources of Scripture and tradition. Chapter 8 presents some of the evidence that John Paul finds in Scripture to "enrich and illumine" this argument, here defended in terms of natural law.

The Difference between Contraception and Natural Family Planning

Several of the earlier discussions have touched on the differences between contraception and natural family planning, but a fuller discussion of this topic is certainly warranted. Many, even the most prominent moral theologians, have claimed that there is no significant moral difference between the use of contraception and the use of methods of natural family planning (NFP). These methods involve abstaining from sexual intercourse when the woman is determined to be fertile and reserving sexual intercourse for the periods when she is determined to be infertile. Some theologians claim there is no moral difference, because the intentions of the couples using contraception and those using NFP are the same; both intend not to have a baby and take means to ensure that such will not happen. Many also claim that it is just as unnatural to use charts and thermometers as it is to use the pill, the IUD, and so on.

Humanae Vitae devotes an entire section, section 16, one of its lengthier sections, to this question. The discussion remains brief, of course, but it includes the fundamental principles necessary for locating the differences between contraception and natural family planning methods. It reiterates that there is no objection to Man's using his intellect to help ensure greater family harmony and peace and to make better provisions for children already born. There is the stipulation, of course, that this "must be done in accord with the order of reality established by God."

It identifies as moral the method of determining the cycles of fertility and of then timing intercourse to correspond with these cycles. To distinguish this practice from contraception it says: "These two situations are essentially different. In the first, the spouses legitimately use a faculty that is given by nature; in the second case, the spouses impede the order of generation from completing its own natural processes."

First let us establish that there is not anything necessarily wrong with the intention of spouses not to have a child (HV 16 explicitly acknowledges this). Indeed, on occasion it would certainly be responsible for spouses to decide not to have a child or another child at a certain time. The Church is careful not to define very precisely what would warrant postponing having a child and leaves the decision to the spouses (see *Gaudium et Spes* 50); HV 16 alludes to the "physical or psychological condition" of the spouses or to certain external conditions. The reasons, though, must be serious (the Latin text speaks of *seriis causis* (serious reasons) [HV 10], *iustae causae* (just reasons) [HV 16], *honesta et gravia argumenta* (worthy and weighty reasons) [HV 16], *probabiles rationes* (defensible reasons) [HV 16], and *iustas rationes* (just reasons) [HV 16]). Indeed, *Humanae Vitae* does not speak so much of limiting family size as of "spacing offspring." This phrase is important. The assumption is that spouses will want to have children but for good reason may wish to "space" (Italian *distanziare*; Latin *intervallandi*) their children.

While the Church does not explicitly lay out what it considers to be good and moral reasons for "spacing" one's children, popes since Pius XI have given their ever-increasing enthusiastic endorsement of methods of natural family planning. While "serious reasons" is the appropriate colloquial English translation for the various phrases used in the Latin, "just reasons" is perhaps a more precise translation of the concept. Clearly, spouses are not to avoid having children for selfish or trivial reasons. But what constitutes a good reason for avoiding pregnancy? The virtue of justice does seem to come into play. That is, spouses should ask: Would it be just—to God, to our marriage, to the children we already have, to the child we might have, and even to society—were we to have a child or another child at this time?

Now clearly they may achieve their ends by recourse to either contraception or abstinence whether periodic or complete. But what is absolutely essential to recognize is that in any moral decision, not only must one's end be moral but so must be the means chosen to achieve that end. A simple and clear example should suffice to illustrate this claim. Two men may wish to support their families and thus both have identical ends for their actions. But one chooses to get a job at a bank and another chooses to rob a bank. Clearly one has chosen moral means to his end; the other has chosen immoral means. The various versions of the natural law arguments against contraception attempted to demonstrate why it is an immoral means. Here let us elaborate a bit on why NFP is a moral means.[37]

Let us first consider what natural family planning entails. Although there are various methods of NFP, they differ primarily in the means used to determine when a woman is fertile or infertile; they use indications of temperature, changes in mucus, changes in the cervix, or a combination of these to determine fertility.[38] The couple is then advised to abstain during the fertile days if desiring to avoid a pregnancy, or to have intercourse during these days if desiring to achieve pregnancy. NFP is truly a method of family *planning* for it helps one to conceive as well as to avoid conception. These methods differ from what is known as the "rhythm method" because they are equally effective for women with regular or irregular cycles. Methods of NFP are remarkably reliable, whereas the old "rhythm method" was not. (Indeed, one author, Michel Rouche, believes that it was the testimony of spouses who found "rhythm" unreliable that most led the papal commission advising Paul VI to recommend that the Church allow contraception. Rouche notes that it is unfortunate that the commission seemed not to take into account the programs conducted in the 1960s on the Mauritian Islands, which were remarkably successful in reducing the growth of the population.[39])

Determining when a woman is infertile is an act of human intelligence, but it is an act of human intelligence that works in accord with nature, that does not violate nature. Some argue that using a thermometer and keeping charts is "unnatural," as unnatural as taking a pill or using a condom. But there is an equivocation on the term *unnatural* here, noted in Chapter 3. Common parlance often uses *natural* to refer to what is normal or to what is spontaneous. Women do not usually chart their fertility cycles, and NFP reduces somewhat the spontaneous participation in sexual intercourse of spouses, so in these terms, perhaps, NFP is as "unnatural" as contraceptive devices and drugs—and as eyeglasses and penicillin, too. But the Church is not using the words *natural* and *unnatural* in these philosophically imprecise ways. Drugs and devices are "natural" when they work in accord with nature and restore something to its natural condition. Thus, for instance, the use of eyeglasses and penicillin is natural because they restore health or full operation to the body. What is "unnatural" works against nature: by this token, as we have stated, contraception is unnatural for it renders infertile an individual who enjoys the healthy and natural condition of fertility. The couple using contraception intends not just to avoid having a baby but to have sexual intercourse and to thwart the natural end of sexual intercourse. The couple using NFP also intends not to have a baby, but they do not tamper with the ordination of the sexual act; it remains whatever nature has made it to be, fertile or infertile. NFP respects the natural fertility cycle of a woman and in this way is fully natural; it leaves her fertile when nature would have her be fertile and it leaves her infertile when nature would have her be infertile.[40] So there is nothing unnatural in a woman's learning the details of her fertility cycle: she is simply charting a natural process.

Perhaps the most straightforward way of seeing the moral permissibility of NFP is to engage in the following line of reasoning. (1) There is nothing wrong with spouses' wanting for good reasons to limit their family's size; (2) there is nothing wrong with married couples' either having sexual intercourse or not having sexual intercourse; (3) thus, since it is not wrong to want to limit family size and there is nothing wrong with not having sexual intercourse, it would seem peculiar to argue that there is something wrong with not having sexual intercourse because of the intent (the moral intent) to limit family size. Again, spouses are doing nothing immoral when they are not having sexual intercourse. If they are not having sexual intercourse because one or the other is sick, that is not immoral; if they are not having sexual intercourse because one or the other is not in the mood, that is not immoral; if they are not having sexual intercourse because the house is full of guests, that is not immoral. Similarly, if they are not having sexual intercourse because at this point they do not wish to have children, why would this decision be immoral?

Nor is there anything wrong for spouses in having sexual intercourse at will (within the dictates of reason, of course!). They may have sexual intercourse during the times when the woman is fertile and the times when she is not; therefore, having sexual intercourse during the infertile periods is moral. G. E. M. Anscombe offers this line of reasoning:

In contraceptive intercourse you intend to perform a sexual act which, if it has a chance of being fertile, you render infertile. *Qua* your intentional action, then, what you do *is* something intrinsically unapt for generation and, that is why it does fall under that same condemnation. There's all the world of difference between this and the use of the "rhythm" method. For you use the rhythm method not just by having intercourse now, but by not having it next week, say; and not having it next week isn't something that does something to today's intercourse to turn it into an infertile act;

today's intercourse *is* an ordinary act of intercourse, an ordinary marriage act.[41]

NFP, then, is moral (1) since it proceeds from a good motive and (2) since neither having sexual intercourse in the infertile periods nor refraining from having sexual intercourse in the fertile periods is immoral.

Let us play this out a bit more. A couple decide for good reasons that now is not a good time for them to have a child or another child. So on a given day a woman determines that she is infertile. That evening her husband becomes amorous. Is there any reason for her to discourage him from pursuing the act of sexual intercourse? Are they doing anything immoral in having sexual intercourse during the infertile time? A few days later, this same woman may determine that she is fertile. Her husband shows signs of interest in having sexual intercourse. She gently informs him that if they were to have sexual intercourse now she may become pregnant, and they have decided that it would not be a good time to have a baby. They decide to go for a walk instead. Have they done anything immoral?

The preceding scenario reveals another distinction between the acts of those who abstain periodically and those who contracept. Whereas with methods of contraception one or the other of the spouses, usually the wife, carries the burden, be it a burden of dangers to health, inconvenience, lack of aesthetic pleasingness, or the like, couples using natural family planning methods bear together the burden of abstaining. Both must cooperate for the method to work. Mary Rosera Joyce expresses well this feature of the differences between the two actions:

As the generation of new persons is a marital action shared by two persons contemporaneously, the regulation of conceptions should be a marital act shared by two persons at once. Conception regulation by periodic continence is impossible without both persons sharing the choice and responsibility at once. For this reason, it is proportionate to the marriage relationship itself. With contraception, on the other hand, one person at a time can easily use means for preventing conception.

Besides engaging both persons together, the art of periodic continence involves the total person of each. It includes psychic, mental and spiritual action as well as physiological consideration. While contraception is an investment of birth control in devices and chemicals, periodic continence is an investment in the whole person. Devices such as the calendar and thermometer are used as helps for integrating the process of ovulation into personal knowledge and understanding. Conception regulation, if it is to be proportionate to the person and to the marriage relationship between two persons, should be as psychological and spiritual as it is physical. And it should be as psychic, spiritual, physical and interpersonal *in its method* as marital love itself.[42]

NFP, then, is a shared endeavor that employs the full faculties of the human person. In this light, contraception is more truly the action that views sexual intercourse in a "biologistic" or "physicalistic" way; if intercourse is simply a physiological act, then it may be modified in a strictly physiological way. Yet, since it is not solely a physiological act, it seems to require a fuller human response that takes into account its fully human dimensions.

Clarifications of the difference between contraception and natural family planning can also be made using the description of sexual intercourse as a kind of language through which the truth must be spoken. As was mentioned, John Paul calls contracepted sexual intercourse a lie since it does not tell the truth, the truth of total self-giving that is proper to spousal intercourse. When they are abstaining, couples using NFP can be compared to those who remain silent when it is better not to speak. They think it better not to speak the full language of love since this language may have results, that is, conception of a child, that they think it right not to invite at a given time. They are not falsifying an act that means total self-giving; they are refraining from such an act. And although it is clear that spouses having sexual intercourse during the infertile periods are not giving quite as fully of themselves as they are during fertile times, they are not falsifying the act itself. They tell all the truth that is to be told at a given time; they have given all there is to give at the time.

One of the purposes of marriage is to bring forth children, and the couples pledge as part of their marriage vows that they will welcome children. What if a couple who do not intend to be true to such vows use NFP? Is their use of NFP immoral? In a general way, it would seem not, for, as mentioned, couples may have sexual intercourse and may refrain from having sexual intercourse when they choose. Thus, considered in isolation of the whole, the individual acts of sexual intercourse would not be wrong as such. But, nonetheless, these actions may be tainted to some extent by the spouses' repudiation of one of the essential purposes of marriage. It would be difficult to determine which particular acts of sexual intercourse of the aforesaid couple are immoral, but their motive is clearly immoral. Their objective acts may be moral (assessed as kinds of acts, at any rate), but since they are not in the least open to children their subjective will is immoral. They have done a good (or indifferent) act for bad reasons. We are not unaccustomed to judging acts in this way. For instance, consider someone who might care for the poor simply so that she might acquire a reputation as a trustworthy person but intends to use this reputation eventually to exploit people. Her acts of helping the poor are not in themselves evil, but her motive is. It may seem strange to say that each of her acts of helping the poor is immoral, but surely her overall intention is.

G. E. M. Anscombe provides a further analogy for demonstrating the moral difference between NFP and contraception.[43] She speaks of a worker who to protest unfair conditions decides to "work to rule." He does what he has contracted to do and does not violate his contract. She contrasts this action with that of a worker who decides to sabotage the work of the factory, say by breaking the machine he works on; he violates his contract. Both may have the same end, but one pursues it in an honorable way; the other does so in a dishonorable way.

It should also be observed that although some moral theologians claim there is little difference between the two methods, those who use the different methods perceive significant differences of several kinds, differences that suggest that the moral evaluation of the two must also differ. Those who use contraception do not easily switch to using NFP; those using NFP rarely switch to using contraception. Both sets of couples believe that such a switch would require a whole new way of viewing the prospect of childbearing, of relating to each other, and even of viewing the world.[44] Indeed, the couple using contraception feel very much in control of their fertility and do not want to relinquish that control; couples using NFP believe they are cooperating with God and do not want to cease that cooperation.

Most of them sense that it would be an affront to their dignity and their spouse's to use a contraceptive. One woman expresses most vividly the difference she experienced with the different methods:

Though my hands are full with children (three) and with work outside the home (retail clerk), I feel moved to write in defense of the sexual sensibilities of those millions of us who are not PHDs or DREs or [Phil] Donahue dissent superstars or even wanna-be's.

Yes, I was alive and fertile in 1968. I was 19 and *knew* the pill was a gift from God and *Humanae Vitae* was a real crock. The pill was going to eliminate teenage pregnancy, marital disharmony and world population problems, bring a new era, etc.

By my five-year reunion (high school), those of us who had been so confident about contraception had gone from euphoria to anger. Nothing seemed to work. I'd been on the pill less than two years before I'd quit. The pill depressed us. Or scared us (especially those of us who were smokers) because of the "stroke" factor. I didn't want to keep taking it year after year, or on-again, off-again after I broke up with my college lover. So I decided to live a minimally healthy life-style and quit both smoking and oral contraceptives.

The "safer" IUD (copper-T) gave me cramps and heavy periods. I was lucky. A friend of mind got such a ghastly infection from her IUD she lost her uterus, tubes, ovaries—the works. The woman was devastated. She felt like a gutted shell. Now they've taken them all off the market.

I tried the diaphragm. Hard to keep motivated on that one. . . . I felt wadded up with junk, inwardly disgusted. I wanted to be delectable, like a Haagen Dazs ice cream cone; instead, I was a spermicidal sump. . . .

By the 10th high school reunion, my friends were still fiddling with this method and that, they'd had abortions, and/or their marriages were falling apart. Mine almost did.

Then my husband and I settled on the condom plus periodic abstinence. But we depended on the condom in a way that made it easy to rationalize some "fudging" on abstinence. ("I'm probably fertile, but hey, we've got the ol' rubber so what harm can it do?") You know what "fudging" can lead to. Thank God I didn't have an abortion, but I did have one hell of an untimely pregnancy.

Are you getting my point, fantasy-land theologians?

Finally, my husband and I reached a turning point. At a very low point in our marriage, we met some great people who urged us to really give our lives to the Lord and to be chaste in our marriage.

That blew our minds. We thought it meant "give up sex." That's not what it means. It means respecting bodily union as a sacred act. It meant acting like a couple in love, a couple in *awe*, not a couple of cats in heat.

For my husband and me, it meant NFP with no rubber, no "fudging." And I won't kid you, it was a difficult discipline.

NFP and a chaste attitude toward sex in marriage opened up a new world for us. It bonded my husband and me in a way that is so deep, so strong, that it's hard to describe. Sometimes it's difficult, but that makes us even closer. We revere each other. And when we do come together, we're like honeymooners.

Sad to say, I was past 35 when I finally realized that the Church was right after all. Not the grab-your-sincerity-and-slide church of Charlie Curran, but the real church, the church we encountered through laypeople in the Couple to Couple League, the *Catholic* church. The Church is right about contraception (it stinks), right about marriage (it's a sacrament), right about human happiness (it flows—no it *floods* when you embrace the will of God). It gave us depth. It opened our hearts to love.

Put *that* in your graduate seminar and smoke it.[45]

There is some interesting experiential evidence of the differences between the use of NFP and contraception. There is evidence that it is very rare for couples using NFP to divorce, whereas over 50 percent of all marriages end in divorce.[46] Indeed, one researcher attributes 50 percent of the rise in the divorce rate from the early sixties to the midseventies to the increased use of contraception.[47] Moreover, it is very rare for women who are using NFP to have abortions, whereas most women having abortions have used contraception. Surely the reasons for these situations are complicated, but such information may well suggest that the differences between the two methods of limiting family size are profoundly different not only as acts but in their effects. Respect for the procreative meaning of sexuality seems to strengthen marriages and deepen respect for life.

Couples practicing NFP also tend to have more children than couples who contracept, not because the method is more unreliable but because these couples come to appreciate the importance of children to their marriage and they want to become "generous with God." NFP, in fact, used by well-instructed and highly motivated couples, is every bit as effective as the most effective forms of contraceptive.[48]

These observations about how NFP affects marriage and relationships bear out the claims of John Paul in *Familiaris Consortio*. There he states:

When . . . by means of recourse to periods of infertility, the couple respect the inseparable connection between the unitive and procreative meanings of human sexuality, they are acting as "ministers" of God's plan and they "benefit from" their sexuality according to the original dynamism of "total self-giving", without manipulation or alteration.

In the light of the experience of many couples and of the data provided by the different human sciences, theological reflection is able to perceive and is called to study further *the difference, both anthropological and moral,* between contraception and recourse to the rhythm of the cycle: it is a difference which is much wider and deeper than is usually thought, one which involves in the final analysis two irreconcilable concepts of the human person and of human sexuality. The choice of the natural rhythms involves accepting the cycle of the person, that is the woman, and thereby accepting dialogue, reciprocal respect, shared responsibility and self-control. To accept the cycle and to enter into dialogue means to recognize both the spiritual and corporal character of conjugal communion, and to live personal love with its requirement of fidelity. In this context the couple comes to experience how conjugal communion is enriched with those values of tenderness and affection which constitute the inner soul of human sexuality, in its physical dimension also. In this way sexuality is respected and promoted in its truly and fully human dimension, and is never "used" as an "object" that, by breaking the personal unity of soul and body, strikes at God's creation itself at the level of the deepest interaction of nature and person. (FC, sec. 32)

Most couples report that the use of NFP does require significant self-denial. Those who were chaste before their marriages tend to find the abstinence more tolerable than those who were not. For some the abstinence leads to periods of some irritability and strain within the marriage. For others, it leads to greater opportunity for communication and for displays of affection that do not lead to intercourse. Many report significant improvements in their marriages as the result of use of NFP. John Paul attributes this improvement to the virtue of self-mastery gained through use of NFP; he notes that when one has control over one's sexual desires, gained through the disciplined pursuit of the goods of marriage, one's sexual acts are then more a result of respectful love for one's spouse than of uncontrollable or hard to control sexual urges that may not respect the spouse. He notes, too, that control over one's sexual desires may permeate the whole of one's life and create greater harmony in the home and elsewhere. Chapter 8 reports in greater detail John Paul's defense of the teachings of *Humanae Vitae*.

FIVE

Some Theological Considerations

H umanae Vitae 4 states that the teaching of the Church concerning marriage is a teaching "rooted in natural law, illuminated and made richer by divine revelation." This chapter takes up a few of the theological considerations of the encyclical. First, it examines briefly the scriptural foundations for Humanae Vitae and shows how these "illuminate and enrich" (HV 4) its natural law foundations. Then follows a theological discussion of a very different sort. The word munus (which means variously, "gift," "reward," "duty," "task," and "mission," among other possibilities) and the concept it captures, as shaped in the documents of Vatican II, are explored. We shall see that this concept greatly enriches our understanding of the Church's valuation of childbearing and its consequent condemnation of contraception. The final portion of this chapter is on the questions of conscience and infallibility. Conscience is not strictly a theological concept, but insofar as violation of conscience in the Catholic tradition constitutes not simple wrongdoing, but sin, that is, an offense against God, it seems appropriate to discuss conscience along with other theological matters. And certainly, if the teaching of Humanae Vitae has been proclaimed infallibly, special constraints will be felt by the Catholic conscience to accept this teaching.

Scriptural Foundations for the Teaching of Humanae Vitae[1]

Scripture, of course, does not provide any statement that explicitly states, "Thou shalt not contracept."[2] Those in the Protestant tradition may be troubled by this, but in the Catholic tradition lack of explicit condemnation is no insuperable barrier to claiming that a teaching has scriptural foundation. Scripture also says nothing, for instance, about the morality of directly bombing civilian sites, but such an action clearly violates the Fifth Commandment, "Thou shalt not murder (that is, directly and deliberately kill the innocent)." The Church argues that both natural law and Scripture make clear the immorality of such an action.

The scriptural basis for the condemnation of contraception is not quite so straightforward as the example just given. Nonetheless, there are at least four themes in Scripture that provide strong evidence that contraception does not fit within God's plan for human sexuality. These are (1) the extreme value given to procreation, (2) the portrayal of sterility as a great curse, (3) the condemnation of all sexual acts that are not designed to protect the good of procreation, and (4) the likening of Christ's relationship to His Church to that of a bridegroom to his bride, a union that is meant to be a fecund relationship, one that will bring forth many sons and daughters of God. There is a wealth of scriptural material on all these issues; here it will be sufficient simply to sketch out how this evidence works to show the immorality of contraception. And let this caution be stated: Scripture is always open to various interpretations; particular readings of various texts here may be controversial and perhaps on occasion, highly questionable, though every effort has been made to offer interpretations that are not speculative but altogether straightforward. The hope is that the general thrust of the argument is not without warrant.

It is of no small significance that the first relevant texts are located at the very beginning of Scripture, in the very first chapters of Genesis. There we see God first as a creator, as one who brings about the existence of everything, as one who produces life. What we first learn about Man is that he is made in the image and likeness of God when "male and female He created them." It would not seem that the male alone images God, but that "male and female" do. In the context this suggests that Man images God in His creative powers as much as in any of His other powers. Indeed, once God has created male and female and thus brought about the actuality of human sexuality, His first directive to Man is "Be fertile and multiply; fill the earth and subdue it" (Gen. 1:27). We also quickly learn that man and woman are to become "one flesh." This seems to refer to the union that they achieve through having a child, which is one flesh of their two, as much as to the conjugal act itself, which makes two "one flesh."

Man is to share in God's abundance and fruitfulness through his procreative power. Thus, fertility and fruitfulness seem to be part of the covenant that Man has with God. When God renews His covenant with Man through Noah (and again when He makes a covenant with Abraham), He repeats His initial mandate: "Be fertile and multiply and fill the earth" (Gen. 9:1). Certainly, the other creatures are to multiply, too, but they are under the dominion of Man whereas Man is under the dominion of God. Animals reproduce, but Man procreates.

Throughout the Old Testament, fertility and family are portrayed as great goods, as evidence of faithfulness to God, as rewards for faithfulness to God. One of God's promises to Abram was "I will make your descendants like the dust of the earth; if anyone could count the dust of the earth, your descendants too might be counted" (Gen. 13:16). God was not quick to deliver on this promise; Abram's wife Sarai was barren until her old age. When Abram was ninety-nine years old, God made a covenant with him and made this His first promise: "I will render you exceedingly fertile; I will make nations of you . . ." (Gen. 17:6). Sarah at this point was ninety, but she bore Abram a son. God clearly wanted to show that He was lord of life, that fertility was His great gift. Children were not viewed as a burden but as a sign of favor and wealth. This is so throughout the Old Testament. Perhaps Psalm 127 says it best:

Unless the Lord build the house, they labor in vain who build it.
Unless the Lord guard the city, in vain does the guard keep vigil.
It is vain for you to rise early, or put off your rest,
You that eat hard-earned bread for he gives to his beloved in
     sleep.
Behold, sons are a gift from the Lord; the fruit of the womb is a
     reward.
Like arrows in the hand of a warrior are the sons of one's youth.
Happy the man whose quiver is filled with them; they shall not be
     put to shame when they contend with enemies at the gate. [3]

In this context contraception could be seen as a rejection of a gift from God, as an action stunting the growth of God's chosen people, for which reason, to this day, Orthodox Judaism rejects contraception.

Passages indicating and singing the praises of fruitfulness could be multiplied abundantly, but let us here turn to the point that the opposite of fruitfulness, sterility or barrenness, is considered a great hardship and even a curse. Many of the key figures in Scripture suffered from infertility. Sarah's story has been told; Hannah, eventual mother of Samuel, prayed day and night to bear a child; Rachel was finally "remembered by God" and bore Joseph; Elizabeth in her old age bore John the Baptist. Since fruitfulness was so much a part of participation in the work of the chosen people, in God's plan, sterility was often considered a sign of disfavor or sinfulness; thus women begged God to relieve them, not of the burden of childbearing but of the burden of childlessness. Psalm 113 praises the Lord in this way:

> He raises up the lowly from the dust; from the dunghill he lifts
> up the poor
> To set them with princes, with the princes of his own people.
> He establishes in her home the barren wife as the joyful
> mother of children.

Again, contraception does not fit into this picture of the value of fertility; insofar as contraception renders one at least temporarily infertile, users of contraception would seem to be voluntarily putting themselves in a highly unenviable position.

Scripture does not explicitly condemn contraception, but it does condemn sexual relationships that are not designed to serve the good of procreation. Fornication, adultery, homosexual acts, and bestiality are typically included on the list of serious sins. In Romans 1:2 homosexuality is called an unnatural act, seemingly because the sexual acts of homosexuals are not ordained to procreation, the natural end of the sexual organs. Followers of Yahweh are not to participate in such acts; those who worship false gods regularly do. Misuse of sexuality seems to result whenever Man severs his relationship with God. Reestablishing right sexual relationships is part of the work of getting right with God again.

Finally, the great good of marriage is sung repeatedly throughout Scripture. The prophets regularly liken God's relationship to His people to a marital one: it is to be fruitful. It is jarring to think of contraception being a part of that relationship, to think of God's withholding His creative power from His chosen one. When He does, it is as a punishment for sin. Hosea at 4:7–10 warns:

> One and all they sin against me, exchanging their glory for
>   shame.
> They feed on the sin of my people, and are greedy for their guilt.
> The priests shall fare no better than the people: I will punish
>   them for their ways, and repay them for their deeds.
> They shall eat but not be satisfied, they shall play the harlot but
>   not increase,
> Because they have abandoned the Lord to practice harlotry.

The new covenant instituted by Christ is, as were all the covenants, a marital one, to be marked by great fruitfulness. We might note that the first miracle that Christ performed, the changing of water into wine, was at a wedding feast. It was a miracle that celebrates abundance, as were many of the miracles of Christ (think, too, of the multiplication of the loaves and fishes). There is not a hint in Scripture that marriage or sexuality used properly is bad. Marriage, especially fruitful marriage, is a great good. Again, just as it is jarring—not to say scandalous—to think of contraceptives coming between God and the Israelites, so, too, is it jarring to think of any obstacle to the loving union of Christ and his Church. Insofar as married couples are to image that relationship (compare Ephesians 5), it would seem that the use of contraception violates the image they are to be.

Marriage, procreation, fertility, and fruitfulness, then, are all values sung in various ways throughout Scripture. Sterility and barrenness are not marks of those with God but of those separated from Him. Where is there room for contraception in this picture of God's plan for human sexuality, of God's plan for marriage, of God's plan for His people?

Scriptural Foundations for Specific Natural Law Arguments

Chapter 4 set forth four different arguments based on natural law principles that purport to show the immorality of contraception. All these versions—the intrinsic worth of human life argument, the special act of creation argument, the contraception is contralife argument, and the violation of the unitive meaning of the conjugal act argument—all can be greatly strengthened by reference to Scripture. The value that Scripture puts on human life because of both its nature and its destiny, the view of God as author of life, the view of God as author of nature, and the understanding of God as an "unconditional" lover all illumine and enrich natural law arguments.[4]

Natural law can certainly establish the intrinsic value of human life, since there are rational grounds for valuing human beings above all else. But Scripture gives us even further warrant for treating human life as something of great intrinsic worth. For instance, it teaches us that Man is made in the image and likeness of God. God also has great plans for Man, namely eternal union with Him. The Christian view of God as one who created a universe precisely because He wanted to share His goodness with others puts a value on fertility far beyond what natural reason can readily discover. God clearly wants multitudes with whom to share His goodness, to be with Him in eternal union. In this light, contraception can be seen as being a kind of denial of God's plan that Heaven be populated through love, His love and the love of spouses. *Humanae Vitae* 8 states: "Conjugal love most clearly manifests to us its true nature and nobility when we recognize that it has its origin in the highest source as it were, in God, Who 'is Love' and Who is the Father, 'from whom all parenthood in heaven and earth receives its name.' " Footnote references to this passage cite 1 John 4, "The man without love has known nothing of God, for God is love," and the passage from Ephesians cited previously. The relationships of God, love, and family, then, are greatly underscored by Scripture. Thus by respecting Man we are respecting God.

The story of creation and all the revelations of God's special intervention in the creation of new life, in the miraculous conceptions of infertile women, all portray God as the Lord of Life. Through Scripture God is referred to as the Lord of Life. *Humanae Vitae* 8 cites Ephesians 3:15: "[God, Who is Love] is the Father from whom every family in heaven and earth is named." Psalm 139 gives beautiful testimony to God's interest in life long before birth:

Truly you have formed my inmost being: you knit me in my
  mother's womb.
I give you thanks that I am fearfully, wonderfully made; wonderful
  are your works.
My soul also you knew full well; nor was my frame unknown to
  you
When I was made in secret,
  when I was fashioned in the depths of the earth.
Your eyes have seen my actions; in your book were they all written; my days were limited before one of them existed.
How weighty are your designs, O God; how vast the sum of them!
Were I to recount them, they would outnumber the sands; did I
  reach the end of them, I should still be with you.

As Psalm 139 manifests, the God of Scripture is not the distant
God of the philosophers, who is the God behind nature, an unmoved
mover who set this ordered world in motion. The Judeo-Christian
God is a "hands-on" creator, who pronounces His creation "good"
and who takes an ongoing interest in it. The miracles of Scripture,
such as the parting of the Red Sea, Christ's calming of the wind and
sea, multiplication of loaves and fishes, and healings, all suggest a
God who is master of nature. Thus, again, by respecting nature we
are respecting God.

The natural law argument (version F), which argues that contraception is wrong because it violates the unitive meaning of the
conjugal act, is also much strengthened by Scripture. The concept
of marriage as requiring total self-giving is one that Man may be
able to grasp through his reason. Scripture, however, manifestly
portrays marriage in this light, especially in the portrait (given
previously) of God's covenantal relationship with His people. Several sections of Humanae Vitae assure spouses that grace is available
to them in their attempt to live their marital life in accord with
God's will.[5] God gives totally and abundantly to His people and will
assist them in giving totally to one another. Again, it seems difficult
if not impossible to consider contraception a part of a relationship
of total giving.

Scripture, then, illuminates and enriches the natural law understanding of marriage, sexuality, and contraception in many different
ways. If the preceding interpretations of Scripture are correct, those
who accept Scripture as a revelation of God's will should be greatly

strengthened in their reasoned conviction that contraception is immoral. Catholic theology, though, works with more than Scripture. Through the tradition of the Church certain themes are developed in such a way that they greatly illumine the proper role of a Christian in this world. In fact the concept of *munus* is one of those very concepts that clarify how we are best to live a Christ-centered life.

The Concept of *Munus*[6]

Let us draw on the concept of *munus* to assist us in understanding the claim that spouses are turning their back on God when they use contraception. This concept may "enrich and illumine" our understanding of the natural law arguments against contraception. First we shall need to establish the meaning of this concept and to suggest how it weaves together some of the themes of earlier Church documents on marriage and *Humanae Vitae*. Then we shall make a particular application of this concept to the condemnation of contraception.

The word *munus* has a fairly technical meaning in the documents of the Church. One appearance, most relevant to our concerns, helps to close the section of *Gaudium et Spes* pertaining to marriage. "Let all be convinced that human life and [the *munus* of] its transmission are realities whose meaning is not limited by the horizons of this life only; their true evaluation and full meaning can only be understood in reference to man's eternal destiny" (GS 51).[7] The first line of *Humanae Vitae* speaks of "the most serious duty [*munus*] of transmitting human life," a phrase that clearly picks up this final portion of GS 51. Here let us first determine the meaning of this word and then consider how it might shed light on the relationship between the procreative values of marriage and the personalist values. This word seems to give us access to a dimension of the encyclical often neglected, a dimension that stresses the positive aspect of having children.

As we have seen, childbearing is a very important part of the responsibility of spouses. It flows not only out of the love that the spouses have for each other but from the love that God has for spouses and for the new life they bring forth. Childbearing is, in fact, a "special assignment," a *munus*, which God has entrusted to spouses. A proper understanding of this term should help illuminate the claim that childbearing is not only an act that spouses perform as a natural outcome of their love for each other but at the same time a service they perform for God. It will also assist us in understanding how the personalist values of marriage are intimately linked with the procreative good of marriage and how, by fulfilling the *munus* of having children, the spouses are advancing the perfecting of their persons.

As noted, the word "*munus*" appears in the very first line of *Humanae Vitae* (*Humanae vitae tradendae munus gravissimum* . . .). This line is usually rendered "The most serious duty of transmitting human life. . . ." The translation "duty" for *munus* is not incorrect, but it is inadequate, as is any one word, to capture all its important connotations. (Indeed, there is good reason to believe that the translation "duty" is not of *munus* but of the Italian *dovere*, for most English translations are primarily from the Italian text.)[8] The chief problem with the translation "duty" is that for many modern English-speaking people the word has a negative sense. A duty is often thought of as something that one ought to do and something that one often is reluctant to do; those who are responsible will perform their duties and may enjoy so doing, but they are thought to transcend what is negative about duties. The word *munus*, though, truly seems to be without negative connotations; in fact, a *munus* is something that one is honored and, in a sense, privileged to have. "Duty" is more properly the English translation of *officium*, one of the possible synonyms of *munus*.[9] It seems fair to say that a *munus* often confers or entails *officia*; that is, when one receives a *munus* one also is then committed to certain duties. What, then, is a *munus*? (Throughout most of the following analysis "*munus*" [plural, *munera*] is used, rather than any single English word or a multiplicity of words; for the references to the documents of Vatican II, both Flannery's[10] and Abbott's[11] translations are given in parentheses, in that order.)

One who knows classical Latin would as readily translate *munus* as "gift," "wealth and riches," "honor," or "responsibility" as "duty." Other English translations commonly used are "role," "task," "mission," "office," and "function"; indeed all of these are on occasion legitimate translations, and on a few occasions the word embraces all of these connotations. One common classical Latin use of the word that captures most of these connotations designates a public office or responsibility that has been bestowed on a citizen. Being selected for such an office would entail certain duties, but ones that the recipient willingly embraces. The word is also often used synonymously for "gift" or "reward";[12] it is something freely given by the giver and often, but not always, with the connotation that the recipient has merited the gift in some sense; it is given as a means of honoring the recipient. In Scripture and in the writings of Aquinas *munus* refers both to gifts that Men consecrate to God and to gifts and graces that Men receive from God. For instance, Ephesians refers to the different gifts (*diversi status et munera*), such as being an apostle, prophet, or teacher, with which Men are endowed to serve the Church and God. Rather than being a burdensome duty, a *munus* is much closer to being an assignment or mission that is conferred as an honor on one who can be trusted and who is chosen to share the responsibility of performing good and important work.

The words *vocation* (*vocatio*), *mission* (*missio*), *ministry* (*ministerium*) (which seems often to be a synonym for *apostolate* [*apostolatus*]), *munus*, and *duty* (*officium*) are often linked and occasionally interchangeable; the order of the list just given suggests a possible ranking of these words as far as comprehensiveness is concerned: that is, all Christians have the mission of bringing Christ to the world; they do so through different ministries or apostolates that involve various *munera* and carry certain duties. The second section of *Apostolicam Actuositatem* (*On the Apostolate of Lay People*) illustrates well one variation of the interconnection of these terms:

The Church was established for this purpose, that by spreading the kingdom of God everywhere for the glory of God, she might make all men participants in Christ's saving redemption, and that through them the whole world might truly be ordered to God. All apostolic [*apostolatus*] activity of the Mystical Body of Christ is directed to this end, which the Church achieves through all of its members, in various ways; for the Christian vocation [*vocatio*], by its very nature is a vocation [*vocatio*] to an apostolate [*apostolatus*]. Just as in the make-up of a living body, no member is able to be altogether passive, but must share in the operation of the body along with the life of this body, so too, in the body of Christ, which is the

Church, the whole body must work towards the increase of the body, "according to the function and measure of each member of the body" (Eph. 4, 16). Indeed in this body the connection and union of the members is so great (cf. Eph. 4, 16), that the member which does not contribute to the increase of the body according to its own measure, is said to benefit neither itself nor the Church.

There is in the Church a diversity of ministries [ministerii] but a unity of mission [missionis]. The munus of teaching, sanctifying, and governing in the name and with the power of Christ has been conferred by Christ on the Apostles and their successors. But the laity, having been made participants in the priestly, prophetic, and kingly munera, are to discharge their own share in this mission of the whole people of God, in the Church and in the world. (AA 2)[13]

The documents of Vatican II make liberal use of the word munus; the index lists 248 appearances of it. One primary reference of the word is seen in the preceding passage; it is to the triple munera of Christ as being Priest, Prophet, and King (LG 31). Christians, in their various callings, participate in these munera; they do so by fulfilling other munera, specifically entrusted to them. For instance, Mary's munus (office, role) is being the Mother of God (LG 53), which also confers on her a maternal munus (function, duty) toward all Men (LG 60). Christ gave Peter several munera: for instance, Peter was given the munus (office, power) of binding and loosening and the grande munus (office, special duty) of spreading the Christian name, which was also granted to the apostles (LG 20). The apostles were assigned the munera (exalted functions, great duties) of "giving witness to the gospel, to the ministration of the Holy Spirit and of justice for God's glory" (LG 21). To help them fulfill these munera, they were granted a special outpouring of the Holy Spirit (LG 21). By virtue of his munus (office), the Roman pontiff has "full, supreme, and universal power" in the Church (LG 22), and also by virtue of his munus (office) he is endowed with infallibility (LG 43). Bishops, by virtue of their episcopal consecration, have the munus (office) of preaching and teaching (LG 21). The laity, too, sharing in the priestly, prophetic, and kingly munera of Christ, have their own missio (mission); they are particularly called (vocantur) by fulfilling their munera (own particular duties, proper functions) of to "contribute to the sanctification of the world, as from within like leaven. . . . Thus, especially by the witness of their life, resplendent in faith, hope, and charity they must manifest Christ to others" (LG 31). *Munera* are conferred by one superior in power on another; it is important to note that Christ is routinely acknowledged as the source of the *munera* for each of the groups mentioned. *Munera* are not man-made but God-given.

Forms of *munus* appear ten times in the five sections of *Gaudium et Spes* that speak about the role of married people in the Church. There we learn that spouses and parents have a *praecellenti . . . munere* (lofty calling) (GS 47); that conjugal love leads spouses to God and aids and strengthens them in their *sublimi munere* (lofty role, sublime office) of being a mother and father (GS 48); that the sacrament of marriage helps them fulfill their conjugal and familial *munera* (role, obligations); that spouses are blessed with the dignity and *munus* (role, office) of fatherhood and motherhood, which help them achieve their *officium* (duty) of educating their children (GS 48); that young people should be properly and in good time instructed about the dignity, *munus* (role, duty), and *opere* (expression) of conjugal love (GS 49). The next occurrence appears in a paragraph that brings together several of the terms that are of concern here: "Married couples should regard it as their proper mission [*missio*] to transmit human life [*officio humanam vitam transmittendi*, etc.] and to educate their children; they should realize that they are thereby cooperating with the love of God the Creator and are, in a certain sense, its interpreters. This involves the fulfillment of their role [*munus*] with a sense of human and Christian responsibility. . ." (GS 50). Later in the same section, there is mention of "the *munus* [duty] of procreating"; of fulfilling "this God-given *munus* [mission, task, *commissio a Deo*] by generously having a large family" (GS 50). And we meet again the passage at the close of GS 51: "Let all be convinced that human life and its transmission [*munus eam transmittendi*] are realities whose meaning is not limited by the horizons of this life only. . ." (GS 51).

The Interiority of *Munus*

To this point the discussion of *munus* has focused largely on its external dimensions, on its status as a task bestowed as an honor on Man by God. What is needed now is a consideration of the kind of internal benefits gained by one who eagerly embraces and seeks to fulfill his or her vocation, mission, or *munus*. What we need to do is focus on the interior changes, the growth in virtue and perfection, in the individual who lives his or her married commitment faithfully. And we wish to place particular emphasis on the role of children in fostering these interior changes. When *Humanae Vitae* 9 asserts that one of the defining characteristics of marriage is its fruitfulness, it states: "[Conjugal] love is fruitful since the whole of the love is not contained in the communion of the spouses, but it also looks beyond itself and seeks to raise up new lives." *Humanae Vitae* 9 cites further from *Gaudium et Spes* (50): "Marriage and conjugal love are ordained by their very nature to the procreating and educating of children. Offspring are clearly the supreme gift of marriage, a gift which contributes immensely to the good of the parents themselves."

Let us elaborate on this claim of *Gaudium et Spes* and *Humanae Vitae* that children contribute immensely to the good of the parents. The fundamental point is that having children and raising children are sources of great good for the parents, that having to meet the responsibilities entailed in the *munus* of transmitting human life works to transform individuals into more virtuous individuals and also works an attitudinal change that enables them to be better Christians. Here we will be drawing on the work of John Paul II, in particular from passages in his book *Sources of Renewal*, which he wrote (as Karol Wojtyla) as a commentary on Vatican II, and from *Familiaris Consortio*, itself, in some parts, a marvelous commentary on *Humanae Vitae*. In these works, John Paul puts a great deal of emphasis on Man's internal life, on his need for transformation in Christ.

The focus on interiority is characteristic of John Paul; it flows from his emphasis on personalist values, from his interest in the kind of self-transformation one works on one's self through one's moral choices. John Paul has labored hard to draw the attention of moralists to personalist values, the values of self-mastery and generosity, for instance, that are fostered by moral choices. He repeatedly depicts life as a continuous process of transformation. For instance, in *Familiaris Consortio* he states, "What is needed is a continuous, permanent conversion which, while requiring an interior detachment from every evil and an adherence to good in its fullness, is brought about concretely in steps which lead us ever forward. Thus a dynamic process develops, one which advances gradually with the progressive integration of the gifts of God and the demands of His definitive and absolute love in the entire personal and social life of man" (FC 9). [14] The task of life, then, is to become ever more like Christ through fidelity to the demands of one's calling in life.

In *Sources of Renewal,* Wojtyla places great stress on the "attitude of participation" required from Christians in Christ's mission, which he calls the "central theme of the Conciliar doctrine concerning the People of God."[15] There he refers to Christ's threefold power or *munus* as priest, prophet, and king in which Christians must participate. He maintains that sharing in this power of *munus* is not simply a matter of sharing in certain tasks; rather it is more fundamentally a participation in certain attitudes. He tells us that Man has the power or " 'task' or 'office' (cf. Latin *munus in tria munera Christi*) together with the ability to perform it [the Latin is cited in Wojtyla's text]." He goes on to observe: "In speaking of participation in the threefold power of Christ, the Council teaches that the whole People of God and its individual members share in the priestly, prophetic and kingly offices that Christ took upon himself and fulfilled, and in the power which enabled him to do so. . . . The Conciliar teaching allows us to think of participation in Christ's threefold office not only in the ontological sense but also in that of specific attitudes. These express themselves in the attitude of testimony and give it a dimension of its own, as it were an interior form derived from Christ himself—the form of his mission and his power."[16] The claim that participating in a *munus* not only involves the power to act and the responsibility to complete an external act but also requires an internal attitudinal change by Christians adds another dimension to the complexity of this word. In *Sources of Renewal* Karol Wojtyla outlines the different attitudinal changes required to be faithful participants in Christ's threefold *munus.* He identifies a certain attitude associated with each of the three *munera* of priesthood, prophet, and king.

It is possible to crystallize these attitudes in the following way. In conjunction with the *munus* of *priesthood* shared by the laity, the attitude needed is a sacrificial one, whereby "man commits himself and the world to God." To explain this attitude, he cites part of a key passage in *Gaudium et Spes*: "It follows, then, that if man is the only creature on earth that God has wanted for its own sake, man can fully discover his true self only in a sincere giving of himself" (GS 24). Sharing in the *prophetic munus* of Christ requires that spouses work to bring the truth of Christ to the world, through evangelization. And the *kingly munus* is best exercised by Man not in rule over the world but in rule over himself. Thus, to be a priest, one must be self-sacrificing; to be a prophet, one must evangelize; and to be a king, one must govern—and govern one's self above all.

It is in *Familiaris Consortio* that we find more detailed instruction about how spouses are to participate in the threefold *munera* of Christ; how they are to be priests, prophets, and kings; or how they are to be self-sacrificing, evangelical, and self-mastering. *Familiaris Consortio* speaks specifically about the family's part in the threefold *munus* of Christ:

The Christian family also builds up the Kingdom of God in history through the everyday realities that concern and distinguish its *state of life*. It is thus in *the love between husband and wife and between the members of the family*— a love lived out in all its extraordinary richness of values and demands: totality, oneness, fidelity, and fruitfulness—that the Christian family's participation in the prophetic, priestly, and kingly mission of Jesus Christ and of His Church finds expression and realization. Therefore love and life constitute the nucleus of the saving mission of the Christian family in the Church and for the Church. (FC 50)

In the remainder of *Familiaris Consortio*, he explains how the family fulfills their participation in Christ's threefold *munus*. He identifies the *prophetic* office with the obligation of the family to evangelize, especially to its own members. The pope rehearses the obligation of parents to be educators of their children, especially in matters of the faith. *Familiaris Consortio* refers to the evangelization of children as an original and irreplaceable ministry (FC 53): "The family must educate the children for life in such a way that each one may fully perform his or her role [*munus*] according to the vocation received from God." For the family, the *priestly* office is fulfilled by engaging "in a dialogue with God through the sacraments, through the offering of one's life, and through prayer" (FC 55). And the *kingly* office is fulfilled when the family offers service to the larger community, especially to the needy. Note this powerful passage:

While building up the Church in love, the Christian family places itself at the service of the human person and the world, really bringing about the "human advancement" whose substance was given in summary form in the Synod's Message to families; "Another task for the family is to form persons in love and also to practice love in all its relationships, so that it does not live closed in on itself, but remains open to the community, moved by a sense of justice and concern for others, as well as by a consciousness of its responsibility towards the whole of society." (FC 64)

The family participates in the threefold *munus* of Christ by being true to its own *munus*. In the previous sections of *Familiaris Consortio*, which laid the foundation for the discussion of the family's participation in the threefold *munus* of Christ, John Paul sketched out the interior changes to be gained when the family is true to its *munus*. What John Paul hopes for from marriage is that it will result in the formation of a new heart within the spouses, the children, and ultimately all of society. This heart will be one that is loving, generous, and self-giving (FC 25). The family serves to build up the kingdom of God insofar as it is a school of love; as John Paul puts it, "The essence and role [*munus*] of the family are in the final analysis specified by love" (FC 17). He goes on, "Hence the family has the mission to guard, reveal and communicate love." *Familiaris Consortio* states: "The relationships between the members of the family community are inspired and guided by the law of 'free-giving.' By respecting and fostering personal dignity in each and every one as the only basis for value, this free giving takes the form of heartfelt acceptance, encounter, dialogue, disinterested availability, generous service and deep solidarity" (FC 43).

The text also states: "All members of the family, each according to his or her own gift [*munus*], have the grace and responsibility of building, day by day, the communion of persons, making the family 'a school of deeper humanity': this happens where there is care and love for the little ones, the sick, the aged; where there is mutual service every day; when there is a sharing of goods, of joys and of sorrows" (FC 21).

A key phrase for our purposes is the next line: "A fundamental opportunity for building such a communion is constituted by the education exchanged between parents and children, in which each gives and receives" and "Family communion can only be preserved and perfected through a great spirit of sacrifice. It requires, in fact, a ready and generous openness of each and all to understanding, to forbearance, to pardon, to reconciliation." These passages suggest the kinds of virtues needed for and cultivated by good family life. Successfully adapting to family life fosters love and generosity, ability to forgive, and many other related virtues. Both the parents and the children and ultimately the whole of society stand to grow in these virtues as the family attempts to be true to its nature.

The *munus* of transmitting life, of educating children, of being parents, then, yields multiple goods. Creating a family in which self-giving and all the virtues might begin to flourish is an activity that has multiple purposes. Certainly, it works toward achieving God's end of producing more individuals to share with Him eternal bliss. Having children also helps parents mature and acquire many of the virtues they need to be fully human and fully Christian. Furthermore, building families is to the good of the whole of society because generosity and love should flow from the family to the larger community, especially to the poor and needy.

What is key here for an understanding of *Humanae Vitae* is to recognize that to reject the procreative power of sexual intercourse is not simply to reject some biological power; it is to reject a God-given *munus* and all that it entails. The resistance to the procreative power of sexual intercourse that accompanies the desire to use contraception predictably involves an underestimation of the value of the family: to God, to the spouses, and to the larger society. Ultimately spouses must come to realize that to reject the *munus* of transmitting life, to limit the number of children they have for selfish reasons, is to limit the number of gifts and blessings that God gives to them; it is to limit the gifts that they return to God and their opportunities and ability to grow as Christians.

An Application of *Munus* to *Humanae Vitae*

An analogy drawn around the concept *munus* may help us better understand the teaching of *Humane Vitae*. This analogy requires us to imagine a good and generous king of a country who has asked one of his worthy subjects to help him build his kingdom. The king needs a responsible individual to perform this task since it is important, indeed, essential, to the kingdom to keep contact with a distant borough. He chooses to honor his subject George with the *munus* (mission) of maintaining contact with one of the outlying boroughs. In order for George to perform this service, the king gives him the use of a fine horse and buggy that will enable him to travel to the distant borough. The king needs someone to spread goodwill and cheer in this community and wants George to undertake this *munus*. He makes it clear that George should never go to the borough unless he attends to the king's business when he is there. The king has another motive for providing George with the horse and buggy, for he also wishes George to prosper. The horse and buggy will enable George to attend to his own business when he travels to the distant borough. The king makes it clear that those who live in the borough, and George himself, will fare better if George uses the horse and buggy as designated, for the king knows that it is quite impossible for George and him to prosper without each other. So George achieves two ends by the use of the horse and buggy; he advances his own prosperity and that of the kingdom. The king also tells George that business is closed in the outlying borough one week of every month and during that week George may continue freely to use the horse and buggy for his own purposes. Moreover, since the horse and buggy are handsome and efficient it is pleasurable for George to employ them, but pleasure is an added benefit to the use of the horse and buggy, not its purpose. The king more or less leaves it up to George how often and when he visits the borough; he asks him to be generous but to use his own good judgment. Now, if George were to accept this *munus* and the horse and buggy that go with it but refuse to drive to the outlying borough, then he would be reneging on the *munus* that he accepted. And if he were to go to the borough but refuse to attend to the king's business while there, he would again be failing to live up to the demands of his *munus*.

There are parallels here with the *munus* of transmitting human life. God has given this *munus* to spouses because He wishes to share the goods of His kingdom with humans and He has chosen to call on spouses to share with Him the work of bringing new life into the world. This work is an honor entrusted only to those willing to embrace the responsibilities of marriage. Those who perform the responsibilities of marriage in accord with God's will benefit both themselves and the rest of society. The spouses achieve the good of strengthening their relationship through sexual intercourse, that is, the good of union, and they achieve the good of having children, that is, the good of procreation. Both goods also benefit God's kingdom for He wishes love between spouses to flourish and He desires more people with whom to share the goods of His kingdom. Thus, sexual intercourse is a part of the *munus* of transmitting human life, a *munus* that is intimately bound with other goods. Those who accept this *munus* need to respect the other goods that accompany it.

Still, in the same way that the good king allowed George to use the horse and buggy even when business was not in session in the outlying borough, God has so designed human fertility and human sexuality, that humans are sometimes fertile and sometimes not. It is permissible for spouses to enjoy marital intercourse at any time, whether they are infertile or fertile. God seems to have designed the human system this way to foster greater union and happiness between spouses. He has also asked them to be receptive to new life, generously but in accord with their best judgment, and not to fail to fulfill the *munus* that He has given them. To refuse absolutely to have children is like refusing ever to go to the outlying district. It is to renege on the *munus* that accompanies marriage. To have contraceptive sex is like driving to the outlying borough and ignoring the king's business. The contracepting couple is repudiating the *munus* of their own fertility and altering the functioning of the body. They are pursuing pleasure while emphatically rejecting the good of procreation. They may not feel that they are engaging in an act of emphatic rejection of the good of procreation, but in terms of their *munus*, that is exactly what they are doing. (It is also true that the good they achieve, pleasure, is not identical to the good of union, for that can be achieved only if the procreative good is also respected.) But the good king allowed George to use the horse and buggy when business was not in session, and that is exactly what the couple who are having sexual intercourse during the infertile period is doing. They are pursuing one good, the good of union, *when another is not available.* Again, the contracepting couple is repudiating a *munus* that they have accepted; the noncontracepting couple, on the other hand, is cooperating with the complexity of the *munus* that God has entrusted to them.

This analogy and argument allow us to see how a theological concept can "illuminate and enrich" our understanding of the Church's condemnation of contraception.

In the second portion of this chapter, we shall turn to the question of the role of conscience in a Catholic's response to *Humanae Vitae* and to the question of the infallibility of the teaching of *Humanae Vitae*.

Humanae Vitae and Conscience

When *Humanae Vitae* was issued, some Catholic theologians immediately rejected the encyclical largely on the basis of the claim that the natural law understanding of the encyclical was inadequate.[17] Yet the immediate aftermath, for the most part, was not characterized by the attempt to establish more adequate formulations of natural law. Rather, one of the chief responses to the encyclical was the development of the argument that Catholics were permitted to practice contraception if their consciences so directed them. Indeed, in 1969, one theologian, John Milhaven, announced that in a sense *Humanae Vitae* had become a dead letter: Catholics felt perfectly free to use contraception as an act of conscience.[18] As Milhaven noted, the statements of several bishops' conferences following the promulgation of *Humanae Vitae* seem to have offered support for such a response.

The statement of the French bishops portrays the reason for countenancing the use of contraception by Catholics as the result of a "conflict of duties" and states that "traditional wisdom makes provision for seeking before God which duty in the circumstances is the greater."[19] Although this statement is frequently given as an instance of justifying departure from the teaching of the encyclical on the basis of conscience, it seems rather to draw on the principle of the toleration of the lesser evil, a principle that is explicitly rejected by *Humanae Vitae* 14 as not being properly applicable to the issue of birth control.[20] Statements from other bishops' conferences, however, do seem to have a "conscience clause." The Canadian statement is perhaps the most straightforward in this regard:

It is a fact that a certain number of Catholics, although admittedly subject to the teaching of the encyclical, find it either extremely difficult or even impossible to make their own all elements of this doctrine. . . . We must appreciate the difficulty experienced by contemporary man in understanding and appropriating some of the points of this encyclical, and we must make every effort to learn from the insights of Catholic scientists and intellectuals, who are of undoubted loyalty to Christian truth, to the church and to the authority of the Holy See. Since they are not denying any point of divine and Catholic faith nor rejecting the teaching authority of the church, these Catholics should not be considered, or consider themselves, shut off from the body of the faithful. But they should remember that their good faith will be dependent on a sincere self-examination to determine the true motives and grounds for such suspension of assent and on continued effort to understand and deepen their knowledge of the teaching of the church.[21]

Further on it states:

Counselors may meet others who, accepting the teaching of the Holy Father, find that because of particular circumstances they are involved in what seems to them a clear conflict of duties, e.g., the reconciling of conjugal love and responsible parenthood with the education of children already born or with the health of the mother. In accord with the accepted principles of moral theology, if these persons have tried sincerely but without success to pursue a line of conduct in keeping with the given directives, they may be safely assured that whoever honestly chooses that course which seems right to him does so in good conscience.[22]

To round out the picture let us note portions of a few other statements, those by the Austrian and U.S. bishops. The Austrian bishops observe:

Since the encyclical does not contain an infallible dogma, it is conceivable that someone feels unable to accept the judgment of the teaching authority of the Church. The answer to this is: if someone has experience in this field and has reached a divergent conviction after serious examination, free of emotion and haste, he may for the time being follow it. He does not err, if he is willing to continue his examination and otherwise affords respect and fidelity to the Church. It remains clear, however, that in such a case he has no right to create confusion among his brothers in the faith with his opinion.[23]

The U.S. bishops speak of dissent only in respect to theologians: "There exists in the Church a lawful freedom of inquiry and of thought and also general norms of licit dissent. This is particularly true in the area of legitimate theological speculation and research. When conclusions reached by such professional theological work prompt a scholar to dissent from noninfallible received teaching, the norms of licit dissent come into play." It seems only fair that the next sentence be cited as well: "They [the norms of licit dissent] require of him careful respect for the consciences of those who lack his special competence or opportunity for judicious investigation."[24] This portion of the statement of the U.S. bishops, although not immediately relevant to the question of conscience, allows us to make an important distinction. What needs to be noted here is that scholarly dissent on a theoretical level by learned theologians is not at all the same as dissent on a practical level by individuals untrained in theology. Offering reasons why one thinks a teaching is faulty differs radically from living in contradiction to that teaching. Our primary concern in this section is not to determine the proper status of theological dissent but to determine whether Catholics can practice contraception in good conscience. Momentarily we shall note that the U.S. bishops had within their statement a quite developed view of conscience that does not allow much room for divergence from the Church's teaching.

The perspective of over twenty years' distance from the issuance of these statements may put them in a different light. The Austrian bishops on March 29, 1988, issued a statement that seems to repudiate their statement of 1968.[25] The recent statement emphasizes and clarifies further the acknowledgment of the 1968 document "There is freedom of conscience but no freedom from building a correct conscience." A greater stress is put on the obligation to form one's conscience in accord with what the Church teaches. The Austrian hierarchy promised further clarification of the nature, function, and formation of conscience.

The Canadian bishops seemed to have sensed the inadequacy of their statement somewhat earlier, for in 1974 they issued a statement on conscience that puts forward a view of conscience that suggests that a Catholic would have a very difficult—if not impossible—time rejecting the Church's teaching in good conscience.[26] We shall note some of the teachings of the Canadian bishops' statement on conscience shortly, but first let us review, if only in a very sketchy way, the Church's teaching.

First, it must be noted that the Church teaches that one must follow his conscience, even if this conscience is wrong.[27] Conscience and practical reason are very closely related: conscience informs an individual whether an action he is about to perform or has performed is one that is in accord with morality. If a Man is not following his conscience, he is following something (for instance, one of his passions) or someone else, and these evidently are urging him to oppose his conscience. An individual may have various passions and desires directing him to do this or that, but the conscience is an act of reason and determines whether those passions are guiding him toward what is moral or what is immoral; the conscience should also determine whether advice he is getting from another coheres with the dictates of morality; he should only follow the advice of another when this advice does not conflict with his conscience. To say that a Man should always follow his conscience is to say that he should always do what he believes to be moral and not do what he believes to be immoral. Certainly, because of ignorance, neglect, or a variety of other causes, an individual may have a conscience that is not making a good judgment about what is moral. Nonetheless, it is the conscience that says, "This is moral and that is immoral," and it should be the guide of one's action, otherwise one is acting against what one believes to be moral.

There are two other corollaries that are important to note here. Although one must follow one's conscience whether one's conscience is correct or not, this does not necessarily free one of all moral responsibility for one's action. One may be acting out of ignorance, but it may be culpable ignorance;[28] an individual may have neglected to acquire all the information necessary to make a good decision; for instance, a man may be hunting and may shoot at a moving figure that he thought to be a deer; he may be acting in good conscience; he may think he has done no wrong. But he may have killed a human being going for a walk in the woods. If the hunter failed to take due care to determine whether what he was shooting at was a deer or a human being, he may have acted in good conscience, but he is still guilty of wrongdoing. Second, even if one acts from a good conscience and is in no way culpable for wrongdoing, one's action may still be objectively evil. For instance, a woman may have an abortion without knowing that she has taken a human life. She may have consulted a doctor and even a clergyman and theologian who assured her that her action was moral. But if she has an abortion, although she may not be morally culpable, she has still performed an action that is objectively evil.[29] Thus, although one must always follow one's conscience, this does not guarantee that one is not morally responsible for what one has done or that one will never do what is objectively evil.

There is a modern distortion of the teaching that one must always follow one's conscience that is most pernicious; some draw the false inference that if one does not feel guilty that means that one has not acted in contradiction to one's conscience. Many moderns tend to think that they are following their conscience if they feel comfortable about, or feel no guilt about, their chosen behavior. Some may steal or commit adultery and claim that they feel no guilt. It would seem that their consciences do not trouble them. But it is more likely that they have not troubled their conscience, that is, that they have never pondered whether what they are doing is moral or immoral; they have simply acted on their desires. Furthermore, some may not properly form their consciences and thus not feel guilt for what they do, but they cannot rightly be said to be acting in "good conscience."

Let us also recall that the conscience is one's guide to moral behavior; it does not *decide* the principles of moral behavior but *discovers or learns* them and then judges whether a particular action is moral or immoral.[30] One of the best and most succinct statements on conscience is to be found in *Gaudium et Spes*:

Deep within his conscience man discovers a law which he has not laid upon himself but which he must obey. Its voice, ever calling him to love and to do what is good and to avoid evil, tells him inwardly at the right moment: do this, shun that. For man has in his heart a law inscribed by God. His dignity lies in observing this law, and by it he will be judged. His conscience is man's most secret core, and his sanctuary. There he is alone with God whose voice echoes in his depths. By conscience, in a wonderful way, that law is made known which is fulfilled in the love of God and of one's neighbor. Through loyalty to conscience Christians are joined to other men in the search for truth and for the right solution to so many moral problems which arise both in the life of individuals and from social relationships. Hence, the more a correct conscience prevails, the more do persons and groups turn aside from blind choice and try to be guided by the objective standards of moral conduct. Yet it often happens that conscience goes astray through ignorance which it is unable to avoid, without thereby losing its dignity. This cannot be said of the man who takes little trouble to find out what is true and good, or when conscience is by degrees almost blinded through the habit of committing sin. (GS 16)

Conscience, then, is not the faculty by which each man or woman tries to determine what he or she thinks moral or immoral; it is the faculty by which an individual attempts to discern what God holds to be moral or immoral.

For a Catholic, the magisterium of the Church plays a definite role in assisting him or her in determining what God holds to be moral or immoral. As the following discussion hopes to establish, if the magisterium is not forming the conscience of the Catholic, again something else (one's own reason, perhaps) or someone else is. The Catholic who rejects the teaching of the Church has, in effect (though possibly not deliberately), decided that something or someone else is a more authoritative teacher than the Church.

Although many dissenters contest it, it has been and remains the claim of the Church to be an authentic teacher on matters of morals (and faith). The Canadian bishops speak of the Catholic's relation to Church teaching in this way: "A believer has the absolute obligation of conforming his conduct first and foremost to what the Church teaches, because first and foremost for the believer is the fact that Christ, through His Spirit, is ever present in His Church—in the whole Church to be sure, but particularly with those who exercise services within the Church and for the Church, the first of which services is that of the apostles." A Catholic presumably knows and accepts the nature of the Church to which he or she belongs; this Church claims to teach for Christ and to have special guidance from the Holy Spirit in its teachings on faith and morals. This, too, is a decision of conscience; one decides that it is right to become or remain a Catholic.

Some claim that the Catholic has an obligation to follow the Church's teaching only when that teaching has been declared infallibly (the next section of this chapter will discuss the infallibility of the teaching). Those who contest this claim, as do the Canadian bishops, regularly draw on *Lumen Gentium* 25:

Bishops who teach in communion with the Roman Pontiff are to be revered by all as witnesses of divine and Catholic truth; the faithful, for their part are obliged to submit to their bishops' decision, made in the name of Christ, in matters of faith and morals, and to adhere to it with a ready and respectful allegiance of mind. This loyal submission of the will and intellect must be given, in a special way, to the authentic teaching authority of the Roman Pontiff, even when he does not speak *ex cathedra* in such wise, indeed, that his supreme teaching authority be acknowledged with respect, and sincere assent be given to decisions made by him, conformably with his manifest mind and intention, which is made known principally either by the character of the documents in question, or by the frequency with which a certain doctrine is proposed, or by the manner in which the doctrine is formulated.[31]

The preceding statements rest on a claim noted earlier and reiterated in these various statements: that the Church speaks for Christ. Thus, when a Catholic wrestles with a problem on which the Church speaks one way and his own thoughts or various advisers speak another, it is much as if he were to hear Christ Himself say one thing and himself and others say another. At the least, he is hearing those Christ has designated to speak for Him. Whom should he trust?

Again, as noted, one must always follow one's conscience, even if it is wrong. But should a Catholic feel free to think his conscience is correct if it departs from a Church teaching (one that adheres to the criteria of *Lumen Gentium*)? The U.S. bishops' statement that followed *Humanae Vitae* cites the famous statement of John Henry Newman in regard to what a Catholic should do when he or she disagrees with a teaching/mandate of the Church.

I have to say again, lest I should be misunderstood, that when I speak of conscience, I mean conscience truly so called. When it has the right of opposing the supreme, though not infallible authority of the Pope, it must be something more than that miserable counterfeit which, as I have said above, now goes by the name. If in a particular case it is to be taken as a sacred and sovereign monitor, its dictate, in order to prevail against the voice of the Pope, must follow upon serious thought, prayer, and all available means of arriving at a right judgment on the matter in question.

And further, obedience to the Pope is what is called "in possession": that is the *onus probandi* (burden of proof) of establishing a case against him lies, as in all cases of exception, on the side of conscience. Unless a man is able to say to himself, as in the presence of God, that he must not, and dare not, act upon the papal injunction, he is bound to obey it and would commit a great sin in disobeying it. *Prima facie* it is his bounden duty, even from a sentiment of loyalty, to believe the Pope right and to act accordingly. . . .[32]

What the preceding seeks to establish is that Catholics who find that they cannot agree in conscience with the Church's teaching on contraception find themselves with a second crisis of conscience on their hands: That is, what are they to make of the Church's claim to be a reliable and authoritative teacher in matters of morals when they in practice have rejected the Church as teacher? According to the Church is this a teaching that can be disobeyed in good conscience? If not, what now is their relationship to their Church?

Now let us give some caveats here. The preceding presupposes, of course, Catholics who share the traditional understanding the Church has of its role in teaching on matters of faith and morals. The reality, however, is far from the ideal. It is perhaps true to say that many if not most Catholics have not been taught what the Church claims in regard to its status as a teacher or what the proper role of conscience is. They may not realize that their decision to reject the teaching of the Church puts them in such a quandary. With the example and counsel of dissenting theologians, their subjective state may diverge considerably from the objective reality, and their culpability may in fact be slight.

The Infallibility of *Humanae Vitae*

Since the earliest moments of its promulgation, many theologians have justified dissent from *Humanae Vitae* by arguing that the document and its teaching are not infallible. Most acknowledge the teaching of the document to be authoritative and deserving of respect but not as having the claim on Catholics that an infallible teaching would have. Indeed, Monsignor Ferdinando Lambruschini, a member of the Papal Commission who sided with the majority and who presented *Humanae Vitae* to the press on its promulgation, claimed that the document did not have the "theological note of infallibility."[33] Although he was never publicly corrected on this statement, Rev. Ermenegildo Lio, reportedly one of the authors of *Humanae Vitae*, reports that Lambruschini had not been authorized to make such a statement and that the views were strictly his own. Lambruschini's statement about the "noninfallibility" of the encyclical was omitted from the report in *L'Osservatore Romano* on the press conference.[34]

Although there were multitudes of articles on the issuance of the encyclical that attempted to define the nature of the authority of the document,[35] with perhaps one or two exceptions,[36] there was no immediate attempt in the scholarly literature to challenge Lambruschini and the widespread consensus that the teaching of *Humanae Vitae* was not infallible. Lio has since taken up the challenge[37] by arguing that Pope Paul VI used language in *Humanae Vitae* meant to indicate that he was making a solemn definition of Church doctrine and that infallibility extends to such definitions. To date it seems that there have been no responses to Lio's work, a work at this time available in Italian only.

Lio was not the first to make the argument that the teaching of *Humanae Vitae* has been infallibly pronounced. On very different terms, in 1978 John C. Ford, S.J., and Germain Grisez made such an argument; they do not argue that *Humanae Vitae* was an infallible declaration; rather they argue that the condemnation of contraception was already an infallible teaching by virtue of the way it had been taught through the ordinary magisterium. Their argument has met with some vigorous criticism to which Grisez has as vigorously replied.[38] Both the arguments of Grisez and Ford and those of their critics are complex and lengthy. Thus, a thorough recounting of the debate would be out of place here. A brief sketch of its nature will have to serve.

The Minority Report of the Papal Commission had included the argument that the Church could not have erred through all the centuries (not even through one century) in its condemnation of contraception, a condemnation that imposed "very heavy burdens under the grave obligation of the name of Jesus Christ." The strong implication is, that if the Church were wrong about such a matter it would have to relinquish its claim to being the authoritative interpreter of Christ's teachings. Grisez and Ford "sought to develop and complete" this argument in their study.[39] They argued that the teaching of Humanae Vitae meets the criteria of Lumen Gentium 25 for a teaching that is infallible not by virtue of being defined so in an ex cathedra fashion but by virtue of being constantly proclaimed by the universal ordinary magisterium. They articulate what they believe to be Vatican II's criteria for a teaching to be proclaimed infallibly by the universal ordinary magisterium: "First, that the bishops remain in communion with one another and with the Pope; second, that they teach authoritatively on a matter of faith or morals; third, that they agree in one judgment; and fourth, that they propose this judgment as one to be held definitively."[40] Building on the work of John Noonan that demonstrated that the Church has constantly proclaimed contraception to be evil (a nearly uncontested claim), Grisez and Ford came to the conclusion that the condemnation against contraception has infallible status:

At least until 1962, Catholic bishops in communion with one another and with the Pope agreed in and authoritatively proposed one judgment to be held definitively on the morality of contraception: Acts of this kind are objectively, intrinsically, and gravely evil. Since this teaching has been proposed infallibly, the controversy since 1963 takes nothing away from its objectively certain truth. It is not the received Catholic teaching on contraception which needs to be rethought. It is the assumption that this teaching could be abandoned as false which needs to be rethought.[41]

Francis Sullivan, S.J., questions several claims that he believes Grisez and Ford to be making: (1) he questions the claim that throughout the centuries the faithful have accepted the Church's teaching on contraception *as a matter of faith;* (2) he objects that if their argument holds, then "If the magisterium speaks in a definitive way about something, it must necessarily be the case that what they speak about is a proper object of infallible teaching"; (3) he registers a doubt that Grisez and Ford have succeeded in showing that the teaching on contraception is a secondary object of infallibility (one that is not revealed but necessary to guard revealed truths); (4) he questions that the Church has truly taught *definitively* on contraception; (5) and he doubts that the Church has the authority to teach infallibly on "concrete norms" of natural moral law.[42]

In another extensive article, Grisez responds to each of these difficulties[43]: it would be quite otiose to cover them here. One point of central interest, though, would seem to be whether the teaching of the Church is truly rooted in norms expressed in Scripture and whether it has a necessary connection with truths that are necessary for salvation. To this point, Grisez cites a speech by John Paul, wherein he makes precisely the claims Grisez has labored to defend.

The Church teaches this norm, although it is not formally (that is, literally) expressed in Sacred Scripture, and it does this in the conviction that the interpretation of the precepts of natural law belongs to the competence of the Magisterium.

However, we can say more. Even if the moral law, formulated in this way in the Encyclical *Humanae Vitae*, is not found literally in Sacred Scripture, nonetheless, from the fact that it is contained in Tradition and—as Pope Paul VI writes—has been "very often expounded by the Magisterium" (HV, n. 12) to the faithful, it follows that this norm *is in accordance with the sum total of revealed doctrine contained in biblical sources* (cf. HV, n. 4).

4. It is a question here not only of the sum total of the moral doctrine contained in Sacred Scripture, of its essential premises and general character of its content, but of that fuller context to which we have previously dedicated numerous analyses when speaking about the "theology of the body."

Precisely against the background of this full context it becomes evident that the above-mentioned moral norm belongs not only to the natural moral law, but also to the *moral order revealed by God*: also from this point of view, it could not be different, but solely what is handed down by Tradition and the Magisterium and, in our days, the Encyclical *Humanae Vitae* as a modern document of this Magisterium.[44]

Grisez draws three points out of this passage: "The fact that the norm excluding contraception is in accord with the sum total of revelation *follows from* its being contained in tradition and its often being expounded by the magisterium; the norm belongs to the moral order *revealed by God;* and it *could* not be different." The preceding, of course, does not constitute an argument or even lay out the lines of an argument: it does, though, serve to indicate what the issues of the debate are.

Garth Hallett, S.J., is one of the few who contest that the Church has had a constant teaching against contraception. He categorizes moral expressions into those that are prescriptive (those that attempt to command or forbid behavior) and those that are descriptive (those that explain why behavior is good or bad). He argues that although the Church has consistently opposed contraception, that is, provided prescriptive teachings against it, it has not provided consistent descriptive accounts about the immorality of contraception. He claims that infallibility does not extend to prescriptive teachings.

In reply Grisez questions Hallett's acceptance of the categorization of moral expressions popular with one school of modern philosophy. Although Grisez grants (not concedes) that moral language is complex, he argues that we are not without resources to determine what the moral expressions of various periods mean. He denies that the Church is without a common criterion to determine morality. He further notes that if Hallett is correct about incoherence in the Church's teaching on contraception, the same would hold true of its teaching about any moral behavior, such as killing the innocent or loving one's enemies.

This last claim by Grisez is a challenging one. Those who uphold the Church's teaching on contraception note that the Church has taught few moral norms with as much consistency and zeal as it has the norm against contraception. Thus, they reason, if the Church is wrong about contraception, it is possible to call into question most if not all of its other moral norms. As other portions of this book demonstrate, since *Humanae Vitae*, most if not all of the other moral norms taught by the Church, especially those regarding sexuality, have been called into question.

One further important argument needs to be noted. Nearly all of those who assert that *Humanae Vitae* does not contain infallible teaching in fact think that that teaching is not only not infallible but wrong. But they are not troubled in the same way as their opponents for they generally believe that the Church has been wrong in its teaching many times in the past. The statement issued by Charles Curran and other dissident theologians on the issuance of *Humanae Vitae* provides a good example of this view: "The encyclical is not an infallible teaching. History shows that a number of statements or [sic] even greater authoritative weight have subsequently been proven inadequate or even erroneous. Past authoritative statements on religious liberty, interest-taking, the right to silence, and the ends of marriage have all been corrected at a later date."[45] What must be noted here is that there is certainly no complete agreement with the claim that teachings promulgated with the same gravity and weight as the condemnation of contraception have been "proven inadequate or even erroneous."[46] Many have contested the very examples given in the preceding statement (given with no supporting argumentation). The arguments generally take three forms: either the claim is made that the Church has not in fact changed its teaching on a given issue (arguments in this respect have been made about the Church's teaching on religious liberty);[47] or that the other teachings were wedded to certain cultural conditions that no longer exist (arguments in regard to usury generally take this line);[48] or that development of a teaching has been of a sort not to contradict or cancel an earlier teaching but to expand and illuminate it (analyses of the new emphasis on personalist values in marriage often take this form[49]).

To this day, there is much debate on what the proper response would be for a Catholic to the teaching of *Humanae Vitae*. From the moment of its promulgation it met with a very mixed response; the next two chapters examine the critical theological response.

SIX

The Aftermath of *Humanae Vitae* and the "Revision" of Natural Law

OPE PAUL VI'S reaffirmation of the constant Church teaching was a surprise and a disappointment to many, though, it might also be said that an abandonment of Church teaching would have been an even greater surprise, even to those who ardently desired a change. Many theologians and lay people registered their dissent from *Humanae Vitae* nearly before the ink was dry.[1] To this day, *Humanae Vitae* remains a source of bitter debate within the Church. It was widely observed even at the time that *Humanae Vitae* was issued that never before had a papal statement met with such a reception. Bernard Haering expressed this view slightly less than a month after the document had been issued: "No papal teaching document has ever caused such an earthquake in the Church as the encyclical *Humanae Vitae*. Reactions around the world—in the Italian and American press, for example—are just as sharp as they were at the time of the *Syllabus of Errors* of Pius IX, perhaps even sharper. There is the difference, of course, that this time anti-Catholic feelings have been rarely expressed. The storm has broken over the heads of the curial advisors of the Pope and often of the Pope himself."[2]

Even the manner of the release of the document was a source of turmoil and confusion. Ferdinando Lambruschini, who presented the document to the press and was among the majority on the commission, in his prepared text twice stated that the teaching was not presented infallibly: "Attentive reading of the encyclical *Humanae Vitae* does not suggest the theological note of infallibility . . ."[3] and "[The pronouncement] is not infallible but it does not leave the questions concerning birth regulation in a vague problematic state."[4] At the same time he asserted that no one could claim that there is any doubt about the Church's teaching and that it was owed "loyal and full assent, interior and not only exterior, to an authentic pronouncement of the magisterium, in proportion to the level of the authority from which it eminates [sic]—which in this case is the supreme authority of the Supreme Pontiff—and to its object, which is most weighty since it is a matter of the tormented question of birth regulation."[5] *Humanae Vitae* was not received as an authoritative document; Lambruschini's statement was not received as an authoritative one; many refused to give either loyal or full assent, exterior or interior.

Charles Curran quickly, within twenty-four hours of the release of *Humanae Vitae*, issued, with eighty-six others, a statement of protest against the teaching of the document, which was signed by two hundred theologians within the week and ultimately by over six hundred. Their statement made several points: they claimed that the encyclical was not infallible; that the ecclesiology and methodology of the encyclical were incompatible with Vatican II; that the experience of Catholic couples was neglected; that it paid insufficient attention to modern science; that it had a narrow view of papal authority and an inadequate concept of natural law; that it disregarded the world population problem. The preceding is a partial list of its complaints. As noted earlier, the final conclusion of the statement, unaccompanied by any theological or philosophical support, was: "Spouses may responsibly decide according to their conscience that artificial contraception, in some circumstances is permissible and indeed necessary to preserve and foster the values and sacredness of marriage."[6] Hans Küng called the encyclical "another Galileo case."[7] Karl Rahner explained at some length how dissent from the document could be justified.[8] Maintaining that *Humanae Vitae* was written under the undue influence of conservative theologians, Bernard Haering stated that the pope was "walled in" and issued a call to "rescue the Pope."[9]

There were, of course, theologians who publicly supported *Humanae Vitae*. For instance, Austin Vaughan, president of the American Catholic Theological Society at the time, gave it his full support as he stated, "I don't think that it is possible that what has been laid down in this document could be anything else than what the Holy Spirit, who guides our use of our resources with his providence, wants and expects of us as Catholics, at this moment in the plan of salvation, apart from what direction the course of that plan might take in the future. If it were, the guidance of the Holy Spirit, promised to the magisterium, according to the *Constitution on the Church* would be an illusion."[10] Pedro Arrupe, general of the Society of Jesus, invoking "our duty as Jesuits," called on Jesuits to respond with "an attitude of obedience, which is at once faithful, loving, firm, open, and truly creative." He explained what he meant: "A teaching such as the one that [Pope Paul VI] presents merits assent not simply because of the reasons he offers, but also, and above all, because of the charism which enables him to present it. Guided by the authentic word of the Pope—a word that need not be infallible to be highly respected—every Jesuit owes it to himself, by reason of his vocation, to do everything possible to penetrate, and to help others to penetrate, into a thought which may not have been his own previously; however, as he goes beyond the evidence available to him personally, he finds or will find a solid foundation for it."[11]

The bishops both in the United States and around the world,[12] for the most part, issued supportive statements, counseling Catholics to form their consciences in accord with the teaching of the Church. Some, however, indeed possibly as many as a third, were pointedly qualified, implying that Catholics could in good conscience use contraception (see, for instance, the statements of bishops' conferences from Canada, France, West Germany, Belgium, Holland, Austria, Switzerland, Italy, Scandinavia, and Indonesia). Still, the way that the bishops rallied around the pope was quite remarkable, to the point that it provoked the headline, in reference to the U.S. bishops, "BISHOPS UNITED BEHIND PAUL" in the *National Catholic Reporter.*[13]

The lay reaction was mixed. Several of the lay people who had been members of the Papal Commission issued statements of dissent, most notable among them John Noonan's.[14] A statement issued by Dennis Landis, president of the twelve-thousand member National Association of Laymen, called the document "tragic" and stated that the teaching "becomes a further reason why more and more people no longer take seriously the authority image of the magisterium of the church."[15] A Gallup poll showed that 54 percent of lay Americans opposed the teaching, 28 percent favored it, and 18 percent had no opinion. A poll of Italians showed that 42.8 percent opposed the teaching, and 31.5 percent favored it.[16] Some would find the percentage supporting the teaching surprising.

The document caused other furor. Cardinal O'Boyle in Washington, D.C., was faced with many dissenting priests and theologians at The Catholic University of America. His attempts to discipline them were largely ineffective. Bishop Shannon of Minneapolis resigned his position over this issue.

Pope Paul VI and *Humanae Vitae*

The delay between the completion of the work by the Papal Commission and the issuance of *Humanae Vitae* led some to conjecture that Paul VI had been considering reversing the Church's teaching. The preponderance of evidence seems to refute this view. He was by nature, it seems, a man who deliberated long and carefully over complex questions. In conversations with Jean Guitton that took place several years before *Humanae Vitae*, we find these revealing remarks, which explain his slowness to react to the report of the commission in contrast to the speed of the reaction of many theologians against *Humanae Vitae*: "Burning questions are also complex ones. Simple honesty demands that they be considered without haste. We should have respect for the complexity of things, listen, weigh them. If the past teaches us anything, it is that it is better to wait, to risk disappointing the impatient, than to make hasty improvisations. And the higher the authority, the more it must wait. It is easy to study, difficult to decide."[17] In these dialogues with Guitton, the pope speaks freely about his views on marriage and expresses his reasons for valuing the fruitfulness of conjugal love:

> In love there is infinitely more than love. We would say that in human love there is divine love. And that is why the link between love and fecundity is deep, hidden, and substantial! All authentic love between a man and a woman, when it is not egoistic love, tends toward creation of another being issuing from that love. To love can mean 'to love oneself,' and often love is no more than the juxtaposition of two solitudes. But when one has passed beyond that stage of egoism, when one has truly

understood that love is shared joy, a mutual gift, then one comes to what is *truly* love.

If it is true that love is what I tell you it is, one can understand that it cannot be separated from the fruit of love. Even Plato taught us that love's spring is in the generation of souls in beauty, for the education of spirits. Love reaches out toward fecundity. It imitates the creative act. It renews. It gives life, it is a sacrifice on behalf of life.[18]

In what is his most direct reference to contraception he states: "When one uses a technique of dissociating the act of love from its end, one must be aware that something has been subtracted from happiness."[19] The preceding is just a small sampling of the nearly poetic musings of Pope Paul VI on marital love. In subsequent remarks he acknowledges that the question is currently under study, but the context of his remarks makes clear that he was not truly in doubt over the permissibility of contraception.

Pope Paul VI makes several subsequent references to *Humanae Vitae*. In a speech given to a general audience just a few days after the encyclical was issued he speaks of his thoughts and feelings during the four years of study that preceded its publication.[20] He insists that the encyclical is "not just a declaration about a negative moral law . . . : it is above all a positive presentation of conjugal morality in relation to its mission of love and fruitfulness . . . ."[21] He speaks of the "grave feeling of responsibility" that "caused Us no small measure of mental anguish. We never felt the weight of Our office as much as in this situation. We studied, read, and discussed all We could; and We also prayed a great deal."[22] He mentions "being swamped by [a] wave of documents" and of feeling "Our own humble inadequacy in the face of the formidable apostolic task of having to speak out on this matter."[23] In spite of all these expressions of anguish in the face of the task before him, Paul VI sounds a note of manifest confidence in his encyclical:

We invoked the enlightenment of the Holy Spirit and put Our mind at the complete disposal of the voice of truth, striving to interpret the divine law that rises from the intrinsic requirements of genuine human love, from the essential structures of the institution of marriage, from the personal dignity of the spouses, from their mission in the service of life and from the holiness of Christian marriage. We reflected on the enduring elements of the traditional doctrine in force in the Church, and then in particular on the teachings of the recent Council. We pondered the consequences of one decision and the other; and We had no doubts about Our duty to set forth Our decisions in the terms expressed in the present encyclical.[24]

Then on August 4 at an Angelus recitation, he reports "As far as we recall, the Pope has never received so many spontaneous messages of gratitude and approval for the publication of a document as on this occasion. These messages have poured in from every part of the world and from every class of people."[25] He acknowledges that there have been voices raised in opposition and notes that such is to be expected for a teaching that is so contrary to modern mores. He reminds his audience that the teaching is not his own but one "derived from the law of God, a law that is compatible with true peace and harmony, with the purity of love and the purpose of married life." And at his Angelus recitation of August 11, 1968, he refers again to *Humanae Vitae* and asks for prayers for those who have rejected it: "Let us ask the Lord to strengthen Our *magisterium* with His authority, His serenity and His goodness. May all those who accept it be blessed, and also those who oppose it, so that their consciences may be enlightened and guided by true, higher doctrinal and moral rectitude; if nothing else, We will have invited them to reflect upon a subject of vital importance."[26] He himself delivered a fairly lengthy meditation and explanation on the Church's teaching on marriage in a speech to a group known as Teams of Our Lady. He makes only one explicit reference to *Humanae Vitae*:

> There is no married love which in its deepest joy is not an impetus towards the infinite and does not by reason of its very dynamism aim to be total, faithful, exclusive, and fruitful [a reference to *Humanae Vitae* 9].
> It is in this perspective that the sexual appetite finds its full significance. Sexual intercourse is as much a means of expression for husband and wife as it is a means for them to know each other and to commune with each other. Intercourse supports and strengthens their love, and then in the fruitfulness of this act the couple finds its total fulfillment: in the image of God the couple becomes a source of life.[27]

Paul VI, then, in no way retreated from the teaching of *Humanae Vitae*[28] although he was greatly vilified for his stand.

Still, although these events are interesting for the sociological dynamics of the Church, for the philosopher and theologian what is of greatest interest are the arguments made in behalf of or against the conclusions of *Humanae Vitae*. But, again, as has been observed earlier, there was little true examination of the arguments of *Humanae Vitae* itself; most of the debate immediately following the issuance of the encyclical focused on the status of the encyclical as infallible or authoritative, on the role of conscience and the legitimacy of dissent. Nor did theologians later often take up the issue of contraception itself; rather they questioned all the more radically the very principles on which the teaching on contraception and indeed the teaching on all moral matters had been traditionally based. Yet here we should note what was the shape of the arguments that were made against *Humanae Vitae* soon after its promulgation.

Dissident Theological Response

For as much discussion as there was of "birth regulation" in the years preceding *Humanae Vitae,* in some ways the debate on the morality of contraception, such as it was, did not really get started until after the publication of *Humanae Vitae.* Certainly, it must be remembered that the reports of the Papal Commission, examined in Chapter 1, were not intended for publication and were not written as polished and complete justifications of the conclusions they advocated. Thus, of necessity, they do not provide a full defense of their positions. There are other reasons, though, for the readily apparent incompleteness of their defenses. In the perspective of Church history, the debate about contraception is relatively new. Until recent decades there had been no serious challenge to the Church's teaching on contraception. It is not unusual in the history of Church teaching on a given topic for the conclusions to precede the arguments and for a development of the arguments in support of a teaching to await the stimulus of dissenting objections. The arguments about contraception are still being developed and undoubtedly will continue to be developed for some time. For this reason, both the positions of those defending the teaching and those challenging it have occasionally been based on assumptions not satisfactorily supported in the eyes even of those who hold them. They have had some sense, some conviction, that justification can be found for some of the arguments, and their work has been to find these justifications.

The primary focus of this chapter and the next will be the challenges made to *Humanae Vitae*. Again, the target of the critique has been not so much the encyclical itself or its specific teaching. Rather, dissenting theologians regularly challenge the principles on which they believe the conclusion of the encyclical is based, as well as a whole host of other teachings on moral matters. These challenges have been many and various and proposed by a large number of theologians substantiating their critiques through widely varying justifications. Thus, it would be impossible to survey the literature on this topic, impossible even to survey the major works of the most well-known critics. Since limitations are necessary, here only some of the more constant criticisms will be reviewed. The first portion of this chapter will be directed to the early challenges made to natural law. These challenges were not directed toward repudiating natural law but to revising certain premises of traditional law theory. Indeed, most of the dissenting theologians would claim that they are natural law theorists[29] but that in certain key respects they reinterpret some of the premises of natural law (most notably, the premise that some kinds of actions are intrinsically wrong). Those who consider themselves to be traditional natural law theorists argue that in spite of the claim of the dissenting theologians to be revising and not repudiating natural law, their revision is so radical as to amount to a rejection.

To some extent this chapter reviews criticisms of natural law in general but focuses chiefly on how these criticisms are directed toward the arguments of *Humanae Vitae*. The criticisms are themselves subject to criticism largely based on the claim that the critics have misrepresented the natural law theory they are critiquing. Perhaps even more importantly the claim will be made that revisionists, too, at crucial junctures, must employ the very natural law claims they have purported to have proved false. This chapter addresses the following major criticisms of natural law: that natural law is based on a static view of nature and does not exhibit the historical consciousness developed in the modern age; that it sees grace as something "imposed" on nature; that it is "physicalistic"; that its reasoning is a priori and deductive rather than a posteriori and inductive. The arguments of Charles Curran and Bernard Haering will have primacy of place for several reasons: they have long had an interest in the Church's teaching on sexual ethics, an interest that predates *Humanae Vitae*, and they were perhaps instrumental in fostering the view that the Church could and would change its teaching on contraception;[30] they have applied their criticisms more directly and thoroughly to *Humanae Vitae* than have other theologians; and both have had an undeniably great impact on Catholic moral theology. Furthermore, to this day they have not ceased making a public case against the Church's teaching on contraception; in 1986 Charles Curran was relieved of his post at The Catholic University of America for his constant open dissent from the Church's teaching on contraception[31] and Bernard Haering in 1989 helped marshal support from a number of European theologians to a mandate now called the Declaration of Cologne which urged the pope to appoint an international commission to reconsider the Church's opposition to contraception.[32]

Chapter 7 presents a fairly detailed appraisal of the debate about whether there are exceptionless moral norms, whether any kind of actions can be deemed "intrinsically evil," and whether the use of contraception is one of these actions. This debate began just before the issuance of *Humanae Vitae* and has continued nearly unabated since.[33]

Nature and Grace

One of Charles Curran's objections to traditional natural law theory is that it portrays the relation between nature and grace improperly.[34] Curran first applauds natural law theory for "recognizing a source of ethical wisdom for the Christian apart from the explicit revelation of God in Christ Jesus. This recognition remains a most important and lasting contribution of Catholic thought in the area of theological ethics."[35] (The source of this ethical wisdom, has, of course, generally been considered to be the workings of nature; it remains to be seen whether Curran's rejection of "physicalism" does not also undermine a common source of ethical understanding between Christians and non-Christians.) He observes that the most difficult question for this perspective is reconciling it with the distinctively Christian way of viewing reality. The chief deficiency that he has found in attempts to this effect has been an "unnuanced understanding of the relationship between nature and grace. . . . A simplistic view of the supernatural sees it as something added to the natural."[36]

He finds this deficiency in section 4 of *Humanae Vitae*, which states, "All the moral law" is explained as "not only, that is of the law of the Gospel, but also of the natural law, which is also an expression of the will of God. . . ."[37] He also cites the call in section 7 of *Humanae Vitae* for an anthropology based on "an integral vision of man and his vocation, not only of his earthly and natural, but also his supernatural and eternal, vocation."[38] He argues that these statements are opposed to the Christian view, wherein "nature and creation are relativized by the transforming Christian themes of redemption and final resurrection destiny [sic] of all creation."[39] He concludes, "In the total Christian perspective there is a place for the 'natural,' but the natural remains provisional and relativized by the entire history of salvation."[40]

No definition of what it means for nature to "remain provisional and relativized" is offered here, but the context suggests that Curran thinks that natural law restricts the kind of free and creative response to nature that the Christian view legitimates. The defense for this position seems to be that Christ came to redeem nature and thus that Man is called to participate in this redemption by "perfecting" nature. Therefore, nature would be relative to the good of mankind and provisional because there are no absolute restrictions on Man's intervention. Again, this is not the place to attempt to justify or critique Curran's position; the task here is to evaluate Curran's response to *Humanae Vitae*.

Does *Humanae Vitae* exhibit a "both/and" view of nature and grace? Does it "absolutize" nature? Truly no more than on the surface level of the passages cited. The tradition out of which *Humanae Vitae* grew is not susceptible to the charge that it posits a gulf between nature and grace, between the natural and the supernatural. One fundamental thesis of traditional natural law theory is that the same God created both the natural and the supernatural and for that very reason there can be no great disjuncture between them; it is for that very reason that traditional natural law theory believes that much can be learned about God by observing the world that He created; it is for that very reason that traditional natural law theory believes that in giving nature the respect due to it, one is respecting God's will. Nor is grace imposed on nature. For instance, it is natural that one love one's family and friends, but Christ commands us to love our neighbors and enemies as well. Certainly we are to do *both* the first *and* the second, but God's grace can also transform both the first and the second. The grace of God allows us to perfect our natural love for our friends and our family so that now we also love them not just as *ours*, but as God's; and the love we have for them helps us to know how to love our neighbors and enemies *both* as brothers and sisters *and* as God's beloved creations. There is no dichotomy or disjuncture here; we do find grace perfecting nature and transforming it, not violating it. Chapters 2 and 3 review some of the truths that Man can know about marriage through natural law, through the power of his own reasoning. He knows, for instance, that having children is good for Man and that marriage is a good institution for providing for those children. What does he learn about marriage from revelation? That the best analogue for understanding marriage is the relationship that God has with His people, Christ has with His Church, one of complete fidelity and unwavering concern and love; this is not just "added to" what is known about marriage but clearly transforms all that is known about marriage; the husband and wife must learn to love each other with a new depth (made possible by grace) and raise their children to be more than securities for their own future. Revelation and grace perfect the natural inclinations of Man.

Humanae Vitae 4 also states that the Church is to be the proper interpreter of natural law and that compliance with the natural law is necessary for salvation. What can this mean? The response to this question answers another of Curran's criticisms, as well. He states that *Humanae Vitae* does not sufficiently recognize the "disrupting influence of sin [that] colors all human reality."[41] Acknowledging that *Humanae Vitae* notes that sin adversely affects the will, he finds fault with the document because "No mention is made of the fact that sin affects reason itself and the very nature on which natural law theory is based."[42] But, in truth, the claim of *Humanae Vitae* that the Church is the proper interpreter of the natural law grows directly out of the realization that Man's reason is flawed and that he may, thus, misinterpret natural law. A passage from *Casti Connubii* (referred to by *Humanae Vitae*, footnote 1) expresses the view informing *Humanae Vitae* as well:

[God] has constituted the Church the guardian and the teacher of the whole of the truth concerning religion and moral conduct; to her therefore should the faithful show obedience and subject their minds and hearts so as to be kept unharmed and free from error and moral corruption, and so that they shall not deprive themselves of that assistance given by God with such liberal bounty, they ought to show this due obedience not only when the Church defines something with solemn judgment, but also, in proper proportion, when by the constitutions and decrees of the Holy See, opinions are prescribed and condemned as dangerous and distorted.

Wherefore, let the faithful also be on their guard against the overrated independence of private judgment and that false autonomy of human reason. For it is quite foreign to everyone bearing the name of a Christian to trust his own mental powers with such pride as to agree only with those things which he can examine from their inner nature, and to imagine that the Church, sent by God to teach and guide all nations, is not conversant with present affairs and circumstances. . . .[43]

Humanae Vitae, then, in conformity with *Casti Connubii* well understands the fallibility of human reason; however clear the natural law might be, Man is yet often incapable of discerning this; he needs the guidance of the Church. And since the Church speaks for God and speaks the same truth that a proper use of human reason should be able to discern, there can be no true conflict between Church teaching and proper use of human reason.

Curran, of course, recognizes the importance of the Christian understanding of sin, but his definition of it exhibits certain inadequacies or at least certain departures from the tradition. He states, "Sin can simply be described . . . as a lack of love and an alienation from God and others."[44] Again, this description is not wrong, but it and his discussion of sin do little to explain what is the source of sin in the human person. The tradition has placed it in both a weakness of the will and a darkness of the intellect. The failure to recognize the effect of original sin on the human intellect seems to have led Curran to ignore or to underplay the sinfulness of human reason and to attribute rather extreme powers of accurately judging the truth to it. Whereas the Church teaches that Man's reason is fallible and needs the guidance of the Church, Curran's position tends to judge the Church's teaching on the validity of the reasons offered for it and to suggest that if individuals do not see or accept these reasons they need not accept the Church's teaching. It does not seem that his perspective makes provision for the sinfulness or flawed reasoning ability of those evaluating the validity of the Church's justifications for its own positions. The Church understands that Man's reasoning ability, though a great gift from God and the source of the discovery and understanding of many truths, is nonetheless subject to err because of either sin or ignorance. Ultimately the Church does not believe there can be any true conflict between the proper use of Man's reason, his recourse to conscience, and his submission to Church authority; such a belief stems from a view of Man's reason and Church authority that Curran does not seem to share.

Curran not only finds natural law incompatible with the Christian view of reality but considers natural law methodology in general "subject to severe negative criticism."[45] He singles out three areas for criticism: "1) a tendency to accept natural law as a monolithic philosophical system with an agreed upon body of ethical content which is the source of most, if not all, of Catholic moral teaching; 2) the danger of physicalism which identifies the human act with the physical or biological structure of the act; 3) a classicist worldview and methodology."[46] In his elaborations of these criticisms, he inserts several others, such as the charges that the Church's view of natural law is based on a primitive, not a technological view of reality, that it uses an a priori rather than an a posteriori method of reasoning, and that it is too concerned with certitude. These criticisms will be dealt with here insofar as they bear on his criticism of *Humanae Vitae*.

A Monolithic System of Natural Law

The first charge is the claim that there is no monolithic system of natural law and that therefore the Church's moral teaching cannot be based on natural law.[47] Curran notes, "The vast majority of Catholic teaching on particular moral questions came into existence long before Thomas Aquinas enunciated his theory."[48] This undeniable assertion seems to be meant to suggest that the earlier teachings of the Church could not have been based on natural law reasoning since Aquinas did not write about natural law until the thirteenth century. This is a curious suggestion, since Aquinas claims that Man quite naturally reasons in accord with the principles of natural law and that he does not need special instruction in natural law theory to reason in this way. Early teachings of the Church may have been based on sources other than natural law (such as revelation), but they may also have been based on natural law, even if they preceded Aquinas. Again, it is the very core of Aquinas's natural law theory that humans *naturally* reason in accord with natural law principles and thus that Man need not be taught some system of moral reasoning before he begins to reason about what is morally good for him. That is, Man naturally knows that good ought to be sought and that evil ought to be avoided, and he comes to know what is good and what is evil for him by the natural act of reflecting on his own natural inclinations (physical, psychological, intellectual, spiritual, and so on). Natural law theory holds that when Men do so they will agree on some fundamentals, such as that "innocent human life ought never to be taken directly."

Nor does natural law theory claim that natural law reasoning generates a "monolithic system with an agreed upon body of ethical content."[49] Certainly there are some certain non-negotiable fundamentals such as the one already mentioned: that "innocent human life ought never to be taken directly." But problems and situations faced by Men are often so complex that to imply that no further reasoning is necessary beyond knowing the fundamentals of natural law is to falsify the sophistication of traditional natural law theory. Proper application of natural law principles requires considerable understanding not only of universal human nature and the goods that perfect it but of many other realities, such as a knowledge of the culture in which one lives and of the contingencies that bear on the moral decision that one must make. It is difficult to understand what justice there is in the charge that the method of reasoning dictated by natural law theory is "monolithic."

When Curran evaluates *Humanae Vitae* in terms of this criticism he states, "The reasoning of the Encyclical does not admit that there is a pluralism in understandings of the natural law and in the conclusions which can be derived from different natural law theories. The impression lingers in *Humanae Vitae* that the natural law is a coherent philosophical system with an agreed-upon body of content."[50] The force of this criticism is not clear. Admitting that there is a pluralism of understandings, of course, would not entail that the one used by the encyclical is not coherent and defensible. Perhaps the criticism that *Humanae Vitae* does not admit to a pluralism in natural law understandings means that some individuals reading the document would not be able to recognize which natural law principles (Stoic, Thomistic, Suarezian) were being used to justify the conclusions of the document. But are these "systems" so different and so identifiable that it is possible to put a label on which natural law "system" any natural law theorist is using? Are there not fundamental characteristics of all natural law theories that may or may not be applied in ways characteristic of individual theories? Chapters 3 and 4 of this text attempt to show that a careful reading of the encyclical gives sufficient indication of the kind of natural law principles it relies on and to demonstrate several different applications of these principles used to construct arguments against contraception.

But as the preceding analysis suggests, the criticism means more than that *Humanae Vitae* does not make clear which natural law system it is using. It seems to be an objection to an overreliance or an unjustifiable reliance on natural law arguments by the document. Is this charge true? Certainly *Humanae Vitae* for its explanation of its teaching uses much natural law terminology and principles out of the natural law tradition(s). *Humanae Vitae* does not claim or assume a monolithic philosophical system; it does claim and assume that the principles of moral reasoning that it uses are reasonable, that its understanding of reality is sound, and that it applies these principles properly. But it must also be kept in mind that the encyclical does not state or assume that natural law is the only source of Church moral teaching, nor that there are not other methods or terminologies that could express the truth of its teaching. Indeed, as many of the preceding discussions have shown, *Humanae Vitae* and much of the supportive literature on *Humanae Vitae* use arguments and principles, that, although not incompatible with natural law reasoning, are more generally considered characteristic of reasoning based on "personalist" values. The Church certainly recognizes that the truth can be expressed in different philosophical "languages." Indeed, it has been common practice for the Church, although not abandoning its preference for natural law terminology, to adopt freely other terminology and methodologies associated more commonly with other "systems." For instance, there has been a proliferation of "rights" talk in Church documents accompanied by constant declarations that Man has natural rights of many different descriptions. This way of talking was not a part of the earlier formulations of the natural law tradition and may well be construed as a legitimate development of natural law thinking. That is, "natural law" is not a set or closed system; rather it can readily appropriate terminology and concepts that disclose truths about Man and his nature and his proper moral behavior.

Physicalism

Curran's second charge is one that perhaps has greater currency. He notes in Aquinas "a definite tendency to identify the demands of natural law with physical and biological processes."[51] In the areas where he went astray, Aquinas, in Curran's view, relied too heavily on Ulpian. Ulpian, he tells us, saw humanity as something layered on top of animality.[52] He sees the influence of this view as being most pernicious in sexual morality, where he sees "nature" as understood to be "synonymous with animal or biological processes and not as denoting human actions in accord with the rational, human nature."[53] There would seem to be room here to question Curran's understanding both of Ulpian and of the extent and nature of Aquinas's reliance on him, but here let us just suggest that it seems that this view is far from anything that appears as influential on *Humanae Vitae*.

Curran asserts that Ulpian's view of nature means that Man may not interfere in the animal processes and finalities of his body. In contrast to this, he states his own views thus: "Rationality does not just lie on top of animality, but rationality characterizes and guides the whole person. Animal processes and finalities are not untouchable. Our whole vocation, we have come to see, is to bring order and intelligence into the world, and to shape animal and biological finalities toward a truly human purpose."[54] Curran's charge of "physicalism," here, the charge that natural law theory simply "layers" rationality on top of animality combined with an excessive respect for the physical processes of nature, is hard to square with the fact that the Church holds that it is permissible to intervene much more freely with the biological processes of animals than with those of Man. As we have noted, sterilization, abortion, contraception, in vitro fertilization, and production of animals for "farming" of organs for transplantation are all permissible for animals. Yet the Church finds none of these actions permissible for Man. Again, it is because of the nature of *Man*, not because of the nature of the biological processes per se, that Man must not interfere with these processes. It is because the generative biological processes of Man mean something much greater for Man than they do for animals that these biological processes are evaluated differently. As noted in Chapter 3, few defenders of the Church's teaching on contraception make arguments that focus solely on the ordination of the biological organs or processes. Rather, the more prominent arguments are based on the value of the human person and on the importance of his actions respecting the fullness of his dignity as a human person. To treat him as another animal would justify contraception, not condemn it. On the other hand, defenders of *Humanae Vitae* think it is the defenders of contraception who treat the generative processes of Man as merely physical, for allowing the use of contraception seems to suggest that only the organs or processes are violated; that the deeper dimensions of the human person do not enter into these generative acts and thus are not harmed by contraception.

Curran, though, seems to acknowledge in at least a minimal way that the physiological ordination of the act is not entirely without relevance: he avers, "One must, of course, avoid the opposite danger of paying no attention to the physical structure of the act or to external actions in themselves."[55] He also cautions, "In the last few years the ecological crisis has made us aware of the danger of not giving enough importance and value to the physical aspects of worldly existence. We are not free to interfere with nature any way we see fit. Just as it is wrong to absolutize the natural and the physical, so too it is wrong to give no meaning or importance to the natural and the physical."[56] When he is rejecting the "physicalism" of *Humanae Vitae*, he avers, "Note that the fact that the moral aspect of the act may coincide with the physical structure of the act is not denied in this [Curran's] presentation."[57] One looks in vain, though, for any indication of what attention ought to be paid to physical structures or why attention ought to be paid to them; no explanation of what importance, value, or meaning the physical aspects of worldly existence have is given. No examples of which acts are to be judged morally in accord with their physical structure and why they are to be so judged are presented.

In proving that the arguments of *Humanae Vitae* are guilty of physicalism, Curran cites several passages where spouses are enjoined to respect the "intimate structure of the conjugal act" (HV 12) and where "the use of means directly contrary to fecundation is condemned as being always illicit" (HV 16). He also draws our attention to the passages where it is claimed that it is by the design of God that these conjugal acts have their nature (HV 12). The "core practical conclusion" in his telling is that which prohibits abortion and direct sterilization; he goes on to say: "Similarly excluded is every action which, either in anticipation of the conjugal act, or in its accomplishment, or in the development of its natural consequences, proposes, whether as an end or as a means, to render procreation impossible" (HV 14). From this evidence he concludes, "The natural law theory employed in the encyclical thus identifies the moral and human action with the physical structure of the conjugal act itself."[58]

Surely, he speaks too strongly when he says that the encyclical "*identifies* the moral and human action with the physical structure" (my emphasis). Certainly, the natural law theory employed by *Humanae Vitae* holds that the physical structure of the act is *one* identifying element of the conjugal act, but only one: rather the conjugal act takes its proper and full meaning from the fact that it is *humans*, humans attempting to achieve the goods of conjugal love and responsible parenthood, who are engaging in an act with this physical structure. Curran seems generally to ignore the portions of the encyclical that lay the groundwork for the condemnation of contraception, the sections commenting on what are designated as the "two important elements" of married life: conjugal love and responsible parenthood (HV 7). *Humanae Vitae* 9 lays out four ennobling characteristics of conjugal love and four concerns of responsible parenthood. It does not trace the purpose of sex in the animal or biological world through to the human realm; rather, it starts out with a view of Man and a view of the human and spousal mission entrusted by God to Man. Curran notes these passages not at all, nor does he inform us why they do not merit his consideration in evaluating the teaching of *Humanae Vitae*. He criticizes natural law theory (here Ulpian's) for having a "notion of nature [that] easily leads to a morality based on the finality of a faculty independent of considerations of the total human person or the total human community."[59] But it is unclear that *Humanae Vitae* is guilty of such a fault, if one takes into account the whole of the document, rather than citing a few passages out of context.

Furthermore, most theologians put great weight on another passage that does not receive Curran's notice; this is the claim that there is an indissoluble nexus between the unitive and procreative meanings of the conjugal act (HV 12). The unitive meaning, which is generally taken to be the more "spiritual" meaning of the conjugal act, is weighted as equally essential with the procreative element; neither may be deliberately removed, and both, it is argued, are violated by the use of contraception. Thus, it seems difficult to sustain Curran's claim "*Humanae Vitae* identifies the moral and human action with the physical structure of the conjugal act itself."

The charge that natural law is guilty of "physicalism" has been taken up by other theologians, whose arguments differ substantially from those provided by Curran. Curran is rather alone in arguing that there is no premoral evil in the use of contraception; indeed, he calls contraception a "limited good."[60] Others maintain that there is some "premoral" or "ontic" evil in the use of contraception but contend that this evil does not make the use of contraception intrinsically evil; the intention of the spouses may render the choice to use contraception moral. The chief contours of this argument will be drawn in Chapter 7.

A Classicist View of Nature versus Historical Consciousness

The third major deficiency of natural law theory that bears on the teaching of *Humanae Vitae* is, in the eyes of Curran, its reliance on a classicist worldview that, he claims, has been replaced by a more historically conscious worldview. He describes the classicist worldview as emphasizing "the static, the immutable, the eternal, and the unchanging."[61] He illustrates this view by likening it to the Platonic world of ideas: "Everything is essentially spelled out from all eternity, for the immutable essences, the universals, exist in the world of ideas. Everything in this world of ours is a participation or an accidental modification of the subsistent ideas. We come to know truth and reality by abstracting from the accidents of time and place, and arriving at immutable and unchangeable essences. Such knowledge based on immutable essences is bound to attain the ultimate in certitude."[62] On the other hand, the "more historically conscious worldview emphasizes the changing, developing, evolving, and historical. Time and history are more than mere accidents that do not really change essential reality."[63]

Curran describes two methodologies "created" by classicist and historically conscious worldviews:

The classicist methodology tends to be abstract, *a priori,* and deductive. It wants to cut through the concrete circumstances to arrive at the abstract essence which is always true, and then works with these abstract and universal essences. In the area of moral theology, for example, the first principles of morality are established, and then other universal norms of conduct are deduced from these.

The more historical methodology tends to be concrete, *a posteriori,* and inductive. The historical approach does not brush by the accidental circumstances to arrive at the immutable essence. The concrete, the particular, and the individual are important for telling us something about reality itself.[64]

Surely this portrayal of the natural law theory and its concept of essences and its understanding of the role of particulars and universals is a caricature of natural law. (Even as a reading of Plato it is highly suspect.) Natural law does hold, of course, that there is something that we understand to be human nature, an immutable "essence" that humans share with Adam and all members of the species *Homo sapiens* who are descended from Adam. But natural law theorists do not on the basis of this nature create some abstract definition of Man from which they then deduce moral laws. The natural law understanding of Man is deeply rooted in an experiential understanding of how Man responds to his environment. As Man understands his own experience and environment better he learns better what is good for him, what is in accord with his nature and what is not. The natural law tradition certainly understands that different cultures and different periods in time have various notions of what is good for Man, but it believes that these differences must be assessed in accord with the fundamental dignity of Man. It holds that no historical or cultural conditions could justify some actions, such as rape and murder. An example of an important change in moral understanding based on a deeper understanding of Man is the prohibition of slavery, not always recognized by Man to be seriously wrong.[65] Man's understanding of the natural law, then, is advancing with progress in Man's understanding of his own nature and a more deepened appreciation of his fundamental dignity.

Moreover, natural law theory considers the moral life to be a lifetime enterprise; each individual human being throughout his life is developing his moral character; he is engaged in a veritable transformation of himself; change is not only allowed but required. Charges that the natural law tradition is "static" have legitimacy only insofar as natural law theory does hold that there are an essential human nature and some exceptionless moral norms, but in every other regard these charges are a distortion of natural law theory. Curran's understanding of the role of "concrete particulars" is also highly questionable; for instance, the virtue of prudence, which enters into all ethical action, requires a true and right understanding of concrete particulars.

When Curran turns these charges against *Humanae Vitae*, he notes, "The natural law methodology employed in the Encyclical is excessively deductive and does not leave enough room for the inductive."[66] It would be quite a chore to go through the document and to analyze which arguments are deductive and which inductive, but what might be said is that in traditional natural law theory, most deductive reasoning is preceded by extensive inductive reasoning; the principles from which deduction proceeds are derived from induction, or reflection on experience and knowledge of the world around one. Definitions of natural things and processes are not taken from some a priori source but are derived from observation of the way these things and processes operate. It is simplistic to call one worldview and its methodology deductive and the other inductive.

Curran notes that the document does acknowledge that times have changed and that new social conditions have raised new questions, but he questions whether sufficient attention has been paid to these changes. As evidence that perhaps it has not he notes that none of the footnotes of the document gives references that would indicate "any type of dialogue with other Christians, non-Christians and the modern scientists."[67] Other criticisms of the document are that it does not give due weight to the difficulty that abstinence creates for married couples (as observed in *Gaudium et Spes* 51);[68] that its teaching may be based on an outmoded biology that did not recognize that because of the rhythms of fertility and infertility very few sexual acts can actually result in conception,[69] that there was too much insistence on single act analysis, and that insufficient attention was paid to problems of overpopulation.[70] It would be otiose to take up each of these claims; perhaps the discussions in Chapters 3 and 4 and in the commentary (Appendix 2) suffice to show that *Humanae Vitae* is not guilty of these charges; they are cited to show what historical conditions Curran thinks should have served to alter Church teaching.

Evolutionary Historical Consciousness

The term *historical consciousness* is used variously by theologians, to make two different types of distinction about change. One is simply social change, the kind that societies undergo in their development, which produces the differences among cultures. Curran's claim is that those living in modern times are much more aware of how culturally based are many of our moral perspectives and that this historical consciousness leads us to realize that our moral perspectives should change with the changes in society. The other sense in which *historical consciousness* is used is in reference to the theory of evolution understood in reference to both biology and spirituality. In this view Man, as are all other species, is an evolved and evolving creature whose physical and spiritual nature is in a state of flux; thus, deducing moral norms from a "static" human nature is considered to be false to reality. Haering's early objections to *Humanae Vitae* exhibited this understanding of historical consciousness.

Haering clearly desires some version of natural law to be a guide to ethical analysis. This desire, though, does not serve to change the fact that he consciously, explicitly, and radically departs from the view of reality or nature that informs *Humanae Vitae*. The portions of his work that are most relevant to our purposes here are the sections of his *Medical Ethics*, especially the chapters "Human Nature and the Understanding of Medicine"[71] and "The Inseparability of Unitive-Procreative Functions of the Marital Act," in the volume *Contraception: Authority and Dissent* edited by Curran. Although the chapter from *Medical Ethics* was written later, it gives a fairly thorough account of his view of nature, one that informed his earlier rejection of *Humanae Vitae*. In these works Haering exhibited a firm conviction that nature is evolving and that Man may creatively intervene in this evolving process.

Haering shares Curran's view that the traditional view of natural law was based on static essences, whereas a more biblically centered theology, one more in accord with evolutionary science, requires that we see a dynamic and changing design in nature. Perhaps the thrust of his view can be seen in the following passage:

Today's theology pays greater attention to the biblical account of creation where, at the beginning, there was only chaos which gradually yielded to a magnificent order of things. That God entrusted nature to man reveals his intention that man, as an adorer and a loving being, overcome the chaotic tendencies in the world around him. Medicine, then, can envisage its task as that of subduing the disorderly powers of human 'nature' in view of the most desirable redeemed order.

The biblical perspective of creation makes it possible for theology to meet with modern man who, to some extent, considers himself as "his own self-creator, for in a sense man is unfinished and capable now of creating himself."[72] Of course, theology must be alert to the danger of man's turning a deaf ear to God's express design by wanting to be *independently* his self-creator. Theologically speaking, this would mean that man chose to seek his self, his true "nature" by existentially separating himself from the very Truth that gives him life. Man can find his true nature only by going back to the source of life. In his limited realm, then, man can share in God's creativity.[73]

Man, then, is mandated by God to make order out of chaos, and insofar as he deems his physiological functions as disorderly, he should intervene creatively to order them to the goods he seeks.

Although he does not use the label *physicalism,* he shares Curran's rejection of the traditional natural law evaluation of the ethical importance of the natural ordination of biological processes.[74] He argues that medicine needs to see that bodily and spiritual goods are interconnected and that they both need to be served. These views lead him to this position: "The biological nature of man as a partial aspect of his being does not bear any definite normative character. It can never set an intangible limit but it does, very often, have an indicative character. In most situations, biological laws would stand the test of serving the good of the total person. Medicine usually imitates them or brings them to full function whenever possible, but it cannot always attain this goal. It is at this juncture that bold challenges and new questions confront modern medicine."[75]

Haering sees nature as evolving and Man as having a divine mandate to mold nature creatively:

The physician of today no longer defines his *role* by the Hippocratic notion of "servant of nature" or servant of the ordered potentialities and powers of nature. He is acquiring a greater consciousness of his own creative status. He increasingly considers himself an architect and sculptor of the given stuff of nature. He scrutinizes nature in its manifold trends of development, in its positive potentialities and dangers of decay, and he tries to meet all these by creative interventions. My first thesis, then, is that we should prefer a conscious and responsible moulding of the *physis* to all those changes that happen through lethargy or sloth. In more sociological terms, I favour "planned" change over "natural" change.[76]

He does not mean for Man to have absolute freedom over the forces of nature. He offers as the primary criterion for judging when creative change is morally permissible the principle of totality, which he admittedly redefines:

The traditional use of the principle of totality justified intervention in view of physical health and functioning. Medical ethics for the future must rest on an all-embracing concept of "totality": *the dignity and well-being of man as a person in all his essential relationships to God, to his fellowmen and to the world around him.* In view of the breadth and depth of the human vocation, man can and must use his knowledge and art to manipulate the chaotic forces of the *physis* for the creation of a more humane order not only in the physical world but also in his psychosomatic nature. If it is more humane, it is also more pleasing to God. The mere observance of the impersonal and sub-personal laws and tendencies of "nature" cannot guarantee such an increasingly humane order of development.[77]

As the discussion in Chapter 3 indicates, the principle of totality has had a precise meaning in moral theology that served to evaluate moral treatment of parts of the body in relation to the whole. This principle was based on a view of the parts of the body as having value insofar as they served the whole of which they were an *organic* part. The Schema and Majority Rebuttal both attempted to expand the meaning of this principle to justify their judging conjugal acts as parts of the whole of marriage and not as individual acts to be judged individually.[78] In this passage Haering is not speaking directly of marriage but of the parts of the body, not as parts of the body but as parts of the whole person. Therefore, if a certain manipulation or intervention of biological processes could be argued to be in the service of the whole person, this would be permissible even if this manipulation or intervention violated the nature of the processes. These would be "humane interventions." He does not explain what standard is to be used to determine what is a humane intervention.

But even more importantly, is this a proper or an improper application of the principle of totality? Again, Haering uses the principle to justify manipulating parts of the body, the procreative parts, in service of the whole person. Yet he fails to acknowledge the customary distinction that although most body parts may have an instrumental function in respect to the whole of the body, neither the parts nor the whole is instrumental to the person. The human person is, after all, a unity of body and soul. The body does not exist simply to serve the person; in an important sense, it is the person, though not the whole of the person. There are, of course, important distinctions to be made here. Cosmetic surgery, that is, surgery performed for the purposes of making less unattractive some physical deformity that is not health-threatening, is customarily justified as being for the sake of the psychological well-being of the whole person. Could not contraception be justified for a similar reason? The cosmetic surgery, however, is undertaken to restore the body to its more natural condition, whereas contraception alters what is natural. The psychological harm in the first case is that a bodily part does not look as it ought; the psychological harm in the second is that the procreative organs are operating as they ought. Moreover, as has customarily been taught, the procreative organs are not like other organs: they serve purposes beyond the good of the individual; they have interpersonal value; they serve to foster union with a beloved spouse and to engender children from these loving unions. Thus, one is not tampering simply with some minor physical part but with a power and faculty that have meaning far beyond those of other bodily parts. Haering does not consider that it may be inherently "inhumane" to treat human procreative organs as instruments; it may be inherently opposed to the dignity of the human person for him to solve his psychological or social problems by subjecting his body to treatment appropriate for animals.

He in fact reads *Humanae Vitae* as justifying contraception, at least implicitly, on the basis of his understanding of the principle of totality. In his reading of the text of *Humanae Vitae* 10, one of the key passages is the following: "In relation to biological processes, responsible parenthood means the knowledge and the respect of their functions; the human intellect discovers in the power of giving life biological laws which are part of human nature." He comments on this text, "I think that it is possible to give this text an acceptable interpretation in the sense that biological processes must not be ignored, which medicine never does."[79] (If medicine *never* does this, it would seem that this is a needless instruction and the controversy would seem to be over nothing.) Later he draws attention to the passage in *Humanae Vitae* 14 that allows the therapeutic use of drugs or medical procedures that have a contraceptive effect. The therapeutic effect is allowed for the sake of the *corpus*. (This word is often translated as "the organism," though more literally it means strictly "the body.") But Haering takes *corpus* in what he calls the "Semitic" sense, to refer to the whole person.[80] Thus, he argues that the permission to use medicine for therapeutic reasons that have a contraceptive effect also amounts to permission to allow contraception when it is in the service of the whole person.[81] This interpretation seems to be a very free reading of the text and is an admitted reinterpretation of the principle of totality.

His earlier interpretation of *Humanae Vitae*, written shortly after the encyclical was written, argued that it was morally permissible to use contraception for the good of the whole person, but at that time he did not see this as the intended meaning of the text of *Humanae*

Vitae. He noted that the encyclical seemed to give Man no dominion over biological functions related to the transmission of life.[82] He reported what has been the justification for this view: the claim that the respect that Man owes to life must be extended to those processes connected with the creation of life. His comment on this reflects the depth of his conviction that the biological processes of Man are, even now, evolving:

In spite of the unreliability of biological laws and rhythms, the encyclical seems to consider them as a part of the human person. It seems to go so far as thoroughly to subordinate the whole human person and the marriage itself to the absolute sacredness of biological laws which have only recently become better known. It has, in fact, been learned that they are not "unchangeable" but are constantly subject to change. We know, for example, that certain animals capable of begetting offspring two or three times a year adjust rapidly when transferred from tropical or subtropical regions to northern areas with a long winter. By a change in their biological "laws and rhythms" they adjust the process of begetting to once a year. Man's biological nature differs from that of lower animals; it is slower in its changes. However, man survives precisely because he can make use of such artificial means as clothing, modern technology, and most importantly, medicine in adjusting in a typically human way.[83]

Throughout his early writing on these matters, Haering showed an optimistic faith in the relentless and inevitable progress in the evolutionary development of biological processes and in the progressive ability of medicine to improve Man's lot. His reasoning about contraception as an advance for Man would seem to be the result of this kind of reasoning; since it is good for Man to have control over the processes of generation, nature will be evolving to provide Man with this control; until it does, or to help it along, Man may intervene in the processes of nature to give himself control now over his generative processes. (A question occurs to this reader: Is it not possible that medical progress may impede the evolution of biological processes? That is, if Man artificially provides a good for himself that nature would provide once Man more fully evolves, will nature continue to evolve to provide this good for Man?) For Haering, the standard of judgment of moral acts seems to be wedded to the prophetic ability to discern the direction of biological evolution (which takes place slowly over millions of years). But this seems to be a problematic standard at best and perhaps an impossible one. Should we not treat biological processes in accord with the nature we now know them to have, rather than in accord with the nature that we think they are coming to have—and think they ought to come to have?

Haering's justification of intervention in biological processes based on an evolutionary view of nature has important implications. His position requires that we be able to discern the course of evolution and to operate in accord with the emerging progressive changes. We need not be bound by what we discern are presently the purposes of our biological processes; we need to be guided by our creative projections of how they will be evolving. How he or anyone knows the direction of evolution and what constitutes an advancement is not explained. (In recent years, it is extremely rare to find theologians stressing the evolutionary character of nature; indeed, it seems to be absent even from Haering's more recent work. The debate now lies elsewhere.)

What Haering also needs to make clear is whether he thinks that contraception used to be wrong but no longer is, or whether he means to say that it was always morally permissible but was not recognized as such. If it was always morally permissible but not recognized as such, we need to be informed what caused the ancients to miss this truth. If it was once wrong but no longer is, we need to know precisely how human nature has changed and how this change now makes contraception morally permissible. Simply saying that "things have changed" does not warrant a change in moral behavior unless we learn what the changes are and their relevance to the point in question.

He performs the service of providing an example of a case where he believes the therapeutic use of contraception would be morally permissible in accord with his principles. He speaks of a woman who is suffering a postpartum psychosis or a psychotic fear of a pregnancy.[84] He asks, "How else can a woman in either instance be helped and her capacity to render the marital due be restored if not by an interference into her biological 'laws and rhythms' so as to ascertain avoidance of a pregnancy?"[85] He believes that contraception could be an intervention justified for the sake of the whole person, which is his application of the principle of totality. He seems to believe that the woman must render her "marital due" and must be free of fear of pregnancy in order to do so. There are, perhaps, other ways to achieve this end: her husband could be counseled to be loving and patient; she could, perhaps, be assisted by psychoanalysis to discover the source of her psychosis. Subjecting her to contraception and the notion that she must always be available to "her man" in spite of a debilitating psychosis may do more to form in her an image of herself as an instrument for her husband's pleasure and thus increase her reasons for psychosis rather than decrease them. (In the end, Haering's argument reduces to a kind of consequentialism or proportionalism: if sufficient good can be wrought by an action in proportion to the evil endured, such an action can be justified. This position is critiqued in Chapter 7, but note that Haering's argument relies on such reasoning.)

Such cases certainly present problems, but like some of the cases that serve to make abortion seem a very appealing choice, these cases cannot, in themselves, provide a true challenge to the traditional evaluation of these acts. It is true that cases can be found for every act that one deems to be immoral (for instance, rape, murder, or racial discrimination) where this act would seem to be a response that could possibly protect goods one wishes to protect. Many of the challenges of living a moral life are rooted in the tension created by cases of just this sort: how does one remain true to one's moral principles when it seems that much good will result if one suspends them? But if the action that one contemplates is truly immoral, then the Church teaches it ought not to be done, for it has been a constant of Church teaching that one must never choose an immoral means to a moral end. The revisionists, of course, do not think they are counseling immoral means to a moral end, for they redefined the method by which one determines the morality of actions; this debate is discussed in Chapter 7.

Haering's reasons for rejecting the view of nature that has informed the natural law theory invoked by Catholic moral theology are clear, as is his own view of nature. What is unclear is what standards his view of nature supplies for judging human actions. The phrases that he uses, such as, "Man must use his creative capacities only in dependence on God, that is, in a spirit of responsibility for history and for his vocation as a person in community,"[86] are simply not precise and focused enough to be of assistance in evaluating specific actions. This deficiency in Haering's views has been noted by others. For instance, Curran offers some rather sweeping, not to say devastating, critiques of Haering's moral theology. Although he states the view "Haering's work stands as the best existing treatise in moral theology," his next remark is "Throughout the three volumes [of *Free and Faithful in Christ*] there is no consistent philosophical grounding of Haering's thought."[87] Indeed, he finds a "disparaging of the philosophical and the metaphysical" throughout the book.[88] He notes that Haering "agrees with Berdyaev in making freedom rather than being the basis of his philosophy. Unfortunately there is no sustained development of this freedom-based anthropology."[89] And finally, he observes, "The weakest part of Haering's first volume is the discussion of the human act and moral norms. In a sense there is no treatment of the human act and its morality as such."[90] To be sure, Curran holds, "Haering's work stands as the best existing treatise in moral theology," but is it possible to have a truly useful ethical system without a discussion of moral norms, without an anthropology, without a metaphysics, without a philosophy of being?

Curran maintains that we are now in a radically different age from the age in which arguments from natural law were respected, an age that calls for a radically different moral theology. He sketches out some of the possibilities for us: the personalist approach (represented by Bernard Haering), the relational approach (he identifies Johan and van der Marck with this view), and the transcendental method (identified, for instance, with Lonergan and Rahner).[91] That so many possibilities exist indicates the state of flux in which moral theology finds itself. Curran maintains that all these approaches would lead to an evaluation of contraception at odds with that of the official teaching of the Church. Clearly a radical break has been made with the tradition. Moral theologians have been struggling since to establish what will be put in the place of this tradition.

Current Views of Curran and Haering

Since his act of immediate dissent, Curran has not in the least reversed his views on contraception, as is evidenced by his willingness to reprint his original objections. Ten years after *Humanae Vitae*, he was very direct: "On the question of artificial contraception the pope and bishops must be willing to admit publicly that the previous teaching is wrong. . . . For my perspective the issuance of *Humanae Vitae* was a tragic mistake in the life of the church. . . ."[92] In a more recent piece, he announces, "Contraceptive technology in general has been a good for human beings."[93] He notes, though, some problems with contraception, among them the health risks to women and the possibility that they may be more open to exploitation by men. He also cautions that contraception may become a power tool for the rich to use against the poor. In light of this statement his views on population control are surprising. When he speaks of the dangers of overpopulation and the need to take measures to control population growth, he does not rule out entirely that some human freedom may need to be sacrificed for the good of the whole: "In general I am opposed to coercive measures except as an absolutely last resort, but it is necessary to evaluate properly the role and meaning of freedom in this discussion about contraception and population control. Too often freedom in these matters can be poorly understood in an overly individualistic sense. Insistence on reproductive autonomy can forget the social dimensions of human sexuality and procreation. Sexuality and procreation involve a relationship to the human species."[94] Whereas traditionally arguments *against* contraception have depended on appeals to the good of the human species, here appeal to this good is used to justify (at least in principle) *mandating*—coercing—couples to use contraception. And whereas appeals to human freedom have generally been used to justify the use of contraception, we now find that freedom *not* to use contraception is called into question. This, indeed, is a radical break with traditional teaching.

Haering seems, on occasion, to have modified his views somewhat. In his *Free and Faithful in Christ* (critiqued by Curran, earlier), his comments in the section "Fecundity as a Part of the Sexual Language" seem to be much more supportive of the teachings of *Humanae Vitae* than his earlier writings were.[95] Indeed, he begins this section by quoting from *Humanae Vitae*, which says "beautifully," "Love is fecund for it is not exhausted by the communion between husband and wife, but is destined to continue, raising up new lives."[96] In this section Haering expresses no criticism of *Humanae Vitae*. Rather, he deplores modern views of sexuality and notes disapprovingly, "Artificial means of contraception and easily accessible abortion has made possible the severing of unitive and procreative goals."[97] He further expresses his concern about modern society in this remarkable statement:

In this atmosphere, human fertility may be drastically reduced by sex-consumers, people who have lost the true meaning of life. Not needing children for social status or for security's sake, they have no motive for begetting offspring. It seems to me that the present situation is moving towards a profound separation of humankind into two species. On the one hand are those who have no ground or motive to transmit life; or if they do transmit it they only increase the number of competitors and rivals in a consumer society. On the other hand there will be those who firmly make their commitment to genuine love and, moved by their mutual love and sense of life, desire as many children as they can well prepare for life's combat, for this life and the other.[98]

Haering emphatically insists that he does not wish to speak on methods of birth regulation (and adopts for himself the silence of article 50 of *Gaudium et Spes*).[99] He does not explicitly state his views on the morality of methods, but some of his remarks indicate that although he has not completely abandoned his approval of contraception, he has much more respect for the teaching of *Humanae Vitae* than he once had.

He elaborates extensively on the meaning of "responsible parenthood" and the role of generosity to new life that is a part of this criterion. He speaks most admiringly of Martelet's explanations of *Humanae Vitae*'s understanding of sexuality in terms of the paradigm of human language and his emphasis on truth in this language.[100] He speaks against portraying contraception as "betraying life," and his earlier voice is heard most clearly in his insistence "Our physical processes are inherited from prehumanity. Of themselves they have no moral responsibility and can command none."[101] And a few remarks about "conscience" suggest that he allows greater freedom in this area than does *Humanae Vitae*. But remarks such as the following are new: "Pope Paul VI, in *Humanae Vitae*, invokes 'the unbroken tradition.' The encyclical bases its conclusion on tradition and on natural law. It therefore tries to give convincing reasons, since 'natural law' is what is open to the eyes of reason after shared experience and reflection. If the reasons do not convince fully, this does not prove the doctrine wrong. Competent people should probe the possibility of finding more convincing ones."[102]

One would almost think that this is not the voice of a dissenting theologian. But one would be deceived, for in April 1989, Bernard Haering reemerged as a leader in the dissent against *Humanae Vitae* when he gathered the signatures of 169 theologians on a statement urging John Paul II to take a worldwide poll about the views of theologians on contraception.[103]

The voices of dissenting theologians have not quieted in the last twenty years; they have only become more focused. The next chapter follows their saga.

SEVEN

Premoral Evil and Other
Variations on a Theme

GENERATION AFTER the issuance of *Humanae Vitae*, dissatisfaction with the conclusions and method of the tradition has not abated among many theologians. The focus of the debate has become fairly well defined; for the most part, theologians have concentrated their efforts on justifying a rejection of the traditional claim that some kinds of actions, apart from specifying circumstances, are intrinsically wrong, that some kinds of actions should never be freely chosen by human agents no matter what good is intended or foreseen.[1] They prefer instead to speak of "premoral," "ontic," or "physical" evils that cannot be morally defined apart from circumstances. In regard to the specific issue of contraception, the claim is made that although there may be some negative element or premoral evil in the use of contraception, contracepted acts of sexual intercourse are not, from the moral point of view, intrinsically evil acts.[2]

Whether the rejection of the concept "intrinsic evil" constitutes a radical break with the tradition or not is a matter of some dispute. In the early part of this decade Richard McCormick conceded the justice of Germain Grisez's charge that Peter Knauer (recognized as the one of the leaders in the rejection of the concept of intrinsic evil) "is carrying through a revolution in principle while pretending only a clarification of traditional ideas." McCormick stated, "I be-lieve this is true—and Knauer explicitly admits it in this study. The only question, then, is the following; Is the revolution justified? Is it solidly grounded?"[3] But now McCormick and others describe themselves as being in "dialogue" with the tradition. Indicative of their change in stance is their preference for the label *revisionist theologians* rather than the *dissenting theologians* used earlier. Indeed, many of them claim that they are within the natural law tradition and often cite Thomas Aquinas as supporting their views.[4] This revised assessment of the nature of the opposition seems largely to rest on the fact that whereas the tradition has taught that all abortions, all use of contraception, all homosexual sexual intercourse, and all masturbation are wrong, the new way of thinking would allow some abortions, some use of contraception, some acts of homosexual sexual intercourse, some instances of masturbation. But an examination of their position shows that what seems to be a disagreement about absoluteness of wrongness is rather a disagreement about how one determines the morality of actions.

The debate over the morality of contraception seems to have been the primary fuel firing the controversy over whether some kinds of acts are intrinsically immoral.[5] Certainly the concept of intrinsic evil is essential to the Church's teaching on this matter. As we recall, *Casti Connubii* condemns contraception as intrinsically against nature and intrinsically wrong:

But no reason, however grave may be put forward by which anything intrinsically against nature [*intrinsece est contra naturam*] may become conformable to nature and morally good. Since, therefore, the conjugal act is destined primarily by nature [*suapte natura . . . destinatus*] for the begetting of children, those who in exercising it deliberately frustrate its natural power and purpose sin against nature and commit a deed which is shameful and intrinsically vicious [*contra naturam agunt et turpe quid atque intrinsece inhonestum operantur*].[6]

Humanae Vitae speaks of contraception in similar terms:

Nor truly, is it possible to justify conjugal acts deliberately deprived of their fertility by claiming that one is choosing the lesser evil. Nor can one claim that these same acts [those deprived of fertility] can be considered together as a whole with past and future fertile acts and thus [be judged] to share in one and the same moral goodness of these fertile acts. For if it is sometimes permissible to tolerate moral evil, which is the lesser evil, in order that one might avoid a greater evil or so that one might promote a more immediate good, it is never permissible, not even for the most serious reasons, to do evil so that good might result. That is, the willing permission of what by its very nature violates the moral order [*ex propria natura moralem ordinem transgrediatur*] ought for that very reason to be judged unworthy [*indignum*] of man. This is so, even if one has acted with the intent to defend and advance what is good for individuals, for domestic relationships, or for human society. For which reason, it is an error to think that a conjugal act, deprived deliberately [*ex industria*] of its fertility, and therefore which is intrinsically wrong [*intrinsece inhonestum*], is able to be justified by the sexual unions of a whole married life. (HV 14)

The tradition of the Church has used a wide variety of terms to describe the acts that it teaches ought never to be freely chosen by human beings; it teaches that these actions by their very nature are against the natural order and that directly acting against the natural order is destructive to the moral goodness of human beings, is unworthy of their dignity. In the preceding passages we find several variants of terms used to describe these actions: *intrinsece est contra naturam* ("intrinsically against nature"); *ex propria natura moralem ordinem transgrediatur* ("by its very nature transgressing the moral order") and *intrinsece inhonestum* ("intrinsically unworthy"). Among other variants, *intrinsece malum* ("intrinsically evil") is also found in the literature. Finding the appropriate English designation for this concept is not without its problems. "Intrinsically evil" appears quite commonly throughout the scholarly literature, and it seems most accurate in regard to the Latin. But in English the word *evil* is rarely used to refer to any evil other than moral evil, whereas in the Latin *malum* refers to conditions, situations, or relations that are not the way they ought to be: *malum* connotes both ontic and moral evil; that is, it refers both to some flaw in the being of an entity and to the flaws in moral acts and characters of human beings. "Evil," "bad," "wrong," and "unworthy" are all possible translations of *malum*. In this discussion "intrinsically wrong" will be the preferred term, but since different terms appear in Church documents, it is useful to have in mind all the possible variants ostensibly referring to the same concept.

It is fairly widely accepted that most modern theologians reject the designation of "intrinsically wrong" for any *kind* of action. They insist that actions can only be evaluated as concrete particulars and may call some of these intrinsically wrong, but they do not accept the designation of *kinds* of acts as intrinsically wrong (more about this later). McCormick describes "the issue" in this way:

The issue is: What *materia circa quam* (object in a very restricted sense) should count as stealing or murder or lying? This is the issue as I read it in the works of Schüller, Fuchs, Janssens, J.-M. Aubert, W. Molinski, Chirico, John Dedek, F. Böckle, Charles Curran, Pater [sic] Knauer, Scholz, Helmut Weber, K. Demmer, F. Furger, Dietmar Mieth, Daniel Maguire, Henrico Chiavacci, Marciano Vidal, Walter Kerber, Timothy O'Connell, and many others. While these theologians differ in significant ways, they do share a certain bottom line, so to speak: individual actions independent of their morally significant circumstances (e.g., killing, contraception, speaking falsehood, sterilization, masturbation) cannot be said to be intrinsically morally evil as this term is used by tradition and the recent magisterium. Why? Because such concepts describe an action too narrowly in terms of its *materia circa quam* without morally relevant circumstances.[7]

Many of the opponents of the magisterial view, the revisionists, argue that such actions as contraception and sterilization are not intrinsically morally evil but involve ontic evils (premoral or physical evils),[8] that the evils involved are not of a nature to render an action the sort never to be chosen by a human agent. The arguments of the participants in this debate, both of those who accept the traditional claim of the Church that some actions are intrinsically wrong—whom we shall call "traditionalists"—and of the revisionists, have been most edifying in the ever perplexing effort to discern how to evaluate moral behavior. It would be impossible to consider fully the views of even one of these theologians here, let alone to survey or critique the many varieties of arguments devised to refute the claim that some acts are intrinsically wrong.[9] Nor is it possible to do full justice to the attempts of traditionalists to counter the claims of the revisionists. In brief, let us observe that it seems fair to say that the most prominent traditionalists primarily charge revisionists with being "consequentialists." Germain Grisez is perhaps the foremost critic of the revisionists on this ground.[10] He argues that it is unintelligible to attempt to judge actions by their consequences (which is what he understands revisionists to be doing); he argues that one cannot possibly foresee all the likely consequences of one's actions nor is one able to commensurate the goods and evils that different choices may produce. Ultimately, he thinks that consequentialism or proportionalism is an unworkable means of moral evaluation. For the most part, Grisez's critique, in the opinion of this author, has been most effective. The approach in this chapter, however, has a somewhat different focus. Grisez's concern has been to show that the revisionists are consequentialists and that consequentialism is a system of moral reasoning that is ultimately not coordinate with reality. The purpose here, however, is to show that the departure of the revisionists from the claim that some kinds of acts are intrinsically evil by their very nature is a radical departure from the traditional teaching of the Church. And since this author thinks the mode of moral analysis used traditionally by the Church corresponds to the demands of reality, this, too, would constitute a severe deficiency in the views of the revisionists. Again, the Church's teaching on contraception as set forth in *Humanae Vitae* seems to have been very much one of the causes for this departure, a departure that has affected the moral analysis of all moral action, not just contraception. Here we hope to show more precisely how the revisionists have departed from tradition, often by using principles and terminology of the tradition to justify their departure, in their attempt to justify the use of contraception.

The major concerns of this chapter are several. Since the terminology within the debate is so confused, an attempt will be made to clarify the meaning of some key terms. This chapter will examine what is meant by the terms *ontic, premoral,* or *physical evil.* Yet, since the terminology of this debate has been so fluid and imprecise, in order to avoid semantic entanglements, in the discussion itself as much use as possible will be made of illustrative examples. Most of the examples will be taken from the category of sexual acts, since these are the actions that dominate the debate and that are most relevant to the discussion here.

After the clarification of terms, there will be a presentation of the revisionist position with some indication of how it differs from the traditionalist position. Revisionists regularly claim that their views are misunderstood and misinterpreted, so, although it will be cumbersome at times, some extensive citation of their positions will be necessary in order to demonstrate points directly from their own writings. Some detailed attention will also be given to Aquinas's criteria for evaluation of moral action. Our interest in Aquinas is twofold: (1) both revisionists and traditionalists claim him as their forefather in ethical analysis and borrow terms and categories from him; (2) the Church, especially in the documents we are considering, seems to employ his mode of ethical analysis. This discussion should serve to show that the revisionist mode of moral analysis is incompatible with that sketched out by Aquinas.

A final portion of this chapter compares the revisionist evaluation of contraception with that of the traditionalists.

The Revisionist Position

Some of those who object to the description of any kind of actions as being "intrinsically wrong" claim that actions cannot be evaluated morally apart from the intention of the agent. Others speak of the need to take into account the circumstances of the action. Consequences also play a role for revisionists, although, for some, the consequences are subsumed into the intention, and, for others, into the circumstances. As Lisa Cahill states (here referring to "revisionists" as "proportionalists"): "The key difference is that the focus of discussion in the proportionalist approach shifts from the act in itself (the moral 'object') to the act in relation to proportionate or disproportionate circumstances (object, intent, and circumstances considered together)."[11] Traditionalists deny that they ignore the intention of the agent or the circumstances when evaluating a moral action; these certainly have great bearing on the moral evaluation of an action. But they also argue that certain kinds of actions are so directly in violation of what is good for Man that no good intention and no circumstances could render them the sort that ought to be chosen by a human being.

Revisionists hold that some actions are the sort that do bring about evils, but that, apart from human choice, these are premoral or ontic evils. Richard McCormick offers an explanation of the difference between moral and premoral evil: "Moral evil refers to those evils that render the person as a whole bad: e.g., the desire of and will to injustice or unchastity. . . . Premoral evils do not touch directly the moral goodness of the person, but only the person's well-being."[12] Moral evils, then, are by definition those evils that harm the moral agent *qua* moral agent; "premoral" evils are those that are external to the moral character; they may cause Man harm and suffering but they do not harm his moral character. McCormick goes on to say, "[Premoral evils] are relevant to moral goodness.

How? The morally good person will avoid causing them unless there is a *correspondingly serious reason*" (my emphasis). Knauer's description of the difference between physical evil and moral evil is similar to McCormick's description of the difference between a premoral evil and a moral evil:

What is physical evil is known by everyone from experience. Sickness or error or other destruction is never willed for itself but only on account of some other associated good. The question is whether, by reason of this good, the permission or causing of the evil is justified or not. The unjustified permission or causing of evil signifies simply that the evil itself is also intended: then, by intention, the act becomes morally evil.

The principle of double effect, rightly understood, responds to the question whether in a given case the permission or causing of evil is justified or not. In answering this question it reveals itself as a principle which provides the criterion for every moral judgment.

Moral evil, I contend, consists in the last analysis in the permission or causing of a physical evil which is not justified by a commensurate reason. Not every permission or causing of physical evil is a moral evil, but every moral evil depends on the permission or causing of physical evil.[13]

Not all adopt Knauer's "commensurate reason" or McCormick's "correspondingly serious reason": some are devotees of "proportionate weighing of values and disvalues"; indeed, there are a wide variety of terms to express the need of comparative weighing of evils likely to result from an action. In spite of the lack of agreement on terminology, all revisionists think that on occasion one may justifiably choose actions that cause "ontic," "premoral" (and sometimes "nonmoral"), or "physical" evils, if proportionate or commensurate goods would result. Traditionalists agree that on occasion one may choose to perform actions that cause "premoral," "ontic," or "physical" evils, but, as we shall see, many actions that revisionists deem to be in the category of "premoral," "ontic," or "physical" evil are considered by traditionalists to be moral evils. Herein lies the crux of the debate.

Before we continue, let us note that there are many difficulties with the terms *ontic, premoral,* and *physical evil.* Often they are used as though they were synonymous; but it seems that they do not all do the same work in describing kinds of evil. The term *ontic evil* (from the Greek word "being") would seem to have a clear enough meaning: it refers to some lack of being in a thing, some deficiency—considered apart from its possible moral dimensions or inadequacy—that affects the being of something. Lameness, blindness, retardation are all ontic evils suffered by Men. *Premoral* evil seems to have the same referent as *ontic* evil but serves to stress the fact that the evil referred to as ontic is prior to any moral evaluation. The word *ontic*, when so narrowly defined then, is fairly unproblematic. But the fact that some philosophers would consider moral evil to be itself an ontic evil for Man obviously creates problems. These philosophers would argue that the most important perfection of his being that Man can have is moral perfection and thus moral evil would be the worst kind of ontic evil. Although there may be some residual strains of this understanding of ontic evil among revisionists (they occasionally denounce actions that would cause Man to mar his integrity), for the most part revisionists do not seem to understand the term in this sense. Indeed, revisionists use the term to distinguish a certain set of evils from moral evil.

The term *physical evil* is perhaps the most fraught with confusions. The word *physical* itself has several meanings, that, if not clearly distinguished in concept and use, can lead to some troubling confusions. The most common understanding of *physical* is that which is distinct from what is spiritual. It refers most immediately to what is tangible or material or bodily. This is the meaning that the general reader most likely has in mind when he or she reads "physical evil." And certainly and justifiably at times when revisionists are speaking of physical evil, they do indeed refer to evils that are the result of the diminishing of the physical properties of something. But human acts cause many kinds of harm besides harm to material or physical things: they cause heartbreak and fear and misery and loneliness, for example. When *physical evil* is used synonymously with *ontic evil* and *premoral evil*, it is meant to embrace harms of this sort as well. Indeed, the etymological meaning of *physical* allows such an expansion of the meaning of *physical*; the word *physical* has its roots in the Greek word *physis*, which means "nature"; perhaps this is the meaning of "physical" that underlies the term *physical evil*. It often has this sense in the manualist tradition. The revisionists often seem to have this sense in mind when they use the term to refer to any evil in the "nature" or "being" of something, whether the something is material or immaterial. Again, this meaning of "physical evil" is synonymous with the understanding of "ontic evil" given previously.

Revisionists also seem to use the term *physical* to refer to a part of the moral act designated by traditionalists as the "object of the act." Some refer to the object of the act (the *materia circa quam* mentioned by McCormick) as the physical act. Since in English, it is not unusual to use the terms *physical* and *material* synonymously, it should not be surprising that there is some interchanging of these terms. (These words even have senses in Latin that permit them to be used synonymously, but their synonymous meaning is not the same as it is in English.) The Latin needs to be attended to carefully. Again, the "matter" of an act need not be physical at all in the sense of being tangible or bodily in some way. Aquinas is not using the word *materia* to refer to anything physical (in our common use of physical as bodily) when he speaks of the *materia* or matter of a moral act. Indeed, stealing, murder, and lying are all considered the *materia* of moral actions. The word *materia*, or matter, is used in an analogous and technical sense in reference to the object of an act. Aquinas explains moral action by comparing it to a thing that is defined in terms of both its matter and its form; in attempting to describe human action he finds it useful to speak of the object of the act (the external act) as the "matter" and the end (or intention) of the act as the "form" (*Summa Theologiae* I–II; q. 18, art. 6).

We will look at Aquinas's analysis of the moral act in some detail momentarily, but here let us note in a preliminary way that in Aquinas's view a moral act can be assessed in terms of both its object (or its matter) and its end (or its form). Sometimes they share the same moral evaluation, and sometimes they differ (*Summa Theologiae* I–II; q. 20; art. 3). For instance, if one works hard to earn money to give to the poor, both one's object (earning money) and one's end (giving to the poor) are good. But if one directly kills an innocent human being to gain money to feed the poor, the object or the matter of one's act (directly killing an innocent human being) is evil; the end (giving to the poor), the form, is good. Still, in spite of the goodness of one's end, one has done something morally wrong. Later we shall clarify further what Aquinas means by the object and end of an act, but what needs to be stressed here is that Aquinas most clearly did not mean that the matter or object of an act is premoral; rather the matter of an act, the object of the act, is that which determines the "primary goodness" of the action (*Summa Theologiae* I–II; q. 18, art. 2). As we shall see in Aquinas's view moral actions can be evaluated by several different criteria, and the object, the *materia*, the matter, is one of them. In Aquinas's view, the human agent commits to good or evil when he chooses the object of his action as well as the end of this action. If the object of the act is to be considered the physical act, for Aquinas it is not a premoral part of the act: if there is physical evil in an act in the sense that the object (or *materia*) of the act is evil, then the act is a moral evil *for that very reason.* In this context "physical evil" is not synonymous with "ontic evil"; rather when the object of an act is evil, this does not mean that it is merely deficient in its being in some way (say, one mistakenly hands to someone to whom one owes ten dollars a one dollar bill). Rather to say that an action is evil in respect to its object means that it violates right reason, and actions that violate right reason are immoral; that is, it is the kind of action that ought never to be performed by humans.

For the revisionist, on the other hand, simply because the object of the act is evil (say, having sexual intercourse with someone other than one's spouse, which may result in some evil, such as one's child having a parent other than one's spouse) does not suffice to determine the moral status of the act; one must know the intention or the circumstances to evaluate the act.

Let us expand a bit on this confusion about what exactly is being denoted by the terms *premoral, ontic,* or *physical evil.* That is, sometimes it seems that reference is being made to the act itself, so that killing or practicing contraception or telling falsehoods is seen as "evil" because there is some negativity in the act itself; for instance, killing destroys life, contraception impairs fertility, and telling false-hoods denies truth. One could choose these "premoral" evils if sufficient good were to result from one's choice. But at times revisionists seem to think that these actions are not evil in themselves but that they could result in evils: for instance, killing, as well as causing the death of the victim, may harm the victim's family and society; the use of contraception may lead to selfishness; and telling false-hoods may lead to lack of trust in members of society. And all these actions could have good consequences as well (killing could aid one in self-defense; contraception could help one avoid an unwanted pregnancy; lying could save the life of a refugee). Thus the job of the moral agent is to assess the premoral evils and goods that an action may produce and then choose that which actualizes the greater goods and the lesser evils.

Since revisionists frequently fail to provide a precise definition of the term *physical evil,* the confusions that result are considerable. As we have shown, sometimes the term *physical evil* is used (1) to refer to any deficiency in an action; (2) to refer to the "object" of the act (which Aquinas maintains can be specified independently of circumstances or intention but revisionists maintain cannot be evaluated apart from circumstances or intention); (3) or to refer to actions that have bad consequences. Some of these confusions may be at the root of the revisionists' claim that exceptionless moral norms are tautologies and of the traditionalists' claim that the revisionist understanding of moral action justifies choosing a morally evil means in pursuit of a good end. The subsequent discussion attempts to steer clear of the confusions by avoiding problematic terminology as much as possible and by using examples to demonstrate points made.

Are Exceptionless Norms Tautologies?

Revisionists ardently deny that their perspective allows choosing an evil means to a good end or permits "adultery, rape, or murder" if a sufficiently good reason might be provided or if sufficiently proportionate goods might be attained. Their claim is that words such as *adultery, rape,* and *murder* indicate acts that are morally wrong because these very words already specify a defining circumstance.[14] In their view, statements such as "Do not commit murder" are analytical or tautological norms. In their view, these prohibitions simply state, "Do not do that which ought not to be done" and specify the sort of thing that ought not to be done.

Traditionalists would disagree with the description of these norms as tautologies. They would define adultery simply as "a married individual's having sexual intercourse with someone other than his or her spouse." They would claim that this definition is not a tautology. Certainly it does not contain any moral prohibition; it is a purely descriptive definition. Thus, in the view of traditionalists the prohibition of adultery does not amount to saying "Do not have sexual intercourse with those with whom you should not have sexual intercourse" or "Do not have sexual intercourse with someone who is not your spouse without reasonable cause." That it is always wrong to have intercourse with someone who is not one's spouse is a moral judgment made on the basis of an understanding of the nature of marriage and the nature of Man; such an act is judged to be opposed to nature. Different and perhaps interdependent reasons could be given why it is always wrong for a spouse to have sexual intercourse with someone other than his or her spouse; for instance, it could be argued that such an action is wrong because one has made certain commitments to one's spouse that such an act violates; it could be argued that it is wrong because it is an act that is directed toward the creation of offspring for whom the agents are not prepared to be parents. But the point is that the term *adultery* does not carry "within" it a moral evaluation; the claim that adultery is wrong is based on a judgment that adultery does not serve to promote human goods. Demonstrating this point through an example also gives us an opportunity to see the difference between the revisionist and the traditionalist modes of analysis of moral action, in action, so to speak.

Although acknowledging that some evil is involved when a spouse has intercourse with someone other than his or her spouse, revisionists could conceive, at least theoretically, of circumstances in which it would be morally permissible to tolerate this evil, this premoral evil. The example usually given is that of a Mrs. Bergmeier unjustly detained in a prison camp. She was in the quandary of being separated from her family or attaining freedom by becoming pregnant through intercourse with a prison guard. Revisionists approving of her having intercourse with the guard (and not all do) would not call her choice an act of adultery, for her deciding to have intercourse with someone other than her spouse would be morally justifiable by virtue of the circumstances or her intention. Revisionists might have various ways of justifying the action (again, not all justify her action, for some weight the competing goods differently), but most likely many would say she is not really guilty of betraying her husband for she does not intend adultery and would also say that she is prepared to provide a responsible upbringing for the child conceived. In fact, her act of intercourse with the prison guard is for the sake of her husband and family and this good is an overriding good.

Traditionalists would judge Mrs. Bergmeier's choice to be wrong and indeed to be an act of adultery, an act that no circumstances or intention could justify. Certainly circumstances may render her less morally culpable than other women who commit adultery, but nonetheless the traditionalist holds that one ought never to have sexual intercourse with someone other than one's spouse. It is because traditionalists consider any act of deliberately having intercourse with one other than one's spouse as adultery that some of them accuse revisionists of justifying adultery. Their mode of analysis does not depend on weighing the balance of evils that may result from adultery against those that may result from having intercourse with someone other than one's spouse and then deciding for the course of action that causes the least evil. Rather, traditionalists argue that what is most important is that Mrs. Bergmeier respect human goods, that she remain (or become) a human being dedicated to honoring human goods. For they understand marriage to be a covenant with another human being, a convenant that involves the promise to express one's love sexually only with one's spouse. Sexual intercourse is a special expression of love and intimacy that is appropriate only between spouses. To use one's sexuality in an instrumental way, in a way that treats it simply as a means to acquire goods (in Mrs. Bergmeier's case the good is freedom), is to reduce the meaning of sexuality; it no longer is an expression of love exclusively proper for spouses. Moreover, the Church teaches that children have a right to be the product of the incarnational union of loving spouses. Children ought not to be conceived as a means of winning the goods, such as freedom, that one desires.

Thus, for traditionalists, there is no tautology in the phrase "Do not commit adultery." Again, they do not mean by it "Do not have sexual intercourse with anyone other than one's spouse without sufficiently good reason." Rather they argue that committing adultery always violates the promise that one has made to one's spouse, a promise rooted in the special and exclusive relationship one has with one's spouse. To violate that promise would cause harm to one's moral character; to do something that would harm one's moral character is to do moral wrong. Thus, to have intercourse with one other than one's spouse is to do moral wrong. And since it is wrong to choose to do something immoral to achieve some good, Mrs. Bergmeier makes an immoral choice in choosing to have sexual intercourse with the guard. Later we shall attempt to explain why it is wrong to harm one's moral character. What has been said here should be sufficient to show that because of the different criteria by which they judge moral actions, for revisionists, the norm "Do not commit adultery" truly is a tautology, whereas for traditionalists it is not.

Exceptionless Norms and Circumstances

Another way of describing the debate between the traditionalists and revisionists is to see it as a debate between those who claim that there are exceptionless moral norms and those who think there are not. Yet that this is an accurate description is denied by some. Edward Vacek's description of the revisionist position (here called proportionalism) makes these claims:

Contrary to what its critics say, P [proportionalism] is not opposed to the use of the terms "intrinsic evil," "duty," or "absolute," but it uses these terms only for concrete acts. One ought not—"absolutely" ought not—do an act that is wrong. Such an act is "intrinsically evil." In the sphere of concrete moral decisions, P often is experientially indistinguishable from classical act-deontology. What P refuses to do is use these terms for norms or for classes of acts viewed independently of the agent or the circumstances. "Absolutes" commonly refer to a class of acts that are always prescribed or proscribed, i.e., in all circumstances, at all times, in all places, and for all persons without exception. For P, the word "absolute" is reserved for a particular contingent deed that is objectively required. Since no behavioral norm can foresee or include all the possible combinations of values involved in a concrete deed, absolute behavioral norms unjustifiably exclude consideration of features of an act that may be relevant.[15]

This description seems a proper description of the revisionist position: although there are norms that are practically exceptionless, apart from the concrete situation no definitive absolute determination can be made. As Joseph Fuchs states, "An action cannot be judged morally at all, considered purely in itself, but only together with all the 'circumstances' and the 'intention.' "[16] Still, in spite of the preceding statements, Lisa Cahill claims, "I cannot think of any contemporary moral theologians who repudiate exceptionless moral norms entirely. . . ."[17] She gives a few examples: "Do not kill to gain an inheritance (but do so in self-defense)," "Do not tell a falsehood to evade due punishment (but do so to save an innocent)," and "Do not mutilate a child for sadistic pleasure (but do so as life-saving therapy)."[18] She believes these norms are not norms abstracted from circumstances but are norms that regard acts "plus specific immoral circumstances." What is not clear from Cahill's account is why these particular circumstances make an action always wrong. Without an answer to this question, it seems right to speculate that some other circumstances might override the immorality of the circumstances defining these norms. That is, could one kill to gain an inheritance if one had plans for the money that saved many more lives than the life taken? Could one tell a falsehood to evade a due punishment, if one were on a mission to save many lives?

Saying there are exceptionless moral norms implies that the answer to these questions would be no, but it is not clear why—if balancing likely good consequences of actions is the proper way to determine the morality of actions. Thus, although some revisionists would deny that they would permit the actions described previously, the principles articulated by those who count themselves among the revisionists do seem to allow for these possibilities. Richard McCormick comments on the views of one theorist, Sanford S. Levy, who "is not convinced of the immorality of killing an innocent child to end a war and thus save thousands of lives. I think he is wrong here, but it is difficult to make the point persuasively. It would be instructive to see how he would develop his position. Increasingly I am comfortable with the idea that we cannot adequately explain all cases, that no systematic analysis will cover everything, that it may even be a mistake to expect such clarity."[19] Levy's position that—according to McCormick's principles[20]—it would be right to kill an innocent child to end a war and McCormick's claim that he has only his intuition to guide him that this would be wrong are the kinds of positions that lead many traditionalists to argue that revisionists are ultimately consequentialists and that in spite of protestations to the contrary they cannot sustain a claim that there are exceptionless norms, for it seems always possible to conceive of some situation (however unlikely) for which some circumstances could not be conceived to justify violation of the norm. The claim of some revisionists that there are "virtually" exceptionless norms seems, in its own way, to concede the point.

Cahill's position, though, is somewhat distinct from that of other revisionists in that she believes it is possible to evaluate some actions as types, whereas many revisionists, such as those described by Vacek, seem to think that only concrete particular acts can be evaluated morally. The revisionist claims to judge an action in accord with the intention of the agent, the circumstances, and the consequences of the action and only in reference to the concrete particular. Concrete particular actions are understood as actual events that involve identifiable agents, times, places, and so on. Traditionalists, of course, do not exclude consideration of the con-crete particulars in their evaluations of actions and on occasion find them morally determinative of particular actions, but, again, they believe that some actions can be assessed morally apart from such particulars.

In order to understand these distinctions more clearly, let us use as an example the act of having sexual intercourse with an unwilling partner. Again, for a traditionalist, to know that it is an *unwilling* partner with whom sexual intercourse is to be had is enough to determine that such is an immoral action. The traditionalist does not need to know the name of the agent, the name of the victim, the time or the place or the reason for the rape to be able to judge that this or any act of rape is wrong. He or she knows this action to be *contra naturam*, against both the natural dignity of the persons involved and the nature of human sexual intercourse. But revision-ists seem committed to saying that although it is true that most often (*ut pluribus*) such actions are wrong, until one knows the concrete particulars, no definitive judgment can be made. The revisionist would need to know who the rapist was, who was raped, when and where the rape was committed, and why the rape was performed before he or she could evaluate an action. He or she would allow that although "having sex with an unwilling partner" might have a negative element about it, no final judgment can be made until the concrete situation is known.

And conceivably, such information may be sufficient to lead one to judge the act of "having sex with an unwilling partner" a right and moral choice. For instance, suppose Bill Jones believes that Sue Reed would benefit from having sex with him; suppose Bill is a prison guard and knows that if Sue becomes pregnant she will be released and, for the sake of her family, he wishes to see her released. Or suppose that for some reason thousands of lives would be saved if Bill had sexual intercourse with Sue against her will. Has Bill, then, in forcing Sue to have sexual intercourse with him, done a good deed? (The traditional way of viewing Bill's act would assess his exterior act as immoral and his motive, though not his complete action, as good; more about this later.) Suppose even that Bill is successful; that she does become pregnant, is released, and is euphoric to be home with her family; or that thousands of lives are in fact saved. Has Bill, then, done a good deed? Well certainly, if all these things came to pass, one might allow that his act had good consequences, but the traditional way of reasoning would conclude that, nonetheless, no matter how good the consequences, Bill was wrong to have sexual intercourse with Sue against her will. Revisionists generally consider rape to be a virtually exceptionless moral norm,[21] but it seems that it is possible to conceive of circumstances in which more good than evil might result even from rape. I have chosen this example to illustrate what I believe to be the logical conclusion of the revisionist position, a conclusion that they most likely would not readily accept, but that I believe their principles yield.

In spite of possible disagreements of the kind explored, it nonetheless remains true that traditionalists and revisionists would agree on how to evaluate most concrete particular moral choices of such actions as having sexual intercourse with one who is not one's spouse and having sexual intercourse with an unwilling partner. They may be equally appalled at news that Joe Morris, father of six, has left his hard-working, devoted, loving wife, Rachel, to have an affair with the foxy Linda Cress or that the brutal Dan Miller raped the lovely Jane Everett. But there are many classes of actions that would not find the same kind of response from traditionalists and revisionists. Contraception is certainly one of them: traditionalists condemn all uses of contraception, whereas it seems that revisionists, although perhaps condemning contraception used for selfish reasons, would judge that many couples would have good reason to use it.

The Principle of Double Effect

The principle of double effect is also an essential tool of traditional act analysis and one that has been modified by revisionists. This principle clarifies how to decide what to do when one is faced with an action that has both good and bad effects. This principle is discussed in Chapter 3 insofar as it has been used to justify the use of contraception for therapeutic reasons. Revisionists, however, use some of the principles of double effect to justify the deliberate choice to perform actions that are or result in "premoral evils." Let us see how they do so.

First let us briefly review what the principle of double effect is. It gives four conditions that must be met if one is morally to choose to perform an action that has bad effects as well as good ones:

1. The external action performed (that is, the object of the moral act) must be either morally good or at least not morally wrong in itself.

2. The good effect must not be produced through the bad effect (in other words, the bad effect must not be directly intended as a means to the good effect).

3. The good effect and not the bad effect must not be directly intended by the agent.

4. There must be a proportionately grave reason for permitting the foreseen bad effect to occur.

This principle is particularly useful for medical ethics since so many medical procedures involve actions with good and bad effects. A common example is the removal of a fetus from the fallopian tube. The fallopian tube ruptures and the woman dies if the fetus is not removed. The fallopian tube is not a natural or fitting place for the fetus; it has no chance of surviving in the tube. One is not intending the death of the fetus when one removes it; rather one is intending to save the life of the woman. This action is justified because saving a woman's life is a morally good intention (criterion 1) and is a proportionate good to the loss of the baby's life (criterion 4); the clearing of the tube is an acceptable surgical procedure (and would be performed for any other growth in the tube) (criterion 1), and the death of the child is an indirect result of the clearing of the tube: it is not a "means" to clearing the tube or to saving the woman's life (criterion 2). And the death of the child is not what one would have chosen (it is not the intended end, criterion 3). The death of the child is an unintended and indirect side effect of the clearing of the tube. This principle does not justify deliberately killing a baby so that its mother might live (or deliberately killing a mother so that a baby might live) since these actions would be using an immoral means to a good end.

Much of revisionist theology has grown out of a reinterpretation of the principle of double effect.[22] Many claim that the most important criterion of this principle is the fourth: that one must have a "proportionate reason" for performing an action that has bad effects as well as good. They also generally reject the distinction between direct and indirect causing of evil. But what remains most important is their claim that no actions fit in the category of acts that are in themselves against the moral order; no acts are intrinsically wrong. They claim that the principle of double effect justifies choosing actions that have evil effects if one has a proportionate reason. They claim that just as the principle of double effect justifies killing in self-defense, so, too, it could be used to justify such actions as contraception and masturbation if there were a proportionate reason.

It seems, though, that revisionists misunderstand the traditionalist position; traditionalists are not saying that "killing" is a premoral evil that is justified in such circumstances as those that require one to defend oneself. Rather, traditionalists argue that "killing" is an action that in itself is not morally good or evil but that further information must be acquired to determine when killing is bad.[23] Certainly, traditionalists share with revisionists the view that any action that causes the death of another, any act of killing, obviously would rarely be justified, for there are few instances in which the good to be gained is proportionate to the evil of the death of another. Killing in self-defense (and killing for other reasons may be justified, too) is an occasion when the good to be gained is proportionate to the good endangered. But it must also be noted that the life lost in justifiable killing in self-defense must be that of the individual who is threatening one's own life. This principle is not based on the view that one life is equal in value to another but on the view that innocent life deserves defense against one threatening that life. The calculation is not just of one life for another but it is a consideration of justice that is essentially at work in an act of justifiable self-defense.

The principle of double effect serves to justify killing in self-defense in this way: The life of Alice is threatened by Bill, who wants to kill Alice to get her inheritance. It is good and right for Alice to defend herself, for her life is a good worth protecting. Were Alice to shoot Bill in order to defend herself her action would have two effects, one good and one bad; her life would be saved, but Bill's life would be lost. What justifies Alice's shooting of Bill is not that her life is "worth more" than his (she may be terminally ill and he a scientist who alone is capable of discovering a cure for AIDS). What is crucial to the moral analysis is that she is innocent of wrongdoing and thus not deserving to die and that he is guilty of wrongdoing and has thus put himself in a situation in which he is risking his own life. Alice's shooting of Bill is a justifiable means to the effect, or end of her saving her life, a means that has the double effect of threatening Bill's life. But the point here is not that a life has been balanced against a life but that an *innocent* life has been protected from a malevolent threat.

This point can be clarified by noting that it is not permissible to kill someone who is not threatening one's life even if one thereby preserves one's own. If a terrorist commanded a hostage, Alfred, to kill another hostage, Bob, and threatened to kill Alfred if he refused, Alfred would not be justified in killing Bob. Nor would he be justified if the terrorist threatened to kill both Alfred and Bob, if Alfred would not kill Bob. The killing of Bob by Alfred would be an action of "directly killing an innocent human being" that is always morally evil or intrinsically wrong and, thus, can never be chosen as an action, no matter what good effects might come from this act. Bob has done nothing worthy of losing his life and thus to kill him would be not a justifiable act of self-defense but unjust killing.

To say that the justification of killing in "self-defense" is to allow an evil means to pursue a good end, is, then, based on a misreading of the justification of self-defense made by the traditionalist. The traditionalist on occasion allows actions that may result in the death of human beings but never permits an "evil" killing for good ends. Thus, it cannot be said that since the traditionalist allows the "premoral" act of killing on occasion, so too should the traditionalist allow such "premoral" acts as contracepted acts of sexual intercourse, homosexual sexual intercourse, and masturbation. The traditionalist does not put these actions in the category of acts such as killing that cannot be morally defined until further specified. Rather, the traditionalist claims that a parallel is better made between "murder" and "contracepted sexual intercourse, and so on." (One hopes it is not necessary to note that murder is a much greater evil than contraception, and so on. Traditionalists claim that "murder" (maliciously killing a human being) and "contraception" (deliberately rendering infertile an act of sexual intercourse) are actions that can be specified as immoral apart from any circumstances, whereas "killing a human being" cannot be so specified. The traditionalist argues that no application of the double effect would serve to justify the choice to murder. So, too, the traditionalist argues that "contraception, and so on," are the kinds of acts that cannot be justified by the principle of double effect, for one cannot choose an immoral means to a moral end. More will be said about this understanding of "contraception, and so on," later; here the intent is simply to show why a simple appeal to the traditionalist acceptance of killing in self-defense does not serve to justify committing other acts that also generally have bad effects.

Now that we have painted the larger picture of the dimensions of the debate between the traditionalists and the revisionists, let us attempt to focus on some of the more refined points of analysis that may be at the root of the larger disagreements. Let us now review Aquinas's criteria for evaluating the morality of an action. It is, of course, impossible to do complete justice to the complexity of Aquinas's analysis here, but if we keep in mind its main framework we may be able to get closer to the crux of the difference between the revisionists and the traditionalists.

Aquinas's Analysis of Moral Action

Revisionists routinely speak of the evaluation of the *whole* act, as though parts of a human action add up to one complete act that can be evaluated morally. They allow that there may be evil, premoral evil, in one part of an action but that this evil may be justified by the good being pursued. It is extremely important to note that Aquinas *does not evaluate an action as a whole.* He does not evaluate the different "parts" of an action—the "intention," the "object," the "circumstances," and the "end"—and then add up these evaluations to determine the morality of an action as a whole. Nor does he focus on any one of these parts singly and allow that one part to determine the moral evaluation of the whole act. Indeed, in his view actions are not wholes made up of parts; rather, they are wholes that are subject to analysis by several different criteria: the criteria of intention, object, and so forth. Aquinas does not speak of the morality of the whole act; rather he maintains that there is a fourfold goodness in human action: "The first is the goodness an action has in terms of its genus, namely, as an action, for it has as much of goodness as it has of action and being, as we have said. Second, an action has goodness according to its species, which it has from its appropriate object. Third, it has goodness from its circumstances— its accidents as it were. Fourth, it has goodness from its end, which is related to it as a cause of its goodness." He goes on to say: "Nothing prevents an action from being good in one of the ways mentioned above, and not in another. Thus it is possible that an action which is good according to its species or according to circumstances be ordered to a bad end, and vice versa. But an act is not good absolutely unless it is good in all ways, for 'evil results from any one defect, while good results from the whole cause,' as Dionysius says" (*Summa Theologiae* I–II, q. 18, art. 4)[24] When Aquinas speaks of an action being "good absolutely" he means that the action must be judged to be good in accord with all criteria proper for judging a moral action. If an action is bad in any respect it cannot be good absolutely. But acts may be good in some respects and bad in others. There is no formula for weighing which respects are more important and then finally determining the morality of the "whole."

It is no longer customary to speak of an action having a genus, species, accident, and end, but what Aquinas means by these terms is not so very difficult to understand, at least in a general way. Of an action defective in its genus or being, Aquinas gives the example of a blind man who limps and swerves as he walks; his "walking" is deprived of the "being" proper to walking (*Summa Theologiae* I–II, q. 18, art. 1). Thus one could speak of an act of robbing a bank as "good" (*bonum*) insofar as the robbery was successful. One could also speak of a failed rescue attempt of an individual trapped in a burning building as a "bad" act (*malum*), insofar as it was unsuccessful. This is the realm, in fact, where Aquinas would be inclined to use the phrase *ontic evil* to refer simply to the action apart from any moral considerations that might impute moral guilt to the agent for the success or failure of his action.

The terms *object, circumstances,* and *end* will also need some explaining. In brief, the object is the act itself, the action itself (the external act) that the agent intends; the circumstances involve such considerations as the time, place, and manner of the act, which may or may not have significant bearing on its morality (and which may, on occasion, lose their "circumstantial" status and "enter into" or define the object of the act). The end is the *final* intention (there is an intermediate intention in regard to the object, for one intends the object as a means to the end) or purpose for which one undertakes an action. For instance, one may give alms (object, or external act) to a poor man in the public square (circumstances) for the purpose of winning public office (the end). Aquinas's discussion of these terms reveals that they all contribute to the moral evaluation of the act.

Aquinas asks whether the act has its species of good or evil from its end (*Summa Theologiae* I–II, q. 18, art. 6). Aquinas speaks of the end where we more often speak of the intention or reason for the action. Aquinas's word is perhaps more useful since acts have more than one intention. This is an extremely important point and one that is often neglected in discussion of the moral evaluation of an action. The following passage from Aquinas may help us see this more clearly:

Acts are called human insofar as they are voluntary, as we have said. Now there is a twofold act in voluntary action: the interior act of the will and the external act; and each of these has its object. The end is properly the object of the interior act of the will, while that with which the exterior act is concerned is its object. Hence just as the exterior act receives its species from the object it is concerned with, so the interior act of the will receives its species from the end, which is its proper object.

Now that which is on the part of the will is related as form to that which is on the part of the exterior act, for the will uses members as instruments for action; furthermore exterior acts are not counted as moral except insofar as they are voluntary. The species of a human act, therefore, is considered formally in terms of the end, but materially in terms of the object of the external act. Hence the Philosopher says that "he who steals in order to commit adultery is, properly speaking more an adulterer than a thief." (*Summa Theologiae* I–II, q. 18, art. 6)

The terminology in this passage is fairly technical and entangled; what is most important to note is that the will has two (at least two) intentions for each moral action, that which intends the object or external act and that which intends the end (the purpose or motive). The example that Aquinas gives at the end of the passage cited serves to illustrate the contention that an action has two intentions (at least) and thus possibly two moral evaluations. One who steals to commit adultery is *more* of an adulterer (for this was the end of his act) than a thief (the object was to steal), but it is extremely important to note that he is *both* a thief and an adulterer for he intended both to steal and to commit adultery. In the next article Aquinas speaks of the act as having two moral evaluations. To illustrate, he states, "We say that someone who steals in order to commit adultery is guilty of two evils in one act" (*Summa Theologiae* I–II, q. 18, art. 7). His mention of a man's stealing in order to give alms also suggests that giving alms is a good end but that stealing is evil; the end of giving alms does not render the act of stealing moral; this act is both good and evil, in different respects (see also q. 20, art. 1).

Aquinas clearly allows that the end/intention/purpose enters into the moral evaluation of an action. But clearly this is not the only criterion that determines the evaluation; the "object" (external act, or means) also determines the moral evaluation of an action. Note from the preceding discussion of the end that in Aquinas's view the moral evaluation of the object can be independent of and different from the moral evaluation of the end, for it too is a voluntarily intended human action. What is this "object"?

The object is what gives an act its species (*Summa Theologiae* I–II, q. 18, art. 5). It is important to note that Aquinas distinguishes between the natural species of an act and the moral species of an act. For example, having sexual intercourse with one's mistress and having sexual intercourse with one's wife are the same act in respect to their object in one respect—in respect to their natural species: they are both acts of generation. But morally, since the object of the acts can be evaluated as being in accord with right reason or against right reason, they are in different species. The first is an act of adultery, an evil act; the second, an act of conjugal love, a good act. Aquinas notes that an act takes its "primary goodness [or first goodness: *prima bonitas*] from the appropriateness of its object" (*Summa Theologiae* I–II, q. 18, art. 2). What does this mean? The translation of "primary" for *prima* may be somewhat misleading, for primary is ambiguous in English; it can mean both "first" and "most important". *Prima* here does seem to mean "most important"; it seems to mean "first" in the sense that one already has a first evaluation of the moral act simply by knowing the object, apart from any information about the other features of the act. A simplistic but perhaps useful way to think of the "object" of an act is to think of it as what could be described by any observer who does not know the intention of the agent. If one were to see someone bash in the head of a small child, one could safely judge the action to be immoral. As kinds of actions, however, some actions are not specifiable morally without further information: Aquinas gives the examples of picking up a leaf or taking a walk (*Summa Theologiae* I–II, q. 18, art. 8). Revisionists hold that all actions are of this indifferent sort—we can only know them as premoral, ontic, or physical acts—and claim that one needs to know the circumstances or the end in order to know how to evaluate the act. But Aquinas would say that this information would enable us to define the object more precisely and thus to arrive at a moral evaluation (more will be said momentarily about "specifying circumstances"). For instance, if the one who is taking a walk is a man guilty of a crime and escaping from prison, we may have enough information to evaluate his action morally; we need not know his intention or the circumstances. To explain what counts as a circumstance and what enters into the object is difficult (and will be attempted momentarily), but what is important to note is that whereas Aquinas holds that some acts are morally specifiable by their object *as kinds* (he gives making use of what is one's own as an example of an action that is good of its kind and taking what belongs to another as an example of an action that is evil of its kind [*Summa Theologiae* I–II, q. 18, art. 2], the revisionists hold that no acts are morally specifiable as kinds of actions.

Although the act does take its primary goodness from its object, as noted previously, an act can have more than one moral evaluation. Acts that are good by their nature and acts that are evil by their nature can be performed for good or bad ends. We spoke earlier about those who steal (an act bad in respect to its object) in order to give alms (a good end); one could also give alms (an act good in respect to its object) for bad purposes (say, with the final intention of exploiting those one has helped).

An action that is otherwise good can be marred because of the circumstances. *Circumstances* as used by Aquinas (also known as accidents) is a much broader term than it is in our customary usage: it refers to such considerations as performing an action at the right time, in the right place, in the right manner. For instance, one might give alms in such a way as to embarrass the recipient. This defect in manner then would render an act that is good in itself, that is, apart from the circumstances, an imperfect moral act. One is still giving alms, but one is not doing so in the right manner. Thus, in respect to manner of giving, one has done something wrong, but not in respect to the object of one's act.

But some circumstances do not simply "mar" an otherwise good action: as mentioned, they transform the very object or species of the action. These "circumstances" strictly speaking are no longer circumstances for they are not accidents. Aquinas maintains, "A circumstance, taken precisely as a circumstance, does not give an act its species, since it is an accident; but to the extent it becomes a principal condition of the object, it can give species to an act" (*Summa Theologiae* I–II, q. 18, art. 10, ad. 2). There is no technical term for such "specifying circumstances," but they are considerations that cause one kind of action no longer to be that kind of action but to become another kind; let us call them *circumstances[2]*. Aquinas gives the example of stealing from a sacred place, which, because of the circumstance[2] of place, makes this action not simply stealing but sacrilege (*Summa Theologiae* I–II, q. 18, art. 10). Thus circum-stance[2] "enters into" or specifies the object. One viewing some-one's stealing from a sacred place would not have given a full description of all the morally relevant features of the act until he included that the stealing was "from a sacred place." Another exam-ple might make this way of defining an action even clearer. For instance, it is moral for a spouse to have sexual intercourse with his or her spouse, but one must have it in the right time, in the right manner, at the right place, and so on. To have sex with one's spouse in the public square or when the spouse is unwilling to have sex becomes immoral because of circumstance[2]. One is no longer simply having sexual intercourse with one's spouse but performing a radically *different sort* of action: one is now engaging in an action that in the one case may be termed "exhibitionism" and in the other "rape." In these cases the circumstance[2] is no longer considered among the accidents of the act: it is now a feature of the act serving to define its very nature.

Here, too, perhaps, we should note the role of consequences in Aquinas's moral evaluation of an act. Critics of the traditional method of evaluating moral acts have claimed that it does not take into account their consequences. This is untrue. But as with other features of Aquinas's analysis, his response to consequences is more subtle than the dictum that one must do whatever will maximize the good consequences and minimize the bad ones. Aquinas distin-guishes between consequences of several different kinds (*Summa Theologiae* I–II, q. 20, art. 5): He distinguishes consequences that follow per se from the kind of act that it is and for the most part from those that follow accidentally and seldom from one's actions. Having sex with an unwilling partner, for example, has the per se effect of violating the dignity of the agent, of endangering the physical and psychological well-being of the victim, and of jeopardiz-ing the well-being of any future offspring engendered through this act. If there is also good that results from this act—a pregnant woman being released from prison, or thousands of lives being saved—these are "accidental" effects and not those that are per se part of the kind of act that this is. Aquinas maintains that an act is to be judged according to its per se effects, not its accidental effects.

A Comparison with the Revisionists

Now let us return to a comparison with the views of the revisionists. Revisionists, again, hold that, although apart from concrete particular situations some actions may entail premoral evil or ontic evil, no decisive moral judgment may be made of these actions until all their circumstances and purposes are assessed. Again, most revisionists would agree with the traditional condemnation of such actions as adultery, rape, and murder, but they would do so not because these actions are the kind of actions that by their nature violate the goods of human nature, but because they have an overwhelming negative element, generally unidentified but most likely in respect to their consequences, that makes them unworthy to be chosen. But there is a set of actions about which the traditionalists and the revisionists tend to disagree regularly and sometimes radically. Among these actions are the three that we have been considering as a group: contracepted sexual acts, homosexual sexual acts, and masturbation.

Lisa Cahill identifies the traditional condemnation of contracepted acts, homosexual sexual acts, and masturbation as the very kinds of norms under challenge by the revisionists. She describes them as "norms which prohibit a physical act abstracted from circumstances":

Examples are: "Do not use artificial contraception," "Do not masturbate," "Do not abort a fetus." Now we are in much more controversial territory, though perhaps not so controversial as might at first appear. It is agreed, even by revisionists, both that these actions generally are to be avoided, and that not just any sort of reason can justify them. But the question of those who are inclined to revise our traditional understanding of these norms as absolute is whether there are *any* reasons which can justify such acts, e.g., artificial contraception to preserve a woman's health, abortion to save her life, or masturbation as part of medical investigation of and therapy for infertility.

Rather than taking the physical act as the equivalent of a *moral* norm, some would see it as an evil which is "premoral," "ontic," "material," or "physical." Now this is not to say that a "premoral evil" is morally neutral. To the contrary, it is regarded as something generally not fulfilling for human nature, and indeed harmful to it. It always counts as a negative factor in a total moral evaluation. But taken by itself, it is not morally *decisive.* Completion of the evaluation of which it is a part depends on other factors as well. Although there is a presumption that the premoral evil will be avoided, it can be justified in exceptional cases, when there is sufficient reason in the form of an even higher good at stake than that safeguarded by the norm.[25]

First, it is interesting to note that revisionists do acknowledge that there is some evil in such acts as contraception, masturbation, and aborting a fetus. Are they physical evils? The death of the fetus makes clear the evil in abortion, but what is the evil in contraception and masturbation? Is the evil of contraception that it prohibits fertility from achieving its natural/proper end of procreation (does this smack too much of "physicalism"?)? Is it that contraception harms the symbolism of "self-giving" that should be a part of every loving conjugal act? McCormick notes that calls for simple, easily reversible, cheap, medically safe, and so on, contraceptives indicate that disvalues are involved.[26] Is he suggesting that if these demands were met, there would be no disvalue? Why is masturbation a premoral evil that ought to be avoided? Because the sexual organs have a purpose or purposes (procreation and interpersonal expression of conjugal love) that it violates? Although the revisionists regularly allow that contraception and masturbation are "premoral evils," "ontic evils," or "disvalues," they have failed to make sufficiently clear what the evil is in these acts. If these acts and the evil they entail are to be avoided and tolerated only in the pursuit or protection of greater goods, it would seem that a proper evaluation can be made only if one knows what goods one is sacrificing when contracepting or masturbating.

Cahill acknowledges what we have noted earlier: that a legitimate criticism of the revisionists' perspective is that certain key terms such as *value term, premoral evil,* and *physical evil* are not defined clearly enough.[27] And this, I believe, is one of the chief reasons why she and other revisionists do not see that *masturbation* and *contraception* are terms not categorically different from *blasphemy, perjury,* and *murder.* Earlier Cahill stated, "There is a confusion inherent in the way the notion of 'intrinsic evil' traditionally has been explicated. Standard lists of examples tend to include terms which are not really all of the same sort, e.g., 'blasphemy, perjury, masturbation, and murder.' Obviously 'masturbation' denotes a specific physical action apart from accompanying circumstances, while the other three assert that the sometimes licit acts of speaking God's name, telling an untruth, and homicide are accompanied by circumstances which make them immoral."[28] Cahill's claim "Obviously 'masturbation' denotes a specific physical action apart from accompanying circumstances" would not be obvious to a traditionalist (this point will be explained momentarily), for it could be described as the "physical" act of sexual stimulation with the "accompanying circumstance" of being performed by one's self. But, still, in the traditionalist understanding these circumstances are of the circumstances[2] type; they become part of the definition of the action. Such actions then are considered by the tradition to be defined *apart* from circumstances that would be more accidental factors; for instance, *where* one masturbates may or may not enter into the evaluation of the act.

It is also important to note that Cahill here exhibits the revisionist tendency to understand condemnation of such actions as blasphemy as a tautology. She understands *blasphemy* to mean "an immoral use of God's name" and its condemnation to be a tautology. Earlier we considered the difference between the revisionist and the traditionalist understanding of adultery. The difference in the evaluation of blasphemy follows the same lines. A traditionalist understands blasphemy not to mean an immoral use of God's name but an irreverent use of God's name. The judgment that blasphemy is wrong depends on a judgment that God is the kind of entity who deserves to be revered. The condemnation of blasphemy is not a tautology.

Let us here consider the possibility that masturbation and homosexual acts of sexual intercourse and contraception are (1) not descriptions of physical acts only and (2) not tautologies. Let us consider the possibility that like the words *adultery* and *murder* and *blasphemy* they are actions that are condemned because when they are assessed in terms of their coherence with human goods, they are judged to be actions that by their very nature violate a good. Thus, they are actions that humans should never deliberately choose. For instance, murder violates the good of just interaction between humans; blasphemy violates Man's relationship with God; and adultery violates the goods of marriage.

What is masturbation? Described simply as a physical act it is the touching or rubbing of one's own genital organs. This physical act clearly is permissible in some circumstances; for instance, of course, to maintain cleanliness. But obviously not all touching of one's genital organs is masturbation, so the first description offered is inadequate. Is a proper description of masturbation then, "touching of one's genitals that results in sexual stimulation"? No, for one might experience unintended sexual arousal while cleaning one's self. By masturbation is meant "touching of one's own genital organs *for the purpose* of experiencing stimulation that would be no part of a completed act of heterosexual intercourse" (even if there are other ends—bad or good—also intended, such as showing off or collecting sperm for a fertility test). Now experiencing sexual arousal is not in itself bad; indeed in many contexts it is good. What makes it immoral to be responsible for arousing one's self sexually? Because for genital sexual activity for human beings to be good it must be interpersonal; the nature of human sexual activity properly pursued is that it fosters intimacy between spouses and it also is the means for transmitting human life. Solitary sexual activity achieves neither of these ends. To prefer one's momentary physical pleasure is to reject the goods authentically allied with human sexual activity. The evil of masturbation is not that it causes "physical evil"; it is that it is not an action in accord with authentically human sexual activity. Solitary sexual stimulation does not enable one to develop the virtues fostered by spousal sexual intercourse, the virtues, for instance, of generous self-giving, of showing loving concern for another, of assuming the responsibilities that accompany sexual activity. Conceivably it would not be unusual for masturbators to become withdrawn, selfish, and irresponsible, for theoretically the actions in which they engage promote such qualities.

What physical, ontic, or premoral evil is involved in homosexual sexual intercourse? Is intercourse between members of the same sex physically or premorally evil because it is between members of the same sex, rather than the opposite sex? Where is the physical or ontic or premoral evil there? Is it because the genital organs of members of the same sex are not designed for fully satisfactory sexual intercourse? Is it because members of the same sex cannot provide the same psychosexual satisfaction to each other as members of the opposite sex? Traditionalists argue that all of these deficiencies of homosexual intercourse are not the definitive reasons that homosexual intercourse is wrong but are rather the kind of effects one would expect from a wrong action. Homosexual intercourse is wrong because it, like masturbation, does not fulfill the requirements for authentically human sexual activity. Authentically human sexual activity must be expressive of conjugal love and open to the possibility and responsibility of children. Such love is possible only for members of the opposite sex; for humans to choose another kind of sexual intercourse is to choose sexual intercourse that is not authentically human. Whatever is not authentically human is immoral and diminishes or damages the moral character of human beings.

Let us now finally turn to contraception. Revisionists generally allow that there is some negative element or premoral or physical evil in contracepted sexual intercourse.[29] They see this strictly as a physical or premoral evil. Knauer says of contraception, "That a marital act lose its procreative power is a purely physical evil which does not constitute a human act without further content."[30] Most revisionists would consider this physical evil slight and one that ought readily to be tolerated for the sake of other goods such as harmony in a marriage or relief from fear of pregnancy. But traditionalists would not find the evil of contraception a slight one, and, depending on how Knauer is using *physical* (here he seems to be talking of a diminution of the biological power of sex), they would not agree that the use of contraception is just a physical act and not one that engages the whole of the human person. Rather they understand that spouses using contraception for the very purpose of thwarting the procreative power of sex are acting directly against the good of procreation and union. If one uses drugs or devices for the very purpose of thwarting one's procreative capacities, then one is contracepting (contra-conception: [acting] *against* conception); one is deliberately and directly acting against a good inherent in human sexuality. This argument is not based simply on a "perverted faculty" argument, which simply forbids any behavior that prohibits a human physical function from performing in its natural way. The traditionalist holds that rejecting the procreative power and meaning of sexual intercourse is not rejecting some small and insignificant good; it is not just a bemoaning that a sperm did not meet an egg as it otherwise might have. Rather, as Chapters 3 and 4 argue, the procreative meaning of sexual intercourse goes far beyond the good of the reproduction of the species. Once the sperm meets the egg, a new human being exists and with it all that that new life represents, as a good in itself, as a good for the spouses and their relationship, for society and for God's kingdom. The procreative meaning of human sexuality goes far beyond the need to actualize physiological powers: it reflects one's view of the value of life; it reflects one's willingness to cooperate with God; it reflects the type of unitive relationship one wishes to have with one's spouse. To violate this meaning is to do much more than to cause some slight, "purely physical evil."

Traditionalists argue that the refusal to accept and honor fundamental human goods, the willingness to sacrifice these goods in pursuit of other goods, causes great damage to the moral character of Man. Being faithful to the goods that promote what is most fundamentally good for Man is to nourish one's moral character. The traditional analysis, here represented primarily by Aquinas, then, has a complicated and sophisticated mode of analyzing moral actions. For all the effort made by the tradition to understand the moral complexity of human actions, it would be wrong to conclude that the greatest concern in moral analysis is the act. Rather, the chief interest of the tradition is in the person, the acting person and his or her moral character. The focus of Aquinas's moral analysis, for all the attention paid to the act chosen, is not on the act but on the agent. The chief concern is what kind of a person the agent becomes in choosing this kind of act. For Aquinas, the question is, Is Man conforming his will to God's will? The main thrust of this question is not meant to suggest that Man must be wholly submissive to the power of God, though this may be true enough. Rather it is to say that Man's will should become like God's will: that is, a will that chooses only what is good. Man is made in the image of God and perfects himself only through acting in imitation of God's goodness. Only the briefest of explanations of this view is possible here, but even that may help us see how crucial this point is to traditional moral philosophy.

Again, the preceding analysis of Aquinas's method of evaluating moral action has focused on the act, but the importance of the act is not in its consequences or even in its nature: the importance of being able to evaluate an action correctly lies in the effect of that action on the character or the soul of the agent who is choosing. The focus on the action in the *Summa Theologiae* follows many questions that address the question of Man's happiness, both his natural happiness and his eternal salvation. Aquinas speaks of "rectitude of the will" as being necessary for happiness and salvation (*Summa Theologiae* I–II, q. 5, art. 7). The primary concern is that agents choose only those actions that will improve their moral character, not those that will worsen it; actions that will contribute to their being virtuous, not to their being vicious. Paul Quay explains:

Strictly speaking, *no* free act is ever a choice of an existent good, of some pleasurable being or action, or of some person to be loved. Instead, every free choice is a choice of *oneself as related in a given way to this concrete good.* If I seek to make fully explicit the object of my choice, I cannot merely say that I am choosing an apple in preference to an orange. I choose, rather, to take an apple instead of an orange to eat it, or to look at it. More fully still, I choose to be the sort of person who takes or eats or looks at this apple, while knowing that oranges are available. So, John does not, in a strict sense, choose Joan as his wife but chooses to become that kind of person that is himself having entered into marital relationship with Joan.

   The full object, then, is not some concrete good in itself, but oneself as focussed on this good through a relation of seeking it or being ordered towards it, of possessing it corporeally or spiritually, of exercise (say, if the good is an activity chosen for itself, e.g., playing a game, contemplating a painting or mountain, praising God), of fruition, or of union.[31]

Joseph Boyle speaks of moral action as "soul-making" or "self-making." He asserts that for the Christian, "morality is primarily in the heart." He goes on to explain:

It seems . . . that our role in building up the kingdom is primarily a matter of "soul making" or "self making"; it is, less metaphorically, a matter of building up the persons and the interpersonal relationships which are now and forever will be part of the kingdom. This is part of what is meant by the idea that, for the Christian, morality is primarily in the heart. For it is our very selves—both individually and in communion—that are now already, and will be perfectly when the Lord comes, integral parts of the kingdom. And these selves are constituted by our free choices, by what we love and how we set out hearts.[32]

Ultimately the point is that human beings harm their moral character when they deliberately choose actions that they know to be evil.
Individuals form their moral character through their moral choices;
bad moral choices foster vice in the human character and good
moral choices foster virtue. For humans nothing is more important
than to form a good moral character for themselves; it is this character that will make them worthy members of human society, it is this
character that will gain them any true happiness that they will enjoy
in this world, it is this character that makes them eligible for eternal
union with God. As the statement by Boyle suggests, humans must
be perfect as God the Father is perfect; they must exercise their
freedom responsibly; for instance, since God would not choose to
do that which has per se evil effects, neither must Man do so.
Christianity has always taught that one should never do evil so that
good may come of it. This principle simply states the preceding
analysis of human action more succinctly: a good end does not justify
an evil object or means. As many of the traditionalists have argued,
the importance of this dictum resides in the formation of the human
person that results from the deliberate choice to do evil: to choose
evil deliberately is to set one's heart on what one knows to be wrong;
it is to form oneself into an individual who has not yet formed his
or her will to be a will that refuses to choose evil; perhaps an
individual has not yet the courage or love or fidelity to be faithful
to the good that he or she knows, or perhaps one has an intellect
that is confused and not a good guide for the will. But, again, the
traditionalist claims that since God does not choose evil to achieve
good ends, neither should Man. To do so is to *presume* to know that
the evil consequences we foresee and/or fear are so great that we are
justified in choosing to do what we do know to be evil to avoid or
prevent these evil consequences. It is to commit again the sin of
Eve; it is to be so proud as to believe that the good that we hope or
expect will come out of our choice justifies the evil choice that we
know we are making.

Chapter 8 explains more fully how contraception adversely affects
human moral character and how living by the teachings of *Humanae
Vitae* strengthens and ennobles human moral character. But let the
preceding discussion serve to explain why traditionalists believe
that the evil involved in contraception is not just a "physical,"

"premoral," or "ontic" evil. Rather, it is an evil that when deliberately chosen strikes a blow at the very goods that make human existence the noble and worthy endeavor that it is. Evils of this nature are called *intrinsic evils*. In choosing to do intrinsic evils, Man is striking a blow at his own dignity; he is sacrificing what should be the ultimate goal of all his actions: a moral character that can discern and be faithful to the goods that are most authentically human.

The very name that is now worn by those who challenge the tradition, *revisionists*, seems to suggest that for the most part they accept the tradition in which they find themselves and that the changes that they recommend are slight alterations and improvements on the tradition. The preceding analysis began by attempting to demonstrate that the revisionists do not share with the traditionalists a fundamental understanding of the proper method of analyzing moral actions. It has ended with the suggestion that they do not share the traditionalist view of what evils are caused by certain acts, what goods are protected by certain acts. The acts that most concern us here are, of course, acts of contracepted sexual intercourse between spouses. We have begun to see why the traditionalists do not think that these acts cause only some fairly slight "physical" or "premoral" evil, but that they strike at the moral ordination of the human character.

Let us now turn to the writings of Pope John Paul II, who has deeply pondered how contraceptive intercourse harms Man's moral character and how Man becomes more authentically human by his respectful honoring of his procreative powers.

EIGHT

Self-Giving and Self-Mastery: John Paul II's Interpretation of *Humanae Vitae*

T HE MOST energetic proponent and expositor of the doctrine of *Humanae Vitae* in recent years has been Pope John Paul II. In a series of talks given over a period of six years (1979–84), he has laid out an anthropology both philosophically and biblically based that has provided the foundation for his reflections on *Humanae Vitae*.[1] Two of his earlier major works, *Love and Responsibility* (1960) and *The Acting Person* (1969), were foundational for much of the thinking exhibited in this series of talks, as was *Familiaris Consortio* (1981).[2] In *Familiaris Consortio* he issued a "pressing invitation" to theologians "to unite their efforts in order to collaborate with the hierarchical Magisterium and to commit themselves to the task of illustrating ever more clearly the biblical foundations, the ethical grounds and the personalistic reasons behind this doctrine [on proper regulation of family size]."[3] This invitation seems to be based on the call from Vatican II that ethics be better grounded in Scripture: "Let special care be put into perfecting moral theology, so that its scientific exposition, better nourished on the teaching of Sacred Scripture, may shed light on the dignity of the vocation of the faithful in Christ and on their obligation to bear fruit in charity for the life of the world."[4] It may be said that John Paul has led the way in answering this invitation. The more strictly philosophical lines of his argument have been sketched in Chapter 4; here we shall consider the fuller dimensions of his defense of *Humanae Vitae*, which will include theological as well as philosophical considerations.

Much of this chapter will be devoted to explaining such passages as the following: "Man is precisely a person because he is master of himself and has self-control. Indeed insofar as he is master of himself he can 'give himself' to the other. And it is this dimension—the dimension of the liberty of the gift—which becomes essential and decisive for that 'language of the body,' in which man and woman reciprocally express themselves in the conjugal union. Granted that this is communion of persons, the 'language of the body' should be judged according to the criterion of the truth."[5] Many of the most important themes of John Paul's teaching on *Humanae Vitae* are contained in this passage. Self-mastery, marriage as a mutual "giving of self" by the spouses, marriage as a "communion of persons," and the need for truthful "language of the body" are characteristic phrases and themes employed by John Paul. His exposition of these is permeated and supported by an explanation of personalistic values and by extensive exegesis of a few key biblical passages. He also draws regularly on the documents of Vatican II, particularly *Gaudium et Spes,* to support his points. Our presentation of his views will draw on all these sources.

Let us note at the outset that John Paul's understanding of natural law and of personalist values permits no conflict between them. His commitment to explaining the Church's teaching on sexuality in terms of personalist values should not be taken as a rejection or abandonment of natural law reasoning, for all his writings indicate that he finds tight links among natural law reasoning, personalist values, and self-mastery or chastity. Yet, certainly John Paul places the primary focus in his teachings on sexuality, on the human person.

Our intent to explicate John Paul's reflections on *Humanae Vitae* as stated in such passages as that cited is not without its difficulties. As noted, he sets forth the principles of his thinking in widely disparate works, from his very philosophical *The Acting Person* to his weekly audiences. The weekly audience talks make difficult any systematic presentation of his views since they involve much repetition of earlier discussions, much "folding back" to points developed earlier, and a considerable amount of pointing ahead. Some points are developed at great length; others are introduced briefly. Undoubtedly the format of the presentation dictated this style: treatment of these same matters in a book would have taken on a different form. In this single chapter justice cannot possibly be done to the comprehensiveness of John Paul's complicated and sophisticated understanding of the meaning of human sexuality, though an attempt is made to touch at least on the main themes of his analysis.

Another difficulty in presenting John Paul's views is the general unfamiliarity with them both among professional theologians and the general public.[6] Few are familiar with the fairly distinctive terminology that John Paul uses in his teachings, here particularly his teachings on sexuality. This terminology is neither arcane nor abstract—indeed, the terms he uses have a currency in popular speech. But his analysis provides a deep probing of human experience, and thus as he unfolds his views, his key phrases begin to carry the weight of the preceding analysis. Since he uses and reuses these terms in his explanation of his understanding of human sexuality, it is necessary for the reader to recall the analysis out of which these terms and phrases emerged. Much of the work of this chapter involves explicating key terms and phrases. Because of the general lack of familiarity with his writings and the special nature of his terminology, liberal citation from his works is necessary. Citation from his works should assist us in getting a sense of John Paul's thought and style, of the constancy and intricacy of the themes he develops. What the presentation of his views here ultimately hopes to achieve is an understanding of the main lines of his analysis sufficient to enable us to grasp more precisely his understanding of the centrality of self-giving to married life and of the importance of self-mastery as a requisite for being able to give of oneself. Both of these concepts are essential to his affirmation of the teachings of *Humanae Vitae*.

Self-Mastery

As has been shown in the preceding chapters in the analysis of *Humanae Vitae* and the theological debate it spawned, one of the most controversial claims of *Humanae Vitae* is the claim "Each and every act of marital intercourse must remain ordained to procreation" (HV 11). Nearly equally central to the debate is the assertion "The unitive and procreative meanings of the conjugal act are inseparable" (HV 12). Certainly, John Paul labors to clarify and justify these claims, but of greater interest to him and more central to his reflections on *Humanae Vitae* are several passages rarely taken notice of by the critics of *Humanae Vitae*, most notably sections 9 and 21. These sections refer not to whatever limits there may be to Man's control over his fertility but to the characteristics of conjugal love, most particularly to the centrality of "self-giving" to that love (HV 9), and to the benefits for human happiness from the control that Man acquires over himself through proper self-discipline in the realm of sexuality (HV 21).

John Paul defines the central problem that the doctrine of *Humanae Vitae* faces as "maintaining an adequate relationship between what is defined as 'domination . . . of the forces of nature' (HV 2), and the 'mastery of the self' (HV 21) which is indispensable for the human person."[7] He observes, "Modern man shows a tendency to transfer the methods proper to the former to those of the latter." Many of the critics of *Humanae Vitae* have put great emphasis on Man's ability to control nature, to manipulate his biological processes. John Paul, on the other hand, chiefly emphasizes Man's ability to control himself, the human power of self-mastery.

Let us note that the concern for the development of "self-mastery" is not new in Catholic moral theology. It has been foundational in Catholic moral theology that ethical choice not only involves the external good or evil caused by the act performed but is also vitally concerned with the type of character that an individual is forming for himself or herself with his or her choices. John Paul expresses this understanding in the following passage: "In [his] action the person is, owing to self-determination, an object for himself, in a peculiar way being the immanent target upon which man's exercise of all his powers concentrates, insofar as it is he whose determination is at stake. He is in this sense, the primary object or the nearest object of his action."[8] The method of moral evaluation based on this understanding of human action not only labors to calculate the amount of "ontic evil" likely to be caused by an action but is most concerned with the moral evil caused, specifically the evil done to the character of the agent. In fact, according to this perspective what makes an action "intrinsically evil" is not only that it is a violation of nature or of a fundamental good but also and even primarily that it is the kind of action that can never be voluntarily chosen by a human agent without doing harm to the agent's moral character. Rape, murder, and genocide, for instance, not only cause great harm to others, not only violate nature and fundamental goods, but reveal a bad moral character—or at least a moral character that is becoming bad—for they are the kinds of acts that do great damage to the moral character of the agent.

This view is succinctly expressed in *Gaudium et Spes*. After giving a long list of actions opposed to life, such as murder, genocide, abortion, and euthanasia, and of acts that insult human dignity, such as slavery and prostitution, *Gaudium et Spes* states, "[These acts] poison human civilization; and they debase the perpetrators more than the victims and militate against the honor of the creator" (GS 27).[9] Later this view is stressed in another context, the importance of human activity that builds up the world: "Human activity proceeds from man: it is also ordered to him. When he works, not only does he transform matter and society, but he fulfils himself. He learns, he develops his faculties, and he emerges from and transcends himself. Rightly understood, this kind of growth is more precious than any kind of wealth that can be amassed. It is what a man is, rather than what he has, that counts" (GS35). (John Paul developed this theme at some length in his encyclical *Laborem Exercens*).[10] The concern with moral character, the concern with developing "self-mastery," then, should be the foremost ethical concern of Man.

Let us elaborate on this point that with every choice of action Man reveals himself and forms himself. In acting, the person shows himself for what he is and also continues to form himself: he is becoming a better or worse person through his choices.[11] To become a better or worse person means to become one who is more or less able to perceive the truth and to act in accord with it. There is a reciprocity here that is indeed circular: our character and values help determine our choices, our choices determine our actions, and in turn, our actions determine our characters, which determine our values. The ability of Man to determine himself is rooted in both his fundamental freedom and his ability to discern the truth about reality, his ability freely and deliberately to respond to what is good.[12]

John Paul understands "self-mastery" to be a virtue fundamental to the perfection of the human person (he uses various terms synonymously with *self-mastery: self-discipline, temperance, continence, self-*

denial, and *purity*). He draws on the reference to self-mastery in HV 21:

This self-discipline . . . brings to family life abundant fruits of tranquillity and peace. It helps in solving difficulties of other kinds. It fosters in husband and wife thoughtfulness and loving consideration for each other. It helps them to repel the excessive self-love which is the opposite of charity. It arouses in them a consciousness of their responsibilities. And finally, it confers upon parents a deeper and more effective influence in the education of their children. For these latter, both in childhood and in youth, as years go by, develop a right sense of values as regards the true blessings of life and achieve a serene and harmonious use of their mental and physical powers.[13]

Sexual maturity, then, requires and fosters many other virtues per-fective of the human person, for instance, thoughtfulness, charity, and responsibility, which are all conducive to helping spouses be-come good parents. He later remarks that the virtue of chastity "does not appear and does not act abstractly and . . . in isolation but always in connection with the other virtues (*nexus virtutum*), therefore in connection with prudence, justice, fortitude and above all with charity."[14] What is especially important to grasp here is that the virtue of self-mastery is not valuable only insofar as it enables one to abstain from sexual intercourse when necessary. Throughout his writings John Paul emphasizes self-mastery in a way that sees it as more than a useful characteristic for enabling spouses to limit their family size. John Paul teaches that chastity is an essential virtue for the true expression of love; if one is driven by one's passions one will treat one's spouse as an object designed to satisfy those passions, not as a person deserving to be loved. Self-mastery does not free one from one's passions but enables one to put them into the service of one's loving response, of one's best judgment. Man, of course, needs such mastery over not only his sexual passions but all his passions. Indeed, the term *self-mastery* has both a narrow and a broad designa-tion: it refers particularly to chastity, to the control of the sexual passions, and more generally it also refers to moral virtue, or the mastery of any passion. Self-mastery in both senses is essential to the perfecting of the human person. Indeed, it is the very characteris-tic that enables us to make the kinds of choices that are worthy of our personhood, worthy of our human nature.

In his deeper analysis of the virtue of self-mastery or continence, the virtue that controls the powers of concupiscence, in his description of the way that an individual gains this virtue, he elaborates well the meaning of continence:

The personal subject, in order to succeed in mastering this impulse and excitement, must be committed to a progressive education in self-control of the will, of the feelings, of the emotions; and this education must develop beginning with the most simple acts in which it is relatively easy to put the interior decision into practice. This presupposes, as is obvious, the clear perception of the values expressed in the law and the consequent formation of firm convictions which, if accompanied by the respective disposition of the will, give rise to the corresponding virtue. This is precisely the virtue of continence (self-mastery), which is seen to be the fundamental condition for the reciprocal language of the body to remain in the truth and for the couple to "defer to one another out of reverence for Christ," according to the words in Scripture (Eph. 5:21).[15]

He goes on to note that the citation from Scripture here shows that although continence may begin as the capacity to resist the concupiscence of the flesh, the linkage of continence with "reverence for Christ" suggests a deeper value to continence. He notes that this virtue "gradually reveals itself as a singular capacity to perceive, love and practice those meanings of the 'language of the body' which remain altogether unknown to concupiscence itself and which progressively enrich the marital dialogue of the couple, purifying it, deepening it, and at the same time simplifying it."[16] As John Paul concludes: "That asceticism of continence, of which the encyclical speaks (HV 21), does not impoverish 'affective manifestations,' but rather makes them spiritually more intense and therefore enriches them."[17] Again, the value of continence is in not only its "negative" value of controlling the passions but its positive value of enriching the marital relationship through greater sensitivity and love. Both the negative and the positive power of self-mastery aid spouses in achieving the good of self-giving in their marriage.

Basic to John Paul's teaching is the view that the human person, being a creature who can grasp and live by the truth, is exalted, is perfected, only when he is respectful of the objective truths of reality. In *Love and Responsibility* he makes these connections between truth and freedom and self-determination:

Truth is a condition of freedom, for if a man can preserve his freedom in relation to the objects which thrust themselves on him in the course of his activity as good and desirable, it is only because he is capable of viewing these goods in the light of truth and so adopting an independent attitude to them. Without this faculty man would inevitably be determined by them: these goods would take possession of him and determine totally the character of his actions and the whole direction of his activity. His ability to discover the truth gives man the possibility of self-determination, of deciding for himself the character and direction of his own actions, and that is what freedom means.[18]

The truth of the relation between Man's sexuality and love is sometimes difficult to grasp because of the intensity of sexual powers: "A salient feature of sexual love is its great intensity—which indirectly testifies to the force of the sexual instinct and its importance in human life. This intense concentration of vital and psychic forces so powerfully absorbs the consciousness that other experiences sometimes seem to pale and to lose their importance in comparison with sexual love. You only have to look closely at people under the spell of sexual love to convince yourself of this. Plato's thinking on the power of Eros is for ever being confirmed."[19] Self-mastery enables Man to gain some control over his sexual passions and thus some measure of freedom that allows him to respond to the objective realities of his passions and his love.

John Paul stresses the human ability to express the deepest values of his person through his actions and also stresses the need for the human person to "have possession" of himself in order to express himself authentically and in accord with objective truth and to give of himself fully. Self-mastery both depends on and enables Man to make such a response to reality. *Gaudium et Spes* 16 expresses this principle when discussing the necessity of having a well-formed conscience: "Through loyalty to conscience Christians are joined to other men in the search for truth and for the right solution to so many moral problems which arise both in the life of individuals and from social relationships. Hence the more a correct conscience prevails, the more do persons and groups turn aside from blind choice and try to be guided by the objective standards of moral conduct." A mature and responsible human person is to be guided by "objective norms." What are these "objective criteria" in regard to human sexuality, in regard specifically to the use of contraception?

The Objective Criteria for the Wrongness
of Contraception

Gaudium et Spes speaks generally of the objective norms that must govern human sexuality in regard to the regulation of family size. We have cited the crucial passage from section 51: "When it is a question of harmonizing married love with the responsible transmission of life, it is not enough to take only the good intention and the evaluation of motives into account; the objective criteria must be used, criteria drawn from the nature of the human person and human action, criteria which respect the total meaning of mutual self-giving and human procreation in the context of true love; all this is possible only if the virtue of married chastity is seriously practiced."

To determine the "objective standards" by which contraception is to be judged, we must know "the nature of the human person and his acts," the value of "mutual self-giving and human procreation."

John Paul holds that there will be no proper use of sexuality without a fostering of personalist values. In the thought of John Paul, personalist values are rooted in a respect for the very dignity of the human being. John Paul argues that unless we understand the dignity of the human person we will not fully understand the Church's condemnation of contraception, for he believes that the use of contraception is a violation of the dignity of the human person, for a person is one who is able to perceive the objective truth about the relation between the sexes and act in accord with it. As John Crosby notes, "[John Paul II] holds that to the acceptance of artificial contraception there corresponds one vision of the human person, and to the rejection of it there corresponds an entirely different vision of the person."[20] Here, of course, it would be impossible to lay out in any complete way John Paul's understanding of the human person. Perhaps a statement from *Love and Responsibility* serves to clarify the fundamental requirement of personalist values, to reveal John Paul's understanding of the human person. There, when disputing utilitarianism, John Paul[21] speaks of the personalist principle and the personalist norm: "This norm, in its negative aspect, states that the person is the kind of good which does not admit of use and cannot be treated as an object of use and as such the means to an end. In its positive form the personalistic norm confirms: the person is a good towards which the only proper and adequate attitude is love."[22] This, indeed, is a fundamental teaching of John Paul: we are never to treat others as objects to be used but are always to treat them as persons to be loved. A passage from the introduction to *Love and Responsibility* makes explicit his understanding of the priority of the person in his analysis of human sexuality: "Sexual morality is within the domain of the person. It is impossible to understand anything about it without understanding what the person is, its mode of existence, its functioning, its powers. The personal order is the only proper plane for all debate on matters of sexual morality. Physiology and medicine can only supplement discussion at this level. They do not in themselves provide a complete foundation for the understanding of love and responsibility: but this is just what matters most in the relations between persons of different sex."[23] What John Paul is stating is that physiology and medicine do not have an exclusive right to speak on these matters and that philosophy and psychology and theology have understandings of men and women that illuminate the reality of human sexuality. Still, although John Paul puts enormous emphasis on the importance of understanding the human person for understanding human sexuality, he is not suggesting that knowledge of physiology is not also important: he is not saying that the procreative end of human sexuality can be superseded by other values.

Indeed, John Paul considers the procreative end of sexuality to be one of the central objective truths that must govern the moral use of sexuality. He states the Catholic understanding of procreation in this way:

A man and a woman by means of procreation, by taking part in bringing a new human being into the world, at the same time participate in their own fashion in the work of creation. They can therefore look upon themselves as the rational co-creators of a new human being. That new human being is a person. The parents take part in the genesis of a person. A person is, of course, not merely an organism. . . .

The essence of the human person is therefore—in the Church's teaching—the work of God himself. It is He who creates the spiritual and immortal soul of that being. . . .[24]

He summarizes, "The sexual urge is connected in a special way with the natural order of existence, which is the divine order inasmuch as it is realized under the continuous influence of God the Creator. A man and a woman, through their conjugal life and a full sexual relationship, link themselves with that order, agree to take a special part in the work of creation."[25] It is telling that one of the later chapters in *Love and Responsibility* is entitled "Justice towards the Creator." To exclude the power of procreation from sexual intercourse is to exclude God from this act that symbolizes and transmits His creative love.[26]

The procreative purpose of sexual intercourse, of course, is not its only purpose. What continues to be of essential importance for John Paul and for all Church teaching on sexuality is that sexual intercourse is not only the means of procreating new life: it is the appropriate means for the expression of love between the spouses. John Paul insists:

On no account . . . is it to be supposed that the sexual urge, which has its own predetermined purpose in man independent of his will and self determination, is something inferior to the person and inferior to love. The proper end of the sexual urge is the existence of the species *Homo*, its continuation [*procreatio*], and love between persons, between man and woman, is shaped, channelled one might say, by that purpose and formed from the material it provides. It can therefore take its shape only in so far as it develops in close harmony with the proper purpose of the sexual urge.[27]

In this text, written nearly ten years before *Humanae Vitae*, he anticipates the "inseparable connection" of *Humanae Vitae* when he states (in the continuation of the preceding passage): "An outright conflict [of love] with that purpose [of procreation] will also perturb and undermine love between persons. People sometimes find this purpose a nuisance and try to circumvent it by artificial means. Such means must however have a damaging effect on love between persons, which in this context is most intimately involved in the use of the sexual urge."[28]

John Paul denies here and elsewhere that an insistence on the essentiality of procreation to the meaning of sexual intercourse reduces this meaning to one that is strictly biological.[29] Rather, he argues that the use of contraception is what reduces the powers of procreation to a merely biological meaning, one that can be removed or deterred or nullified if other goods are sought. Again, John Paul argues that contraception violates not only the biological meaning of sexual intercourse but also the personalist values that are inseparably linked with procreation. That is, if the procreative power of sexual intercourse is impaired, the ability of sexual intercourse to express and nourish the love between spouses is also impaired. John Paul makes this point clearer later in the text. Since this point is so crucial to his understanding of sexuality, it is proper to give a fairly full explanation of it:

Where the sexual urge is concerned, as in other matters, man cannot triumph over "nature"' by doing violence to it, but only by understanding the laws which govern it, adapting himself to its immanent purposes and making use of its latent possibilities. There is a direct connection between this and love. Since the sexual relationship is grounded in the sexual urge, and since it draws another person into a whole complex of acts and experiences, the attitude to that person and that person's moral value is indirectly determined by the way in which gratification of the sexual urge is geared into the relationship. In the order of love a man can remain true to the person only in so far as he is true to nature. If he does violence to "nature" he also "violates" the person by making it an object of enjoyment rather than an object of love. Acceptance of the possibility of procreation in the marital relationship safeguards love and is an indispensable condition of a truly personal union. The union of persons in love does not necessarily have to be realized by way of sexual relations. But when it does take this form the personalistic value of the sexual relationship cannot be assured without willingness for parenthood. Thanks to this, both persons in the union act *in accordance with the inner logic of love*, respect its inner dynamic and prepare themselves to accept a new good, an expression of the creative power of love. Willing acceptance of parenthood serves to break down the reciprocal egoism—(or the egoism of one party at which the other connives)—behind which lurks the will to exploit the person.[30]

The key sentence in this passage is perhaps "In the order of love a man can remain true to the person only in so far as he is true to nature." It is reminiscent (or, more properly, anticipatory) of the passage in Humanae Vitae that speaks of the necessity of Man's knowing "the laws written into" the natures of male and female (HV 12, cf. HV 10). Those who engage in sexual intercourse should appreciate its possible ordination to new life and the connection of this ordination to the kind of love appropriate for spouses, one that overflows with potential for loving and creative activity.

Perhaps the most pressing question that arises out of this text is, Why must Man respect the "laws" or operations of nature? John Paul acknowledges that few value nature as an "abstract value." He does not insist, though, on nature as some abstract value; rather he directs Man's gaze to the personal authority of God the Creator behind nature.[31] John Paul explains that violating nature violates the justice of God, especially when the "nature" at work is so intimately involved with the human person. John Paul explains that God is the author of nature and thus that respecting nature is respecting God. Again, conversely, to violate nature is to do an injustice to God. As John Paul explains in his *Reflections on Humanae Vitae*, the understanding that God is the author of nature reveals that "the virtuous character of the attitude which is expressed in the 'natural' regulation of fertility is determined not so much by fidelity to an impersonal 'natural law' as to the Creator-Person, the Source and Lord of the order which is manifested in such a law."[32] Thus, the respect for the laws of nature that John Paul counsels is not the product of a legalistic attitude but of a loving attitude; those who love God will love and respect what He has made.

Whereas those who violate the laws of nature do an injustice to God, on the other hand, by conforming to the order of nature, Man becomes *particeps Creatoris*, a sharer in God's creation.[33] When spouses use contraception, they are violating nature and thereby ceasing to be participants in God's nature. Being participants in God's nature, particularly in His act of creation of new being, is clearly an ennobling privilege granted to Man by God. To reject this privilege is unjust not only to God but to one's own noble nature. Thus, in John Paul's view, contraceptive intercourse is unjust both to God and to Man.[34]

As important as it is to understand contraception as a violation of nature and of the justice of God, the passage cited at length elaborates further some of the more immediate personalist values to be safeguarded and fostered through the respect of the procreative power of sexual intercourse. The goods of intimate union and of the breaking down of egoism are safeguarded through having one's acts of sexual intercourse express the willingness to be open to new life. In his later writings and talks, John Paul further clarifies this claim about sexual intercourse and develops a whole new vocabulary to explicate his views; he speaks of it as an impediment to total self-giving, as a violation of the language of the body.[35]

But what is essential to understand here is that when *Gaudium et Spes* and John Paul are speaking of the "objective standards" by which sexuality is to be governed, they are not speaking of the sexual act solely in its physiological aspect; the preceding discussion shows how the physiological aspect of human sexuality has a transcendental aspect in its connection with God's creative act. What we wish to note now is that it is absolutely central to John Paul's understanding of objective reality (here meaning a truth to which all must adhere) to recognize that objective reality in this case includes the subjective. That is, to live one's sexuality authentically includes subjective reality: that is, it includes acting in accord with the interior or spiritual reality of the human person.[36] John Paul calls on spouses to reflect on the deepest realities of their relationship with one another so that they will come to understand that contraception violates the true union that they seek with one another; that it impedes the mutual self-giving of which sexual intercourse is expressive. The primary "objective reality"—with a subjective component—of interest for determining the morality of sexual behavior is an understanding of the spousal relationship, which is defined as one of a "communion of persons," as one of mutual total self-giving. Spouses must come to know that their spousal relationship is one of total mutual self-giving (which is a subjective component of the act that is also a part of its objective reality). What this self-giving is will soon be explained, but first let us consider John Paul's understanding of the "original condition" of Man, which explains why the objective reality of Man includes his (subjective) need to give of himself and why self-mastery is necessary for such self-giving.

The "Original" Condition of Man

There are several fundamental truths about the "person" that Man must know in order to understand himself as a person. That he is rational and that he possesses free will are two of the most important truths. But the truths of foremost interest here are that Man is in need of self-mastery and that he can realize himself fully only through self-giving. These are truths known to Man both through his reflection on his experience and through the sources of revealed truth. The fact that Man needs to achieve self-mastery and to be self-giving is a truth that is discoverable experientially. In his *The Acting Person* John Paul employs the phenomenological method to explore various characteristics of man. But, following the recommendations of Vatican II, he has also sought to ground his anthropology and ethics in biblical teaching as well as in philosophical justification. It is in Scripture that he finds the explanation of the *cause* of Man's need for self-mastery and need for self-giving. God made Man to be self-giving, but it is because of original sin that "historical" Man is not in the "original" human condition; it is because of original sin, because of disorderedness in his passions, that Man needs self-mastery. John Paul analyzes a few key passages from Scripture to explain how recovering an understanding of the original condition assists us in understanding our current condition and the proper response to it.

John Paul's teaching on the original condition of Man is a fundamental element in his theology of the body and of marriage. It emerges from an exhaustive probing of Matthew 19:3ff. (cf. Mark 10:2ff.). Since this is a key passage it should be cited in full:

And the Pharisees came up to him and tested him by asking, "Is it lawful to divorce one's wife for any cause?" He answered, "Have you not read that he who made them from the beginning made them male and female, and said, 'For this reason a man shall leave his father and mother and be joined to his wife, and the two shall become one flesh?' So they are no longer two but one flesh. What therefore God has joined together, let not man put asunder." They said to him, "Why then did Moses command one to give a certificate of divorce, and to put her away?" He said to them, "For your hardness of heart Moses allowed you to divorce your wives, *but from the beginning it was not so.*"[37]

John Paul picks up on Christ's revelation that "from the beginning it was not so." He takes "the beginning" (mentioned twice in the passage) to be a reference to the "original innocence" of Man, to the condition symbolized by the story of Adam and Eve,[38] to the truth about Man revealed in the manner of his creation. Essential to his reflections is the understanding that human nature has two "states": the state of "integral nature" and the state of "fallen nature."

Historical Man now has a fallen nature, although he has not lost his rootedness in his integral nature. For Man to understand who he is now and why he feels and acts as he does, for him to understand how he ought to act and what he needs to do to achieve proper action, it is necessary for him to understand his original condition. For him to have the proper confidence that he can regain this condition, it is also necessary that he understand that Christ has redeemed him from complete subjection to the consequences of the fall.[39] Man needs to "live in the theological perspective of the redemption."[40] And part of that is living with an understanding of what he was "in the beginning."

John Paul speaks of Man's "original solitude" and of the "nuptial meaning of the body" as revealed in Genesis. It is through his body that Man comes to realize who he is. John Paul states that the first human recognition is an awareness of "solitude" or uniqueness. Man realizes that he is different from the rest of the visible world; this is a truth that his body helps him to understand.[41] Many other truths come to him through this awareness of his distinctiveness from the rest of creation. He realizes that he is a subject, that is, that he has self-awareness and thus powers of self-determination. Though this solitude is the source of Man's understanding of himself, God knew that "it is not good that man should be alone" (and here, as elsewhere, John Paul takes *man* to mean both male and female). Man did not have a true identity, a true wholeness, until he was two, until there were both masculinity and femininity. The welcomeness of the union that overcomes solitude is expressed through Adam's first words on seeing Eve: "This at last is bone of my bones and flesh of my flesh" (Genesis 2:23). John Paul elaborates on this remark: "In this way the man (male) manifests for the first time joy and even exaltation, for which he had no reason before, owing to the lack of a being like himself. Joy in the other human being, in the second 'self,' dominates in the words spoken by the man (male) upon seeing the woman (female). All that helps to establish the full meaning of original unity. The words here are few, but each one is of great weight."[42] John Paul, then, understands sexuality to be constituent of the human person[43] and the sexual union of male and female to fulfill their human nature. He also notes that even though the ease and spontaneity of this union "in the beginning" (or in the state of "original unity") were marred by the disorder introduced by original sin, nonetheless "In every conjugal union of man and woman there is discovered again the same original consciousness of the unifying significance of the body in its masculinity and femininity."[44] That is, it is important to note that however flawed John Paul may think male and female relationships are as the result of the fall, he views sexuality as a fundamental human good, both "in the beginning" and now.

Indeed, John Paul clearly has a positive evaluation of the powers of human sexuality for perfecting the human person and creating a community of loving persons that is the very goal of Christianity. Many have charged that the Church has a negative evaluation of human sexuality. The following passage manifests a widely held view of Church teaching about sexuality:

[Catholic theological literature has taught that] sexuality is not an ennobling feature of human nature. It may have a proper and, accidentally, even an honorable place in human existence. But it cannot be considered in itself a proper foundation for human achievement or Christian spirituality. We stop short of concluding that God would have been wiser had he created an androgenous mankind, or if he had disposed otherwise than sexually for the reproduction of mankind. But we do not ordinarily experience vividly, or with awe, God's wisdom in having created man male and female—along with all the personal sexuality of the individual which the generic bi-sexuality of man implies. We are not often *glad*, precisely as Christians and in virtue of our faith, that sexuality exists.[45]

Whether or not this is an accurate assessment of earlier theological literature will not be resolved here, but it most certainly is true that John Paul "experiences with awe God's wisdom in creating man male and female." In his view, the original unity of man and woman was the source of their true identity, a source of their happiness, of their being like God. When John Paul speaks of the "nuptial meaning of the body" he is referring to the fact that the body gives Man the ability to be a unity with one of the opposite sex, to give of himself to one of the opposite sex, and it is through that union that he achieves his identity, his wholeness, his fulfillment.

The positive evaluation of sexuality is also revealed in John Paul's understanding of the meaning of shame. The original nakedness of man and woman was not a source of shame to them: it was a sign of the unity and ease with which they could be together. The shame and the uneasiness that male and female now experience in being together are a result of original sin. One of the goals, then, of Man should be to regain this ease of association with the opposite sex. John Paul speaks of the freedom that the original innocence provided Man:

The root of that original nakedness free from shame, of which Genesis 2:25 speaks, must be sought precisely in that complete truth about man. Man or woman, in the context of their beatifying "beginning," are free with the very freedom of the gift. In fact, to be able to remain in the relationship of the "sincere gift of themselves" and to become such a gift for each other through the whole of their humanity made of femininity and masculinity . . . they must be free precisely in this way.

We mean here freedom particularly as mastery of oneself (self-control). From this aspect, it is indispensable in order that man may be able to "give himself," in order that he may become a gift, in order that (referring to the words of the Council) he will be able to "fully discover his true self" in "a sincere giving of himself."[46]

The task of human life is to regain, with the aid of the graces of Christ, the original freedom that was Man's at the outset. This freedom will enable him to become a "gift giver" as God Himself, the Creator, is a "giver."[47] But this original freedom is not attainable without the virtue of self-mastery.

The Negation of Self-Mastery: Lust

Original sin destroyed the ordered unity of body and soul and introduced, among other sins, lust into the world. One of the best ways to understand what is meant by self-mastery or chastity and to understand what self-giving means is to understand the opposite of self-mastery, which is lust, its negation. In his second series of lectures (entitled *Blessed Are the Pure of Heart* by the Daughters of St. Paul) John Paul probes the phenomenon of lust. Again he does this in the context of analyzing a key passage from Scripture, a passage from the Sermon on the Mount. There Christ taught: "You have heard that it was said, You shall not commit adultery. But I say to you that everyone who looks at a woman lustfully has already committed adultery with her in his heart" (Mt. 5:27–28).[48] Lust is in radical opposition to the "communion of persons" that was Man's before the fall; it became a part of his makeup after the fall. A consequence of the fall was that Man no longer experienced that ordered unity of spirit and body that enabled him truly to offer himself to another. John Paul finds this revealed in Man's response to his sin: "I was afraid because I was naked" (Gn. 3:7). He observes:

In this sense the original shame of the body ("I am naked") is already fear ("I was afraid"), and announces the uneasiness of conscience connected with lust.

The body, which is not subordinated to the spirit as in the state of original innocence, bears within it a constant center of resistance to the spirit, and threatens, in a way, the unity of the man-person, that is of the moral nature, which is firmly rooted in the very constitution of the person. Lust, and in particular the lust of the body, is a specific threat to the structure of self-control and self-mastery, through which the human person is formed. And it also constitutes a specific challenge for it. In any case, the man of lust does not control his body in the same way, with equal simplicity and "naturalness," as the man of original innocence did. The structure of self-mastery, essential for the person, is, in a way, shaken to the very foundations in him; he again identifies himself with it in that he is continually ready to win it.[49]

The evil involved in lust is not that Man enjoys some "illicit pleasure." It is in the diminishment of his proper human powers and in the resultant lack of respect that he shows for another human person. One moved by lust cannot love, since lust takes for oneself whereas love gives of oneself.

Lust is a sexual attitude that reduces the other person to an object, to a thing to be used. It does not emerge from a loving response to another person but from Man's selfish desire to satisfy his passion: " 'Lust' turns away the intentional dimension of the man's and woman's mutual existence from the personal perspectives, 'of communion,' characteristic of their perennial and mutual attraction, reducing it, and, so to speak, pushing it towards utilitarian dimensions, within which the human being 'uses' the other human being, for the sake merely of satisfying his own 'needs.' "[50]

John Paul, of course, does not think that lust is Man's only possible response to his sexuality. In an interesting departure from his usual mode of analysis (which rarely includes mention of current debates), he briefly considers the views of a few modern thinkers, whom he understands to hold that Man is irredeemably self-centered. Following Ricoeur, he calls Freud, Marx, and Nietzsche "masters of suspicion" since they seem to judge and accuse the human heart. In contrast, he sees Christianity as being hopeful about Man's sexuality, for Christianity teaches that through the grace of Christ, Man can be restored to his original unity and master his lust:

Man cannot stop at putting the "heart" in a state of continual and irreversible suspicion due to the manifestations of the lust of the flesh and libido, which, among other things, a psychoanalyst perceives by means of analyses of the unconscious. Redemption is a truth, a reality, in the name of which man must feel called, and "called with efficacy." . . . Man must feel called to rediscover, nay more, to realize the nuptial meaning of the body and to express in this way the interior freedom of the gift, that is, of the spiritual state and that spiritual power which are derived from mastery of the lust of the flesh.[51]

The answer to Man's unruly desires, to his persistent selfishness, is self-mastery, a virtue that requires knowledge of himself. Referring again to Christ's words against adultery in the heart during the Sermon on the Mount, John Paul observes:

Christ's words are severe. They demand from man that, in the sphere in which relations with persons of the other sex are formed, he should have full and deep consciousness of his own acts, and above all of interior acts; that he should be aware of the internal impulses of his "heart," so as to be able to distinguish them and qualify them maturely. Christ's words demand that in this sphere, which seems to belong exclusively to the body and to the senses, that is, to exterior man, he should succeed in being really an interior man, he should be able to obey correct conscience; to be the true master of his own deep impulses, like a guardian who watches over a hidden spring; and finally to draw from all those impulses what is fitting for "purity of heart," building with conscience and consistency the personal sense of the nuptial meaning of the body, which opens the interior space of the freedom of the gift.[52]

Self-mastery, then, is not something that diminishes Man or deprives him of some elemental power of existence. Here using the more traditional terms of *temperance* and *continence*, John Paul makes clear the empowering quality of self-mastery:

Temperance and continence do not mean—if it may be put this way—suspension in emptiness: neither in the emptiness of values nor in the emptiness of the subject. The ethos of redemption is realized in self-mastery, by means of temperance, that is continence of desires. In this behavior the human heart remains bound to the value from which, through desire, it would otherwise have moved away, turning towards pure lust deprived of ethical value. . . . In the field of the ethos of redemption, union with that value by means of an act of mastery, is confirmed or re-established with an even deeper power and firmness.[53]

By freeing one from the power of lust, from lust's demands to treat the other as an object, self-mastery enables one to conform one's behavior to the values that one holds. Self-mastery is empowering, then, because it allows one to put one's sexual passions in service of one's love, because it enables one to respect one's beloved.

The opposite of lust, and the result of self-mastery, is the possession of the gift and the virtue of purity. John Paul refers to the Pauline concept that the body is the "temple" of the Holy Spirit. He praises purity in these grand terms:

Purity, as the virtue, that is, the capacity of "controlling one's body in holiness and honor," together with the gift of piety, as the fruit of the dwelling of the Holy Spirit in the "temple" of the body, brings about in the body such a fullness of dignity in interpersonal relations that God Himself is thereby glorified. Purity is the glory of the human body before God. It is God's glory in the human body, through which masculinity and femininity are manifested. From purity springs that extraordinary beauty which permeates every sphere of men's mutual common life and makes it possible to express in it simplicity and depth, cordiality and the unrepeatable authenticity of personal trust.[54]

Purity, then, issues in beauty, simplicity, depth, cordiality, and trust. He also claims that Man in mastering himself can "become more fully a real gift for another person."[55] What is this "self-giving" that is the joyful result of self-mastery, of purity?

The Gift of Self

Chapter 4 discusses at some length the concept of self-giving. Here let us place this teaching within the more theological and scriptural context of John Paul's reflections.

John Paul's understanding of the need for Man to give of himself to achieve his perfection and happiness, and of the role of human sexuality in this giving, draws on *Gaudium et Spes*.[56] Early in this document we find the following statement: "But God did not create man a solitary being. From the beginning 'male and female he created them' (Gen. 1:27). This partnership of man and woman constitutes the first form of communion between persons. For by his innermost nature man is a social being; and if he does not enter into relationships with others he can neither live nor develop his gifts" (GS 12). The philosophical truth that Man is a social animal is reflected in this passage, but the perspective of the Church goes further than this philosophical truth. Christ's revealing message indicates that Man's need for interpersonal communion is rooted in his being made in the image and likeness of God (more is said on Man's "trinitarian nature" later). The following passage from *Gaudium et Spes* suggests the links among Man's social nature, God as a union of persons, and the need for Man to make a gift of himself: "Furthermore, the Lord Jesus, when praying to the Father 'That they may all be one . . . even as we are one' (Jn. 17:21–22), has opened up new horizons closed to human reason by implying that there is a certain parallel between the union existing among the divine persons and the union of the sons of God in truth and love. It follows, then, that if man is the only creature on earth that God has wanted for its own sake, man can fully discover his true self only in a sincere giving of himself" (GS 24). The footnote to this passage refers to Luke 17:33, where we read, "Whoever tries to preserve his life will lose it; whoever loses it will keep it." Perhaps no other scriptural verse can convey so perfectly what is meant by "giving" oneself to another: it does not mean simply associating with others, or even just being good to them; it means living one's life in service of another (or others), putting another's (or others') concerns and well-being over one's own selfish concerns.

The portion of *Gaudium et Spes* on marriage refers continually to marriage as the spouses' mutual gift of self. Section 48 is particularly replete with such references. The originating cause of marriage is described in these terms: "It is an institution confirmed by the divine law and receiving its stability, even in the eyes of society, from the human act by which the partners mutually surrender themselves to each other; . . ." The most pertinent passage is perhaps the following: "Thus the man and woman, who 'are no longer two, but one' (Mt. 19:6), help and serve each other by their marriage partnership;

they become conscious of their unity and experience it more deeply day by day. The intimate union of marriage, as a mutual giving of two persons, and the good of the children demand total fidelity from the spouses and require an unbreakable unity between them" (GS 48). The passage goes on to state that marriage imitates the love that Christ has for the Church, a love that is characterized by His complete giving of Himself for the Church.

In his teachings on the body, his writings on marriage, and his reflections on *Humanae Vitae*, John Paul elaborates on these themes of *Gaudium et Spes*. Indeed he calls for a "hermeneutics of the gift."[57] John Paul, with the tradition, sees all of creation—and in this case particularly human sexuality—as a gift that flows out of love and that aids the expression of love. Remarking on the passage "God saw what he had made, and behold, it was very good," John Paul states, "Through these words we are led to glimpse in love the divine motive of creation, the source, as it were, from which it springs: only love, in fact, gives a beginning to good and delights in good" (cf. 1 Cor. 13).[58] All of creation then is the result of an act of love and an act of giving. Furthermore, "Every creature bears within him the sign of the original and fundamental gift."[59] Man's existence is a gift and so too is his sexuality: "There is a deep connection between the mystery of creation, as a gift springing from love, and that beatifying 'beginning' of the existence of man as male and female, in the whole truth of their body and their sex, which is the pure and simple truth of communion between persons."[60]

Teaching that the sexes were created in such a way that they could give of themselves to one another, John Paul links Man's "original" solitude and the creation of another human being in this way: "This is the body: a witness to creation as a fundamental gift, and so a witness to Love as the source from which this same giving springs. Masculinity-femininity—namely, sex—is the original sign of a creative donation and of an awareness on the part of man, male-female, of a gift lived so to speak in an original way."[61] God's creation is a gift and, again, Man imitates God in his giving of himself as a gift. Man's sexuality is foundational to his ability to give himself as a gift. John Paul finds that Man will understand his essence better through understanding that he perfects himself through making a gift of himself. In commenting on God's creation of the first woman as a "helper" for the first man, for whom it was not good that he be alone, John Paul observes,

These two expressions, namely, the adjective "alone" and the noun "helper," seem to be really the key to understand the very essence of the gift at the level of man, as existential content contained in the truth of the "image of God." In fact the gift reveals, so to speak, a particular characteristic of personal existence, or rather of the very essence of the person. When God Yahweh says that "it is not good that man should be alone" (Gn. 2:18), He affirms that "alone," man does not completely realize this essence. He realizes it only by existing "*with someone*"—and even more deeply and completely: by existing "*for someone.*"[62]

This norm of existence as a person is shown in the Book of Genesis as characteristic of creation, precisely by means of the meaning of these two words: *alone* and *helper*. It is precisely these words that indicate as fundamental and constitutive for Man both the relationship and the communion of persons. The communion of persons means existing in a mutual "for," in a relationship of mutual gift. And this relationship is precisely the fulfillment of Man's original solitude.[63]

The first man responds to the first woman by saying, "This at last is bone of my bone, flesh of my flesh." And through marriage the two are to become one flesh. Thus the communion between persons is deeply rooted in the bodily nature of Man. The "meaning" of the body is not separate from the "meaning" of sex. Indeed, John Paul makes this explicit: "The theology of the body, which, right from the beginning, is bound up with the creation of man in the image of God, becomes, in a way, also the theology of sex, or rather the theology of masculinity and femininity, which has its starting point here, in the Book of Genesis."[64] John Paul teaches that the "meaning" of the body is a sexual meaning, one that is truly expressed through a nuptial union. This nuptial union of communion of persons that Man is, is made possible by the nuptial meaning of the body and is accomplished through a kind of giving, a giving of male and female to each other. Male and female, through giving themselves to each other, complete each other and fulfill each other: they make each other more perfect "images made in the likeness of God," for now they, too, like God, are a community of persons united by love.

Again, the original unity of man and woman, the original ability they had to be a perfect gift for each other, was marred by original sin. John Paul states this fundamental truth in this way: "It is well known that as a result of the sinfulness contracted after original sin, man and woman must reconstruct, with great effort, the meaning of the disinterested mutual gift."[65] If man and woman do not strive to overcome the effects of original sin, they will treat each other not as gifts from God to be respected as creatures made in the image of God but as objects to be exploited for sexual pleasure. Historical Man needs to regain his ability to be self-giving through the virtue of self-mastery:

The root of that original nakedness free from shame, of which Genesis 2:25 speaks, must be sought precisely in that complete truth about man. Man or woman, in the context of their beatifying "beginning," are free with the very freedom of the gift. In fact, to be able to remain in the relationship of the "sincere gift of themselves" and to become such a gift for each other through the whole of their humanity made of femininity and masculinity . . . they must be free precisely in this way.

We mean here freedom particularly as mastery of oneself (self-control). From this aspect, it is indispensable in order that man may be able to "give himself," in order that he may become a gift, in order that (referring to the words of the Council) he will be able to "fully discover his true self" in "a sincere giving of himself."[66]

Moreover, the mutual giving of self that the nuptial meaning of the body allows serves to lead men and women to respect one another, to "affirm one another" as unique and unrepeatable creations of Love, deserving to be loved:

The human body, oriented interiorly by the "sincere gift" of the person, reveals not only its masculinity or femininity on the physical plane, but reveals also such a value and such a beauty as to go beyond the purely physical dimension of "sexuality." In this manner awareness of the nuptial meaning of the body, is in a way completed. On the one hand, this meaning indicates a particular capacity of expressing love, in which man becomes a gift; on the other hand, there corresponds to it the capacity and deep availability for the "affirmation of the person," that is, literally, the capacity of living the fact that the other—the woman for the man and the man for the woman—is, by means of the body, someone willed by the Creator "for his (her) own sake," that is, unique and unrepeatable: some one chosen by eternal Love.

The "affirmation of the person" is nothing but acceptance of the gift, which, by means of reciprocity, creates the communion of persons.

Gift and Procreation

Man's ability to give himself, to become a "communion of persons," is, as mentioned, a way in which Man shares in the likeness of God, for God is a trinity, a trinity whose goodness overflows into creation. John Paul notes that "from the beginning" this unity of persons, this trinitarian aspect of Man's existence, was linked with sexuality and with the power of procreation (compare Genesis 1:28):

The second narrative [of creation in Genesis] could also be a preparation for the understanding of the Trinitarian concept of the "image of God," even if the latter appears only in the first narrative. Obviously, that is not without significance also for the theology of the body; in fact, it even constitutes, perhaps the deepest theological aspect of all that can be said about man. In the mystery of creation—on the basis of the original and constituent "solitude" of his being—man was endowed with a deep unity between what is, humanly and through the body, male in him and what is, equally humanly and through the body, female in him. On all this, right from the beginning, there descended the blessing of fertility, linked with human procreation (cf. Gn. 1:28).[68]

He observes that Genesis 2:24 "speaks of the finality of man's masculinity and femininity, in the life of the spouses-parents."[69] In his later reflections he describes briefly the connection between the original condition of Man, the mutual union of gift of self, and procreation: "[The original community-communion of persons] should have made man and woman mutually happy by means of the pursuit of a simple and pure union in humanity, by means of a reciprocal offering of themselves, that is, the experience of the gift of the person expressed with the soul and with the body, with masculinity and femininity ('flesh of my flesh'; Gn. 2:23), and finally by means of the subordination of this union to the blessing of fertility with 'procreation.' "[70] The procreative power of sex is a power that further enables Man to share in the loving action of God, the creative action of God: "Procreation is rooted in creation, and every time, in a sense, reproduces its mystery."[71]

Thus, in John Paul's view, to exclude the procreative power of sex from acts of conjugal intimacy is to violate the very meaning of sex, the "nuptial meaning" of the body. It is to thwart the ability of sexual intercourse to be the unique expression of total self-giving of the spouses to each other. John Paul states this position most explicitly in *Familiaris Consortio*:

When couples, by means of recourse to contraception, separate these two meanings [the unitive and procreative] that God the Creator has inscribed in the being of man and woman and in the dynamism of their sexual communion, they act as "arbiters" of the divine plan and they "manipulate" and degrade human sexuality—and with it themselves and their married partner—by altering its value of "total" self-giving. Thus the innate language that expresses the total reciprocal self-giving of husband and wife is overlaid, through contraception, by an objectively contradictory language, namely, that of not giving oneself totally to the other. This leads not only to a positive refusal to be open to life but also to a falsification of the inner truth of conjugal love, which is called upon to give itself in personal totality.[72]

If one is not willing to share one's life-giving power, one's fertility, with another, one is not giving totally of oneself: by negating the procreative meaning of sexual intercourse, one is also negating the unitive meaning of marriage, the meaning of total self-giving. In his final address on *Humanae Vitae*, John Paul has these words of counsel:

Respect for the work of God contributes to seeing that the conjugal act does not become diminished and deprived of the interior meaning of married life as a whole—that it does not become a "habit"—and that there is expressed in it a sufficient fullness of personal and ethical content, and also of religious content, that is, veneration for the majesty of the Creator, the only and ultimate depositary of the source of life, and for the spousal love of the Redeemer. All this creates and enlarges, so to speak, the interior space for the mutual freedom of the gift in which there is fully manifested the spousal meaning of masculinity and femininity.[73]

John Paul, then, teaches that for spouses to enjoy fully the profound meaning of their relationship, they must foster a respect for the meaning of their sexual powers; they must realize the meaning of these powers within the economy of God's salvation. Only then can they prevent their sexual relationship from becoming one of routine, from becoming one that does not fully appreciate the mystery of the beloved, the mystery of sexuality.

Summary

   John Paul has been most concerned throughout his pontificate to bring modern Man to appreciate the wisdom and truth of the Church's teaching on marriage. He has not treated the teaching on contraception as a mere annoying appendage to the Church's teaching on marriage. Rather, he has shown that the doctrine that there is a moral necessity of keeping each and every conjugal act unimpaired for procreation is one that is informed completely by biblical and personalist understandings of the meaning of sexuality, of the body. The preceding analysis gives only a sketch of his rich views, views developed carefully and at length over two decades. In addition to emphasizing personalist values, he makes extensive use of a few biblical passages, most notably passages from Matthew on divorce and passages from Genesis on creation, to unfold a profound understanding of the meaning of the body and the meaning of sexuality. He uses natural law in his insistence on the essentiality of the procreative powers of sexuality to the meaning of sexuality, but he does not speak narrowly of biological laws and powers. Rather, he speaks of the workings of God through human sexuality and speaks of intercourse as a special domain where Man can participate in the creative power of God. The Christian doctrine of original sin is also central to his teaching on sexuality for he asserts that it is essential that Man understand that since the fall his sexual passions have been disordered and his understanding of himself has been flawed. Proper use of sexuality requires the development of the virtue of self-mastery, for it enables one to order one's passions and to acquire a true understanding of the meaning of sexuality. Self-mastery further enables one to express the true meaning of sexuality, one that conveys the loving commitment one has to one's spouse. For this true meaning to be expressed, it is necessary that the procreative power of the conjugal act remain unimpaired; otherwise the truth of the act is thwarted: the spouses are telling a lie with their bodies. Finally, John Paul does not consider the condemnation of contraception a denial that impedes Man's full enjoyment of his sexual powers. Rather, he understands true enjoyment of sexuality to arise from a sexual life that is governed by love for one's spouse and by respect for God's intentions for sexuality. In short, he sees sexuality as a gift that to be used properly must be used as the Giver intended, that is, as a means by which spouses express their exclusive and committed love for one another.

Criticism of the Views of John Paul II

As noted, few revisionist theologians take note of John Paul's analysis of sexual acts and of his defense of *Humanae Vitae*. Lisa Sowle Cahill is one of the few who give evidence of familiarity with his work. In a brief notation of his work in a survey of Catholic teaching on sexual ethics in the last forty or fifty years, she expresses some of her criticisms of John Paul's ideas. She expresses appreciation for his efforts to "engage Catholic sexual morality with Scripture and to explore basic male-female relationships." Although she acknowledges that John Paul's emphasis on mutual self-donation is egalitarian in its treatment of men and women, she finds this in conflict with his recognition of what she calls "gender roles": she is referring to his view that motherhood is the preeminent calling of women. She believes that a full appreciation for biblical and personalist values would lead to conclusions different from those that John Paul draws. At one point she alludes to an "authoritative overemphasis on procreation." But most of her chief objections seem to be expressed in the following passage:

> One suspects that, were it not for a "bottom line" of consistency with *Humanae Vitae*, these personalist insights would lead ineluctably to the conclusions that, *if* mutual "self-gift" is to be the most basic norm of male-female relationship, then (1) interpersonal values are the essence of marriage, to which sex and procreation are linked in firm but subordinate relationships; (2) full interpersonal and sexual reciprocity of women and men implies equality in all spheres of familial and social life; (3) full equality in family, church, and society likewise implies the necessity to control reproduction adequately to permit women as well as men to mesh family life with their contributions in other spheres.[74]

She gives no argument why she thinks these conclusions must follow "ineluctably" from the recognition that mutual self-gift is the basis of the male-female relationship. An attempt would be made here to call into question her reasoning, but since she does not lay out her argument, suffice it to say that her conclusions hardly seem "ineluctable," self-evident, or obvious.

Cahill's final criticism of John Paul's teaching is "The elevated self-gift language . . . romanticizes sexual commitment."[75] Her further remarks suggest that she thinks romanticism is in conflict with practicality; others might think that John Paul sets too high an ideal for the reality of many marital unions.

Certainly the language of "self-giving" is easily accommodated to a romantic usage, but when one recalls that John Paul claims that all Christians are called to "self-giving," one recognizes that the romantic meaning, so appealing to modern Westerners, is not foremost in his mind. He has in mind lives that are lived in the service of one another, of one's family and of society, and urges that all one's acts express "self-giving." Some acts by their very nature have a deeply rooted meaning of "self-giving": the act of marital intercourse is one such act. Though spouses may be at odds with one another, their sexual actions can only assist them in regaining harmony if they are acts truly expressive of the commitment to each other that they have. John Paul, again, is saying that to remove the procreative meaning from sexual intercourse diminishes if not negates the unitive meaning and that spouses are only furthering the alienation they may feel from one another when they are engaging in contracepted intercourse. He is not saying that the spouses must have an attitude of total romantic involvement with the other in each act of sexual intercourse; his demands are not incompatible with the varying degrees of affection that spouses may feel for one another. He teaches only that one's actions must express one's love and commitment; he is not commenting on attitude. Perhaps a trivial example may assist us. A wife may be quite annoyed at her husband for several legitimate reasons, but for his birthday decide to prepare his favorite meal. Her act expresses her love and commitment, despite what tensions there may be between them. Acts of marital intercourse can and should do the same.

It seems that no other revisionist responses to John Paul's teaching on sexuality exist. His remarks do not lend themselves to easy categorization and do not rely on the standard terminology of ethical debate. His reliance on Scripture may also be a deterrent to many theologians, who in spite of their frequent calls for a more biblically based moral theology rarely root their own positions in passages in Scripture.

John Paul II's Continual Reaffirmation of *Humanae Vitae*

As noted at the outset of this chapter, John Paul has been one of the most zealous advocates of the teachings of *Humanae Vitae*. This is not surprising, since he has identified his chief pastoral priority as "the problems of marriage and the family" and seeks to work "most of all with youth."[76] He did not cease his efforts to defend the Church's teaching on sexuality when he completed his series of talks on the theology of the body. Many of his subsequent speeches make glancing reference to the Church's condemnation of contraception and several take *Humanae Vitae* as their chief focus. A review of the chief themes of these speeches and remarks will enable us in this last portion of this last chapter to review the major themes covered in the preceding chapters and to suggest the shape of the current debate.

Natural Law as the Basis of Humanae Vitae

John Paul does not give an in-depth analysis of the place of natural law in the moral evaluation of contraception, but he makes some comments that are extremely suggestive. For instance, he asks:

At a time when so many ecological movements call for respect for nature, what are we to think of an invasion of artificial procedures and substances in this eminently personal field? To resort to technical measures in place of self-control, self-renunciation for the sake of the other, and the common effort of husband and wife, does not this mark a regression from that which constitutes man's nobility? Do we not see that man's nature is subject to morality? Have we measured the whole significance of a continually accentuated rejection of the child on the psychology of parents, bearing as they do the desire for a child inscribed in their nature, and on the future of society?[77]

This passage glances at least three important points: (1) It suggests that use of contraceptives is not ecologically sound; the fact that the contraceptive pill and intrauterine devices have been so harmful to women physically does suggest that these are not ecologically wise measures of birth control for they harm the very nature that they supposedly seek to assist. (2) It also suggests that Man is foolish to rely on artificial procedures when measures of self-control are more in accord with his dignity. Again, one may find substances that will help one to reduce one's weight, but these may be harmful to one's health. A greater degree of self-control may enable one to achieve the same end without taking the same risks. (3) The passage makes the provocative suggestion that an "antichild" mentality may adversely affect the psyches of parents who have an innate desire for a child and may also harm the future of society. The millions of abortions sought by American women testify to the rampant "antichild" mentality of our times, one severely detrimental to our society. That spouses and their families may also suffer when the parents are not willing to accept another child may well be a result of the use of contraception. This passage reinforces the claim that the Church's teaching is not "biologistic" or "physicalistic": that it draws on and shapes the whole of the human person, psychological and social, as well as physiological.

Contraception as a Violation of Self-Giving

John Paul sees the human person as a creature who has the "fundamental and innate vocation" of love. And he generally speaks of love as an act of self-giving. He teaches: "In order to avoid any trivialization or desecration of sexuality, we must teach that sexuality transcends the purely biological sphere and concerns the innermost being of the human person as such. Sexual love is truly human only if it is an integral part of the love by which a man and a woman commit themselves totally to one another until death. *This full self-giving is possible only in marriage.*"[78]

The Theological Grounding of Humanae Vitae

Humanae Vitae has a theological grounding as well as a philosophical one. Chapter 4 lists the arguments against contraception based on the description of the sexual act as one that provides God an opportunity to perform His creative act of creating new life. In the act of sexual intercourse, then, spouses become "cooperators with the Creator and co-administrators in the work of creation"[79] with God. John Paul gives an eloquent statement of this argument:

At the origin of every human person there is a creative act of God. No man comes into existence by chance; he is always the object of God's creative love. From this fundamental truth of faith and reason it follows that the procreative capacity, inscribed in human sexuality is—in its deepest truth—a cooperation with God's creative power. And it also follows that man and woman are not the arbiters, are not the masters of this same capacity, called as they are, in it and through it, to be participants in God's creative decision. When, therefore, through contraception, married couples remove from the exercise of their conjugal sexuality its potential procreative capacity, they claim a power which belongs solely to God: the power to decide *in a final analysis* the coming into existence of a human person. They assume the qualification not of being cooperators in God's creative power, but the ultimate depositaries of the source of human life. In this perspective, contraception is to be judged objectively so profoundly unlawful, as never to be, for any reason, justified. To think or to say the contrary is equal to maintaining that in human life situations may arise in which its lawful not to recognize God as God.[80]

As this passage makes clear, in contracepting spouses do wrong not so much in violating the biological finality of sexual intercourse, or even so much in disrespecting God as the author of that finality, but in excluding God from an action in which He may directly perform a creative action; they do not recognize God as one who has an action to perform.

Status of the Church's Teaching

John Paul has been firm on the authoritativeness of the Church's doctrine on contraception. For spouses, he places the teaching in the context of their general call to holiness:

In the first place, there must be no deception regarding the *doctrine of the Church*, such as it has been clearly set forth by the Magisterium, the Council, and my predecessors, I am thinking especially of Paul VI's encyclical *Humanae Vitae*, of his address to the Notre-Dame Teams on 4 May, 1970, and of his numerous other interventions. It is necessary to set one's course constantly by this standard of perfection for imitation in conjugal relations, governed by and respectful of the nature and finalities of the conjugal act, and not according to a more or less wide, more or less avowed, concession to the principle and practice of contraceptive morals. God calls spouses to the holiness of marriage, for their own good and for the quality of their witness.[81]

John Paul makes several salient points bearing on the status of the teaching. Speaking to moral theologians, he admonishes them to keep to the fundamental truth that: "There are moral norms that have a precise content which is immutable and unconditioned. You are undertaking a rigorous reflection on some of these in the course of this Congress: for example, the norm that prohibits contraception or that which forbids the direct killing of an innocent person. To deny the existence of norms having such a value can be done only by one who denies the existence of a *truth* about the person, of an immutable nature in man, based ultimately on the creative Wisdom which is the measure of all reality."[82] And further he states: "To appeal to a 'faith of the Church' in order to oppose the moral Magisterium of the Church is equivalent to denying the Catholic concept of Revelation. Not only that, but one can come to violate the fundamental right of the faithful to receive the doctrine *of the Church* from those who teach theology by virtue of a canonical mission and not the opinions of theological schools."[83] He bemoans the confusion that constant questioning of the teaching or dissent from the teaching cause the faithful:

In their effort to live their conjugal love correctly, married couples can be seriously impeded by a certain hedonistic mentality widespread today, by the mass media, by ideologies and practices contrary to the gospel. This can also come about, with truly grave and destructive consequences, when the doctrine taught by the Encyclical is called into question, as has sometimes happened, even on the part of some theologians and pastors of souls. This attitude, in fact, can instil doubt with regard to a teaching which for the Church is certain; in this way it clouds the perception of a truth which cannot be questioned. This is not a sign of "pastoral understanding," but of *misunderstanding the true good of persons*. Truth cannot be measured by majority opinion.[84]

He denies that a proper use of conscience could truly lead one to reject the Church's teaching:

With the passing of time it is ever more evident how certain positions on the so-called "right to dissent" have had harmful repercussions on the moral conduct of a number of the faithful. "It has been noted"—I mentioned in my address last year to the bishops gathered in Los Angeles— "that there is a tendency on the part of some Catholics to be selective in their adherence to the Church's moral teachings." Some people appeal to "freedom of conscience" to justify this way of acting. Therefore, it is necessary to clarify that it is not conscience that "freely" establishes what is right and wrong. Using a concise expression of John Henry Newman's Oxford University sermons, we can say that conscience is "an instrument for detecting moral truth." *Conscience detects moral truth: it interprets a norm which it does not create.*"[85]

In the speech in Los Angeles, to which he refers in the preceding passage, he states: "It is sometimes claimed that dissent from the magisterium is totally compatible with being a 'good Catholic' and poses no obstacle to the reception of the sacraments. This is a grave error that challenges the teaching office of the bishops of the United States and elsewhere."[86] His insistence on the truth of the teaching of *Humanae Vitae* and the obligation of theologians to teach this truth and of spouses to live by it seems to become ever stronger:

> [The doctrine of *Humanae Vitae*] is not, in fact, a doctrine invented by man: it was stamped on the very nature of the human person by God the Creator's hand and confirmed by him in Revelation. Calling it into question, therefore, is equivalent to refusing God himself the obedience of our intelligence. It is equivalent to preferring the dim light of our reason to the light of divine Wisdom, thereby falling into the darkness of error and resulting in the undermining of other fundamental principles of Christian doctrine.[87]

And further, "Since the *Magisterium of the Church* was created by Christ the Lord to enlighten the conscience, then to appeal to that conscience precisely to contest the truth of what is taught by the Magisterium implies rejection of the Catholic concept both of the Magisterium and moral conscience."[88]

The Need for Continual Nourishing of Love and Spiritual Growth in Spouses

The need for couples to be faithful to the truth of their love for one another is best met, in the thought of John Paul, through an ongoing effort to foster and nourish their love, an effort that he believes needs much prayer to succeed. In a speech to several recently married couples, he states:

> To carry out the commandment of love means accomplishing all the duties of the Christian family: fidelity and conjugal virtue, responsible parenthood and education. The "little Church"—the domestic Church—means the family living in the spirit of the commandment of love; its interior truth, its daily toil, its spiritual beauty and its power. But to live this poem of love and unity in this way you absolutely need to pray. In this sense prayer becomes really essential for love and unity: in fact, prayer strengthens,

relieves, purifies, exalts, helps to find light and advice, deepens the respect that spouses in particular must mutually nourish for their hearts, their consciences and their bodies, by means of which they are so close to each other.[89]

The Good of Natural Family Planning

As in his speeches on modern life, in John Paul's talks on marriage and the family he regularly warns against the dangers of materialism, which causes young people "to live their love under the banner of impermanence and sterility."[90] Yet he realizes that often couples may need to limit their family size and repeatedly calls on scientists to help perfect methods of determining fertility and urges on the work of groups that promote the various methods of natural family planning.

The constant attention that John Paul pays to the Church's doctrine on marriage and contraception is a natural result of his view that happy marriages and family life are essential to human well-being and that should we secure these, we will have gained great ground in combatting many, if not most, of the other evils to which human life is peculiarly subject. He understands the Church, its bishops, theologians, and laypeople, to have a peculiar responsibility to seek a deeper understanding of this teaching and to promote it. He has provided all with abundant resources for doing so.

Afterword

THE NEGLECT by philosophers and theologians of the issue of contraception is not easily explained in light of the complexity of the issue and the magnitude of the question. In light of the Church's perpetual condemnation of contraception, it would seem that Catholic philosophers and theologians would have a special impetus for considering the issue. This book has attempted to assess the status of the question: It has sought to place the Church's condemnation within the context of its teaching on marriage and to show how it draws on principles fundamental to Catholic moral teaching. It claims that the challenges to the Church on contraception have resulted in or at least run parallel to a challenge to the fundamentals of Catholic moral reasoning. The analysis offers some positive arguments to show the moral impermissibility of contraception; it critiques the arguments of revisionists who find contraception morally permissible; and on occasion it points out the weaknesses of some of those who support the Church's teaching but not well. The middle chapters of this book are, I think, the most important, for they attempt to show that traditional natural law arguments against contraception are stronger than have customarily been granted.

Of great importance, too, are the sections that explain Pope John Paul II's innovative defense of *Humanae Vitae*. His arguments are especially effective and blend together truths based on natural law with what has come to be known as personalist values. He has offered a rich source of insights for those attempting to understand why contraception is immoral and a powerful challenge to those who think it is not.

While I was writing this book, during the twentieth anniversary year of *Humanae Vitae*, I received and accepted many invitations to speak around the country about the encyclical. I spoke to university professors and students, to NFP groups, and to many Church groups. I found that interest in this document is strong and that when presented with the arguments that defend the document, most readily admit that the Church is not imposing some outdated, rigid, and arbitrary teaching. Whether or not they ultimately agree with the teaching or the arguments, most allow that they have an admirable consistency and force in terms of their philosophical rigor and additional strength in their theological foundations.

Many bemoan that so little effort has been made to make the teaching and the arguments supporting it known to the Catholic faithful and the public at large. As noted at the outset in chapter 8, John Paul II has been among the most energetic proponents and most innovative interpreters and teachers of the teachings of *Humanae Vitae*. If the teaching is true and if such interpreters as John Paul are correct that a great deal of the unhappiness in marriages is attributable to a neglect of this teaching, and if it is true that unhappy marriages make for unhappy families and that unhappy families make for unhappy societies, we would do well to attempt to understand better and to live better by the teachings of *Humanae Vitae*.

I have attempted to reintroduce contraception into the marketplace of debate as an ethical issue of tremendous import and one that greatly needs our careful consideration. I suspect that if future generations learn from the generation that followed *Humanae Vitae* they will not so readily embrace contraception as a guarantor of an anxiety-free sex life but will begin to suspect it as a threat to the intimacy and love sought in marriage.

Translation of *Humanae Vitae*

Translator's Introduction

The currently available English texts of *Humanae Vitae* are based extensively, if not primarily, on the Italian version of the encyclical.[a] Since the encyclical was originally composed in Italian and French, this is understandable. Nonetheless, Latin remains the official language of the Church and thus the Latin version of *Humanae Vitae* is the official text. The following translation of *Humanae Vitae* is based on the Latin text.

[a]The claim that *Humanae Vitae* was written in Italian and French is made by Lucio Brunelli, "The Pill That Divided the Church," *Thirty Days* 4 (July–August 1988), p. 66. A comparison of some of the Italian phrases with the Latin can be found in Innocentius Parisella, "Latinae Quaedam Voces Locutionesque in Encyclicis Litteris *Humanae Vitae* Occurrentes cum Sermone Italico Comparatae," *Ephemerides Iuris Canonici* 24 (1968) 265–270, and reprinted in *Latinitas* 17 (1969) 115–120.

In preparation for this translation reference was made to six English translations. The most commonly available is that first published in the English edition of the *L'Osservatore Romano* when *Humanae Vitae* was released and made widely available in this country through the Daughters of Saint Paul (hereafter referred to as the "usual translation" and designated by DSP). Popular, too, is the translation by Marc Calegari, S.J., *Humanae Vitae* (San Francisco: Ignatius Press, 1978) (hereafter IP). The Catholic Truth Society sponsored a translation, by Rev. Alan C. Clark and Rev. Geoffrey Crawfurd (London: Catholic Truth Society, 1968) (hereafter CTS), with a revised edition in 1970 (hereafter CTS2); a revised version of the CTS translation is also to be found in *The Pope Speaks* 13:4 (1969) 329–46 (hereafter CTS3). (It is difficult to determine the extent of the revisions, but they seem not very significant, except for the crucial last line of *Humanae Vitae* 11; see the comment on this section in the following notes.) A text that seems to be identical to CTS2 is published in *Vatican Council II* vol. 2, ed. by Austin Flannery, O.P. (Northport, N.Y.: Costello Publishing Co., 1982), 397–416, though the claim is made that the translation was done by the Vatican Press Office (p. 414). Although the CTS translation is accompanied by the notice that it was made on the basis of the Latin text it seems to this reader to be truer to the Italian, except in a few crucial passages. The only translation that used the Latin as the primary base is that by A. Durand, " 'The Encyclical'—A Fresh Translation," *Homiletic and Pastoral Review* 69:11 (Aug. 1969) 851–864 (hereafter HPR), which seems to this reader to be quite a free translation. I am indebted to these translators for felicity of phrasing that I have "borrowed" on occasion. The translation published here is based on the Latin, though on a few occasions, when the Latin seemed irrecoverably obscure, recourse was made to the Italian.

For the most part the Italian and Latin texts do not differ substantially, though there are several important differences in tone and in some key phrases. Moreover, the Latin has important correspondences with earlier Church writings and serves better to show the continuity and development of certain arguments. For instance, the fourth word in the Italian text is *dovere*, which is properly translated "duty" in English. In Latin, one would have expected to have found *officium* (duty). But one finds *munus*, meaning "reward," "honor," "gift," "responsibility," "task," "office," "function," and so on; this choice is not surprising because it is a word that, as Chapter 5 seeks to substantiate, has a distinguished history in Church documents. My studies have led me to believe that "mission" captures best the word's many connotations. Since *munus* is so central to my interpretation of *Humanae Vitae*, all occurrences of the word have been noted by the insertion of the Latin in the translation.

Even more significant is a difference in the crucial passage in section 11 usually translated "Each and every marriage act must remain open to procreation." The Italian reads "Che qualsiasi atto matrimoniale deve rimanere aperto alla trasmissione della vita." The Latin substitutes the words *per se destinatus* ("in itself destined") for the Italian *aperto* ("open"), though the Latin *apertus* ("open") would easily have worked here. As the commentary in Chapter 3 argues, the phrase *per se destinatus* is philosophically more precise and more in keeping with the context.

The Latin of the document has no identifiable source of reliable decipherment; it is a kind of "modern" or "Church" Latin, which is an odd combination of classical Latin and the language the Church has developed over the centuries. The method of translation employed here has involved consultation of classical and medieval dictionaries, reference to arguably representative classical and medieval authors, tracing of the word being considered through the documents of Vatican II, consideration of the appearance of a word in other Church documents, cross-reference to other uses of a word within *Humanae Vitae* itself, reference to the Italian "original," and reference to other translations. I have included Latin words or phrases when I thought the reader with a little Latin might like to know how the Latin reads.

As any who have attempted to translate Latin know, it is a language that loves long and intricate sentences. The form of these sentences is not easily or wisely transported into English. Consequently, I have customarily broken down long sentences into at least three English sentences. Certainly, this translation attempts to follow the Latin closely, but some slight liberties were taken when necessary for respecting English idiom. Some stiltedness and convolutedness inevitably remain. I have also taken the liberty of breaking some of the paragraphs into smaller units in the hopes that this will enable the reader to see the structure of the argument more easily.

Subtitles are given periodically throughout the Italian text. These do not appear in the Latin text. But since they are accurate and useful, I have decided to employ them here.

The numbered notes are to the documents that are cited by the encyclical. The lettered notes are explanatory of my reasons for preferring certain translations.

And, as is the practice throughout the body of this book, when *Man* is capitalized it is to be understood to be the generic use of the word *man*, that is, inclusive of both males and females.

HUMANAE VITAE
An encyclical letter on the proper regulation
of the propagation of offspring [addressed]
To the Venerable Patriarchs, Archbishops, Bishops
and to all the local Ordinaries,
Who are in peace and communion with the Apostolic See
to the Clergy and the Christian Faithful of the
whole Catholic realm [*totius Catholici Orbis*]
and to all Men of goodwill.
Pope Paul VI
To Our venerable brothers and beloved sons,
Greetings and [Our] apostolic blessing

The Transmission of Life

1. God has entrusted spouses with the extremely important [*gravissimum*]
mission [*munus*][b] of transmitting human life. In fulfilling this mission
spouses freely and deliberately [*consciam*] render [*tribuunt*] a service [*opera*]
to God, the Creator.[c] This service has always been a source of great joy,
although the joys are, at times, accompanied by not a few difficulties and
sufferings.

Fulfilling this mission [*munus*] has always raised some difficult questions
[*quaestiones*][d] for the consciences of married couples. Furthermore, in recent

[b]See Chapter 5 for a discussion of the word *munus*.

[c]This second line has been translated "for which married persons are the free and responsible
collaborators of God the Creator." The Italian word for "collaborators" appears in the Italian
and may be an echo of *Gaudium et Spes* 50.2, which refers to the duty of transmitting and
educating human life (*in officio humanam vitam transmittendi atque educandi*) and speaks of
spouses as cooperators and interpreters of God's love in this duty (*cooperatores . . . amoris Dei
Creatoris*). But in Latin the phrase is *tribuunt operam*. *Operam* is from *opera*, not *opus*; the
Lewis and Short Latin dictionary notes, "*Opus* is used mostly of the mechanical activity of
work, as that of animals, slaves, and soldiers; *opera* supposes a free will and desire to serve."
Opera is more properly translated as "service." *Tribuunt* has very much the sense of "pay back"
or "render"; "transmitting life" is, indeed, something that the spouses do *with* God, but the
way it is stated here puts some emphasis on the fact that in doing so, they perform a service
or give a return to God for the *munus* He has entrusted to them. This interpretation coincides
with the meaning of *munus* as a task that God delegates to Man, and, in a sense, needs him
to do, so that He may advance His kingdom.

Consciam is the word that later in the document is allied with *paternitas* (paternity or
parenthood) and with it is translated as "responsible parenthood." Humans, when engaging
in sexual intercourse, are capable of knowing that a result of this intercourse may be the
conception of a child. To engage in sexual intercourse responsibly they must be prepared to
be good parents to a child. More is said about responsible parenthood in section 10, but the
presence of the word *consciam* here indicates that "transmitting human life" involves more
than simple reproduction.

[d]This first sentence of the second paragraph has been translated: "At all times the fulfillment
of this duty has posed grave problems. . . ." This translation again follows the Italian rather

times, the evolution of human society has brought with it changes that raise new questions. The Church cannot ignore these questions, for they concern matters intimately connected with human life and happiness.

Part 1. New Aspects of the Question and the Competence of the Magisterium

2. The various changes that have taken place [in modern times] are truly of great importance. In the first place, there has been a rapid increase in population, an increase that causes many to fear that the population of the earth will grow faster than its available life-sustaining resources. This [disparity] could result in even greater hardships for many families and for many developing nations. Public authorities may easily be tempted to fight the danger by rather severe methods. Moreover, contemporary conditions of work and housing, as well as increased expenses involved in providing for, raising, and educating children, often make it burdensome to support a large family adequately.

It must also be noted that there have been changes in how we view the person of woman and how we view her role [*munere*] in society; indeed there have even been changes in the value we place on conjugal love and on how we understand the meaning of acts of sexual intercourse [*actibus coniugum*]ᵉ in light of this love.

Finally, and above all, it must be noted that because Man has made such remarkable progress in controlling [*moderandis*] the forces of nature and in rationally organizing them, he also strives to extend this control [*moderationem*] to the whole of his life: that is, to his body, to the powers of his mind [*ad sui animi vires*], to his social life, and even to the laws that regulate the propagation of life.

3. This state of affairs gives rise to new questions. [Some ask:] Given the conditions of life today and given the importance of marital intercourse

---

than the Latin. "Problems" is the English cognate of the Italian *problemi*, but it is not perhaps the best translation even of the Italian. In Italian the word is closer in meaning to the English "questions" (a cognate of the Latin used here), which means a query that one might raise about something; it is more neutral than "problems," which connotes that one has some difficulty with something. Indeed, there is the suggestion here that it is not always easy for spouses to understand the *munus* that is theirs and that at times it can be difficult for them to accept it, but it is important not to stress the acknowledgment that a *munus* may involve difficulties without, at the same time, stressing what an honor it is.

ᵉ*Actibus coniugum* is variously translated as "conjugal acts" (DSP, IP, CTS3) and "intimate married life" (CTS1 and CTS2). Conceivably "conjugal acts" could refer to activity in married life other than sexual intercourse, but it does not seem to be too presumptuous to assume that such is its meaning here.

for marital harmony and fidelity, is it not appropriate to reconsider [*recognoscere*]ᶠ the moral norms that have obtained up to now? Is not a reconsideration especially appropriate if it is believed that these norms cannot be observed without serious sacrifices [*gravia incommoda*], sometimes heroic sacrifices?ᵍ

Or, is it not possible to apply the so-called principle of totality to this problem? Would it not be possible to use this principle to justify using one's reason to reduce one's fertility? Would not an act that causes sterility become a licit and prudent way to limit one's family size? That is, would it not clearly be right to consider the goal [*finem*] of having children to pertain more to the whole of married life than to each and every act [of sexual intercourse]? And, again, given the fact that moderns have an increased sense of their responsibilities, [they ask] whether it is not right for them to entrust the mission [*munus*] of transmitting life more to their reason and will, than to the biological rhythms [*certis . . . vicibus*] of their bodies?

Competence of the Magisterium

4. Certainly, questions of this kind require that the Magisterium of the Church give new and deeper consideration to the principles of the moral teaching concerning marriage, a teaching that is rooted in natural law, illuminated and made richer by divine revelation.

Let no one of the faithful deny that the Magisterium of the Church is competent to interpret the natural moral law. For it is indisputable—as Our predecessors have often declared[1]—that when Jesus Christ imparted

1. Pius IX, encyclical *Qui Pluribus*, Nov. 9, 1846, in Pii IX P. M. Acta, I, 9–10; St. Pius X, encyclical *Singulari Quadam*, Sept. 24, 1912, in AAS 4 (1912) 658; Pius XI, encyclical *Casti Connubii*, Dec. 31, 1930, in AAS 22 (1930), 579–81; Pius XII, "Address to the Episcopate of the Catholic World," Nov. 2, 1954, in AAS 46 (1954) 671–72; John XXIII, encyclical, *Mater et Magistra*, May 15, 1961, in AAS 53 (1961), 457.

ᶠThe Italian here refers to a need for a *revisione* of the norm. Both DSP and IP translate *recognoscere* as "revise," which, although a cognate of the Italian, perhaps in English suggests a greater change than the text intends to suggest. CTS uses "review," which I believe is closer to the Latin. "Revise" is certainly what many wanted the Church to do; "review" or "reconsider" is what in fact the Church did.

ᵍThe translation for *incommoda* as "sacrifices" has been adopted from DSP and IP, which are following the Italian *sacrifici*. The Latin *incommoda* has the connotation more of "inconvenience" than of "sacrifice"; "difficulties" would perhaps be a more precise translation. A literal English translation would read: "serious difficulties which are sometimes a worthy [challenge] for the strongest men and women [*fortissimis viris digna*]." But, since it does not work in English to say "heroic difficulties," I have stayed with the more idiomatic "heroic sacrifices." The question of the morality of asking spouses to make heroic sacrifices was part of the concern of the Schema.

His divine authority [*potestatis*] to Peter and the other apostles and sent them to all nations to teach His Commandments,[2] He established those very men as authentic guardians and interpreters of the whole moral law, that is, not only of the law of the Gospel, but also of natural law. For natural law [as well as revealed law] declares the will of God; [thus] faithful compliance [*fidelis obtemperatio*][h] with natural law is necessary for eternal salvation.[3]

Moreover, the Church has always been faithful in fulfilling this command. In recent times, she has more amply provided an integrated teaching [*congrua documenta*][i] on the nature of marriage, on the moral use of conjugal rights, and on the duties of the spouses.[4]

Special Studies

5. Conscious of Our responsibility [*muneris*] in this regard, We approved and enlarged the commission established by Our venerable predecessor John XXIII in March of 1963. In addition to many experts in the relevant disciplines, the commission also included married couples. The commission was to consider opinions and views concerning married life and, in particular, [it was to reflect upon] the legitimate means of controlling family size [*rectem progignendae prolis temperationem*].[j] It was to report the results in due

2. Cf. Matt. 28:18–19.
3. Cf. Matt. 7:21.
4. Cf. *Catechismus Romanus Concilii Tridentini*, part II, ch. 8; Leo XIII, encyclical, *Arcanum*, Feb. 19, 1880, in *Acta Leonis XIII*, II (1880) 26–29; Pius XI, encyclical *Divini Illius Magistri*, Dec. 31, 1929, in AAS 22 (1930), 58–61; Pius XI, encyclical *Casti Connubii* in AAS 22 (1930) 545–46; Pius XII, "Address to the Italian Medico-Biological Union of St. Luke," Nov. 12, 1944 in *Discorsi e Radiomessaggi di S. S. Pio XII* 6, 191–92; Pius XII, "Address to the Italian Catholic Union of Midwives," Oct. 29, 1951, in AAS 43 (1951) 835–54; Pius XII, "Address to the Congress of the Family Front and of the Association of Large Families,"

[h]CTS translates *obtemperatio* as "observance"; DSP uses "fulfillment"; I have chosen "compliance" since I believe that "observance" seems somewhat weak and vague. "Obedience" would not be wrong, but since modern Americans, at least, seem to think all obedience is servile, I have selected "compliance" since this seems to capture both the sense of necessary adherence and the notion of voluntary cooperation.

[i]There is quite a variation on the translation of the phrase *congrua documenta*: DSP reads "has provided a coherent teaching on"; IP reads "has provided an integrated teaching on" and CTS1 and CTS2, "has always provided consistent teaching"; CTS3, "has always issued appropriate documents."

[j]All the translations use "birth regulation" or "regulation of births," which is true to the Italian. The Latin *rectem progignendae prolis temperationem*, which strictly translated reads "the correct regulation of having offspring," may be equivalent to "birth regulation." Neither "birth regulation" nor "birth control" is equivalent to "contraception," since they both refer to any methods that spouses might use to regulate the number of children that they are to have and therefore could include natural methods. Yet this phrase "birth regulation" may be the cause of some confusion since in English it is too easily equated with birth control, which,

time to the Magisterium so that it could provide a fitting response to the
faithful and to people worldwide who were awaiting an answer.[5]

The investigation of the experts and the opinions and advice from
Our confreres in the Episcopate—some spontaneously offered and some
solicited by Us—enabled Us to consider very thoroughly all aspects of this
complex subject. For which reason We offer Our most sincere thanks to
all.

The Response of the Magisterium

6. We could not, however, consider the conclusions of the commission
in themselves as carrying the force of a certain and definite judgment; nor
could their judgment relieve Us of Our duty [officium] of deciding a question
of such great importance through Our own consideration. There were
several reasons why this was necessary. First, there was no full consensus
within the commission concerning what moral norms ought to be proposed.
And even more importantly, certain methods and criteria [viae rationesque]
were used in answering the question that departed [discedentes] from the
firm and constant teaching of the Magisterium on what is moral within
marriage.

We have carefully evaluated the findings sent to Us and most thoroughly
considered this matter. Now, after assiduous prayer, We think it right,
through the power given to Us by Christ, to give an answer to these
weighty questions.

Part 2. Doctrinal Principles

A Total Vision of Man

7. The question of having children,[k] like other questions regarding
human life, cannot be addressed adequately by examining it in a piecemeal

---

Nov. 28, 1951, in AAS 43 (1951) 857–59; Pius XII, "Address to the Seventh Congress of
the International Society of Hematology," Sept. 12, 1958, in AAS 50 (1958) 734–35; John
XXIII, encyclical *Mater et Magistra* in AAS 53 (1961) 446–47; Second Vatican Council,
Pastoral Constitution, *Gaudium et Spes*, Dec. 7, 1965, nos. 47–52, in AAS 58 (1966) 1067–
74; *Code of Canon Law 1917*, Canons 1067, 1068.1, 1076.1–2.

5. Paul VI, "Address to the Sacred College of Cardinals," June 23, 1964, in AAS 56

---

in turn, is too easily identified with contraception. "Contraception" refers to devices or drugs
that actively work *against* conception and, therefore, does not include natural methods of
family planning.

k The translation of the first clause of this section is problematic. The Latin reads: *De* way, that is, by looking at it through the perspectives of biology, psychology, demography, and sociology. Rather, [the question] must be addressed in such a way that the whole Man and the whole mission [*munus*] to which he has been called will be taken into account, for this [mission] pertains not only to his natural and earthly existence but also to his supernatural and eternal existence.

Many who attempt to defend artificial ways of limiting the number of children[1] give as their reason the demands of conjugal love or their duty to responsible parenthood [*paternitatis sui officii consciae*]. [Therefore] it is necessary to provide a precise definition and explanation of these two important [*gravia*] elements of married life. As We undertake to do this, We will keep foremost in Our minds what was taught about this matter with the highest authority in *The Church in the Modern World* [*Gaudium et Spes*], the pastoral constitution recently issued by the Second Vatican Council.

Conjugal Love

8. Truly, conjugal love most clearly manifests to us its true nature and nobility when we recognize that it has its origin in the highest source, as it were, in God, Who "is Love"[6] and Who is the Father, "from whom all parenthood [*paternitas*] in heaven and earth receives its name."[7]

It is false to think, then, that marriage results from chance or from the blind course [*cursu*] of natural forces. Rather, God the Creator wisely and providently established marriage with the intent that He might achieve

---

(1964) 588; Paul VI, "Address to the Commission for the Study of Population, the Family and Birth Regulation," Mar. 27, 1965, in AAS 57 (1965) 388; Paul VI, "Address to the National Congress of the Italian Society of Obstetrics and Gynecology," Oct. 29, 1966, in AAS 58 (1966) 1168.

6. Cf. 1 Jn. 4:8.

7. Eph. 3:15.

---

propaganda prole questio. The Italian reads: *Il problema della natalità.* It is translated variously; DSP has "the problem of birth"; IP, "the problem of birth regulation"; CTS1 and CTS2, "the question of the birth of children"; CTS3, "the question of human procreation." I have chosen "the question of having children," since I think the question being addressed here is larger than the question of *limiting* how many children one has: it touches on, for instance, why one should have children and the responsibilities of having children.

[1]This phrase differs considerably in the Latin and the Italian. The Latin phrase *artificiosas vias . . . quibus liberorum numerus coerceatur* corresponds to the Italian phrase *i metodi artificiali di controllo delle nascite*; the usual translation is "artificial methods of birth control." But the Latin is more concrete in speaking of the "artificial ways by which the number of children is limited." I think this concreteness, that it is children who are being "limited" rather than the more abstract "birth," is important.

His own design of love through Men. Therefore, through mutual self-giving, which is unique [*propriam*] and exclusive to them, spouses seek a communion of persons [*personarum communionem*]. Through this communion, the spouses perfect each other so that they might share with God the task [*operam socient*]ᵐ of procreating and educating new living beings.

Moreover, for the baptized, matrimony is endowed with such dignity that it is a sacramental sign of grace representing the union of Christ and His Church.

Characteristics of Conjugal Love

9. When these matters are placed in the proper light, we can clearly see the characteristic marks and requirements of conjugal love. It is of the greatest importance to have an exact understanding of these.

First of all, [this] love is *human* and therefore both of the senses and of the spirit. For which reason, it is a product not only of natural instinct and inclinations [*affectuum*]; it also and primarily involves an act of free will. Through this act of free will [the spouses resolve] that their love will not only persevere through daily joys and sorrows but also increase. Therefore it is especially important that they become one in heart and soul, and that they obtain together their human perfection.

Next, this love is *total* [*pleno*]; that is, it is a very special form of personal friendship whereby the spouses generously share everything with each other without undue reservations and without concern for their selfish convenience. One who truly loves his spouse not only loves her for what he receives from her but also for her own sake. This he does joyfully, as he enriches [his beloved] with the gift of himself.ⁿ

Furthermore, conjugal love is both *faithful and exclusive* to the end of life. Such, in fact, do the bride and groom conceive it to be on the day of their marriage, when they freely and consciously [*planeque conscii*] unite themselves by means of the marital bond [*matrimoniali se vinculo devinxer-*

ᵐThe phrase *cum Deo operam socient* is a bit peculiar. The Italian text speaks of the spouses being collaborators with God, as do several of the translations; others note that spouses "cooperate" with God. Again, I thought it important to note that *operam* is not the word for "work" but for "service." *Socient* means that there is a sharing of the service. This notion, again, is at the root of the word *munus* (mission), which refers to a task that God entrusts to others, needs them to do, and will help them to achieve.

ⁿThe final sentence presents difficulties to the modern translator who works in an atmosphere where all masculine pronouns are taken to refer to the male. This is especially awkward when speaking of marriage, which clearly involves the reciprocal responsibilities of both sexes. The Latin easily includes the obligations of both sexes to each other, whereas it is impossible to convey this in modern-day English.

unt]. Even if fidelity at times presents difficulties, let no one deny that it is possible; [rather] fidelity is always noble and of much merit. The example of many spouses throughout the ages has proved that fidelity is in accord with the very nature of marriage; even more, it has proved that intimate and lasting happiness flows from fidelity, just as from a fountain.

And finally, this love is *fruitful*, since the whole of the love is not contained in the communion of the spouses; it also looks beyond itself and seeks to raise up new lives. "Marriage and conjugal love are ordained [*ordinantur*] by their very nature [*indole sua*] to the procreating and educating of children. Offspring are clearly the supreme gift [*donum*] of marriage, a gift that contributes immensely to the good of the parents themselves."[8]

Responsible Parenthood

10. For the above reasons, conjugal love requires that spouses be fully aware of their mission [*munus*] of responsible parenthood [*paternitatem consciam*]. Today's society justly calls for responsible parenthood; thus it is important that it be rightly understood. Consequently, we must consider the various legitimate and interconnected dimensions [*rationibus*] of parenthood.

If we consider biological processes first, responsible parenthood [*paternitas conscia*] means that one knows and honors [*observantiam*] the responsibilities [*munerum*] involved in these processes.° Human reason has discovered that there are biological laws in the power of procreating life that pertain to the human person.[9]

If then we look to the innate impulses and inclinations of the soul, responsible parenthood asserts that it is necessary that reason and will exercise mastery over these impulses and inclinations of the soul.

If we look further to physical, economic, psychological, and social conditions, responsible parenthood is exercised by those who, guided by prudent consideration and generosity, elect to accept many children. Those are also to be considered responsible who, for serious reasons [*seriis causis*]

8. Second Vatican Council, Pastoral Constitution, *Gaudium et Spes*, no. 50, in AAS 58 (1966) 1070–72.

9. Cf. St. Thomas, *Summa Theologiae*, I–II, q. 94, a. 2.

°The phrase *munerum ad eos [biologicos processus] attinentium* is difficult to capture. *Munerum* is translated by DSP and IP and all the CTS versions as "functions," which seems to reflect the Italian *funzioni*. Durand (translating from the Latin) renders it "obligations associated with these [biological processes]." See also *Humanae Vitae* 17 for two other instances of forms of *munus* used in reference to physical processes.

and with due respect for moral precepts, decide not to have another child for either a definite or an indefinite amount of time.

The responsible parenthood of which we speak here has another intrinsic foundation [*intimam rationem*]ᴾ of utmost importance: it is rooted in the objective moral order established by God—and only an upright conscience can be a true interpreter of this order. For which reason, the mission [*munus*] of responsible parenthood requires that spouses recognize their duties [*officia*] toward God, toward themselves, toward the family, and toward human society, as they maintain a correct set of priorities.ᵠ

For this reason, in regard to the mission [*munere*] of transmitting human life, it is not right for spouses to act in accord with their own arbitrary judgment [*arbitratu suo*], as if it were permissible for them to define altogether subjectively and willfully [*modo ominino proprio ac libero*] what is right for them to do. On the contrary, they must accommodate their behavior to the plan of God the Creator, a plan made manifest both by the very nature of marriage and its acts and also by the constant teaching of the Church.[10]

Respect for the Nature and Finality of the Conjugal Act

11. The conjugal acts by which spouses intimately and chastely unite [*copulantur*], and by which human life is transmitted, are, as the recent council reiterated, "good and worthy of human dignity."[11] Conjugal acts do not cease being legitimate if the spouses are aware that they are infertile for reasons not voluntarily caused by them; these acts remain ordained [*destinatio*] to expressing and strengthening the union of the spouses. Indeed, as experience shows, new life does not arise from every act of conjugal union. God has wisely arranged the natural laws and times of fertility so

---

10. Cf. Second Vatican Council, Pastoral Constitution, *Gaudium et Spes*, nos. 50–51, in AAS 58 (1966) 1070–73.

11. Cf. ibid., no. 49, in AAS 58 (1966) 1070.

ᴾIt is difficult to determine a literal reading of *intimam rationem* (it is used again in HV 12); perhaps "most profound justification" would serve; *ratio* has many legitimate translations. Following the Italian *un più profondo rapporto*; DSP and IP have "a more profound relationship." CTS1 and CST2 have "a further and deeper significance of paramount importance"; CTS3 has "one further essential aspect of paramount importance." Durand has "is chiefly characterized by another and intimate quality."

ᵠThis last phrase is translated a bit loosely. The Latin is *rerum bonorumque ordine recte servato*, which literally means "with the order of affairs and goods having been kept rightly." DSP and IP, following the Italian *in una giusta gerarchia dei valori*, have "in a correct hierarchy of values." All CTS versions have "keeping a right order of priorities," and Durand has "all in due order."

that successive births are naturally spaced. But the Church, which interprets natural law through its unchanging doctrine, reminds men and
women that the teachings based on natural law must be obeyed [*observandis*]
and teaches that it is necessary that each conjugal act [*matrimonii usus*]
remain ordained in itself [*per se destinatus*] to the procreating of human
life.[12] [r]

Two Inseparable Aspects: Union and Procreation

12. The doctrine that the Magisterium of the Church has often explained
is this: there is an unbreakable connection [*nexu indissolubili*] between the
unitive meaning and the procreative meaning [of the conjugal act], and
both are inherent in the conjugal act. This connection was established by
God, and Man is not permitted to break it through his own volition.

Therefore, because of its intrinsic nature [*intimam rationem*][s] the conjugal
act, which unites husband and wife with the closest of bonds, also makes
them capable of bringing forth new life according to the laws written into
their very natures as male and female. And if both essential meanings
[*ratio*] are preserved, that of union and procreation, the conjugal act fully
maintains its capacity for [fostering] true mutual love and its ordination to
the highest mission [*munus*] of parenthood, to which Man is called. Men
of our time, we think, are especially able to understand that this teaching
is in accord with human reason.

Faithfulness to the Design of God

13. People rightly understand that a conjugal act imposed on a spouse,
with no consideration given to the condition of the spouse or to the

12. Cf. Pius XI, encyclical *Casti Connubii*, in AAS 22 (1930) 560; Pius XII, "Address to
the Congress of the Italian Catholic Association of Midwives," in AAS 43 (1951) 843.

'There is little doubt that the last sentence of this section has caused translators the most
difficulty. See Chapter 3 for a discussion of this sentence. The DSP translation reads, "[The
Church] teaches that each and every marriage act must remain open to the transmission of
life." The IP translation is identical to the DSP translation. CTS1 reads, "[The Church]
teaches as absolutely required that *any use whatever of marriage* must retain its natural potential
to procreate human life." CTS2 reads, "[The Church] teaches as absolutely required that *in
any use whatever of marriage* there must be no impairment of its natural capacity to procreate
human life." CTS3 reads, "[The Church] teaches that each and every marital act must of
necessity retain its intrinsic relationship to the procreation of human life." And the Durand
translation reads, "[The Church] teaches the following necessary principle: every single act
of marriage must retain all of its natural potential to generate human life."

'In paragraph two of this section *intimam rationem* remains problematic. DSP and IP,
following the Italian *intima struttura*, have "intimate structure." CTS1 and CTS2 have

legitimate desires of the spouse, is not a true act of love. They understand that such an act opposes what the moral order rightly requires from spouses. To be consistent, then, if they reflect further, they should acknowledge that it is necessarily true that an act of mutual love that impairs the capacity of bringing forth life contradicts both the divine plan that established the nature [normam] of the conjugal bond and also the will of the first Author of human life. For this capacity of bringing forth life was designed by God, the Creator of All, according to [His] specific laws.

Thus, anyone who uses God's gift [of conjugal love] and cancels, if only in part, the significance and the purpose [finem] of this gift is rebelling [repugnat] against either the male or female nature and against the most intimate relationship [intimae necessitudini]; for this reason, then, he is defying the plan and holy will of God. On the other hand, the one who uses the gift of conjugal love in accord with the laws of generation acknowledges that he is not the lord of the sources of life but rather the minister [ministerium] of a plan initiated by the Creator.

In fact, Man does not have unlimited power over his own body in general. So, too, for good reason, he clearly does not have power over his generative faculties as such [genitalium virium], for they by their very nature are directed to bringing forth human life, and God is the source of human life. Indeed, "Human life must be recognized as sacred by all Men" as Our Predecessor John XXIII declared; "Indeed, from its very beginning it requires the creative action of God."[13]

Morally Impermissible Methods of Regulating Birth

14. Thus, relying on these first principles of human and Christian doctrine concerning marriage,' we must again insist [edicere] that the direct interruption of the generative process already begun must be totally rejected as a legitimate means of regulating [temperandi] the number of children. Especially to be rejected is direct abortion—even if done for reasons of health.[14]

13. John XXIII, encyclical *Mater et Magistra* in AAS 53 (1961) 447.
14. Cf. *Catechismus Romanus Concilii Tridentini*, part 2, chap. 8; Pius XI, encyclical *Casti Connubii*, in AAS 22 (1930) 562–64; Pius XII, "Address to the Italian Medico-Biological Union of St. Luke," Nov. 12, 1944, in *Discorsi e Radiomessaggi di S.S. Pio XII*, 6, 191–92;

"fundamental structure," and CTS3 has "fundamental nature." Durand has "inherent structure."
'The Latin here reads *primariis hisce principiis*, or "first principles." The Italian reads *con questi capisaldi*, or "with this foundation stone." The English translations are disparate: DSP reads "landmarks," CTS2 uses "first principles," and IP uses "fundamental elements." "First

Furthermore, as the Magisterium of the Church has taught repeatedly, direct sterilization of the male or female, whether permanent or temporary, is equally to be condemned.[15]

Similarly there must be a rejection of all acts that attempt to impede procreation," both those chosen as means to an end and those chosen as ends. This includes acts that precede intercourse, acts that accompany intercourse, and acts that are directed to the natural consequences of intercourse.[16]

Nor is it possible to justify deliberately depriving conjugal acts of their fertility by claiming that one is choosing the lesser evil. It cannot be claimed that these acts deprived of fertility should be considered together as a whole with past and future fertile acts and thus that they [should be judged to] share in one and the same moral goodness of the fertile acts [of marriage]. Certainly, it is sometimes permissible to tolerate moral evil — when it is the lesser evil and when one does so in order that one might avoid a greater evil, or so that one might promote a greater good.[17] It is never permissible, however, to do evil so that good might result,[18] not even for the most serious reasons. That is, one should never willingly choose to do an act that by its very nature violates the moral order [*ex propria natura moralem ordinem transgrediatur*], for such acts are unworthy of Man for this very reason. This is so even if one has acted with the intent

Pius XII, "Address to the Italian Catholic Union of Midwives," Pastoral Constitution, in AAS 43 (1951) 842–43; Pius XII, "Address to the Congress of the Family Front and of the Association of Large Families," in AAS 43 (1951) 857–59; John XXIII, encyclical *Pacem in Terris*, Apr. 11, 1963, in AAS 55 (1963) 259–60; Second Vatican Council, Pastoral Constitution, *Gaudium et Spes*, 50, in AAS 58 (1966) 1072.

15. Cf. Pius XI, encyclical *Casti Connubii*, in AAS 22 (1930) 565; Pius XII, Decree of the Holy Office, Feb. 22, 1940, in AAS 32 (1940) 73; Pius XII, "Address to the Italian Catholic Union of Midwives," in AAS 43 (1951) 843–44; Pius XII, "Address to the Seventh Congress of the International Society of Hematology," in AAS 50 (1958) 734–35.

16. Cf. *Catechismus Romanus Concilii Tridentini*, pt. 2, chap. 8; Pius XI, *Casti Connubii*, in AAS 22 (1930) 559–61; Pius XII, "Address to the Italian Catholic Union of Midwives," in AAS 43 (1951) 843; Pius XII, "Address to the Seventh Congress of the International Society of Hematology," in AAS 50 (1958) 734–35; John XXIII, encyclical, *Mater et Magistra*, in AAS 53 (1961) 447.

17. Cf. Pius XII, "Address to the Fifth National Congress of Italian Catholic Jurists," Dec. 6, 1953, in AAS 45 (1953) 798–99.

18. Cf. Rom. 3:8.

principles" should be the preferred translation since it captures the technical philosophical sense of *principiis*. A proper inquiry must proceed from first principles; without agreement on these principles, no progress can be made in reasoning about the matters which the principles undergird.

"For the phrase translated here as actions that attempt "to impede procreation," the Latin is *ut procreatio impediatur*; the Italian is *di rendere impossibile la procreazione*.

to defend and advance some good either for individuals or for families or for society. Thus, it is a serious error to think that a conjugal act, deprived deliberately [*ex industria*] of its fertility, and which consequently is intrinsically wrong [*intrinsece inhonestum*], can be justified by being grouped together with the fertile acts of the whole of the marriage.

Morally Permissible Therapeutic Means

15. The Church, moreover, does allow the use of medical treatment necessary for curing diseases of the body although this treatment may thwart one's ability to procreate. Such treatment is permissible even if the reduction of fertility is foreseen, as long as the infertility is not directly intended for any reason whatsoever.[19] ᵛ

The Morality of Recourse to the Infertile Period

16. Nevertheless, there are some in our times who oppose the teaching of the Church concerning conjugal morality, as we noted above (HV 3). [They claim] that it is the right and function [*munus*] of human reason to restrain the irrational forces of nature and to direct them to achieving ends that are beneficial to Man. Now some may ask: in the present day, is it not reasonable to use artificial birth control in many circumstances? Suppose family peace and harmony might better be achieved and better provisions might be made for educating the children already born? This question deserves a clear answer: the Church, of course, is the first to praise and commend the use of the human intellect in an endeavor that allies Man, rational creature that he is, so closely with his Creator. But the Church affirms that this must be done in accord with the order of reality [*rerum ordine*] established by God.

Certainly, there may be serious reasons [*iustae causae*] for spacing offspring ʷ; these may be based on the physical or psychological condition of

19. Cf. Pope Pius XII, "Address to the Congress of the Italian Association of Urology," Oct. 8, 1953, in AAS 45 (1953) 674–75; Pius XII, "Address to the Seventh Congress of the International Society of Hematology," in AAS 50 (1958) 734–35.

ᵛThis is a short but important paragraph. I decided to cast the principle here in the positive rather than the negative. It may also be important to note that whereas most translators prefer "licit" and "illicit," which are cognates of the Latin, I have chosen to use "morally permissible" and "morally wrong."

ʷThe Italian speaks of *seri motivi* for spacing children, whereas the Latin speaks of *iustae causae*; the translations that have been given for this are "serious motives," "well-grounded reasons," and "reasonable grounds." (See Chapter 4 for a discussion of the morality of the use the spouses or on external factors. The Church teaches that [in such cases] it is morally permissible [for spouses] to calculate [their fertility by observing the] natural rhythms inherent in the generative faculties and to reserve marital intercourse for infertile times. Thus spouses are able to plan their families without violating the moral teachings set forth above.[20]

The Church is not inconsistent when it teaches both that it is morally permissible for spouses to have recourse to infertile periods and also that all directly contraceptive practices are morally wrong, even if spouses seem to have good and serious reasons [*argumenta . . . honesta et gravia*] for using these. These two situations are essentially different. In the first, the spouses legitimately use a faculty that is given by nature; in the second case, the spouses impede the order of generation [*ordo generationis*] from completing its own natural processes.*

It cannot be denied that the spouses in each case have, for defensible reasons [*probabiles rationes*], made a mutual and firm decision to avoid having a child; and [it cannot be denied that] each of them is attempting to ensure that a child will not be born. Nevertheless, it must also be acknowledged that only in the first case are the spouses strong enough to abstain from sexual intercourse during the fertile times, when, for good reasons [*iustae rationes*], offspring are not desired. And then, when the time is not apt for conception, they make use of intercourse for the sake of manifesting their mutual love and for the sake of maintaining their promised fidelity. Clearly when they do this, they offer a witness to truly and completely upright [*recti*] love.

Serious Consequences of the Use of Artificial Methods of Birth Control

17. Responsible individuals will quickly see the truth of the Church's teaching [about contraception], if they consider what consequences will follow from the methods of contraception and the reasons given [*vias*

---

20. Pius XII, "Address to the Italian Catholic Union of Midwives," in AAS 43 (1951) 846.

---

of natural family planning.) For the most part the Italian for this passage is much more translatable than the Latin.

*There are some interesting discrepancies between the Italian and the Latin in this paragraph. One choice of Latin seems to be inappropriate; where the Italian states, "the two cases are essentially different" ("Tra i due casi esiste una differenza essenziale"), the Latin reads, "these two causes differ exceedingly" ("hae duae causae inter se maxime discrepant"). The meaning of *causae* (reasons, motives, purposes, sources) does not seem appropriate here; it seems that *casus* (cases) is what is needed, and "essentially" seems somewhat more precise than "exceedingly."

rationesque] for the use of contraception.' They should first consider how easy it will be [for many] to justify behavior leading to marital infidelity or to a gradual weakening in the discipline of morals.² Not much experience is needed to understand human weakness and to comprehend that human beings, especially the young, are so susceptible to temptation that they need to be encouraged to keep the moral law. It is wrong to make it easy for them to violate this law. Indeed, it is to be feared that husbands who become accustomed to contraceptive practices will lose respect for their wives. They may come to disregard their wife's psychological and physical equilibrium and use their wives as instruments for serving their own desires. Consequently, they will no longer view their wives as companions who should be treated with attentiveness and love.

And then [let reasonable individuals] also carefully consider that a dangerous power will be put into the hands of rulers who care little about the moral law. Would anyone blame those in the highest offices of the state for employing a solution [contraception] considered morally permissible for spouses seeking to solve a family difficulty, when they strive to solve certain difficulties affecting the whole nation? Who will prevent public authorities from favoring what they believe to be the most effective contraceptive methods and from mandating that everyone must use them, whenever they consider it necessary? And clearly it will come about that Men who desire to avoid the difficulties that are part of the divine law, difficulties that individuals, families, or society may experience, will hand over to the will of the public authorities the power of interfering in the most exclusive and intimate mission [*munus*] of spouses.

Therefore, if we do not want the mission [*officium*] of procreating human life to be conceded to the arbitrary decisions of Men, we need to recognize that there are some limits to the power of Man over his own body and over the natural operations [*munera*] of the body, which ought not to be transgressed. No one, neither a private individual nor a public authority, ought to violate these limits. For these limits are derived from the reverence

---

'The second portion of this first sentence is translated variously. The Latin is *quae secutura sunt vias rationesque, ad natorum incrementa artificio coercenda adhibitas.* CTS1 and CTS2 have "the consequences of methods and plans for the artificial restriction of increases in the birth rate"; the other (IP), based on the Italian text (*alle conseguenze dei metodi di regolazione artificiale delle natalità*) is "consequences of the use of methods of artificial birth control." Although abortion may also be intended to be included here, it seems that contraception is the issue at hand and it would be the most succinct and accurate translation.

'The translation of this sentence has generally relied on the Italian (*allo abbassamento generale della moralità*). Most translations render this "a general lowering of morality." The Latin is, *ad morum disciplinam passim enervandam,* which literally means "to a little by little weakening of the discipline of habits."

owed to the whole human body and its natural operations [*naturalibus muneribus*], according to the principles acknowledged above and according to a proper understanding of the so-called principle of totality, as explained by Our Predecessor, Pius XII.[21]

The Church, the Guarantor of Authentic Human Values

18. It is possible to predict that perhaps not everyone will be able to accept a teaching of this sort easily. After all, there are so many critical voices—broadcast widely by modern means of communication—that are contrary to the voice of the Church. Therefore, it is not surprising that the Church finds herself a *sign of contradiction*[22]—just as was [Christ,] her Founder. But this is no reason for the Church to abandon the duty entrusted to her of preaching the whole moral law firmly and humbly, both the natural law and the law of the Gospel.

Since the Church did not make either of these laws, she cannot change them. She can only be their guardian and interpreter; thus it would never be right for her to declare as morally permissible that which is truly not so. For what is immoral is by its very nature always opposed to the true good of Man.

By preserving the whole moral law of marriage, the Church knows that she is supporting the growth of a true civilization among Men. She encourages Man not to abdicate human duties by overreliance on technology. In this way, she safeguards the dignity of spouses. Devoted to the example and teaching of the Divine Savior, the Church shows her sincere and generous love for Men as she strives to help them, even during their earthly pilgrimage, "to share, as sons [and daughters], the life of the living God, the Father of all Men."[23]

Part 3. Pastoral Directives

The Church as Mother and Teacher

19. We would hardly be adequately expressing the thoughts and solicitude of the Church, the Mother and Teacher of all nations, if after

---

21. Cf. Pius XII, "Address to the Congress of the Italian Association of Urology," in AAS 45 (1953) 674–75; Pius XII, "Address to the Directors and Members of the Italian Association of Cornea Donors and of the Italian Association of the Blind," May 14, 1956, in AAS 48 (1956) 461–62.

22. Lk. 2:34.

23. Paul VI, encyclical *Populorum Progressio*, Mar. 26, 1967, no. 21, in AAS 59 (1967) 268.

encouraging Men to keep and respect the law[s] of God concerning marriage, We did not also offer them support in morally permissible methods of regulating their family size; [after all,] ours is a time when families and nations face harsh conditions. But the Church can only conduct herself as did the Divine Redeemer; she knows mankind's weakness; she has compassion on the multitude, and she forgives their sins. She cannot, however, do otherwise than to teach the law that is proper to human life restored to its original truth and guided by the Spirit of God.[24]

The Possibility of Observing the Divine Law

20. The teaching of the Church about the proper spacing of children is a promulgation of the divine law itself. No doubt many will think this teaching difficult, if not impossible, to keep. And truly, just as with all good things outstanding for their nobility and utility, [keeping] this law requires strong motivation and much effort from individual Men, from families, and from society. Indeed, this law is not able to be kept without the abundant grace of God, on which the good moral choices [bona voluntas] of Men depend and from which they get their strength. Moreover, those who consider this matter thoroughly will see that [their] efforts [to keep God's law] increase human dignity and confer benefits on human society.

Self-Mastery

21. Moral family planning requires that spouses recognize and value the true goods of life and the family and also that they acquire the habit of complete mastery of themselves and their desires [motibus]. In order to control the drives of nature, the spouses need to become self-denying [asceseos] through using their reason and free will. Only then will the manifestations of love appropriate for married couples be what they ought to be. Self-mastery is especially necessary for those who practice periodic abstention.

Truly, discipline of this sort—from which conjugal chastity shines forth—cannot be an obstacle to love. Rather, discipline imbues love with a deeper human meaning. Although [such control] requires continuous effort, it also helps the spouses become strong in virtue and makes them rich with spiritual goods. And this [virtue] fosters the fruits of tranquility and peace in the home and helps in the solving of difficulties of other

24. Cf. Rom. 8.

kinds. It aids spouses in becoming more tender with each other and more attentive to each other. It assists them in dispelling that inordinate self-love that is opposed to true charity. It strengthens in them an awareness of their responsibilities [munerum exsequendorum]. And finally it provides parents with a sure and efficacious authority for educating their children. As [their] children advance through life they will come to a correct appreciation of the true goods of Man and employ peacefully and properly the powers of their mind and senses.

Creating an Atmosphere Favorable to Chastity

22. We would like to take this opportunity to advise educators and all others whose right and duty it is to be concerned about the common good. They need to work to create conditions favorable to the cultivation of chastity, so that the norms of the moral order might be kept and true freedom might prevail over license.

Therefore, all those who are concerned with improving civilization and all who wish to protect the most important human goods should condemn with one voice all the forms of entertainment in today's modern society that arouse Man's [base] passions and that foster dissolute morals, such as obscene literature and corrupt theatrical and film productions. It would be perverse if anyone were to attempt to defend depravity of this kind by appealing to the needs of art or learning[25] or by appealing to arguments of "freedom of expression" concerning what authorities may permit in the public arena.

Appeal to Public Authorities

23. And We must also address the rulers of nations, since they have chief responsibility for the common good and are able to work toward safeguarding good morals. [We say to them:] Do not allow the worthy morals of your own people to be corrupted; do not allow the law to be used to introduce into the family—that primary unit of the state—practices opposed to the natural and divine law. For surely civil authority can find and ought to use other means to resolve the problem of the increase of population: namely, they should legislate laws protective of the family and they should wisely educate the populace to safeguard both the moral law and the [true] liberty of the citizens.

25. Cf. Second Vatican Council, Decree *Inter Mirifica*, Dec. 4, 1963, nos. 6–7, in AAS 56 (1964) 147.

Indeed We know well what a source of great difficulty [overpopulation is] for leaders of a state, especially in the developing nations. Indeed, We had these justifiable concerns in mind when We issued the encyclical letter *Populorum Progressio.* But here let Us reiterate the words of Our Predecessor, John XXIII: "It is necessary to solve these problems in such a way that Man does not use methods and means opposed to the dignity of Man. [State authorities] ought not to fear rejecting [the views] of those who hold that Man himself and his life are in every respect only material realities. We think this problem ought to be resolved only through economic and social progress that both respects each and every individual and the whole of society and that also increases goods deserving of the name."[26] Truly it would be a grave injustice to attribute to Divine Providence what seems, on the contrary, to be the result of unwise government policies, or of a rather weak sense of social justice, or of a hoarding of goods for one's selfish use, or finally of a careless negligence in undertaking the labors and tasks by which every people and all their offspring achieve a better standard of living.[27] Certainly some authorities have already begun to renew impressive efforts in regard to these matters; all authorities should energetically join these efforts. All members of the great human family should increase their zeal for coming to one another's assistance; [indeed] We think the opportunity for involvement by international aid organizations is nearly unbounded.

Appeal to Men of Science

24. Let Us also encourage scientists, who "are able to do much for the good of marriage and family and are able to assist peace of conscience if with their united efforts they attempt to clarify the conditions which favor a moral ordering of human procreation."[28] This ought especially to be hoped for—a request made earlier by Pius XII—that medical science, through the observation of natural cycles [of fertility], strive to establish a satisfactorily clear basis for the moral regulation of offspring.[29] In this way scientists—and especially those who proudly claim to be Catholic—will make it clear through their own work that, as the Church teaches, "No

26. John XXIII, encyclical *Mater et Magistra,* in AAS 53 (1961), 447.
27. Paul VI, encyclical *Populorum Progressio,* Mar. 26, 1967, no. 21, in AAS 59 (1967) 281–84.
28. Second Vatican Council, Pastoral Constitution, *Gaudium et Spes,* no. 52, in AAS 58 (1966) 1074.
29. Cf. Pius XII, "Address to the Congress of the Family Front and of the Association of Large Families," in AAS 43 (1951) 859.

true contradiction exists between the divine laws for transmitting life and those for fostering true conjugal love."[30]

Appeal to Christian Spouses

25. Now Our attention must be directed in a particular way to Our sons and daughters and especially to those whom God calls to serve Him in the state of matrimony. For the Church, who teaches the inviolable conditions of the divine law, also proclaims salvation and through the sacraments unlocks the sources of grace. [For it is by these means that] Man is made a new creature who responds with charity and true liberty to the heavenly plan of his Creator and Savior and who finds the yoke of Christ to be sweet.[31]

Therefore, let Christian spouses humbly obey the voice of the Church and remember that their proper vocation [*vocationem*] in the Christian life began with baptism and was more fully specified and confirmed anew with the sacrament of marriage. For by the sacrament of marriage spouses are strengthened and, as it were, consecrated so that they might faithfully fulfill their duties [*munia*], so that they might bring their vocation [*vocationem*] to its perfect end and so that, as befits them, they might openly offer the world a Christian witness.[32] To them the Lord entrusts [*committit*] the mission [*munus*] of making manifest to Men the holiness and indeed sweetness of the law that unites their mutual love and generous service [*adiutrice opera*] closely to the love of God, the author of human life.

Certainly We do not wish to ignore the difficulties, the sometimes serious difficulties, that Christian spouses might encounter, since for them, as for everyone, "the gate is narrow, and the way is difficult that leads to life."[33] Nevertheless their way will be illuminated by the hope of this life, just as by the clearest light, as long as they strive courageously "to live wisely and justly and piously in this world,"[34] knowing that "the form of this world passes away."[35]

Therefore, let spouses willingly take up the labors that have been assigned [*destinatos*] to them, strengthened both by faith and by hope, which "do not disappoint: because the charity of God is poured into our hearts

---

30. Second Vatican Council, Pastoral Constitution, *Gaudium et Spes*, no. 51, in AAS 58 (1966) 1072.

31. Cf. Mt. 11:30.

32. Cf. Second Vatican Council, Pastoral Constitution, *Gaudium et Spes*, no. 48, in AAS 58 (1966) 1067–69; Dogmatic Constitution *Lumen Gentium*, no. 35, in AAS 57 (1965) 40–41.

33. Mt. 7:14; cf. Heb. 12:11. 34. Cf. Tit. 2:12.

35. Cf. 1 Cor. 7:31.

through the Holy Spirit who is given to us."[36] Let them constantly pray for divine assistance. And let them especially drink of grace and charity from the eternal font of the Eucharist. If, however, they are hampered by their sins, let them not lose heart, but let them humbly and constantly flee to the mercy of God, which the sacrament of penance abundantly provides. It is by this way of life that spouses will be able to advance toward perfection in their married life, which the Apostle explains in these words: "Husbands love your wives, just as Christ loved the Church. . . . Therefore also husbands ought to love their wives as their own bodies. For he who loves his wife, loves himself. Indeed, no one is able to hate his own flesh; but he nourishes it and cares for it, as Christ does for the Church. . . . And this is true for each and every one of you: let everyone love his wife as he loves himself; and let wives respect their husbands."[37]

Apostolate of Spouses

26. Moreover, great fruits are to be expected when the divine law is kept by a devout soul. The most outstanding of these fruits results from the frequent desire of spouses to share their experience with other spouses. Thus it happens that a new and especially worthy kind of apostolate is added to the already ample vocation of the laity: like will minister to like. That is, spouses fulfill their apostolic mission [munus] in behalf of other spouses by becoming guides for them. Among all the forms of Christian apostolate this apostolate seems most suitable today.[38]

To Doctors and Health Care Professionals

27. Let Us express Our highest admiration for doctors and those health professionals who, in performing their mission [munus], desire to safeguard what is compatible with their Christian vocation rather than what corresponds to some human advantage [utilitatem]. Therefore let them constantly pursue only those solutions that are in accord with faith and right reason. And let them strive to gain the agreement and the compliance [observationem] of their colleagues in this matter. Moreover, let them consider it their

---

36. Rom. 5:5.
37. Eph. 5:25, 28–29, 32–33.
38. Cf. Second Vatican Council, Dogmatic Constitution *Lumen Gentium*, Nov. 21, 1964, no. 35, 41, in AAS 57 (1965) 40–45. [Father Calegari persuasively argues that AAS pages for *Lumen Gentium* should be 40–41 and 45–47.] Pastoral Constitution *Gaudium et Spes*, 48–49, in AAS 58 (1966) 1067–70; Decree, *Apostolicam Actuositatem*, Nov. 18, 1965, no. 11, in AAS 58 (1966) 947–49.

special mission [*munus*] to acquire all necessary learning in this difficult area. Thereby they may be able to give good advice to spouses seeking their counsel and to direct them along the right path. Spouses rightly seek such direction from them.

To Priests

28. With complete confidence We call upon you priests, Our beloved sons, you who are the advisers and spiritual guides of individuals and families. For it is your great and manifest mission [*munere*]—and We address especially those of you who are moral theologians—to promote completely and clearly the teaching of the Church concerning marriage. In performing your ministry you must be an example of the sincere obedience [*obsequii*] that must be given both inwardly and outwardly to the Magisterium of the Church. For truly, you know that you are bound to such obedience [*obsequio*] not only for the reasons given [in behalf of a teaching] but also on account of the light of the Holy Spirit, whose guidance the Fathers of the Church particularly enjoy when setting forth the truth.[39] Nor let it escape you that it is of the utmost importance for safeguarding the peace of souls and the unity of the Christian people, that in moral as in dogmatic matters, all should obey the Magisterium of the Church and should speak with one voice. Wherefore, adopting the anxious words of the great Apostle Paul, We call upon you again with Our whole heart: "I beg . . . you brothers through the name of our Lord Jesus Christ: that you might all speak as one and that there might be no division among you: that you may be united in the same mind and the same judgment."[40]

29. Refusal to compromise anything concerning the saving doctrine of Christ is an outstanding act of charity to souls; yet at the same time it is necessary always to combine this with tolerance and charity. When He spoke and associated with Men, the Redeemer Himself exemplified this truth. Coming not to judge the world but to save it, He was severe against sin but patient and merciful to sinners.[41]

Therefore, let spouses in their times of trouble find in the speech and hearts of their priests the image of the voice and love of our Redeemer.

So Beloved Sons, preach with full confidence and be certain that the Holy Spirit of God, who guides the Magisterium in its teaching, will

---

39. Cf. Second Vatican Council, Dogmatic Constitution *Lumen Gentium*, no. 25, in AAS 57 (1965) 29–31.
40. 1 Cor. 1:10.
41. Cf. Jn. 3:17.

illuminate the hearts of the faithful and invite them to give their assent. Teach spouses the indispensability of prayer; instruct them properly so that they may come regularly and with great faith to the sacraments of the Eucharist and of penance and that they may never become discouraged because of their weakness.

To Bishops

30. Now, at the conclusion of this encyclical letter, Our mind reverently and lovingly turns to you [Bishops], beloved and venerable Brothers in the episcopal mission [*munus*]; with you We share very closely the care of the spiritual good of the people of God. We make this urgent request of you: We ask all of you to take the lead with the priests who assist your sacred ministry and all your faithful. With complete zeal and no delay, devote yourselves to keeping marriage safe and holy, so that the life of married couples may draw more closely to its proper human and Christian perfection. Truly consider this as the greatest responsibility [*opus*] of your mission [*munus*] and the greatest work [*onus*] committed to you at the present time. As you well know, [your] mission [*munus*] requires a certain coordination of pastoral ministry in all areas of human activity, including economic, social, and cultural matters. If progress is gained on all these fronts at the same time, then not only will family life of parents and children be more tolerable, it will be easier and happier. Once the plan God conceived for the world is faithfully kept, fellowship in society will be richer in fraternal charity and more safely grounded in a true peace.

Final Appeal

31. Venerable Brothers, most beloved sons, and all men and women of goodwill, We now call you to the splendid work of education and growth in charity. Relying on the unshakable [*firmissima*] teaching of the Church, We, as the successor to Peter together with the whole Brotherhood of Bishops, faithfully guard and interpret it. Truly this is a great work, for it affects the good of the world and the Church. None can achieve true happiness, the happiness that they desire with the strength of their whole soul, unless they observe the laws inscribed on their nature by the Most High God. To be happy Man must prudently and lovingly cultivate these laws. Therefore, on this important work and on all of you and most especially on married couples, We invoke a wealth of supernatural graces

given by our most holy and merciful God. As a pledge of these graces, We freely give you Our Apostolic blessing.

Given at Rome, from St. Peter's on the twenty-fifth day of July, on the feast of James the Apostle, in the year 1968, the sixth year of Our Pontificate.

POPE PAUL VI

Commentary on *Humanae Vitae*, with Summary of Footnote Citations

This appendix provides a commentary on the text of *Humanae Vitae*. It proceeds section by section with some commentary on each section or referral to material in the main body of this book that covers the topic of the section. The primary purpose of this commentary is to provide a brief summary of the material cited in the footnotes of *Humanae Vitae*. These footnotes often include several citations. In this commentary, discussion of the material in the footnotes has been designated by [Footnote x]. Several documents may be discussed in each section. The numbered footnotes give bibliographical references for these official citations and to any further references cited in the commentary. Much of the supporting material for the claims of the document appears in the footnotes. Chapter 3 discusses much of the supporting materials for sections 4 to 17; this commentary does not repeat the earlier discussions but makes cross-references to them.

Humanae Vitae is divided into three parts. The first part, composed of the first six sections, presents the reasons for the Church's interest in the topic. The second part, sections 7 to 18, sketches out some of the reasons for the doctrine on the moral means of limiting family size. And in the third part, sections 19 to 31, some pastoral guidance is given for effective presentation of this teaching to married couples.

Introduction

Humanae Vitae 1: *The* Munus *of Transmitting Human Life*

Humanae Vitae begins by asserting that God has entrusted spouses with the extremely important mission [*munus*] of transmitting human life. It speaks of this *munus* as a service that spouses render to God and acknowledges that although having children can be a great joy it also has inherent difficulties. Chapter 5 provides an extensive analysis of the meaning of the word *munus*. There we see that a *munus* is a special assignment that one is honored to have and that entails certain significant responsibilities and duties. And as suggested there, the appearance of this word in the first line of *Humanae Vitae* serves to link the encyclical with the sections of *Gaudium et Spes* on marriage that ended with reference to the "*munus* of transmitting human life."[1] Furthermore, its appearance in the first line suggests that the document is not narrowly about "birth regulation" but also about the role of spouses in the transmission of human life and the importance of that role. We must understand the good that contraception violates before we can understand why that violation is a serious wrong. And, too, it is very important to note the mention that spouses "freely and deliberately" embrace this *munus*; it is not a "duty" or "role" imposed against their will; it is a calling to which they give a free and deliberate response. Once they accept this calling they must then accept the responsibilities that it entails.

HV 1 also notes that conditions in society have raised new questions about childbearing (it takes up these in the next section). The document begins to comment on the current conditions that have provoked this document; changes have taken place that make it the pastoral duty of the Church to answer questions that bear so closely on human happiness. The Church has often been accused of being obsessed with sex; yet it recognizes that a great deal of human happiness and indeed, preparation for salvation, depend on a healthy and moral integration of one's sexuality.

Humanae Vitae 2: *Situation Provoking the Encyclical*

Overpopulation

The encyclical continues to acknowledge the conditions that provoked its writing. The first paragraph of this section acknowledges concern with the population "explosion" and with economic realities that would seem to militate against large families. Indeed, concern for overpopulation was a dominant fear in the 1960s, a fear that since that time has somewhat abated, if not reversed.[2] There are those who now argue that especially in

---

1. Forms of the word *munus* appear twenty-one times in *Humanae Vitae*, for example, in reference to the *munera* of women (2.15), of the Church (5.1), of all Men (7.6), of biological processes (10.7), of the medical profession (27.2 and 9), of priests (28.2), and of bishops (30.10). It is used four times in reference to the *munus* of transmitting human life, three times to the *munus* of responsible parenthood, and once to the apostolic *munus* that spouses have to other married couples. It seems fair to say that the *munus* of "transmitting human life" and the *munus* of "responsible parenthood" are one and the same: the second phrase simply specifies and clarifies the first. As Chapter 2 notes, the Church has always linked the begetting of life with the obligation to educate and guide the life begotten.

2. For arguments and evidence that parts of the world are suffering from underpopulation,

developed countries the fall-off in births threatens the long-term economic growth and stability of these countries. Many argue that even in developing countries, the problem is not too many children but the effective and fair distribution of goods. Nonetheless, in the 1960s many of the symposia preceding the issuance of *Humanae Vitae* had as one of their major concerns the perceived population problem. The argument was made that having too many children was an unreasonable hardship for families in developing nations and that some relief might be found in the distribution of contraceptives. The rather in-passing observation in this passage that the fear of overpopulation could easily lead public officials to "severe solutions" seems prophetic in light of the forced sterilization campaigns in countries such as India and the forced abortion policies in China.[3]

Humanae Vitae returns to the question of overpopulation in section 23.

Feminism and Conjugal Love

This section also acknowledges two further changes that prompted a reconsideration of the place of children within marriage. The feminist movement was experiencing significant growth in the 1960s; more women were seeking employment outside the home. The argument was made that for women to be equal to men they needed the "reproductive freedom" offered by contraceptives. Also mentioned is the "changing evaluation of the place of love within marriage." As Chapter 2 notes, some theologians had argued that a greater emphasis on the importance of conjugal love in marriage may serve to legitimize contraception.

Man's Control over His Body

Finally, section 2 raises this concern: Man has used his intelligence to achieve some measure of control over other forces in nature; why would it not be right for him to use this same power to control his fertility? God, in Genesis, ordered Man to subdue the earth. Many have claimed that technological advances are among the greatest achievements of Man's intellect. Many argue that the discovery of drugs and devices that are capable of giving Man some measure of control over his reproductive capacities is in accord with the scriptural command to govern nature. Later in the encyclical the instruction that all technological advances must respect the order of nature or reality established by God is repeatedly stated.

see Ben Wattenburg, *The Birth Dearth* (New York: Pharos Books, 1987), Julian Simon, *The Ultimate Resource* (Princeton, N.J.: Princeton University Press, 1981), and Jacqueline Kasun, *The War against Population* (San Francisco: Ignatius Press, 1988).

3. An excellent resource for an evaluation of population concern and coercive contraceptive and abortion policies is Germaine Greer, *Sex and Destiny: The Politics of Human Fertility* (New York: Harper & Row, 1984). See also Steven W. Mosher, *Broken Earth: The Rural Chinese* (New York: Free Press, 1983).

Section 2 does not seek to give answers to the concerns raised here; indeed, it discusses them in such an even-handed way that there is virtually no hint of the proposed responses.

Humanae Vitae 3: *New Questions*

New Norms Needed?

Section 3 poses some of the questions the encyclical endeavors to answer. It asks whether new conditions in society do not warrant a reconsideration by the Church of the moral norms for marital intercourse, especially since it seems that sometimes heroic sacrifices must be made by those adhering to these norms.

The Principle of Totality

The most common justification for the moral permissibility of contraception is that based on the principle of totality. Extensive discussion of this principle is given in Chapter 3. See also Chapter 1.

Humanae Vitae 4: *Natural Law and the Competence of the Magisterium*

Natural Law

The competence of the Church to interpret natural law is covered in Chapter 3. See also Chapter 1.

Reason and Faith

[FOOTNOTE 1] Pius IX asserts the Catholic principle that there can be no conflict between the truths of faith and the truths of reason or nature. In rejecting the claim that philosophy that finds truth in nature ought to reject the truths of revelation, he states:

Without doubt, nothing more insane than such a doctrine, nothing more impious or more opposed to reason itself could be devised. For although faith is above reason, no real disagreement or opposition can ever be found between them; this is because both of them come from the same greatest source of unchanging and eternal truth, God. They give such reciprocal help to each other that true reason shows, maintains and protects the truth of the faith, while faith frees reason from all errors and wondrously enlightens, strengthens and perfects reason with the knowledge of divine matters.[4]

Pius X, in *Singulari Quadam* (September 24, 1912), announced "Through [Our] awareness of [Our] apostolic duty, We understand it to be Our

4. In *Pii IX P. M. Acta, I,* 9–10. The translation is from *The Papal Encyclicals 1740–1878,* vol. 1, trans. by Claudia Carlen Ihm (Raleigh, N.C.: McGrath Publishing Co., 1981), 277–284.

sacrosanct mission [*munus*] to work toward and bring it about that Our beloved sons preserve Catholic doctrine pure and whole [*sinceram et integram*], and not in any way to allow the Faith itself to be endangered."[5]

A fairly lengthy portion of Pius XI's *Casti Connubii* is mentioned. This passage picks up the point made in the excerpt from *Qui Pluribus*, that the truths of reason are safeguarded by revelation; were it not for revelation, Man might not employ his reason well. A portion from this reference states:

For Christ Himself made the Church the teacher of truth in those things also which concern the right regulation of moral conduct, even though some knowledge of the same is not beyond human reason. For just as God, in the case of natural truths of religion and morals, added revelation to the light of reason so that what is right and true, "in the present state also of the human race may be known readily with real certainty without any admixture of error," so for the same purpose He has constituted the Church the guardian and the teacher of the whole of the truth concerning religion and moral conduct; to her therefore should the faithful show obedience and subject their minds and hearts so as to be kept unharmed and free from error and moral corruption. . . .(DSP 53)[6]

Pius XII, in "Address to the Episcopate of the Catholic World" (November 2, 1954), made the point that the Church must protect the truths of reason because these are often preludes to the faith; those who are faithful to the truths of reason should move more easily to accept the truths of faith:

The power of the Church is not at all contained within the limits of what is strictly religious, as some are accustomed to say. But the whole matter of natural law, its institution, interpretation, application, to whatever extent questions of morals pertain, are in the Church's power. Obedience to natural law out of respect for the order established by God, points to the way which ought to lead Man to his supernatural end. Therefore, truly the Church is the leader and guardian of men along this path which leads to Man's supernatural end.[7]

The point here is that since obedience to law is necessary for salvation and since the Church is responsible for helping Man attain salvation, it is right that the Church be guardian and protector of the law.

Several of the passages cited previously (e.g., *Casti Connubii*, DSP 54) are also close to statements that Catholics must obey the Church even when the Church does not speak solemnly but should trust the Church as a guide and teacher in matters of religion and morals. The passage from

5. *Singulari Quadam*, Sept. 24, 1912, in AAS 4 (1912) 658; my translation.
6. AAS 22 (1930), 579–81. This and all translations are from Pius XI, *Casti Connubii: Encyclical Letter of Pius XI on Christian Marriage* (Boston: St. Paul Editions, 1930); page numbers are given in the text, with the designation DSP.
7. In AAS 46 (1954) 671–72; my translation.

Mater et Magistra (May 15, 1961) takes this claim a bit further in asking for prompt obedience from Catholics in practical judgments of the Church:

Those who profess Catholicism must take special care to be consistent and not compromise in matters wherein the integrity of religion or morals would suffer harm. Likewise, in their conduct they should weigh the opinions of others with fitting courtesy and not measure everything in the light of their own interests. They should be prepared to join sincerely in doing whatever is naturally good or conducive to good. If, indeed, it happens that in these matters sacred authorities have prescribed or decreed anything, it is evident that this judgment is to be obeyed promptly by Catholics. For it is the Church's right and duty not only to safeguard principles relating to the integrity of religion and morals, but also to pronounce authoritatively when it is a matter of putting these principles into effect.[8]

[FOOTNOTE 2] The preceding passages do not offer arguments for the Church's claim that it is fit to interpret the natural law. Again, the presupposition is that the Church has proper competence over all that pertains to Man's salvation and thus over the natural law. Justification for this claim must be found in theological argumentation based on Scripture and tradition. For instance, this same section contains two references to passages in Scripture to justify the claim that Jesus Christ imparted his authority to Peter and the apostles: "Jesus came forward and addressed them in these words: 'Full authority has been given to me both in heaven and on earth; go, therefore, and make disciples of all the nations. Baptize them in the name of the Father and of the Son, and of the Holy Spirit' " (Matt. 28:18–19).[9] The Catholic Church understands this passage to support the claim that Christ gave special powers to His apostles and that this power has been faithfully transmitted to the bishops and priests.

[FOOTNOTE 3] *Humanae Vitae* also cites Matthew 7:21: "None of those who cry out, 'Lord, Lord,' will enter the kingdom of God, but only the one who does the will of my Father in heaven." "Those who cry out, 'Lord, Lord' " refers to those who have faith but do not act on it. This passage indicates that faith alone is not enough for salvation; believers must also follow the will of God. Since natural law is part of the will of God, it, as well as any revealed laws, must be observed.

The Church's Teaching on Marriage

HV 4 also informs the reader that the Church has at all times provided a coherent teaching on (1) the nature of marriage, (2) the correct use of

8. In AAS 53 (1961), 457. The translation is from the edition published by the Daughters of Saint Paul, 67. All subsequent translations are also from this edition and indicated in the text with DSP.

9. Translations from Scripture are from *The New American Bible* (Camden, N.J.: Thomas Nelson, 1971).

conjugal rights (*iurium*), and (3) the duties of husband and wife. Here we shall review the content of the footnote to this passage. Although some of the points repeat material discussed in Chapter 2, it is important to look at what *Humanae Vitae* specifically cites in defense of its claim.

[FOOTNOTE 4] The Catechism of the Council of Trent[10] gives a fairly thorough treatment of all three categories mentioned in *Humanae Vitae*: (1) It defines marriage as "the conjugal union of man and woman, in which the two persons lawfully contract to live together until death."[11] In explaining this definition, the Catechism notes that by referring to "*conjugal union*," the definition includes the notion that the union must be voluntary and indissoluble. Those who are "qualified" must be of a certain age and free of all of the impediments to marriage (discussed later). As the Catechism explains the nature of marriage, it notes that marriage is a natural contract that is indissoluble, freely entered for the purposes of companionship, mutual assistance, offspring, and is "an escape from sinful lust."[12]

Marriage as a sacrament perfects marriage as a natural contract: "As something purely natural, marriage was instituted in order to insure the propagation of the human race. Elevated to the supernatural dignity of a sacrament, its purpose now is to procreate and educate a holy people in the faith and worship of the one true God and of Christ our Savior."[13] With the fall of Man, marriage too fell, to the point that the Jews permitted polygamy and divorce; through the sacrament Christ restored marriage to its original unity and indissolubility.[14] The three blessings of marriage are progeny, both bearing and educating them; fidelity, which fosters a special, holy, and pure love between the spouses; and sacramentality, or indissolubility that represents the union of Christ with His Church.

Another reference to the Council of Trent speaks to the second category mentioned in *Humanae Vitae*: the correct use of conjugal rights. It speaks with some delicacy of the "correct use of marriage" and gives two lessons: "The first is that marriage should not be used out of the sole motive of sensual pleasure. Rather, the motive should reflect—and remain within— the purposes of marriage as instituted by God. . . ."[15] Spouses are also to be taught sometimes to abstain from the marriage debt, in order to devote themselves to prayer.[16] Talk of the "marriage debt" is peculiar to modern ears, but it refers largely to the instruction given by St. Paul, "The husband

---

10. Translations for the Catechism of the Council of Trent are from *The Roman Catechism* trans. by Robert I. Bradley, S.J., and Eugene Kevane (Boston, Mass.: St. Paul Editions, 1985). The chapter numbers of this translation do not correspond to the original text.

11. Ibid., 328.	12. Ibid., 333.
13. Ibid., 334.	14. Ibid., 336.
15. Ibid., 343.	16. Ibid., 343.

should fulfill his conjugal obligations toward his wife, the wife hers toward her husband. A wife does not belong to herself but to her husband; equally, a husband does not belong to himself but to his wife" (1 Cor 7:3–4).

The word *debt* poses some difficulties, as does its close counterpart in this context, the word *right* (Latin *ius*). Indeed, canon law speaks of the *ius in corpus* (right of the body), which is availed by marriage. In the minds of most, these words are more closely associated with a business contract than with the loving relationship of marriage. And to speak of a "right" over someone else's body too easily evokes an image of slavery. But these words have quite a different sense in this context. They arise from a Roman context where "rights" bore a certain resemblance to privileges: they were what free men had. They were connected with law, but with law as protecting the dignity of the free Man, not with law as exploitative or confining. Thus *ius* as "privilege" indicates the intimacy and closeness of the marriage bond.[17] The body, of course, is considered an integral part of the person, and, truly, others do not have a "right" to one's body in the sense that they own it. In marriage two become one flesh; thus a reasonable person would no more exploit or dominate the body of his or her spouse than he or she would abuse his or her own body. In other words, since one is to protect and respect the integrity of one's body, this concept of *ius in corpus* serves to elevate the relationship one has with one's spouse, not to denigrate it. Indeed, St. Paul instructs the husband to respect his wife as he does his own body (Eph. 5:28), not to denigrate the wife but to indicate the closeness that they have and the extreme respect that is due the wife. Spouses in marrying do promise to engage in sexual intercourse with each other, "on demand." But this is a "demand" that is to be made in love and granted out of love; again, it is not meant to be a license to exploit or dominate one's spouse.

The Catechism draws on the epistles of St. Paul and St. Peter to clarify the duties of the husband and wife. The husband is first told "to treat his wife generously and honorably"[18] and is portrayed as the head of the household who is to provide for it financially and to guide his family in living morally and in performing their duties. The wife is counseled to be subject to her husband and to give particular attention to the raising of children and to domestic concerns.[19]

17. John C. Ford, S.J., and Gerald Kelly, S.J., maintain that *ius*, or right, is properly conceived as a relationship that entitles one to certain privileges and commits one to certain obligations, with a view to the mutual benefit of the partners; *Contemporary Moral Theology* vol. 2 (Westminster, Md: Newman Press, 1964), 58–63.

18. *The Roman Catechism*, 340.

19. Ibid., 341.

The popularity of feminism most certainly may cause these counsels to be offensive to modern ears. Many will argue that the Church has a history of denigrating women, but others will suggest that the Christian message is precisely the message that has most served to elevate women to an equality with men. There is no denying that the role and proper treatment of women are sensitive topics. Nor is there any denying that the Church has taught that a wife is to be subject to her husband. This teaching is based not on a view of woman as inferior to man but on an understanding of the kind of relationship that marriage is. Church documents regularly maintain that the family is of extreme importance. It is considered to be like a small state (or church) that in order to be governed properly needs a head, a position it sees to be the husband's role. Yet, there is a persistent effort to provide assurance that placing the husband at the head is not to suggest that the wife is inferior, or her role unimportant. *Casti Connubii*, in commenting on St. Paul's injunction for wives to be subject to their husbands (Eph. 5:22, 23), states:

This subjection, however, does not deny or take away the liberty which fully belongs to the woman both in view of her dignity as a human person, and in view of her most noble office [*muneribus*] as wife and mother and companion; nor does it bid her obey her husband's every request if not in harmony with right reason or with the dignity due to a wife; nor, in fine, does it imply that the wife should be put on a level with those persons who in law are called minors, to whom it is not customary to allow free exercise of their rights on account of their lack of mature judgment, or of their ignorance of human affairs. But it forbids that exaggerated liberty which cares not for the good of the family; it forbids that in this body which is the family, the heart be separated from the head to the great detriment of the whole body and the proximate danger of ruin. For if the man is the head, the woman is the heart, and as he occupies the chief place in ruling, so she may and ought to claim for herself the chief place in love. (AAS 549, DSP 15)

The effort to stress the equality of women with men and the dignity of their role has certainly been a topic of increasing focus in the Church. John Paul II speaks of the importance of "underlining the equal dignity and responsibility of women with men" (*Familiaris Consortio* 38)[20] and asserts that the "history of salvation, in fact, is a continuous and luminous testimony of the dignity of women" (39). He expresses equal concern that women be provided full access to positions of responsibility and that society be so arranged that the family will not suffer undue hardships, should a wife and mother choose not to work outside the home (39):

20. The translation here is from John Paul II, *The Role of the Family in the Modern World* (Boston: St. Paul Editions, 1981); the numbers in the text refer to the pages of this edition.

Without intending to deal with all the various aspects of the vast and complex theme of the relationships between women and society, and limiting these remarks to a few essential points, one cannot but observe that in the specific area of family life a widespread social and cultural tradition has considered women's role [*munus*] to be exclusively that of wife and mother, without adequate access to public functions [*muneribus*], which have generally been reserved for men.

There is no doubt that the equal dignity and responsibility of men and women fully justifies women's access to public functions. On the other hand the true advancement of women requires that clear recognition be given to the value of their maternal and family role [*munus*], by comparison with all other public roles and all other professions. Furthermore, these roles [*munera*] and professions should be harmoniously combined, if we wish the evolution of society and culture to be truly and fully human. (39–40)

John Paul II develops some of these observations about the role of women in his apostolic letter *Mulieris Dignitatem* or *On the Dignity and Vocation of Women*. There he reiterates the point that men and women are equal: "One must speak of an essential 'equality,' since both of them—the woman as much as the man—are created in the image and likeness of God. Both of them are equally capable of receiving the outpouring of divine truth and love in the Holy Spirit. Both receive his salvific and sanctifying 'visits.' "[21] But he also stresses that men and women are not identical: "The personal resources of femininity are certainly no less than the resources of masculinity: They are merely different. Hence a woman, as well as a man, must understand her 'fulfillment' as a person, her dignity and vocation on the basis of these resources, according to the richness of the femininity which she received on the day of creation and which she inherits as an expression of the 'image and likeness of God' that is specifically hers."[22] Throughout this apostolic letter the pope speaks of the marital relationship as one of a communion of persons that requires mutual self-giving and interprets the famous passage in Ephesians 5 as counseling a "mutual subjection" of each to the other.[23]

Further Topics about Marriage

The remaining references in footnote 4 cover a wide variety of topics relating to the Church's teaching about marriage. We learn about the right of the Church to legislate matters pertaining to marriage, about the family's primary right to educate, about the reasons the Church has been opposed to contraception, and about the reasons marriage may be considered invalid.

Leo XIII's *Arcanum* (February 19, 1880) was written to oppose encroach-

---

21. In *Origins* 18:17 (Oct. 6, 1988) 273.
22. Ibid., 269.   23. Ibid., 278.

ments of the state on the Church's right to legislate concerning marriage.[24] It gives a "salvation history" of marriage as it traces the corruption, characterized largely by polygamy and divorce, that marriage underwent with the fall of Man. It tells the story of Christ's returning marriage to its proper natural state of monogamy and indissolubility, a state that also worked to promote great mutual love between the spouses and protected the rights of the wife along with those of the husband. Leo XIII explains that the various impediments to marriage that the Church has decreed are designed "to safeguard marriage, as much as possible, from error and violence and deceit."[25] He writes largely with the purpose of refuting those who seek to "attribute all power over marriage to civil rulers, and allow none whatever to the Church."[26] In fact, he argues that the best of civil laws about marriage are civil adaptations of Church laws.[27] This document maintains that God intended marriage to be "a most fruitful source of individual benefit and of public welfare":

Not only, in strict truth, was marriage instituted for the propagation of the human race, but also that the lives of husbands and wives might be made better and happier. This comes about in many ways: by their lightening each other's burdens through mutual help; by constant and faithful love; by having all their possessions in common; and by the heavenly grace which flows from the sacrament. Marriage also can do much for the good of families, for, so long as it is conformable to nature and in accordance with the counsels of God, it has power to strengthen union of heart in the parents; to secure the holy education of children; to temper the authority of the father by the example of the divine authority; to render children obedient to their parents and servants obedient to their masters. From such marriages as these the State may rightly expect a race of citizens animated by a good spirit and filled with reverence and love for God, recognizing it their duty to obey those who rule justly and lawfully, to love all, and to injure no one.[28]

He also strongly urges the point that without the sacramental graces of marriage, it is predictable and understandable that spouses may find the difficulties of marriage too great to bear. Abandoning God, he states, has lead to the legalization of divorce and "It is hardly possible to describe how great are the evils that flow from divorce."[29]

Pius XI in *Divini Illius Magistri*[30] (December 31, 1929) makes two major points: He speaks of the Church as having received from Christ its *munus* as educator in matters of religion and morals; the *munus* of the family is in

---

24. In *Acta Leonis* 13, 2 (1881) 26–29. The translation is from *The Papal Encyclicals 1878–1903*, vol. 2, ed. by Claudia Carlen Ihm (Raleigh, N.C.: McGrath Publishing Co., 1981), 29–40.

25. Ibid., 32.   26. Ibid., 33.
27. Ibid., 34.   28. Ibid., 35.
29. Ibid., 36.   30. In AAS 22 (1930), 58–61.

remarkable harmony [*mirifice concordat*] with the *munus* of the Church for the family has even a more primary responsibility to educate, since in the order of nature God has joined the principle of life and the principle of education. The second point based on the same principle is that the state does not have the right to usurp this responsibility from parents.

The responsibility that spouses have to children is a constant and central theme of *Humanae Vitae*. The portion of *Casti Connubii* referred to here stresses a point made much of in Chapter 2: that the responsibility of parents does not end with educating their offspring for prosperity in this life: they must seek "to raise up fellow-citizens of the Saints, and members of God's household" (DSP 9).

The Church's Prohibition against Contraception

The next four references all concern the Church's prohibition against contraception in varying degrees of directness.

Pius XII in his "Address to the Italian Medico-Biological Union of St. Luke" (November 12, 1944) discusses the purpose of sexual intercourse. This speech is discussed in Chapter 3.[31] Pius XII in "Address to the Italian Union of Midwives" (October 29, 1951) reiterates the teaching in *Casti Connubii* against contraception and elaborates more on the proper use of the sterile period in marriage.[32] In instructing midwives about the nobility of their apostolate, he teaches them how to guide couples who wish for assistance in limiting their family size. He makes several points. (1) Certainly couples are permitted to have sexual intercourse on the sterile days "for by so doing they neither hinder nor injure in any way the consummation of the natural act and its further natural consequences."[33] (2) He notes that if from the start of the marriage, one of the spouses intended only to use this period and to refuse to have sex during the fertile periods, this would render the marriage invalid.[34] (3) However, if the couple marry with the intent to have sexual intercourse only during the infertile periods but would be willing to accept a child if conception occurred in spite of precautions, they would have a valid marriage. They may, though, be offending against marriage by their unwillingness to be positively directed toward fulfilling the work of marriage.[35] (4) He acknowledges, "There are serious motives, such as those often mentioned in the so-called medical, eugenic, economic, and social 'indications,' that can exempt for a long

31. In *Discorsi e Radiomessaggi di S.S. Pio XII* 6, 191–92.

32. AAS 43 (1951) 835–54; a translation is available in Vincent A. Yzermans, *The Major Addresses of Pope Pius XII* vol. 1 (St. Paul, Minn.: Worth Central Publishing Co., 1961), 160–76.

33. Ibid., 168.　　　　　　　　　　34. Ibid., 168.

35. Ibid., 168–69.

time, perhaps even the whole duration of the marriage, from the positive and obligatory carrying out of the act [of having children]."[36] But he warns that the motives must truly be serious and not the product of selfishness. (5) Finally, he addresses the very difficult cases "in which the risk of motherhood cannot be run or must be avoided completely, and in which, on the other hand, observing the sterile periods either does not give sufficient security or has to be abandoned for other reasons."[37] Here he counsels that if this is truly the case, complete abstinence is the only moral response. To the objection that such is impossible, he insists that heroism is possible and assures us that God will provide the necessary graces. He observes, "It is wronging men and women of our times to deem them incapable of continuous heroism."[38] Those who believe that Man's chief or greatest or only happiness is to be found in the goods of this world will find this teaching impossible to accept. It is only the conviction held by Christians that this life is to be lived in preparation for the next that makes this teaching intelligible. It is also a great comfort that better and more reliable forms of natural family planning enable the vast majority of women to determine with accuracy their fertile times so that occasions on which such heroism is necessary are much less common.

Pius XII in "Address to the Congress of the Family Front and the Association of Large Families"[39] (November 28, 1951) observes that he has "affirmed the legitimacy and at the same time the limits—which are indeed very wide—of a regulation of offspring, which unlike what is termed 'birth control,' is compatible with the law of God. It may even be hoped (but in such a field the Church, of course, leaves judgment to medical science) that the latter will succeed in giving this legitimate method a sufficiently sure basis, and the most recent information seems to confirm such a hope."[40] Many still believe that the only alternative to mechanical devices or contraceptive pills is the rhythm or calendar method. But in recent decades techniques for discerning a woman's period of fertility have greatly advanced. There are a variety of "natural family planning" methods that do not depend on a somewhat unreliable counting of the days of the month as does the rhythm or calendar method. These newer methods depend on a much more reliable reading of different bodily indications signifying that ovulation is about to take place.[41]

36. Ibid., 169.   37. Ibid., 169.
38. Ibid., 170.
39. In AAS 43 (1951) 857–59; a partial translation is available in *The Pope Speaks* ed. by Michael Chinigo (New York: Pantheon Books, 1957), 41–45.
40. Ibid, 45.
41. Two useful texts for an introduction to these methods are Nona Aguilar, *No-Pill, No-Risk Birth Control* (New York: Rawson, Wade Publishers, 1980), and John and Sheila Kippley,

In his "Address to the Seventh Congress of the International Society of Hematology," (September 12, 1958) Pius XII addresses the problems that arise for married couples when it is determined that one is a carrier of hereditary diseases.[42] He addresses the question of the morality of sterilization in this instance. Acknowledging that it is moral to remove reproductive organs when these are diseased (in which case sterilization is an indirect consequence, one not willed although foreseen), he reiterates a constant principle that sterilization cannot be directly intended as a means or an end.[43] He thus asserts that it is not licit to remove "glands . . . or sexual organs for the purpose of impeding the transmission of defective hereditary characteristics."[44] Nor is the use of anovulant drugs permitted for this purpose. [Drugs that have an anovulant effect are morally permitted for treatment of diseases of the reproductive organs, for, again, this effect is indirect.] A "*direct* and therefore illicit sterilization results when ovulation is stopped to protect the uterus and the organism from the consequences of a pregnancy which it is not able to sustain."[45] Pius XII informs couples who find themselves with this problem that complete abstinence or the use of periods of infertility is morally permissible even for the duration of a marriage. He also counsels adoption.

The passage from *Mater et Magistra* by Pope John XXIII reads as follows:

We strongly affirm that human life is transmitted and propagated through the instrumentality of the family which rests on marriage, one and indissoluble, and, so far as Christians are concerned, elevated to the dignity of a sacrament. Because the life of man is passed on to other men deliberately and knowingly, it therefore follows that this should be done in accord with the most sacred, permanent, inviolate prescriptions of God. Everyone without exception is bound to recognize and observe these laws. Wherefore, in this matter, no one is permitted to use methods and procedures which may indeed be permissible to check the life of plants and animals.

Indeed, all must regard the life of man as sacred, since from its inception, it requires the action of God the Creator. Those who depart from this plan of God not only offend His divine majesty and dishonor themselves and the human race, but they also weaken the inner fibre of the commonwealth. (DSP 55)

This passage asserts that what may be permissible intervention in the reproductive processes of plants and animals is not necessarily permissible intervention in the "reproductive" processes of human beings. As explained

---

The Art of Natural Family Planning (Cincinnati, Ohio: Couple to Couple League International, 1985, 3d edition).

42. AAS 50 (1958) 734–35; translations are from *The Pope Speaks* 6 (1958) 392–400.
43. See Chapter 3 for a discussion of the principle of double effect.
44. Ibid., 395.
45. Ibid., 395.

in Chapter 3, a human is not just another animal and therefore "methods and procedures" that are permissible to limit the number of offspring of plants and animals are not immediately permitted for human beings. The same claim is true, of course, of other medical techniques; for instance, animals may be produced in the laboratory for the purpose of providing organ transplants for other animals, but human beings may not. The moral dimension of these techniques must be assessed. How does the human being differ so that what is morally permissible for creatures whose organs share or resemble the purposes of human organs is not permissible for human beings?

Let us pursue this further. Animals have a purpose beyond themselves; they are members of an animal kingdom in which one species often serves the survival of another; big fish eat small fish, lions eat mice, and human beings subsist on many other forms of life. Thus often these forms of life may morally be reproduced simply for the purpose of fostering another species; chickens are grown with the sole purpose of feeding human beings. But human beings are not "reproduced" for the benefit of any other species or even for their own species; they have a value—in the Christian view an infinite value in their own right—because they are destined for eternal life with God. Thus when humans have sexual intercourse, they are engaging in a very different act from that of animals; it entails essentially different responsibilities and thus has an essentially different moral dimension.

Sections 47–52 of *Gaudium et Spes* discuss married life and the family. Since ample reference to this document is made elsewhere in Chapter 2, no attempt is made to summarize it here.

Canons 1012–1143 of the old canon law code refer to matrimony.[46] Canon 1067 reads as follows: "(1) A valid marriage cannot be contracted by a man before he has completed the sixteenth year of his age, by a woman before she has completed the fourteenth year. (2) Although a marriage contracted after the completion of the aforesaid ages is valid, nevertheless pastors of souls shall make every effort to prevent the marriage of youths before that age at which, according to the accepted usage of the country, marriage is customarily contracted."[47] The portion of Canon 1068 referred to states: "(1) By the very law of nature a marriage is rendered invalid by antecedent and perpetual impotence on the part of either the man or the

---

46. Translations are from John A. Abbo and Jerome D. Hannan, *The Sacred Canons: A Concise Presentation of the Current Disciplinary Norms of the Church* vol. 2 (Canons 870–2414) (St. Louis: B. Herder Book Co., 2nd revised ed., 1960).

47. Ibid., 253.

woman, whether it is absolute or relative."[48] The portion of Canon 1076 referred to reads as follows: "(1) In the direct line of consanguinity marriage is invalid between all in the ascending and the descending line, whether of legitimate birth or not. (2) In the collateral line marriage is invalid to the third degree inclusively, but the impediment is multiplied only as often as the common ancestor is multiplied."[49] It is not immediately clear why the author of *Humanae Vitae* chose to cite these particular canons. Perhaps they are intended to be representative samples of the kinds of restrictions that protect the good that marriage is to advance. For instance, Canon 1067 states that restrictions of age are required both by the nature of the spouses—for they must be able to consummate the marriage—and by the nature of the contract—for they must be of an age at which they can freely consent to the obligations they are assuming. The Church understands there to be several impediments to a marriage; Canon 1068 concerns impotency, which prohibits the union that is proper to marriage. The Church has a very nuanced view of what constitutes impotency; since all have a natural right to marry, it generously gives the benefit of the doubt to those wishing to marry. Canon 1076 deals with the impediment of consanguinity; individuals closely related by blood are not permitted to marry each other since one purpose of marriage is to multiply the unions of love; blood relatives already have a bond of love.

Humanae Vitae 5: The Papal Commission

This section is discussed briefly in Chapter 1.

[FOOTNOTE 5] Paul VI in his "Address to the Sacred College of Cardinals" (June 23, 1964) attempted to clarify the status of the birth control question, some four years before he issued *Humanae Vitae*.[50] Acknowledging that the question is a grave and pressing one, he notes that he is drawing on the advice of many from relevant areas of expertise. There was a proliferation of publications at the time, both in academic journals and in the popular media, that suggested that the Church was soon going to abandon its traditional condemnation of contraception. A few used this speculation to call into play the principle of probabilism which allows that when there is no clear Church teaching against a specific action, Catholics are free to proceed in accord with the dictates of their own consciences. Paul VI instructed:

48. Ibid., 256.
49. Ibid., 281.
50. In AAS (1964) 588; a translation of this document is to be found in *The Pope Speaks* 9 (1965) 349–56.

Meanwhile let Us say in all frankness that so far We do not have sufficient reason to regard the norms laid down by Pius XII on this matter as superseded and therefore no longer binding. So these norms must be considered valid, at least until We may feel obliged in conscience to modify them. In a matter of such importance it seems right that Catholics desire to follow one single law propounded authoritatively by the Church. So it seems advisable to recommend that for the present no one should arrogate to himself the right to take a stand differing from the norm now in force.[51]

Yet, this statement, delivered in such tentative terms, served to foster speculation rather than to quell it. Phrases such as "from the norm now in force" were understandably taken as evidence that there was a real possibility that the norm would change.

Paul VI in his "Address to the Commission for the Study of Problems of Population, Family, and Birth" (March 27, 1965) greeted the members of the papal commission.[52] He again acknowledged how important and pressing was their study and indicated his awareness of what great difficulty the uncertainty posed for married couples. He recognized two "levels" on which their research was to be situated: "a better knowledge of physiological laws, psychological and medical data, population shifts and social upheavals; on the other hand, and above all, the level of the higher light cast upon these facts by the data of Faith and the traditional teaching of the Church." He stated the problem before them in these terms: "In what form and according to what norms ought married couples, in exercising their love for each other, to fulfill this life-giving function to which their vocation calls them?" These remarks again served to foster the widespread expectation that there would be a change in the Church's teaching.

In his "Address to the National Congress of the Italian Society of Obstetrics and Gynecology"[53] (October 29, 1966) Pope Paul VI explained that though he had received a report from the papal commission, he was not yet prepared to issue a final decision. Although the Schema that he had received counseled change, he indicated possible reasons for his hesitancy to accept this report. After noting that the traditional norms were still in place, he referred to *Gaudium et Spes*, issued nearly a year earlier (December 7, 1965): "The recent Ecumenical Council supplied some elements of judgment which are very useful for integrating Catholic doctrine on this most important subject, but they are not of such nature as to change its substantial terms. Rather they are suited to explain it and

51. Ibid., 356.
52. In AAS 57 (1965) 388; the translations for this text are found on p. 226 in *The Pope Speaks* 10 (1966) 225–27.
53. In AAS 58 (1966) 1168; the translations from this text are found on pp. 401–2 in *The Pope Speaks* 11 (1967) 401–8.

to prove, with authoritative arguments, the supreme interest the Church attaches to questions concerning love, marriage, birth and the family."[54] Paul VI was largely responsible for this slant to *Gaudium et Spes* (see Appendix 3 on the papal *modi* to *Gaudium et Spes*). Moreover he was troubled by the implications of change in Church teaching: "We still feel that these conclusions [of the commission] cannot be regarded as definitive, because they present grave implications for a good number of other weighty questions of a doctrinal as well as a pastoral and social nature which cannot be isolated and set aside, but must be logically considered in the context of what has been subjected to study."[55] Since the question was so complex and serious, he announced that he needed to study it further and that his response would be delayed. He reiterated that Catholics were still bound by traditional norms: "The norm taught by the Church until now, rounded out by the wise instructions of the Council, calls for faithful and generous observance. It cannot be considered not binding, as if the magisterium of the Church were now in a state of doubt, while it is in a moment of study and reflection on what has been put forward as worthy of the most attentive consideration."[56] It was nearly two years later that Paul VI issued *Humanae Vitae*, more than a year after copies of the Schema and Minority Report were leaked to the *National Catholic Reporter* (April 17, 1967).

Humanae Vitae 6: *Paul VI's Response to the Papal Commission*

This section is treated in Chapter 1.

Doctrinal Principles

The first part of *Humanae Vitae* put the problem of management of family size in the context of the demands and concerns of modern society. It explained why the Church felt constrained to speak on this topic and clarified the procedure for arriving at a decision. The second portion deals directly with the specific moral principles involved in discerning the moral means of limiting one's family size. It links *Humanae Vitae* with *Gaudium et Spes*; it defines "conjugal love," and "responsible parenthood"; it explains what kinds of behavior violate the goods of marriage; it discusses the principle of totality, the principle of choosing the lesser evil, and the principle of double effect; it justifies the use of the infertile period and predicts what evils will result should the Church's teaching be ignored.

54. Ibid., 401.   55. Ibid., 402.
56. Ibid.

Humanae Vitae 7: *Presuppositions*

Section 7 points out what kinds of concerns govern the Church's teaching about moral matters. It takes into account not only what is good for Man's biology or psychology, what is good for population control or for society, but also the mission or *munus* that is Man's. The appearance of *munus* here is significant, for it would, perhaps, be more predictable to find a reference to Man's nature or his dignity. This word is suitable for the claim is that the arguments offered in the document will not only refer to what is good for Man and society "in this earthly existence" but take into account God's will and Man's supernatural destiny.

This section functions as an introduction to the following sections. It notes that since those who wish to legitimate the use of contraception argue from the values of conjugal love and responsible parenthood, these very values must first be defined in order to determine whether indeed they do legitimate the use of contraception. *Gaudium et Spes* spoke about both of these values and thus is a primary source for the principles governing the document.

Humanae Vitae 8: *Conjugal Love*

Procreation and God's Love

[FOOTNOTE 6] Section 8 first makes the point that conjugal love is not "Man-centered," nor is it divorced from parenthood. Immediately a connection is made between conjugal love and procreation. Conjugal love has its source in God as Love and in God as the Father. The passage from 1 John 4:8 cited here reads, "The man without love has known nothing of God, for God is love." Many passages could have been cited to the same effect; this verse was most likely chosen since the remainder of this letter of John is a kind of hymn to God as love. It explains that it is through love of one another that we come to know God. The love of the spouses, then, is not only a source of self-knowledge and knowledge of the other but also of knowledge of God.

[FOOTNOTE 7] A passage from Ephesians that tells us that all parenthood derives its name from God is cited. In this section from Ephesians Paul is speaking of how Christ came to save both Gentiles and Jews. He is teaching that we are all brothers and sisters in the Lord. Paul tells us that he kneels before "[the Father,] from whom every family in heaven and on earth takes its name" (Ephesians 3:15). This notice anticipates the later claim that the two meanings of conjugal love, union and procreation, are inseparable (see HV 12). Union and procreation are both meanings that reflect the divine source of conjugal love, God, Who is truly one. The main point is that God's power is an expression of His love; He is the font of both love and fruitfulness.

Marriage and Mutual Self-Giving

The second paragraph of this section rejects the view that marriage is simply a result of chance or the outcome of natural forces. Rather, God established marriage for the purposes of fostering love among mankind. Marriage achieves this end both through the love of the spouses for each other and in the procreation of new life. Only spouses make a *total* gift of themselves to each other; this is an act appropriate only to spouses. (John Paul II expounds at length on this phrase; see Chapters 4 and 8.) This gift of self aids the spouses in perfecting themselves. This means that through their faithful love for each other they become more loving and selfless and they are thereby able to be better spouses and better parents. Both Chapters 4 and 8 discuss "self-giving" as a proper characteristic of conjugal love.

Marriage as Sacrament

The third paragraph discusses marriage as a sacrament. All marriages of baptized persons are sacramental. The implications of this point are many. The love between spouses is considered to be holy and a source of grace for them. Just as Christ's love for the Church is constant and eternal, so too must married love be unconditional and marriages be indissoluble. The Church realizes that the challenges of marriage are many but assures Man that grace is available to help him meet these challenges. Much will be said later in the document about the need for constant recourse to the sacraments to strengthen the sacrament of marriage. This passage locates conjugal love on the plane of redeemed reality where Man is assisted with a multitude of supernatural aids in pursuing the goods proper to him.

As Chapter 2 notes, many have claimed that *Humanae Vitae* abandoned talk of the "ends" of marriage that were traditionally taught to be offspring, fidelity, and sacrament. Section 8, without explicitly mentioning these as ends, incorporates them into the discussion. The first paragraph speaks about procreation, the second about mutual self-giving, and the third about sacrament. The end of "fidelity" is not explicitly mentioned but surely it can be found in the mention of mutual self-giving. Although no ranking of ends is done here, the mention of procreation and the sacrament in this same section indicates perhaps that *Humanae Vitae* is not abandoning these as goods of marriage. The purpose of this document is not to rank the goods or ends of marriage but to show their inseparable connection.

Humanae Vitae 9: *The Four Characteristics of Conjugal Love*

Section 9 expounds on the four "characteristics and requirements" of conjugal love; it is human, total, faithful and exclusive, and fruitful. This passage is the section of *Humanae Vitae* most directly reminiscent of *Gaudium et Spes* (discussed in Chapter 2). It is clearly intended to link *Humanae Vitae* with *Gaudium et Spes*. All of the characteristics of conjugal love noted here are also noted there, though *Gaudium et Spes* is not quite so systematic in its discussion of these characteristics. The greater precision here is necessitated by the need to define the term *conjugal love* as precisely as possible so that the claim that contraception is compatible with and fosters the goods of conjugal love can be properly appraised.

Conjugal Love as Human

It may seem odd that the first characteristic of conjugal love that must be defined is that it is "human." The importance of asserting this follows from a fairly usual confusion about the Church's teaching about sex. The Church does not maintain that because sexual intercourse is an activity in which both humans and animals engage therefore sex is an "animal" activity. All human activity that issues from a rational and free choice differs radically from the action of other animals. Certainly physiological instincts and desires are clearly motivational forces in seeking marital intercourse, but spouses choose to have sexual intercourse not only and not primarily to satisfy these desires but to express their love for each other. Whereas animals copulate with no intention of expressing their love, increasing their love, or committing themselves to lifelong unions (in fact, strictly speaking, animals have no intentions at all), humans do. Moreover, sex is not just a "release" of passion for humans but a means by which they might foster their human perfection. This section stresses that conjugal love is not just an animal instinct but a fully human relationship.

Conjugal Love as Total

Humans enter into many different kinds of loving relationships, but conjugal love is a special kind, proper only to spouses. Conjugal love is a friendship, but unlike other friendships, which involve some limitations on the extent of the sharing and giving and union, the friendship of spouses is total: it has no limitations of the usual kind and requires sharing that is most extraordinary, for this sharing goes far beyond the sharing of possessions, as it requires the sharing of one's very self. The theme of making a "gift" of one's self to one's spouse recurs throughout the document. See Chapters 4 and 8 for further discussion of this characteristic.

Conjugal Love as Faithful

Clearly this passage stresses the good of fidelity for marriage, a fidelity that spouses intend at the time of their marriage. The reference here to the spouses' "uniting themselves with the marital bond" is important. The definition of marriage as a bond (*vinculum*) is an ancient one. The word conveys the strength of the commitment of marriage; it is one that yokes together, *binds* together the spouses; it is not dissoluble. If marriage is essentially a bond, this explains how even "bad" marriages are still marriages. The couple has pledged a lifetime union, and for better or worse, they are bound to be true to this pledge. Much as a parent is always the parent of his or her child, so too, a spouse is always married to his or her spouse. Again, it is acknowledged that being faithful to this bond is not always easy; nonetheless it is possible. It is asserted that much happiness flows from fidelity with no further clarification of the nature of this happiness. It seems fair to say that the trust and security that result from faithful marriages are a substantial source of human happiness.

Conjugal Love as Fruitful

[FOOTNOTE 8] See Chapter 4 for a fuller discussion of this paragraph. A major point of this paragraph is that, just as God's love overflows into His creation of new beings, so too does the love of spouses extend beyond themselves into the creation of new life. The passage closes by citing a portion of *Gaudium et Spes*, section 50, which brings together the theme of marriage and conjugal love as "being *ordained* by their very nature" to children and the theme of spouses making a gift of themselves to each other. This "gift" leads to the perfection of spouses, which, in turn, leads them to share the gift of life with children. The circle is complete insofar as having children further promotes the good of the parents. Thus the gift that spouses seek to give to each other and God becomes a gift to themselves as well.

Humanae Vitae 10: *Responsible Parenthood*

The Munus *of Responsible Parenthood*

Section 7 notes that the two topics of most importance for considering the question of having children are conjugal love and responsible parenthood, concepts that assume a new prominence in *Gaudium et Spes*. Again, many had argued that the demands of responsible parenthood legitimated the use of contraception. Section 10 attempts to define "responsible parenthood" in order to provide a means for assessing this argument. The first line of *Humanae Vitae* notes that spouses have the *munus* of transmitting human life. Here spouses are said to have the *munus* of responsible parent-hood. It seems fair to conclude that fulfilling the *munus* of transmitting human life entails the *munus* of responsible parenthood. To determine how this responsibility is best met, *Humanae Vitae* strives to provide a precise description of this term.

Knowledge of Biological Processes

The second paragraph of section 10 is most interesting. It may surprise some to find that the discussion of responsible parenthood begins with talk of biological processes. But the point being made here is a basic one; as we have remarked several times, humans, unlike animals, are capable of having a quite remarkable knowledge of their own fertility. Since they are aware that having sexual intercourse is connected with having offspring, they cannot act responsibly in regard to sexual intercourse unless this power of sex is respected and all the responsibilities that flow from it are accepted. That is, the knowledge that sexual intercourse is linked to the bringing forth of new human life should be a major factor for those considering whether or not to engage in sexual intercourse. This paragraph seems a clear attempt to show that in *Gaudium et Spes* 51 the "nature of the person and his acts" are the objective criteria that must determine the morality of means used to limit family size. These criteria include consideration of the nature of human biology.

[FOOTNOTE 9] The footnote reference here is to a portion of the text on natural law in Aquinas's *Summa Theologiae* (I–II, q. 94, art 2). This passage reinforces what was said previously: that Man is an animal and thus shares many biological processes with animals, but Man is not simply an animal. He is a rational animal, which means that he is not subject simply to the instincts of animals but that insofar as possible all his inclina-tions are to be ruled by reason. The first precept of natural law is "Good is to be done and evil is to be avoided." This Man knows and acts on naturally. Aquinas tells us that Man has natural inclinations to sexual intercourse and education of his offspring, which are inclinations he shares with other animals. But since Man is rational, he must submit his inclina-tions to rational guidance and not act on them simply from impulse.

It is also interesting that this section of *Humanae Vitae* speaks of bio-logical processes as having *munera* ("missions") (cf. HV 17). In this con-text *munera* is generally translated as "functions" (probably from the Ital-ian *funzioni*). This is not a bad translation, for strictly speaking it does not seem proper to speak of biological processes as having *munera*. But the use of the word *munera* here may be a projection onto the processes of the responsibilities tied up with the processes. The word suggests the more elevated purpose of the generative organs over the purposes of other organs.

Self-Mastery

Responsible parenthood is said to require that "reason and will exercise mastery over . . . impulses and affections." What are these "innate impulses and affections of the soul [*impulsos innatos et ad animi affectus*]"? What is perhaps surprising here is the suggestion that impulses and affections are "of the soul." The Latin here differs considerably from the Italian, which refers to *alle tendenze dell'istinto e delle passioni* ("instinctive tendencies and passions"), an emphasis that fits with the modern view that sexual feelings are primarily physical or bodily. But the psychology (study or theory of the soul) traditionally used by the Church would have the soul be the seat of all passions. These feelings then are not simply animal but are human, especially insofar as they are subject to higher powers in the soul, the reason and the will. The term *self-mastery* assumes importance in John Paul II's commentary on *Humanae Vitae*. He argues that the use of periodic abstinence helps Man acquire the virtue of self-mastery. This means that he learns how to govern his impulses and passions so that he can act on them according to his best judgment rather than being driven by them. Here it is interesting that *Humanae Vitae* finds self-mastery to be a characteristic of responsible parenthood. Certainly the primary reference is the usefulness of self-mastery to spouses in being faithful to the abstinence their decisions about family planning may require. But the claim may have a broader application. Spouses who have control of their sexual passions will certainly be good examples to their children in this regard. It may also be assumed that they have good control over their other passions, so that they are able to be patient and loving parents.

Paragraph 4 of this section explodes the myth that the Catholic Church teaches that spouses must have as many children as physically possible without regard to other considerations. It is clearly stated that many factors must be taken into account: physical, economic, psychological, and social conditions may bear on the decision about how many children they have. Nonetheless, responsible parenthood does not mean that spouses are to choose an easy path: we are told that choosing to accept many children is the characteristic mark of responsible parenthood. The language here is revealing: it is not said that spouses "have" children but that spouses "accept" children; in a subtle way this emphasis conveys the concept that children are given to spouses.

Limitation of Family Size

[FOOTNOTE 10] This passage also notes that it is in accord with responsible parenthood to limit family size. What must be noted is that this decision should be the result of serious considerations and, of course, in accord with moral precepts. What are serious considerations for limiting family size? The encyclical gives no explicit guidelines in this regard. The first sentence of this paragraph suggests that there may be physical, economic, psychological, and social conditions that would prompt spouses to decide to forego having more children for a certain or undetermined period. Certainly, the health of the spouses and other family members, the financial situation of the family, the emotional stability of all involved, and the conditions in the society in which one lives may all singly or together constitute serious reasons for limiting family size. The portion of *Gaudium et Spes* stating that the decision of how many children to have is the decision of the spouses alone appears in section 50, a section cited by the footnote to this section.

The next paragraph clarifies, though, that the decision about family size is not strictly a private decision that takes into account only the wishes of the spouses. Spouses are not free to define what responsible parenthood is; they are not free to decide, for instance, that the best choice is for married couples to have only one child. The spouses must recognize that parenthood is not something that can be defined by them: it is a reality established by God. For spouses to be able to interpret this reality correctly they must have an upright conscience. They must recognize that God and their interests and those of the family and human society must also be taken into account in their decision on how to conduct themselves as parents. They must come to recognize the true hierarchy of goods; they must come to learn, for instance, what are true financial strains that might necessitate limiting family size and what is a preference for a luxurious or overly comfortable style of living that would not justify refusing to accept more children. Material goods are goods, but they are a lesser good than the good of large families.

Humanae Vitae 11: Respect for the Nature and Finality of the Marriage Act

[FOOTNOTE 11] The first point made in HV 11 is intended to dispel any misconception that the Church thinks that marital intercourse is a tainted human activity; rather, it is good and worthy of human beings. Note the way that marital intercourse is described: as the activity that unites spouses and propagates human life. This sets the stage for the eventual claim (in HV 12) that these "meanings" of marital intercourse are inseparable. Here a reference is given to *Gaudium et Spes* 49, which states that conjugal acts are "good and worthy" because they "signify and foster" the mutual self-giving of the spouses.

But it is the final sentence of HV 11, the sentence that states, "Each and every marital act must remain ordained to procreation," that causes controversy, perhaps the most controversy of any passage in *Humanae Vitae*. This passage is discussed at some length in Chapter 4.

[FOOTNOTE 12] A passage from *Casti Connubii* that refers to contraception as an intrinsic evil is cited. A passage from Pius XII's "Address to the Italian Catholic Association of Midwives" is also cited. Both passages are cited in Chapter 4.

Humanae Vitae *12: The Inseparability of the Procreative and Unitive Meanings of Marital Intercourse*

HV 12 is nearly as controversial as the preceding section; it, too, is discussed at some length in Chapter 4.

Humanae Vitae *13: Further Arguments Concerning Inseparability*

This section is also discussed in Chapter 4.

[FOOTNOTE 13] The portion of *Mater et Magistra*[57] cited in the footnote reference to this text echoes the concepts conveyed in *Gaudium et Spes* noted in note 10; it is cited in footnote 4.

Humanae Vitae *14: Morally Unacceptable Means of Limiting Family Size*

The document has asserted that only some means of regulating family size are morally acceptable. HV 14 eliminates those that are not.

Abortion

Abortion, which takes a human life, is quickly dismissed. This restriction has more relevancy than might at first be recognized. Certainly, many women today use abortion as a form of birth control, usually but not always, as a backup to contraception. But its greater relevancy is due to the fact that the prohibition of abortion directly rules out some forms of contraception. It is still not widely known, though it was suspected even at the time of *Humanae Vitae*, that many popular forms of contraception are not anovulants but abortifacients: that is, they work not by stopping ovulation but by causing an early-term abortion when conception does

57. AAS 53 (1961) 447.

occur. A woman would not know when she conceives and thus would not know when she is aborting; nonetheless, the action she has chosen causes her child to be aborted. A woman using a form of the pill that works as an abortifacient would be playing a kind of Russian roulette: she may or may not be aborting.

[FOOTNOTE 14] [The footnote reference to this section lists the portions of documents that denounce abortion.] The Roman Catechism (part II, chapter 8) cites the angel who speaks to Tobias about marriage and says: "Take the virgin with the fear of the Lord, moved rather for love of children than for lust, that in the seed of Abraham you may obtain a blessing in children" (Tobit 6:16, 17, 22). The Catechism comments on this passage: "Having children is thus clearly one of the reasons why God instituted marriage from the beginning. Whoever, therefore, in marriage artificially prevents conception, or procures an abortion, commits a most serious sin: the sin of pre-meditated murder."[58]

Casti Connubii condemns therapeutic abortion:

As to the "medical and therapeutic indication" to which, using their own words, we have made reference, Venerable Brethren, however much we may pity the mother whose health and even life is gravely imperiled in the performance of the duty allotted to her by nature, nevertheless what could ever be a sufficient reason for excusing in any way the direct murder of the innocent? This is precisely what we are dealing with here. Whether inflicted upon the mother or upon the child, it is against the precept of God and the law of nature: "Thou shalt not kill." The life of each is equally sacred, and no one has the power, not even the public authority, to destroy it. It is of no use to appeal to the right of taking away life for here it is a question of the innocent, whereas that right has regard only to the guilty, nor is there here question of defense of bloodshed against an unjust aggressor (for who would call an innocent child an unjust aggressor?); again there is no question here of what is called the "law of extreme necessity" which could even extend to the direct killing of the innocent. Upright and skillful doctors strive most praiseworthily to guard and preserve the lives of both mother and child; on the contrary, those show themselves most unworthy of the noble medical profession who encompass the death of one or the other, through a pretense at practicing medicine or through motives of misguided pity. (DSP 32)[59]

Pius XII in his "Address to the Italian Medico-biological Union of St. Luke" (November 12, 1944) condemns abortion as follows:

The fifth commandment, "Thou shalt not kill," synthesizes man's duties toward the life and integrity of the human body. It is a font of knowledge for the professor in his chair and the doctor in practice. The life of an innocent man is inviolable. Any act, therefore, which seeks to destroy this life directly is illicit, whether the

58. *The Roman Catechism*, 333.
59. AAS 22 (1930) 562–64.

destruction is an end in itself or a means to an end, whether there is a question of embryonic life, or life in its full bloom, or life drawing to its close. God alone is master of the life of any man who is not guilty of a crime which demands the death penalty. The doctor has no right to dispose of the infant's life or of the mother's life; . . . His [the doctor's] task is not to destroy but to save. These are basic, unchanging principles which the Church has been forced to vindicate against error many times in recent decades.[60]

In his "Address to the Italian Catholic Association of Midwives"[61] Pius XII explains the intrinsic worth of human life in a lengthy passage. Let me cite just two portions from it:

Every human being, even the infant in the mother's womb, has the right to life *immediately* from God, not from the parent or any human society or authority. . . . The direct destruction of what they call "worthless life" born or unborn, practiced a few years ago on many occasions, can be justified in no way. For this reason, when this practice began, the Church formally declared that the killing, even by order of public authority, of those who although innocent are not only useless to the nation on account of physical or psychic defects but also a burden upon it, is contrary to positive natural and divine right and therefore, illegal.

Pius XII in his "Address to the Congress of the Family Front and of the Association of Large Families" inveighs against abortion and gives the Catholic position on the question whether it is morally permissible to take the life of the unborn child in order to save the life of the mother: "Never and in no case has the Church taught that the child's life must be preferred to that of the mother. It is a mistake to formulate the question with this alternative: either the child's life or the mother's. No; neither the mother's life nor the child's may be submitted to an act of direct suppression. For the one and for the other the requirement can be only this: to make every effort to save the life of both the mother and the child."[62]

John XXIII in *Pacem in Terris*[63] (April 11, 1963) gives a list of human rights, the foremost among them, the right to life (*vitae ius*).

And section 51 of *Gaudium et Spes*[64] condemns abortion in these words: "Life must be protected with the utmost care from the moment of conception: abortion and infanticide are abominable crimes."[65]

Sterilization

Sterilization is condemned next. No reason for the condemnation is given in the text, though there are ample footnote references that do give

---

60. In *Discorsi e Radiomessaggi di S.S. Pio XII* 6 (1944) 191–92; the translation is from *Linacre Quarterly* 23 (Nov. 1956) 109–16, 114.
61. AAS 43 (1951) 842–43. 62. AAS 43 (1951) 857–59.
63. In AAS 55 (1963) 259–60. 64. AAS 58 (1966) 1072.
65. The translations for passages from the conciliar documents are from *Vatican II: The*

reasons. Yet, perhaps understanding even in part the reasons for the condemnation of sterilization would assist in understanding the condemnation of contraception. Sterilization is considered to be a type of mutilation; one disfigures or mutilates a feature of one's anatomy that is good. Fertility is a good, a healthy condition in an adult person. To sterilize oneself is deliberately to deprive oneself of a God-given good. Many forms of contraception cause "temporary sterility"; they deprive one of one's procreative capacity for a temporary period.

[FOOTNOTE 15] [This footnote cites documents that condemn sterilization.] Pius XI in *Casti Connubii*[66] states: "Furthermore, Christian doctrine establishes, and the light of human reason makes it most clear, that private individuals have no power over the members of their bodies than that which pertains to their natural ends; and they are not free to destroy or mutilate their members, or in any other way render themselves unfit for their natural functions, except when no other provision can be made for the good of the whole body" (DSP 35). Again, this passage makes clear that human functions are not to be tampered with except for the good of the whole body. That is, sterilization for the purpose of thwarting procreation is intrinsically wrong, whereas sterilization resulting from removal of a diseased organ would be morally permissible in accord with the principle of double effect and the principle of totality. (Pius XII's distinction between direct and indirect sterilization, discussed later, speaks to this point.)

Pius XII in a Decree of the Holy Office[67] (February 22, 1940) responds to a question concerning whether direct sterilization, permanent or temporary, of male or female, is licit. The response is that it is not licit since it is forbidden by natural law (*prohiberi lege naturae*).

There is a reference to Pius XII's "Address to the Italian Catholic Union of Midwives"; see note 14.

Pius XII in his "Address to the Seventh Congress of the International Society of Hematology"[68] repeats the condemnation of sterilization by *Casti Connubii* and earlier condemnations that he had promulgated. Here he explains: "By direct sterilization We mean an act whose aim is to make procreation impossible whether this is intended as a means or an end; but We do not apply the term to every act which, in fact, renders procreation impossible. Man does not always intend to produce the consequences of his acts, even though he has foreseen them. Thus, for example, the removal of diseased ovaries entails as a necessary consequence the impossibility of

---

Conciliar and Postconciliar Documents, ed. Austin Flannery. O.P.; hereafter the section number is given in the text.

66. AAS 22 (1930) 565.   67. In AAS 32 (1940) 73.
68. AAS 50 (1958) 734–35.

procreation, but this impossibility may not be intended either as an end or as a means."[69] And further: "If a woman takes such medicine [anovulant pills], not to prevent conception, but only on the advice of a doctor as a necessary remedy because of the condition of the uterus or the organism, she produces *indirect* sterilization which is permitted according to the general principles governing acts with a double effect. But a *direct* and, therefore, illicit sterilization results when ovulation is stopped to protect the uterus and the organism from the consequences of a pregnancy which it is not able to sustain. Some moralists contend that it is permissible to take medicines with this latter intention, but they are in error."[70]

Temporary Sterilization

The third paragraph of this section makes more specific the prohibition given in the last paragraph against conjugal acts that are temporarily sterilized. This passage makes it clear that it is not just that some forms of contraception interrupt the act of intercourse that makes contraception wrong. Some theologians speculated that since the pill did not interrupt sex as the condom does, it may be morally permissible. Here we are told that if one does something prior to intercourse (such as take the pill) or during intercourse (such as practice withdrawal) or after intercourse (such as douching with the intent to destroy sperm or taking a morning-after pill), all these acts are wrong. They are wrong because they are a kind of sterilization, a temporary sterilization, and thus share in the moral condemnation of sterilization.

[FOOTNOTE 16] The footnote references here repeat many of the prohibitions against contraception and sterilization given earlier.[71] John XXIII in *Mater et Magistra*[72] insists that methods of fertility control appropriate for plants and animals are not appropriate for Man; see note 4 for citation of this passage. A passage from the preceding section of the encyclical is also pertinent, especially since some argue that John XXIII, had he lived, would have changed the Church's teaching on contraception. In reference to the alleged population problem he states:

Besides, God in His goodness and wisdom has, on the one hand, provided nature with almost inexhaustible productive capacity; and, on the other hand, has endowed man with such ingenuity that, by using suitable means, he can apply

69. Translations are from *The Pope Speaks* 6 (1958) 392–400; 394–95.
70. Ibid., 395.
71. *Catechismus Romanus Concilii Tridentii*, pt. 2, chap. 8; Pius XI, *Casti Connubii* AAS 22 (1930) 559–61; Pius XII, "Address to the Italian Catholic Union of Midwives," in AAS 43 (1951) 843; Pius XII, "Address to the Seventh Congress of the International Society of Hematology," in AAS 50 (1958) 734–35.
72. AAS 53 (1961) 447.

nature's resources to the needs and requirements of existence. Accordingly, that the question posed may be clearly resolved, a course of action is not indeed to be followed whereby, contrary to the moral law laid down by God, procreative function also is violated. Rather, man should, by the use of his skills and science of every kind, acquire an intimate knowledge of the forces of nature and control them ever more extensively. Moreover, the advances hitherto made in science and technology give almost limitless promise for the future in this matter. (DSP 54)

The Principle of Lesser Evil

For an extensive discussion of this principle see Chapter 3.

[FOOTNOTE 17] Pius XII in his "Address to the Fifth National Congress of Italian Catholic Jurists" (December 6, 1953)[73] provides a discussion of an appropriate use of the principle of the toleration of the lesser evil. It is cited in Chapter 3.

[FOOTNOTE 18] Romans 3:8 reinforces the claim of the text that it is never right to choose evil as a means to a good: "Or why may we not do evil that good may come of it? This is the very thing that some slanderously accuse us of teaching; but they will get what they deserve."

The Principle of Totality

For an extensive discussion of this principle see Chapter 3.

Humanae Vitae 15: Morally Permissible Therapeutic Means

HV 15 explicitly makes the point already made in several of the footnote references, that, when necessary for reasons of health, individuals may take drugs that would render them infertile. They would not be doing an intrinsic evil but would be "tolerating" a (lesser) evil. Justification for such action is based on both the principle of totality and the principle of double effect.

[FOOTNOTE 19] One footnote reference is to Pius XII's "Address to the Congress of the Italian Association of Urology"[74] (October 8, 1953), where he addresses a false application of the principle of totality:

It is not unusual, when a surgical intervention involves gynecological complications—or even independently of these—that healthy ovaries are removed or rendered incapable of functioning in order to prevent another pregnancy and the dangers which would result from a pregnancy to either the health or the life of the mother. The cause of these dangers is from other diseased organs such as the kidney, the heart, or the lungs, which would be aggravated by a pregnancy. In order to justify the removal of the ovaries, appeal is made to the principle [of totality] cited above, which states that intervention on healthy organs is morally permissible, when the good of the whole requires it.

73. AAS 45 (1953) 798–99.
74. In AAS 45 (1953) 674–75.

Here, however, the appeal to the principle is wrong. Because in this case, the danger which the mother runs does not come, directly or indirectly, from the presence or the normal functioning of the ovaries, nor from their influence on the diseased organs, kidney, lungs, or heart. The danger occurs only if free sexual activity results in a pregnancy, which possibly threatens the above-mentioned organs which are too weak or diseased. The conditions which permit putting one part [of the body] at the disposal of another for the sake of the whole—on the strength of the principle of totality—are, then, absent. Therefore it is not morally permissible to interfere with healthy ovaries. (my translation)

The passage preceding this gives examples of when it is morally permissible to remove a healthy organ or cause it to stop functioning when the well-being of the whole requires it. If in its *normal functioning* a healthy organ in its exercise should cause harm to a diseased organ, it is morally permissible to remove the organ. Why, then, is it not permissible to remove ovaries, if a pregnancy would cause harm to a woman? It is because it is not the normal functioning of the ovaries (which is an automatic bodily function) that is causing harm: it is the *possible* pregnancy that causes harm. And a pregnancy is not an "automatic" physical function over which humans have no control. It is the result of a sexual act, freely chosen. The principle of totality that permits the removal of healthy organs applies only when *no other means* is possible to prevent the damage that they in their healthy functioning do to weakened or diseased organs. There is another means of preventing harm to the heart, and so on, caused by a pregnancy, apart from the removal of healthy ovaries, and that is periodic or complete abstinence from sexual intercourse.

Pius XII in his "Address to the Seventh Congress of the International Society of Hematology"[75] explains the principle of double effect and argues that a woman may use drugs with a contraceptive effect but may not morally use these drugs for the purpose of preventing pregnancy.[76] He makes the same point made earlier: "It is likewise necessary to reject the view of a number of doctors and moralists who permit these practices when medical indications make conception undesirable, or in other similar cases, which cannot be discussed here. In these cases the use of medication has as its end the prevention of conception by preventing ovulation. They are instances, therefore, of direct sterilization."[77]

---

75. AAS 50 (1958) 734–35.
76. For more on double effect, see Chapter 3.
77. AAS 50 (1958) 734–35.

Humanae Vitae 16: *The Morality of Recourse to the Infertile Period*

This section is discussed in Chapter 4.

[FOOTNOTE 20] Pius XII in his "Address to the Midwives" spoke at some length about the legitimacy of using the sterile periods to avoid pregnancy. Perhaps the most relevant passage is the following:

> There are serious motives, such as those often mentioned in the so-called medical, eugenic, economic, and social "indications," that can exempt for a long time, perhaps even the whole duration of the marriage, from the positive and obligatory carrying out of the act. From this it follows that observing the non-fertile periods alone can be lawful only under a moral aspect. Under the conditions mentioned it really is so. But if, according to a rational and just judgment, there are no similar grave reasons of a personal nature or deriving from external circumstances, then the determination to avoid habitually the fecundity of the union while at the same time to continue satisfying their sensuality, can be derived only from a false appreciation of life and from reasons having nothing to do with proper ethical laws.[78]

Humanae Vitae 17: *The Consequences of Using Contraception*[79]

There are many ways of grasping why an action is wrong. Often arguments are based on the very nature of the action; for instance, lying is said to be wrong because it is an intrinsic violation of the good of truth; it is also said to be wrong because it has dire consequences for society. *Humanae Vitae* has been arguing that contraception is wrong because its violates the goods of conjugal love. Here, it begins to give further reasons based on the consequences of the use of contraception. Humans are particularly weak in the realm of sexual discipline; the use of contraception, it is claimed, will only promote this weakness. This first paragraph notes that infidelity and a general lowering of moral discipline will result, but it focuses on how a husband may come to treat and consider his wife. The primary argument is that men will use their wives for their own selfish pleasures, that they will see their wives as "sex objects" and not fully appreciate them as persons, as friends.

The document expresses the fear that if contraception is considered a solution to a difficulty, public authorities might insist that couples use contraception when they judge it to be necessary for the interests of the state. In a day when forced abortions are routine in communist China, these fears seem realistic. The use of *munus* here is significant. The Italian is

---

78. Pius XII, "Address to Midwives," 169.

79. For an expanded commentary on the consequences of contraception, see Janet E. Smith, "*Humanae Vitae*: A Prophetic Document?" *Crisis* 6:8 (Sept. 1988) 30–35.

settore, regularly translated as "sector." But it is a *munus* that the authorities would be violating, a distinctive assignment given to spouses by God.

The tone of this section grows increasingly emphatic as it comes to a close; there is a repeated call for limits and not permitting violation of these limits. The message is strongly stated that neither individuals nor the state has the right to interfere with the procreative powers of Man and that individuals should not abuse this power if they are not prepared to suffer at the hands of a public authority that may abuse this power.

[FOOTNOTE 21] Again the principle of totality is mentioned.[80] The reason for this repeated reference to this principle is that *Humanae Vitae* wants to make it clear that it is not appropriate to use this principle for justifying the interference of the state ("the whole" or "the totality") in marital acts ("the part"), for these acts are not properly speaking part of the state.[81]

Humanae Vitae *18: The Church, the Guarantor of Authentic Human Value*

[FOOTNOTE 22] Although HV 12 states confidently, "Men of our time are particularly suited to understand that the teaching [of the Church] conforms to human reason," here it is acknowledged that many will find the teaching difficult to accept. The Church understands that she is in opposition to—a sign of contradiction to—many of the "opinion makers" of this world. She accepts this as a consequence of preaching the truth, for such was Christ's fate, too. Indeed, the scriptural passage cited in this section refers to Simeon's prophecy to Mary when she presented Christ in the temple: "This child is destined to be the downfall and the rise of many in Israel, a sign that will be opposed [a sign of contradiction]. . ." (Luke 2:34). Christ repeatedly prophesied that He would be rejected and scorned by Men because of the truth that He taught, for the truth that He taught was in contradiction to the ways of the world.

The point made earlier in HV 4, that the Church is the guardian and interpreter of both the natural and revealed law, is reiterated here. Reiterated as well is a thematic truth of this encyclical—that moral truths are not just remote laws laid down by a remote God, but that they are in

80. Pius XII's "Address to the Twenty-Sixth Congress of the Italian Association of Urology" AAS 45 (1953) 674–75 and his "Address to the Leaders and Members of the Italian Association of Cornea Donors and Italian Association for the Blind" AAS (1956) 461–62 explain the proper application of the principle of totality. Both speeches are discussed in the commentary in Chapter 3.

81. Again, see Chapter 3 for a fuller discussion of this principle.

accord with the true good of Man—thus, although the teachings of the encyclical may present some difficulties and be the source of some suffering for Men, ultimately living in accord with these laws and teachings fosters human happiness. Another theme is introduced here: that the Church cannot change its teaching on this matter for it is not a law "made up" by the Church, but one guarded and interpreted by her (cf. HV 20 and Chapter 3).

[FOOTNOTE 23] The Church again defends her involvement in these matters; it is right that she advise Men and their governments, since, if obeyed, her teaching will assist Man in improving the culture in which he lives. She also fears that Man may come to rely on technology at the expense of his human dignity. The passage from *Populorum Progressio* cited here appears at the close of the second portion of that encyclical. It makes no reference to contraception but speaks against any unbridled confidence that technology will solve all of Man's problems and warns against the dangers that accompany technological prowess. It especially warns that such progress may create a desire for ever more possessions and may foster selfishness and greed. Human life, a life lived in accord with human dignity and human love, is infinitely more valuable than possessions. Contraception is clearly viewed by *Humanae Vitae* as one of those modern "improvements" that may lead to the further dehumanization of Man, that may lead him to value material comfort and well-being more than generosity.

Humanae Vitae 19: The Church as Mother and Teacher

[FOOTNOTE 24] *Humanae Vitae* reiterates the claim that the Church acts for Christ in this world, here both as teacher and as the source of forgiveness for Man's sins. The footnote citation here is most telling; it refers to the whole of Chapter 8 of Romans, a chapter that stresses that although Man is a victim of original sin and subject to temptations of the flesh, we have in Christ one who will supply all our needs and help us overcome our tendencies to sin. It is altogether a hopeful chapter; for instance, verses 26–27 read: "The Spirit too helps us in our weakness, for we do not know how to pray as we ought; but the Spirit himself makes intercession for us with groanings that cannot be expressed in speech. He who searches hearts knows what the Spirit means, for the Spirit intercedes for the saints as God himself wills."

Humanae Vitae 20: *The Possibility of Observing the Divine Law*

This section continues to discuss the themes of the last few sections: that keeping the law of God may be difficult and requires strong efforts from Men but that grace is available to assist Man in finding the strength to do what is to his good.

Humanae Vitae 21: *Self-Mastery*

[FOOTNOTE 25] This section is perhaps one of the most important passages in *Humanae Vitae* although one of the most neglected. As Chapter 8 argues, John Paul II makes this passage one of the focal points of his reflections on the encyclical. This section puts the lie to the claim that the encyclical's purpose is primarily to deliver a negative precept, the condemnation of contraception. Rather, it is an effort to set forth the elevated understanding the Church has of marriage and of human nature. This passage sings the praises of the virtue of self-mastery, a virtue acquired by those who live in accord with the highest values. It lists the many goods, such as harmony in the home and generosity, that are the result of the efforts to be selfless. It notes that those who practice periodic abstinence are particularly well situated to acquire the virtue of self-mastery.

Humanae Vitae 22: *Creating an Atmosphere Favorable to Chastity*

Many of the forms of entertainment in the modern world actively work against the acquisition of the virtue of chastity. This section appeals to educators and those who have influence over modern forms of entertainment to condemn forms of entertainment that "arouse Man's passions and . . . foster dissolute morals."

Passages are cited from the Vatican II document on social communications that encourage the representation of moral evil in the arts but insist, "Moral norms must prevail if harm rather than spiritual profit is not to ensue."[82]

Humanae Vitae 23: *Appeal to Public Authorities*

This section addresses the issue of population growth that was introduced in HV 3 as a reason for considering the question of moral means of birth control. Paul VI insists that whatever means are used to solve population

---

82. Second Vatican Council, Decree *Inter Mirifica*, Dec. 4, 1963, nos. 6–7: AAS 56 (1964) 147.

problems must not violate natural and divine law. Largely he counsels generosity and wise government policies as means to provide for the needy.

[FOOTNOTE 26] He cites John XXIII's *Mater et Magistra*[83] to the effect that human dignity must be respected in whatever means and methods of population control are pursued.

[FOOTNOTE 27] He also refers to several sections of his own *Populorum Progressio;*[84] there, too, he calls on rich nations to help poor nations: "Given the increasing needs of the under-developed countries, it should be considered quite normal for an advanced country to devote a part of its production to meet their needs, and to train teachers, engineers, technicians and scholars prepared to put their knowledge and their skill at the disposal of less fortunate peoples" (DSP 30). He calls for a planned program of action rather than sporadic responses to emergencies. He recommends the establishment of a World Fund "to be made up in part of the money spent on arms." He observes, "Only world-wide collaboration, of which a common fund would be both means and symbol, will succeed in overcoming vain rivalries, and in establishing a fruitful and peaceful exchange between peoples" (DSP 31).

Humanae Vitae 24: Appeal to Men of Science

Paul VI reiterates a plea made by the Church several times before, that scientists work to make moral family planning more reliable for spouses.

[FOOTNOTE 28] He cites *Gaudium et Spes*.[85]

[FOOTNOTE 29] He also cites Pius XII, "Address to the Congress of the Family Front and of the Association of Large Families,"[86] to this effect.

[FOOTNOTE 30] And, citing *Gaudium et Spes,*[87] he offers his expectation that such refinement of natural methods will demonstrate that there is no contradiction between divine love and true conjugal love.

Humanae Vitae 25: Appeal to Christian Spouses

This section calls on Christian spouses to take full advantage of the graces available to them through the sacraments to assist them in living in accord with the natural and divine laws.

83. John XXIII, encyclical, *Mater et Magistra*, May 15, 1961, in AAS 53 (1961), 447.
84. Paul VI, encyclical, *Populorum Progressio*, Mar. 26, 1967, no. 21 in AAS 59 (1967) 281–84.
85. Second Vatican Council, *Gaudium et Spes*, 52, in AAS 58 (1966) 1074.
86. Pius XII, "Address to the Congress of the Family Front and of the Association of Large Families," Nov. 28, 1951; AAS 43 (1951) 859.
87. Second Vatican Council, *Gaudium et Spes*, 51, in AAS 58 (1966) 1072.

[FOOTNOTE 31] A passage from Scripture, Matthew 11:30: "For my yoke is easy and my burden light," is cited to assure spouses that God will assist them and reward them for being faithful to His designs.

[FOOTNOTE 32] Not only do spouses receive assistance from the Church in the form of sacraments; spouses who are responsive to these graces play a role in sanctifying the world. Paul VI calls on *Gaudium et Spes* 48[88] to support this claim. The summary sentences of this section read: "The Christian family springs from marriage, which is an image and a sharing in the partnership of love between Christ and the Church; it will show forth to all men Christ's living presence in the world and the authentic nature of the Church by the love and generous fruitfulness of the spouses, by their unity and fidelity, and by the loving way in which all members of the family cooperate with each other."

Lumen Gentium 35[89] speaks of the prophetic role (*munus*) of Christ and of how the laity share in this *munus*. Of spouses, it states:

The state of life that is sanctified by a special sacrament, namely, married and family life, has a special importance in this prophetic office. Where the Christian religion pervades the whole structure of life with a continuous and ever more profound transformation, there is both the practice and an outstanding school of the lay apostolate. In it the married partners have their own proper vocation: they must be witnesses of faith and love of Christ to one another and to their children. The Christian family proclaims aloud both the present power of the kingdom of God and the hope of the blessed life. Hence, by example and by their testimony, they convict the world of sin and give light to those who seek the truth.

[FOOTNOTE 33] Nonetheless, Paul VI acknowledges that spouses may encounter great difficulties in attempting to be faithful to the demands of their calling. Several passages from Scripture are cited to illustrate that difficulties are a part of the Christian calling. Accompanying the citation of Matthew 7:14 is reference to Hebrews 12:11: "At the time it is administered, all discipline seems a cause for grief and not for joy, but later it brings forth the fruit of peace and justice to those who are trained in its school."

[FOOTNOTE 34] Paul VI also uses Scripture (Titus 2:12) to encourage spouses to live in hope that they will eventually—certainly in the after-life—be rewarded for their faithfulness.

[FOOTNOTE 35] Here he exhorts spouses to live in this hope (1 Corinthians 7:31).

88. Second Vatican Council, *Gaudium et Spes*, 48, in AAS 58 (1966) 1067–69.
89. Dogmatic Constitution *Lumen Gentium*, Nov. 21, 1964, no. 35 in AAS 57 (1965) 40–41.

[FOOTNOTE 36] He again reassures spouses that graces are available to them to assist them in their labors (Romans 5:5).

[FOOTNOTE 37] This footnote reminds spouses of the great calling that is theirs: to be images of the love that Christ has for His Church (Ephesians 5:25).

Humanae Vitae 26: *The Apostolate of Spouses*

This section calls on spouses to assist other spouses in being faithful to their calling and, in fact, calls this outreach to other couples part of their *munus.*

[FOOTNOTE 38] *Lumen Gentium* is mentioned;[90] section 35 is cited in footnote 32. Section 41 teaches that all are called to holiness and says of the calling of marriage:

Christian married couples and parents, following their own way, should support one another in grace all through life with faithful love, and should train their children (lovingly received from God) in Christian doctrine and evangelical virtues. Because in this way they present to all an example of unfailing and generous love, they build up the brotherhood of charity, and they stand as witnesses and cooperators of the fruitfulness of mother Church, as a sign of, and a share in that love with which Christ loved his bride and gave himself for her.

Portions of *Gaudium et Spes*[91] are again cited (a relevant passage from section 48 is cited in footnote 32); a relevant passage from section 49 reads as follows: "Authentic married love will be held in high esteem, and healthy public opinion will be quick to recognize it, if Christian spouses give outstanding witness to faithfulness and harmony in their love, if they are conspicuous in their concern for the education of their children, and if they play their part in a much needed cultural, psychological, and social renewal in matters of marriage and the family."

The whole of number 11 of *Apostolicam Actuositatem*[92] speaks of the apostolate of spouses. In enumerating the multiple activities in which families might participate are mentioned "assisting engaged couples to make a better preparation for marriage" and "supporting married people and families in a material or moral crisis."

90. Cf. Second Vatican Council, Dogmatic Constitution *Lumen Gentium*, Nov. 21, 1964, no. 35, 41 in AAS 57 (1965) 40–45. Calegari persuasively argues that AAS pages for *Lumen Gentium* should be 40–41 and 45–47.
91. *Gaudium et Spes*, 48–49 in AAS 58 (1966) 1067–70.
92. Decree *Apostolicam Actuositatem*, Nov. 18, 1965, no. 11 in AAS 58 (1966) 947–49.

Humanae Vitae 27: *To Doctors and Health Care Professionals*

A special plea is made here to doctors and health care professionals to stay true to Christian principles in the practice of their art. They are asked to attempt to educate their colleagues in this regard and to provide trustworthy guidance to Catholic couples.

Humanae Vitae 28: *To Priests*

Paul VI makes multiple appeals to priests. First he calls on theologians to promote the teaching of the encyclical. He asks for obedience from them, not only because of the strength of the reasons given for it but also because the teaching is promulgated by the magisterium, which is guided by the Holy Spirit.

[FOOTNOTE 39] Reference is made here to *Lumen Gentium* 25, which discusses the authority of the bishops as teachers and the infallibility of the pope. It is not clear whether he cites this section to indicate that the teaching shares in the infallibility of his teaching power or whether he is citing it to remind them that even when a teaching is not promulgated as infallible it is still to be adhered to "with a religious assent of soul."

[FOOTNOTE 40] Paul VI asks for support in his teaching and cites 1 Corinthians 1:10 in his call for a united voice on this matter.

Humanae Vitae 29

This section seems to be designed to remind priests that although they may think permitting contraception would be a compassionate action, defending the truth is true charity. But Paul VI hastens to instruct priests to be compassionate with those who may have difficulty living up to the demands of the truth.

[FOOTNOTE 41] He cites Christ Himself as the perfect example of one who did not compromise the truth but who was loving to sinners (John 3:17). He implores priests to exhort couples to make use of prayer and the sacraments in their endeavor to be true witnesses to the truth of Christian marriage.

Humanae Vitae 30: *To Bishops*

Finally Paul VI makes a special plea to bishops to devote themselves "with complete zeal and no delay" "to keeping marriage safe and holy." He speaks of this as the "greatest responsibility of [their] mission [*munus*] and the greatest responsibility committed to [them] at the present time." He reminds them that they can best achieve this task if they coordinate the many ministries in which they are involved, and if they do so, they will better promote happiness.

Final Appeal

Humanae Vitae 31

In this passage, Pope Paul VI calls on a fundamental principle of natural law, that by living by the truth, people are living in accord with "the laws inscribed on their nature by the Most High" and that "to be happy Man must prudently and lovingly cultivate these laws." He invokes a wealth of graces on those attempting to be faithful to the truth.

The Papal Interventions

A letter delivered to those cardinals and bishops considering a draft of *Gaudium et Spes* from the secretary of state requested in the name of a "higher authority" that explicit mention be made of Pius XI's *Casti Connubii* and of Pius XII's "Address to the Italian Catholic Union of Midwives,"[1] both of which contained strong condemnations of contraception. Four *modi*, or emendations, were added to be included in the text.[2] One noted Vatican II watcher understood these *modi* as expressions of the will of Paul VI on the matter of contraception and read them as "exploding the idea that conjugal love enjoyed equal status with procreation as one of the ends of marriage and reasserting Pius XI's doctrine of *Casti Connubii* banning all and every type of artificial contraception unequivocally."[3] There certainly can be no question that the intent of the emendations was to strengthen the text of *Gaudium et Spes* in the direction of condemning artificial contraception.

The *modi* were somewhat modified by the drafters of the constitution, but did serve to give more negative mention to contraception in *Gaudium et Spes* and to accentuate the importance of children. The first of the *modi* was responsible for adding "illicit practices against human generation" [*illicitis usibus contra generationem*] along with "excessive self love" and the "worship of pleasure" as profanations of married love (GS 47). The phrase is not perfectly clear but, in the context of the Church's teaching, can legitimately be taken to mean contraceptive practices. The second *modus* required the addition of a phrase and the removal of a word from a sentence

---

1. Oct. 29, 1951 in AAS 43 (1951) 857–59.
2. The story of the *modi* or interventions can be found in Father Ralph M. Wiltgen, S.V.D., *The Rhine Flows into the Tiber* (Rockford, Ill.: Tan Books, 1967) 267–78, Xavier Rynne, *The Fourth Session* (London: Faber and Faber, 1965) 210–55, and Robert Blair Kaiser, *The Politics of Sex and Religion* (Kansas City, Mo.: Leaven Press, 1985) 115–21.
3. Rynne, *Fourth Session*, 212.

that subsequently read, "Without intending to underestimate the other ends of marriage, it must be said that true married love and the whole structure of family life which results from it is directed to disposing the spouses to cooperate valiantly with the love of the Creator and Saviour, who through them will increase and enrich his family from day to day" (GS 49).[4] The removal of "*etiam*" or "also" which had been placed before "which results from it," was understood to put procreation on an equal footing with conjugal love, rather than making it subordinate. The phrase "without intending to underestimate the other ends of marriage" was added to the phrase beginning with "it must be said that" to preserve the equality of ends. Also, to stress further the importance of children to marriage, after the sentence in GS 50 reading "Marriage and married love are by nature ordered to the procreation and education of children" was added "Indeed children are the supreme gift of marriage and greatly contribute to the good of the parents themselves."

Modus three (which also incorporated *modus* four) brought about this addition: "[Respect for the total meaning of mutual self-giving and human procreation] is possible only if the virtue of married chastity is seriously practiced. In questions of birth regulation the sons of the Church, faithful to these principles, are forbidden to use methods disapproved of by the teaching authority of the Church in its interpretation of the divine law" (GS 51). Clearly, both the mention of the practice of conjugal chastity and the prohibition of forbidden methods of birth control bow deeply in the direction of repeating the constant teaching of the Church. This impression is reinforced by the references in the famous footnote 14 to this section. This footnote cites the portion of *Casti Connubii* that condemns artificial contraception and Pius XII's "Address to the Italian Catholic Union of Midwives." The third reference is to Paul VI's "Address to the College of Cardinals"[5] and is followed by notice that the pope reserves for himself final judgment about this matter, on completion of the work of the papal commission. These final two references were not requested by Paul VI (though they were approved by him). The address to the cardinals asserted that Pius XII's condemnation of the pill was in force, *for now*. The addition of this reference could certainly be taken to mean that some of those voting for it wished to indicate that the question of contraception was still an open one. Since Paul VI's papal commission was still meeting, it is not clear why he insisted on these emendations. Speculations are (1)

4. The translations for passages from the conciliar documents are from *Vatican II: The Conciliar and Postconciliar Documents*, ed. Austin Flannery. O.P.; the section number is given in the text.

5. June 23, 1964, in AAS 56 (1964) 581–89.

that he had made up his mind that there could be no change in the
Church's condemnation of contraception or (2) that he felt more "interim"
guidance was needed for those who were prepared to stray from present
Church teaching until he received a report from his papal commission and
acted upon it.

What is worth noting is that the whole of footnote 14 is an implicit
conciliar advance endorsement of the process that Paul VI was involved
in with the commission—and so too, it seems of the results of this commission, which was *Humanae Vitae*.

A Critique of the Work of Germain Grisez, Joseph Boyle, John Finnis, and William May

The work in ethics of Germain Grisez and that of his associates, Joseph Boyle, John Finnis, and William May, especially their critique of consequentialism and proportionalism, has made an enormous contribution to contemporary Catholic moral thought.[1] They rightly deserve the title as foremost defenders of the Church's teaching on contraception and have

---

1. Their most recent work is a joint one: John C. Ford, S.J., Germain Grisez, Joseph Boyle, Jr., John Finnis, and William E. May, *The Teaching of Humanae Vitae: A Defense* (San Francisco: Ignatius Press, 1988); hereafter I will refer to this book as TOHV. (John Ford did not participate in the writing of the portion of this book that offers a new defense of *Humanae Vitae*.) These ethicists have a distinguished history of writing in defense of *Humanae Vitae*. I would like to reproduce here the list of their writings on contraception and related questions that is given in footnote 4 in their text (39): Germain Grisez, *Contraception and the Natural Law* (Milwaukee: Bruce, 1964) [hereafter, I will refer to this book as CNL]; "Marriage: Reflections Based on St. Thomas and Vatican Council II," *Catholic Mind* 64 (June 1966): 4–19; "Contraception and Reality," *Triumph*, in 3 parts: Feb. 1968, 21–24; Mar. 1968, 18–21; Apr. 1968, 27–30; *The Way of the Lord Jesus*, vol. 1, *Christian Moral Principles* (Chicago: Franciscan Herald Press, 1983), chaps. 35 and 36; Joseph M. Boyle, Jr., "Human Action, Natural Rhythms, and Contraception: A Response to Noonan," *American Journal of Jurisprudence* 26 (1981): 32–46; John Finnis, "Natural Law and Unnatural Acts," *Heythrop Journal* 2 (1970): 365–87; "*Humanae Vitae*: Its Background and Aftermath," *International Review of Natural Family Planning* 4 (1980): 141–53; "Personal Integrity, Sexual Morality and Responsible Parenthood," *Rivista di Studi sulla Persona e la Famiglia: Anthropos* 1 (1985); William E. May, *Sex, Marriage, and Chastity: Reflections of a Catholic Layman, Spouse, and Parent* (Chicago: Franciscan Herald Press, 1981); *Contraception and Catholicism* Common Faith Tract No. 5 (Front Royal, Va.: Christendom Publications, 1983); *Contraception, "Humanae Vitae," and Catholic Moral Thought* (Chicago: Franciscan Herald Press, 1984); Ronald Lawler, O.F.M. Cap., Joseph M. Boyle, Jr., William E. May, *Catholic Sexual Ethics: A Summary, Explanation, and Defense* (Huntington, Ind.: Our Sunday Visitor, 1985).

An important article by Grisez is omitted from this list: "A New Formulation of a Natural Law Argument against Contraception," *Thomist* 30 (1966) 343–61. For some important more recent articles, see William E. May, "The Sanctity of Human Life, Marriage and the Family in the Thought of Pope John Paul II," *Annales Theologici* 2:1 (1988) 83–97, and "The Moral Methodology of Vatican Council II and the Teaching of Humanae Vitae and Persona Humana," *Anthropotes* 5:1 (1989) 29–45.

written many articles and books directed specifically against contraception, most recently *The Teaching of Humanae Vitae: A Defense*. These ethicists, particularly on the issue of contraception, in spite of their strong affirmation of Church teaching, repudiate traditional means of defending it. Their new book is not a defense of the encyclical, for it does not attempt to root its arguments in it, except in the most minimal way.[2] Rather, they provide a new and provocative argument against contraception.

The seeds for their most recent argument were present in Grisez's 1964 work, *Contraception and the Natural Law*, written before *Humanae Vitae* (1968). It grew out of a dissatisfaction with the traditional arguments against contraception. One purpose of this appendix is to show that Grisez, in his critique of traditional natural law arguments, misconstrued these arguments or, at least, did not see the potential for the legitimate development that was within them. It is my contention that the traditional arguments (and their legitimate successors) are stronger than Grisez envisioned. And it is my contention that Grisez's new arguments in particular have weaknesses not shared by the traditional arguments.

A review of Grisez's early work will show the links with the current work and help us pinpoint the difficulties in the new defense. This appendix has several parts: Parts one and two consider Grisez's early rejection of traditional natural law arguments against contraception and attempt to show that he did not consider what are the strongest formulations of these arguments. Part three examines Grisez's own early attempt to construct an argument against contraception. And part four responds to the new arguments of Grisez, Boyle, Finnis, and May as set forth in their new book, *The Teaching of Humanae Vitae: A Defense*.

Grisez's Evaluation of Traditional Arguments

In 1964, in his *Contraception and the Natural Law* Germain Grisez undertook to critique arguments that he thought were representative of traditional natural law arguments against contraception and to replace them with a more cogent natural law argument.[3] Although Grisez states that his later works supersede his early work,[4] I find the arguments there worthy of analysis for several reasons: (1) they did not receive a response on tradition-

2. In the introduction to TOHV, they state, "Our focus throughout is on the *teaching* rather than on the *document*" (7).
3. Germain Grisez, CNL (Milwaukee: Bruce Publishing Co., 1964).
4. In TOHV, fn. 4, 39.

alist lines when they were proposed; (2) I do not think the versions he offers
of the traditional condemnations do justice to them; (3) understanding how
Grisez understood the traditional arguments better enables us to see why
he has sought to provide a new argument, helps to explain the shape of
the new argument, and perhaps serves to reveal some deficiencies of the
new argument as well.

Admittedly, the traditional arguments against contraception were not
well developed before *Humanae Vitae* and are still undergoing development.
But some of the arguments currently offered build on the traditional arguments in ways that suggest the earlier arguments were not so flawed as
Grisez perceived them to be. After we consider Grisez's rejection of the
traditional arguments we shall briefly review some of the current formulations of these arguments.

Grisez structured a syllogism for what he considered to be the traditional
argument in the following fashion:

Major: To prevent any human action from attaining its natural end is
intrinsically immoral.
Minor: Contraception prevents sexual intercourse from attaining its
natural end.
Conclusion: Contraception is intrinsically immoral.[5]

Let me first state that I think Grisez posited a major premise that, although true, is not easily understood without a proper understanding
of the terms *human action* and *natural end*; philosophical and common
understandings of these terms differ substantially. Grisez argues that it is
difficult to clarify this syllogism in such a way that is valid, for he finds
that all attempts depend on some equivocation in the middle term.[6] He
notes that there are several possible clarifications of the syllogism and first
examines the interpretations that he finds most obvious. Let us consider
his interpretations one by one.

He claims that in one possible clarification, the minor premise "natural
end" refers to the biological, teleological end of reproduction and agrees
that such is a reasonable description of its end.[7] Grisez attempts to give an
"equally obvious[ly]" true rendering of the major premise; he states that it
would be true if "natural end" refers to a good that one is morally required
to seek. He acknowledges that there are such ends, such as performing
the professional tasks assigned to one. He concludes that there is an

5. Grisez, CNL, 20.
6. Ibid., 20.
7. Ibid., 21.

equivocation in the use of "natural end" since the minor premise refers to a biological end and the major premise refers to a morally obligatory end.

Although Grisez does not explicitly portray this interpretation of the syllogism as the one meant by the Church, the fact that he begins with this interpretation suggests that he believes it to be a standard interpretation. It seems to me neither an obvious interpretation nor a plausible or good one. To begin with, this understanding of the major premise reduces it to a tautology. It seems to me that "fail to meet one's moral obligations" is not a proper rendering of "intrinsically immoral." If so, the major premise would mean, to prevent any human act from attaining its morally obligatory end is intrinsically immoral (i.e., is to fail to meet one's moral obligations). This seems to be a tautology. This among other reasons leads me to believe that the major premise that Grisez attributes to the traditional argument is not the proper major premise. Momentarily, in considering current versions of the traditional arguments, we shall see that it is possible to provide a major premise that is not tautological and that does not involve equivocations with the minor premise.

But even more serious is Grisez's interpretation of the minor premise. When the Church speaks of the "natural end" of the sexual act, in the context of its condemnation of contraception, it does not have in mind the mere propagation of the species: it means the procreation of a new human being. All that is entailed in the *procreation* of a new *human* being removes the act far from the mere realm of the biological (see the discussion in Chapter 4 of the intrinsic worth of human life argument [version C] and the special act of creation argument [version D]). As we shall see later, Grisez does not consider this more precise interpretation of the traditional argument.

Grisez offers another possible reading of the minor premise. It may mean, "Contraception is the prevention of the end, procreation, which one who engages in sexual intercourse ought to achieve if it is possible."[8] He rejects this as a suitable premise since it is "by no means obvious that everyone who practices contraception has a real obligation to seek the good of procreation." Observing that those who use rhythm would also be doing wrong if it is wrong to engage in sexual intercourse while seeking to prevent conception, he rejects the notion that there is an individual obligation to seek the good of procreation. I have no disagreement with Grisez on this point and do think it is obvious that not everyone has the obligation to seek the good of procreation.

But Grisez, I think, has set up a straw man here. A more reasonable interpretation of the minor premise is not that one has an obligation *to seek* to

8. Ibid., 22.

achieve pregnancy but that everyone has the obligation *not to impede* the act of sexual intercourse from achieving its natural end of procreation. With the suitable major premise, this minor premise may provide us with a sound argument. But before we construct a better syllogism, let us examine further clarifications of the traditional argument considered by Grisez.

Grisez gives a formulation of a principle that he thinks, if properly understood, is true: Any sexual activity apart from the conditions necessary for it to be suited of itself to the procreation and proper education of children is intrinsically immoral.[9] This could perhaps serve as a new major premise. Although he thinks that this formulation is promising, he thinks it implies a limitation of sexual activity that is too severe. He thinks, "At least within marriage incomplete sexual acts are licit even though they are unsuited to procreation."[10] I am not clear to what he is referring here. It can be argued that spouses ought not to engage in behavior that arouses them to have an urgent desire for sexual intercourse if they are not prepared to carry through on that desire. Certainly, they ought not to engage in sexual activity that arouses the male to ejaculation if no intention for sexual intercourse is present. Thus perhaps this formulation could stand.

He also observes that this formulation does not serve as the sole principle of sexual ethics, if it means "any behavior of significance for reproduction must be performed under conditions of normal intercourse and within wedlock," since it "does not exclude even complete solitary acts of women." It seems that Grisez thinks it not right to describe female masturbation as "sexual activity" since, as he observes, it "has no objective significance for the reproductive function."[11] Masturbation is not sexual intercourse, to be sure, but that is not what the formulation need require. It seems arguable that masturbation is sexual activity and that it has significance for the reproductive function. Certainly, masturbation is activity that arouses the desire for an act, a sexual act, that is suited of itself for procreation and thus ought not to be engaged in since there is no prospect for an act of sexual intercourse. It could be argued, of course, that individuals masturbating or engaging in homosexual sexual activity do not desire the act that is suited of itself for procreation because they do not desire intercourse with a member of the opposite sex. Yet, although they may have no felt desire for union with a member of the opposite sex, is it not true that they have a desire to use their reproductive organs and that the reproductive organs have their proper use in a heterosexual union? Thus, a more precise formulation might be the following: Any freely chosen and willed sexual activity that leads to sexual arousal that is accompanied by the desire to

9. Ibid., 26.   10. Ibid., 26.
11. Ibid., 26.

use the reproductive organs apart from the conditions necessary for it to be suited of itself to the procreation and proper education of children is intrinsically immoral. Perhaps it is necessary to state here that what is meant by "desire to use the reproductive organs" is not any passing desire to have sexual intercourse but the driving and intense desire that accompanies sexual arousal. I think the preceding premise would be suitable for an argument against contraception, but it is not one Grisez considers.

Grisez also offers a refutation of the "perverted faculty" argument. He notes that such an argument would provide the major premise "The exercise of any human function in such a way that its given end is frustrated of attainment is intrinsically immoral."[12] The fact that we think it moral to use earplugs, and so on, has seemed a sufficient counterindication for many in evaluating this argument, and so it seems to Grisez.[13] Yet he does think the perverted faculty argument can be construed in such a way as to make it true, for he notes that he uses it in his own argument.[14] (We shall examine this argument later.) He makes the distinction, though, that the perverted faculty argument is only valid for the reproductive organs, not for all organs.

And this insight, that sexual organs have a special status, is one, I believe, that can assist us in constructing sound arguments against contraception (see Chapter 3). I believe that for the most part it is wrong to violate the natural functions of organs since nature acts for a purpose and that purpose is good. Fertility is a natural state, and a good. Nonetheless it is not always wrong to violate the natural purposes of organs (again, see Chapter 3). The sexual organs are a special case: the fact that contraception is considered to be intrinsically wrong is based on the premise that there is no justification for directly violating the ends of the sexual organs. Rather, there is a special need to protect their function and acts since their function is special. This special function is very much tied up with the uniquely important status of an act that by its nature may result in a new *human* life. Although all other organs and acts serve the good of life in various ways, largely indirect ways, the sexual organs and sexual activity do so in a very direct and immediate way.

This point should lead us to constructing a better representation of the traditional syllogism against contraception.

---

12. Ibid., 27.
13. Most, though, fail to make the distinction between interferences with natural functions that seek to protect these functions (such as use of earplugs or eyeglasses), and those that seek to thwart them.
14. Grisez, CNL, 100.

Better Formulations of Traditional Arguments

Certainly, it is not possible here to defend to the fullest the traditional natural law arguments against contraception. It is hoped that a brief sketch of these arguments will help to show what Grisez missed. The basic form of the argument could be stated in the following fashion:[15]

Major Premise: Unnatural acts are wrong.
Minor Premise: Contraception is unnatural.
Conclusion: Therefore, contraception is wrong.

Let us recall what was stated in Chapter 3:

"Unnatural" in this syllogism means "violates natural law." Since for Man to violate the natural law is to do what is immoral, to call an action "unnatural" is to say that it is not natural. For Man to act against right reason, for him to do something that is not in accord with the dictates of reason, is to violate the natural law; thus, to say that an action violates right reason is to say that it violates the natural law and that it is immoral.[16] The preceding syllogism has been explained and justified in many different ways and also rejected for many different reasons, largely depending on the reasons given for stating that contraception is unnatural, for claiming that it violates the natural law.

In Chapter 4 several versions of the traditional natural law arguments against contraception were discussed. The following are two that are particularly relevant to our concerns here.

VERSION C (Intrinsic Worth of Human Life Argument)
1. It is wrong to impede the procreative power of actions that are ordained by their nature to the generation of new human life.
2. Contraception impedes the procreative power of actions that are ordained by their nature to the generation of new human life.
3. Therefore, contraception is wrong.

VERSION D (Special Act of Creation Argument)
1. It is wrong to impede the procreative power of actions that are ordained by their nature to assist God in performing His creative act that brings forth a new human life.
2. Contraception impedes the procreative power of actions that are ordained by their nature to assist God in performing His creative act that brings forth a new human life.
3. Therefore, contraception is wrong.

---

15. Note the discussion in Chapter 3 of the meanings of the word *evil, immoral,* and *wrong*.
16. For an explanation of the connection of right reason and morality, see Vernon J. Bourke, *Ethics: A Textbook in Moral Philosophy* (New York: Macmillan Co., 1951).

Here is not the place to defend the major and minor premises of these versions (see Chapter 4); suffice it to note that when I speak of "actions ordained by their nature to generate new life" and "actions ordained by their nature to assist God in performing His creative act that brings forth a new human life," I am speaking of actions that proceed from the use of the sexual organs. What I wish to note here is that I do not believe that Grisez considered either version C or D in his early book.

He did, though, anticipate what is given in Chapter 4 as version F, a version that relies on the principle that sexual intercourse is meant to signify the total self-giving of the spouses. Grisez critiqued what he described as the "phenomenological argument." He summarized it in this fashion: "human sexual intercourse represents objectively the mutual, total self-giving of man and woman. No reservations and obstacles must be allowed to interfere with the definitive and exclusive surrender of man and wife to one another. But contraception introduces such an obstacle, for it represents a limitation on the giving and receiving of selves. Hence this practice is an offense against the very meaning of the conjugal act, and for this reason it must be avoided."[17] Grisez stated that one understanding of this argument "assumes at the beginning that the withholding of one's effective generative power, whether or not one's partner approves, is a withholding of part of what *ought* to be given in the mutual self-giving." He asserts that this argument does not prove that contraception is wrong but "proceeds on the assumption that it is."

Is Grisez, though, properly stating the argument? Certainly it assumes several premises, but it does not proceed by assuming that contraception is wrong. A possible syllogistic representation of this argument is the following:

VERSION F

1. It is wrong to destroy the power of human sexual intercourse to represent objectively the mutual, total self-giving of spouses.

2. Contraception destroys the power of human sexual intercourse to represent objectively the mutual, total self-giving of spouses.

3. Therefore, contraception is wrong.

Arguments must be made in behalf of each of the premises, to be sure, but it does not seem right to say that the argument assumes what it seeks to prove.

It is not correct, of course, to hold Grisez accountable for not knowing the modern formulations of the phenomenological argument. It seems that

17. Grisez, CNL, 34.

some of them at least do not exhibit the inadequacies that Grisez finds in their earlier precursors. He speaks of a "pure phenomenological argument" that is based solely on the psychological effect of sexual intercourse as an experience of mutual self-giving.[18] He asserts that such arguments, although illuminative of some of the effects of marital intercourse, do not serve to rule out sexual expression outside marriage or even between members of the same sex. Current arguments state that total self-giving means giving of one's whole self, which includes one's fertility or creative powers. Total self-giving can only occur in marriage for only such a relationship provides the security needed for the trust required for total self-giving and for the possible consequences of total self-giving, emotional dependency and offspring. Sexual intercourse between homosexuals cannot *represent* total self-giving because they are not truly giving of themselves; that is, they are not able, by the very fact of their being of the same sex, to give their fertility to one another.

Grisez's Early Argument against Contraception

In *Contraception and the Natural Law*, Grisez states the basic principle of his own argument against contraception in this way: "The principle violated by contraception is that procreation is a human good worthy of man's pursuit, and that human acts suited to achieve this good should be done. This is a basic moral principle. It is one of the primary sources of all human practical reasoning. It obligates all men and holds true at all times."[19] Grisez observes that to some extent trying to prove that procreation is a fundamental human good is to prove the obvious, but he does offer several "considerations" that support it.[20] The first is "Having and raising children is practically a universal phenomenon."[21] He notes that throughout the world and history the chief work of life has been raising children. His second observation is "From a biological point of view the work of reproduction is the fullest organic realization of the living substance."[22] Certainly Grisez recognizes that man has higher ends but notes that this sort of fulfillment is still human. (Here we see Grisez nearly showing how one might "derive" the procreative good from human nature.)

18. Ibid., 33ff.
19. Ibid., 76.
20. Ibid., 78; he states that he will offer three, but I could only find two identified as such.
21. Ibid., 78.
22. Ibid., 79.

Grisez also argues that Man ought never to act against any of the primary practical goods and maintains that contraception "is a directly willed intervention of any positive kind to prevent the realization of the procreative good when it otherwise might follow from an act of sexual intercourse in which one has chosen to engage."[23] He finds the malice of contraception "in the will's direct violation of the procreative good as a value in itself, as an ideal which never may be submerged."[24]

Grisez then makes an observation that indicates a direction of his thought, one that comes to be more predominant in his later argument. He asks, "How, then, is the malice of contraception intrinsic to the act?" He replies, "It is not primarily intrinsic to the external act in isolation, as if the distortion of the normal behavior pattern were all that is wrong."[25] As if anticipating the objection that he seems to ignore the evil of the external act and to place all the evil in the will, he allows that the external act is nonetheless significant for one must do something to prevent conception. And a little later he notes, "The malice is in the intention, but in an intention which is inseparable from the act, an intention which gives formal unity to its very object."[26]

Here is one of the junctures at which this author departs from Grisez's analysis. As our critique of Grisez's more recent argument will maintain, Grisez seems to lose sight of the traditional understanding that the will becomes evil when it wills an evil act and that the evil of acts—at least those considered intrinsically immoral—can be assessed apart from and prior to knowledge of what the agent wills. It is because the agent intends to perform an action that is evil that he has an evil will, but it is also true that the external act can have a moral specification apart from what is intended by the agent (see the following for a Thomistic defense of this point). In fact, on occasion the external act may be good while the will is evil and vice versa. A more traditional formulation would state, "The *sin* of contraception is in the intention because the will intends to do an action that is intrinsically evil and the goodness or evil of the will depends primarily upon the object of the act."[27] As we shall see in our consideration of Grisez's latest explanation of the malice of contraception, Grisez seems to place the malice ever more exclusively in the will. He seems to be describing the sin involved in the *choice* to contracept, rather than the evil of the *act* of contraception.

One of Grisez's objections to the traditional condemnations of contra-

---

23. Ibid., 91.   24. Ibid., 92.
25. Ibid., 92. Cf. TOHV, 40.   26. Ibid., 93.
27. See St. Thomas Aquinas, *Summa Theologiae* I–II, q. 19, art. 3.

ception was not so much to the application of natural law as to the traditional understanding of the workings of natural law. He argued that traditional arguments committed what has come to be known as the "is/ought" fallacy, or the mistake of moving from fact to value.[28] He seems to share the view of those who advance that it is not proper to move from "is" statements to "ought" statements, from statements of fact to statements of value; that something "is" the case (a fact) has no necessary implications for what "ought" to be the case (value).[29] Many are reluctant to allow that nature is normative in any sense.[30] But defenders of the tradition have argued that there is no fallacy in moving from fact to value and that, indeed, moral argumentation cannot proceed otherwise. For instance, the claim might be made that it is not good for human beings to be overweight

28. In CNL, Grisez rejects arguments based on natural teleology; cf. p. 22 and pp. 27–31. See also John Finnis, *Natural Law and Natural Rights* (Oxford: Clarendon Press, 1980), chap. 2, and *Fundamentals of Ethics* (Washington, D.C.: Georgetown University Press, 1983), chap. 2. For a critique of Grisez's work on this point and in general, see Russell Hittinger, *A Critique of the New Natural Law Theory* (Notre Dame, Ind.: University of Notre Dame Press, 1987). For another critique of the Grisez-Finnis position and a defense of the kind of natural law theory that Finnis and Grisez reject, see Ralph McInerny, "The Principles of Natural Law," *American Journal of Jurisprudence* 25 (1980) 1–15. For a response, see John Finnis and Germain Grisez, "The Basic Principles of Natural Law: A Reply to Ralph McInerny," *American Journal of Jurisprudence* 26 (1981) 21–32. Ralph McInerny has another response to Grisez and Finnis in his *Ethica Thomistica* (Washington, D.C.: Catholic University of America Press, 1982), 40–62. See also, Ralph McInerny, "Naturalism and Thomistic Ethics," *Thomist* 40:2 (Ap. 1976) 222–42.

29. Grisez has repeatedly accused the conventional scholastic natural law theory of making such an error. For instance, he states: "[Scholastic natural law theory] moves by a logically illicit step—from human nature as a given reality, to what ought and ought not to be chosen." And further, "Human persons are unlike other natural entities; it is not human nature as a given but a possible human fulfillment which must provide the intelligible norms for a free choice" (from *The Way of the Lord Jesus*, 105). What this objection fails to take into account is that the tradition was fully aware that it was working with fallen human nature and that it was not taking nature as a given but as a guide to the possibilities of human nature through the supposition that enough goodness remained in human nature that it is a good guide for what is true human goodness, once provision is made for the disorderedness it displays after the fall.

30. Grisez seems to make this claim specifically in regard to conception. He begins his article "A New Formulation of a Natural Law Argument against Contraception" by saying, " 'The naturally given structure of the sexual act'—that is a phrase one often encounters in discussions of contraception. The contention here is that there is no such thing, if we are talking about the *human act*; for human acts have their structure from intelligence. Just insofar as an action is considered according to its naturally given structure, it is to that extent not considered as a *human act*—i.e., as a moral act—but rather as a physiological process or as instinctive behavior. Action with a given structure and acts structured by intelligence differ as totally as nature differs from morality. Nature has an order which reason can consider but cannot make and cannot alter. Morality has an order which reason institutes by guiding the acts of the will." Grisez denies that reason must conform itself to nature. Indeed, he states, "It is futile to argue that any act is right or wrong by appealing to its naturally given structure" (343).

and it may be observed that Joe is overweight. Thus, it seems (if there are no other relevant considerations) proper to conclude that Joe ought to lose weight. The charge has been made against the traditional arguments against contraception that they rely on observations of what "is" the nature of sexual organs and acts and then argue to what "ought" to be. Many, this author among them, argue that all sound arguments against contraception depend on an understanding of the proper ordination of sexual organs and sexual acts. Indeed, one understanding of natural law, the traditional one, holds that all proper moral argumentation on any issue argues from facts about existence and nature to moral norms.

Grisez believes that his argument is free from the (alleged) "is/ought" fallacy. Grisez states his argument as follows:

MAJOR: For one who has sexual intercourse to act in a way that presupposes an intention opposed to the procreative good is intrinsically immoral.

MINOR: Contraception is an act, the prevention or lessening of the likelihood of conception by any positive deed directly willed for this purpose, of one who has sexual intercourse, which presupposes an intention opposed to the procreative good.

CONCLUSION: Contraception is intrinsically immoral.[31]

As mentioned, Grisez admits to using the perverted faculty argument (that the prevention of any act from reaching the end proper to it is intrinsically immoral) but claims it is valid only for the sexual faculty. He notes, "While it is not true of all natural ends, it does happen to be true of the natural end of sexual intercourse, the procreative good, that it grounds moral obligations."[32] Seeming to anticipate the objection that he commits the naturalistic fallacy by arguing "Procreation is a basic good; therefore it ought not to be violated," he avers, "The emphasis of our explanation is on the procreative good as a principle of practical reasoning, and hence as a moral ideal, rather than merely on the generative power and its natural teleology."[33] In his view, procreation is simply posited as an ideal, not derived as a good from nature.[34] Still, it seems that his

31. Ibid., 98.   32. Grisez, CNL, 100.
33. Ibid., 101.
34. John Finnis strongly shares Grisez's principles, and for the most part I consider his work a marvelous defense of the Church's teaching. But I find the same difficulties as well, for instance, with his argument that the value of the basic goods is self-evident, rather than inductively derived from reflection on human nature and human experience. Furthermore, I believe that he, too, roots his arguments in part on the physiological nature of the sexual organs and acts. For instance, he asserts in his condemnation of contraception (and more immediately of driving carelessly): "sometimes I find myself in (or bring myself within) situations which by their brute causal structure require of me an attention or a choice that

argument depends on the natural teleology of the generative power and that it is this teleology that "grounds" moral obligation; is not this a case of using nature to determine value, of moving from "is" to "ought"?[35] I believe that it is, but I also believe that no fallacy is involved.

As I stated at the outset and as my analysis has begun to indicate, I think Grisez's arguments are strong to the extent that they mimic, albeit very implicitly, the very natural law arguments against contraception that he seeks to repudiate. They are weak insofar as they depart from traditional moral analysis. This departure becomes ever more clear in his most recent construction of an argument against contraception.

Contraception as Contralife

In their book *The Teaching of Humanae Vitae: A Defense*, Grisez, Boyle, Finnis, and May argue that contraception is immoral because it proceeds

will be adequately open to a basic value whose realization or violation is, by reason of that structure, at stake or in question in the situation" ("Natural Law and Unnatural Acts," 384). What is the brute causal structure of sexual intercourse other than its basic biological teleology?

35. In his chapter where he sets forward the basics of his position, he seems to be making the very moves he rejects. In assessing the role of natural inclinations in determining morality, he states, "It is very important that we be careful . . . not to commit the usual error of proceeding from a preferred set of facts to an illicit conclusion that those facts imply obligation" (65). He then asserts that as long as we do not identify the inclinations with the principles of practical reasoning, we will see that "our understanding grasps in the inclinations the possibilities to which they point" (65). To this reader, it does seem that here we have the movement from what is to what ought to be, with some sense that nature is a guide to what is moral and what is not. The syllogism that Grisez uses to demonstrate his mode of analysis seems to be the very kind that is understood to be an instance of the "is/ought" fallacy. He tells us, "We form, naturally and without reflection, the basic principles of practical reasoning." (It is unclear why he states that we do so "without reflection"; perhaps to admit that we reflect on the relation would suggest more clearly the movement from "is" to "ought.") He gives us an example: "Life is a good whose requirements are to be served. Actions which promote it should be done; what is opposed to it should be avoided" (65). This seems to me a classic case of moving from "is" to "ought" and one that is not a fallacy.

Russell Hittinger seems to make a very similar criticism in his analysis of Grisez's argument: "Grisez does in fact directly rely upon anthropological, if not metaphysical, evidence for including procreation in the list of basic goods—not as a mere 'reminder' but as a 'determinant' of the practical principle. His conclusion that contraception is 'intrinsically immoral' clearly depends upon an antecedent argument that procreation is an intrinsic good, which itself depends upon a theoretical argument concerning what is essential or accidental to human organicity and how human organicity is related to the nature of being human. It looks very much like the older natural law argument except that it lacks the philosophical apparatus for making, justifying, and sustaining the series of theoretical moves which involve the relationship between the person and the body, the nature of life, and the relative importance of the procreative power in relation to human organicity in general" (*A Critique of the New Natural Law Theory*, 62–63). In an excellent review of Hittinger's book, Rev. R. A. Connor gives from a contralife will (see Chapter 4 for an explanation of their position). In spite of their strong affirmation of Church teaching, these ethicists do not employ the traditional arguments of the Church, arguments that depend a great deal on a Thomistic mode of analysis.

It is right to note that they do not intend to offer a traditional defense. They make no claims to be Thomistic in their approach; indeed, there is some evidence that it was because of perceived deficiencies in traditional arguments that they labored to articulate new ones.[36] Nonetheless, their analysis, especially in its terminology, in many ways resembles traditional modes of analysis[37]; these resemblances can mislead the reader into thinking that their analysis is more aligned with the tradition than, in fact, it is. Here I am concerned to show how it departs from traditional analysis and how this departure renders their argumentation weak.

In brief, they understand contraception to be a *choice* that defines one's act, whereas the tradition considers contraception to be an *act* that defines one's *will*. They understand contraception to be a *choice* that ought never to be made; the tradition understands it to be an *act* that ought never to be chosen. Grisez, Boyle, Finnis, and May believe contraception to be evil (wrong) because it entails a contralife will; here I will argue that their understanding of what constitutes the contralife nature of contraception differs considerably from the tradition, and insofar as it does, it suffers from some significant inadequacies.

Contraception: A Choice or an Act?

One key difficulty in evaluating the argument of Grisez, Boyle, Finnis, and May is their very definition of contraception. They often speak of contraception as a choice, and it seems that sometimes they speak of the choice as the act. Consider their definition of contraception: "Contraception can be defined *only in terms of the beliefs, intentions, and choices* that render behavior contraceptive. To contracept one must think that (1) some behavior in which someone could engage is likely to cause a new life to begin, and (2) the bringing about of the new life might be impeded by

---

further reasons for questioning Grisez's understanding of natural law: *American Journal of Jurisprudence* 33 (1988) 250–56.

36. See Grisez, CNL, 46–53. See also John Finnis, *Natural Law and Natural Rights*, chap. 2, and *Fundamentals of Ethics*, chap. 2.

37. They explicitly acknowledge that their terminology resembles the tradition although their theory differs from it in Germain Grisez, Joseph Boyle, and John Finnis, "Practical Principles, Moral Truth, and Ultimate Ends," *American Journal of Jurisprudence* 32 (1987), 99–151; 99.

some other behavior one could perform"[38] (my emphasis). William May has articulated a similar definition: "Contraception is not a sexual act, but is the *choice* (and in this sense an 'intent') to do something, prior to such a sexual act, during it, or subsequent to it, to prevent the coming-to-be of new human life"[39] (my emphasis). In both passages contraception is defined as a *choice*, though certainly a *choice* to *do something*. There is some lack of clarity about what these authors are describing, for, if contraception were simply a choice, speaking of choosing to contracept, or of "choosing a choice," would not be intelligible. But they do speak this way. Consider this statement by William May: "One can *choose to contracept* for a good end, but the act of contraception, this position holds, is always morally bad, and it is morally bad because someone *choosing to contracept* is adopting *by choice the intelligible proposal* to oppose the good of human life in its transmission. . . ."[40] There seems to be some ambiguity here; is contraception the choice to do something, or is it the something that one chooses to do? Is one choosing an action (defined as a contraceptive action) or is one instead choosing "the intelligible *proposal* to oppose the good of human life in its transmission"? These authors do not seem entirely clear on this, but on the whole, their analysis seems to define contraception in such a way that it is an act of the will, a choice, rather than the act that is performed, that is, what is traditionally known as the external act. And, even if their definition includes the external act, they seem to have few resources for describing what is wrong about that external act apart from the will. Their efforts go into describing what is wrong with one's choice, not what is wrong with the act that one performs.

The tradition speaks very differently of contraception. Consider the following from *Casti Connubii*: "No reason, however grave may be put forward by which anything intrinsically against nature may become conformable to nature and morally good. Since, therefore, the conjugal act is destined primarily by nature for the begetting of children, those who in exercising it deliberately frustrate its natural power and purpose, sin against nature and commit a deed which is shameful and intrinsically vicious." It goes on to say: "Any use whatsoever of matrimony exercised in such a way that the act is deliberately frustrated in its natural power to generate life

38. TOHV, 41. Consider, too, a statement by Grisez in an earlier article: "I do not think of contraception as if it were an act already given, the moral judgment on which could be made apart from and after the understanding of the act. No, I am concerned with a human act, an act which is performed through a specific choice. . . . The act precisely is a choice to behave in a way effectively contrary to that good [the procreative good] ("A New Formulation of a Natural Law Argument against Contraception," 354).

39. William May, letter to the editor in *Crisis* 8 (May 1990), 13.

40. Ibid.

is an offense against the law of God and of nature and those who indulge in such are branded with the guilt of a grave sin."[41] According to *Casti Connubii*, then, contraception is an unnatural act, an act that perverts the natural telos of the sexual act. It is a shameful and intrinsically vicious deed and a grave sin. *Humanae Vitae* 11 states, "But the Church, which interprets natural law through its unchanging doctrine, reminds men and women that the teachings based on natural law must be obeyed [*observandis*], and teaches that it is necessary that each and every conjugal act [*matrimonii usus*] remain ordained [*per se destinatus*] to the procreating of human life." In both documents, and elsewhere, the Church understands contraception to be an *act that violates nature;* it follows the Thomistic mode of categorizing action. One intends *to do something* that will help one achieve one's end (here, limit one's family size). The something that one intends to do (here, to contracept) is either in accord with nature, that is, right reason, or not. If one intends to do something that violates nature (contraception does), one acquires an evil will. But what one intends to do (the external act) is defined as good or bad independently of any act of the will. Thus contraception is an unnatural act that one can either choose or not choose to do. If one knowingly chooses to do something bad, one sins, but one can (say, out of ignorance) do evil without sinning.

But Grisez and his colleagues seem to think that it is the choice that defines the act, not the act that defines the will. Grisez says this about choice:

> It is possible to make a choice and then not act on it. Hence morality, which is centered in choice, is not so much in one's behavior as in one's inner self (see Mt 15.10–20; Mk 7.15–23; Lk 6.45; also see S.T., 1–2, q. 20, aa. 1–2). Nevertheless free choice cannot be separated from action. One chooses to do something. What is in view is generally a positive and appealing fulfillment of some capacity, whether of inner activity or outward behavior. Having chosen, one usually proceeds to do what was chosen. *The outward performance shares in and completes the goodness or badness of the choice* (see S.T., 1–2, q. 20, aa. 3–4).[42] (my emphasis)

Here Grisez talks about the choice "to do something" but does not talk about choosing to do something that is good or bad: he talks about doing something that is "a positive and appealing fulfillment of some capacity";

41. Pius XI, *Casti Connubii: Encyclical Letter of Pius XI on Christian Marriage* (Boston, Mass.: St. Paul Editions, 1930), 28.

42. Germain Grisez, *The Way of the Lord Jesus*, 50. Needless to say, I do not read the last passage from Aquinas in the same light as does Grisez. We evidently understand differently the statement in q. 20, art. 3, that the external act occasionally is "good or evil of itself" and the reference in q. 20, art. 4, to the "goodness or evil that the external act has from its matter and due circumstances."

perhaps he means by this that one chooses something good, something in accord with nature, something in accord with right reason (which would be a Thomistic way of speaking). But the last line suggests something different. Grisez speaks of the act not as something that specifies one's choice as good or bad but as something that "shares in and completes the goodness or badness of the choice." Thus it would seem that the act becomes evil because of one's will rather than that the will becomes evil because of the evil that one has chosen to do.

Grisez, Boyle, Finnis, and May describe the contraceptive choice in this way: "Even when based on good reason, the contraceptive choice by its very definition is contralife. It is a choice to prevent the beginning of the life of a possible person. It is a choice *to do something*, with the intent that the baby not be, as a means to a further end: that the good consequences of the baby's not-coming-to-be will be realized and the bad consequences of the baby's coming to be will be prevented."[43] Again, they speak of the choice *to do something* but it is not the something that one does that defines one's act; rather it is one's *intent*, an intent that a baby not come to be, that defines it. *Choice* refers not to a selection of some means to an end but to *the decision* "to prevent the coming to be of a baby," which then leads a couple to engage in contraceptive behavior. These authors argue that the couple using contraception are doing evil (wrong) not because they are using a contraceptive but because they intend that a child not come to be (this is their choice and what makes the act immoral), and that intention leads them to do something contraceptive.

But, again, traditionally some acts are considered intrinsically evil or intrinsically wrong *apart from* any act of the will. By referring to an act as "intrinsically evil" or "intrinsically wrong" the Church means it is the kind of act that ought never to be chosen directly. Although there is no question that sin refers to an act of the will, the Thomistic tradition holds that the external act can be evil, without reference to the will, insofar as it violates right reason. The position of Grisez and associates serves to provide an explanation (though perhaps not the best explanation) of why the choice to contracept is a sin, but do they have the means to demonstrate that the *act* of contraception is always evil (wrong)? The question arises: Does their analysis provide the resources for demonstrating that contraception is an intrinsically evil action apart from what is willed by the agent?

Again, the claim that the evil of an action resides primarily in the will seems to conflict with the traditional Catholic evaluation of some moral actions. The famous passage from *Gaudium et Spes* 51 is to the point here:

43. TOHV, 84.

"When it is a question of harmonizing married love with the responsible transmission of life, it is not enough to take only the good intention and the evaluation of motives into account; objective criteria must be used, criteria drawn from the nature of the human person and human action, criteria which respect the total meaning of mutual self-giving and human procreation in the context of true love. . . ."[44] Clearly, this passage states that it is not solely the intention or the motive of the agent (not that this is precisely what they mean by "choice") that determines the morality of an action: criteria must be drawn "from the nature of the human person and human action." The Church teaches that some actions are intrinsically evil *apart from* the will of the agent, are intrinsically opposed to the nature of the person and human action. The Church has long taught that some actions such as "having sexual intercourse with someone who is not one's spouse," "having sexual intercourse with someone against that person's will," "directly killing the innocent," and "directly thwarting the per se ordination of the sexual act" are actions that violate nature, are against *ratio recta* (right reason), and are in themselves intrinsically evil. The Church recognizes that individuals may choose to perform these actions out of ignorance and if they are not responsible for being ignorant (this is generally known as "invincible ignorance") they are not guilty of a bad will (see *Summa Theologiae* I–II, q.6, art. 6); they are not guilty of sin, but they are the agents of an evil act. They are doing something wrong, that is, something that ought not to be done.

The claim that the external act can have a good or evil aspect of its own apart from the will is carefully explained by Aquinas in *Summa Theologiae* I–II, q.20, art. 1. There, to the question "Is goodness or evil in the act of the will first or in the external act?" the response makes it clear that the external act (or means) can "derive" its goodness or evil from the will (willing the ultimate end of the act) but that it also may have a goodness or evil in itself, apart from the will:

External acts can be called good or evil in two ways. First, according to the kind of acts they are and the circumstances connected with them; for example, to give alms under the right circumstances is good. Second, an act can be good or bad in relation to the end sought; for example, we say giving alms because of vainglory is evil. Now since the end is the proper object of the will, it is evident that the nature of good or evil, which the external act has from its ordering to an end, is found first in the will, then derivatively in the external act. However, *the good or evil the external act has of itself,* as being concerned with due matter and due circumstances, *is not derived from the will, but rather from reason.* Hence, *if we consider the goodness*

44. Austin Flannery, O.P., ed., *Vatican Council II: The Conciliar and Post Conciliar Documents* (Northport, N.Y.: Costello Publishing Co. 1975), 955.

of the external act as it is in the ordering and apprehension of reason, it is prior to the goodness of the act of the will, but if we consider it as it is found in the carrying out of a work, it is subsequent to the goodness of the will, which is its principle.[45] (my emphasis)

The goodness or evil of the external act is prior to the goodness of the act of the will in the order of intention; that is, it is because the act of murder, as a kind of act, is evil that the willing of murder is evil; the will becomes evil because of the kind of act it has chosen. In the order of execution the evil of the will is prior, for the actual act of murder flows from a murderous will; the act is evil because it is the perfection of an evil act of the will. If Grisez and the others are speaking only of the order of execution, their portrayal of the dynamics of the moral act has some plausibility, but they seem, then, to provide only a partial description of the moral act.

In q. 18, art. 2, Aquinas gives as an example of an act that is evil of its kind, "taking what belongs to another." To take what belongs to another violates right reason. We understand this to be against nature for several reasons: since Man is by nature a social animal, private property is natural and taking what belongs to another harms society and violates what is natural. It is wrong to take what belongs to another. If one takes what belongs to another, he has done evil; he has done wrong. If he chooses to do so, he sins.

Let me illustrate these principles and terms by use of another example. Adultery, or having sexual intercourse with one who is not one's spouse, is intrinsically evil. It is an act that *by its very nature* violates right reason. It is natural for the human person to be married and to be married to only one person. Those married individuals who have sexual intercourse with one who is not their spouse commit adultery. They do something unnatural, something against reason, something evil. If they do so knowingly, they are sinning; if they do so unknowingly (for example, if through amnesia they forget to whom they are married), they are doing something evil but perhaps not sinning (if they are not responsible for their ignorance).

When the Church speaks of contraception's being intrinsically evil, it refers to the act (not the choice) as intrinsically evil, as an act that is against right reason. Intrinsically evil acts are intrinsically wrong: they are the kinds of acts that ought never to be chosen. Chapters 3 and 4 present several versions of arguments designed to prove that contraception is wrong. All versions define contraception as an act evaluated as evil apart from what the spouses will when they participate in this act. It is defined as an act that perverts the proper end or ends of the sexual act.

45. Translations from Aquinas are taken from John Oesterle, *Treatise on Happiness* (Notre Dame, Ind.: University of Notre Dame Press, 1983) 193–94.

Grisez, Boyle, Finnis, and May do not speak of contraception as an act that perverts the natural end of the sexual act. As noted, Grisez and Finnis reject the practice of arguing from the natural end of acts to moral norms. I believe that it is the refusal to acknowledge that actions have natures and to acknowledge that the nature of things bears on the morality of acts, along with a vigorous rejection of consequentialism, that leads them to locate the wrongness of contraception most vitally in the will. If acts are not evil because of their nature or because of their consequences, then it would seem they must be evil because of what the agent wills. Their claim that contraception is wrong because it proceeds from a contralife will serves to establish one criterion by which some decisions to contracept may be faulted. I do not believe, however, that it works as a proper description of many decisions to contracept. If it is possible to contracept without a contraceptive will (as I intend to show), then their claim that what is wrong with contraception is that it entails a contraceptive will fails. Would they then have any means to demonstrate that contraception is intrinsically evil? Furthermore, as we shall see, even the argument that contraception is wrong because it proceeds from a contralife will depends to some extent on an understanding of the physiological end of sexual intercourse: of the end of procreation as being definitive (at least in part) of the nature of sexual intercourse and thus normative for sexual ethics. Without this understanding I do not believe their argument has sufficient grounding.

Still, for all their interest in the will, and in spite of their rejection of nature as normative for ethics, in their argument these authors seem to come close to granting that contraception violates the nature of the sexual act. Let us look again at their description of the decision to contracept: "To contracept one must think that (1) some behavior in which someone could engage is likely to cause a new life to begin, and (2) the bringing about of the beginning of new life might be impeded by some other behavior one could perform. One's choice is to perform that other behavior; one's relevant immediate intention (which may be sought for some further purpose) is that the prospective new life not begin."[46] This description of contraception is carefully stated. A key word here is the *likely* in the first sentence. What do they mean by "likely"? Do they mean "statistically probable"? Most likely they do not, since it is not statistically probable that intercourse will result in conception. It seems more likely that they mean something like "*by nature* this act will result in a new life beginning." If so, then, the first premise would be equivalent to, To contracept one must think that 1) some behavior in which someone could engage is *by its*

46. Ibid., 42.

nature conducive to the bringing forth of new life. . . . If this is a proper reading of their first premise, then they would be allowing that the act of sexual intercourse has a nature and that what is wrong with contraception is that it violates the nature of the sexual act.

But they do not speak this way. Indeed, they deny that contraception is a *sexual act:* "the definition of contraception neither includes nor entails that one who does it engages in sexual intercourse, much less marital intercourse."[47] Earlier passages illustrate this claim: "Assuming contraception is a sin, it is not a sexual sin, such as masturbation, fornication, adultery, homosexual behavior, and so on. A dictator who wanted to control population might contracept by having a fertility-reducing additive put in the public water supply. He would engage in no sexual behavior whatsoever and might not will any such behavior. He might also exhort people to abstain but reason that, if they did not, the additive in the water would prevent the coming to be of some of the possible persons he did not want."[48] This passage is extremely revealing. As is well known, the Church has always taught that contraception belongs in the same class as masturbation, and so on, since all these acts are considered to be perverted sexual acts. Masturbation is engaging in solitary sexual stimulation that leads neither to procreation or union; it perverts the *telos* of the sexual act; adultery is an act suited neither to the responsibilities of procreation nor to the deepening of the marital union and thus perverts the *telos* of the sexual act. Contraception, which also makes sexual intercourse suited neither for procreation nor union, also perverts the *telos* of the sexual act. But Grisez and colleagues do not understand contraception this way.

Their description of the dictator as a contraceptor exemplifies their position. They call him a contraceptor because (in their view) he has a contralife will, because he wills that possible future babies not come to be. Yet, I doubt that the accusation that he is a contraceptor would spring first to the mind of those who wish to accuse him of evil (unless we knew about his own acts of sexual intercourse; unless he, too, drinks the water). Certainly, he is guilty of denying spouses their fundamental right to have children. He is causing others to engage in contracepted acts, against their will; they are the contraceptors (albeit innocent contraceptors); he is the facilitator.

It would seem right, though, to say that although this dictator is not guilty of the *act* of contracepting, he is guilty of the *sin* of contracepting— this is not because he has contracepted but because he is morally responsible

47. TOHV, 42.
48. Ibid., 41; cf. 43.

for the contracepted acts of those who do drink the water. His guilt is a remote guilt wherein he becomes responsible for the contracepted acts of others. Although he, himself, does not contracept in putting the additive in the water (again, unless he too drinks it), it seems that he should be held accountable for the sin of contraception, much as one who pays a murderer is morally responsible for the murder. Those who drink the water and engage in acts of sexual intercourse may not at all be guilty of having a contraceptive will, though they have performed contracepted acts. (Let me also note that according to my analysis, the woman who has taken a contraceptive pill but who has not yet engaged in an *act* of contracepted intercourse has not yet contracepted. Yet she, if fully intending to do so, even if she is thwarted from doing so, is guilty of the *sin* of contracepting. Her act parallels that of a murderer who has loaded his gun with the full intention of murdering: he has not yet murdered until he pulls the trigger and kills his victim; yet if he is thwarted from doing so, he is still guilty of the sin of murder.)

And for all the peculiarity of this description of the dictator does it not suggest that contraception is a kind of sexual act?[49] Is it not precisely because the additive that this dictator puts into the water interferes with sexual acts that they are moved to call his a contraceptive will? Again, it is my argument that contraception is a perverted sexual act; i.e., a sexual act deprived of its proper *telos*.

Contraception and the Contralife Will

As the preceding indicates, Grisez, Boyle, Finnis, and May focus on choices, on the will, in their analysis of the evil of contraception. Their basic argument seems to proceed in the following fashion (note that nature is never mentioned):

1. Acts proceeding from an intention that a prospective new life not come to be are acts proceeding from a contralife will.

2. All acts proceeding from a contralife will are wrong.

3. Contraception proceeds from an intention that a prospective new life not come to be.

---

49. Grisez, Boyle, Finnis, and May allow, "Contraception often is thought of as if it were a sexual act, and the morality of contraception treated as an issue of sexual ethics. The reason is that contraception presupposes and is closely related to sexual acts, since there is not occasion to practice contraception unless someone is likely to become pregnant, and pregnancy rarely occurs apart from some sexual act" (43). To my mind, though, this does not say enough; contraception is not just "closely related to sexual acts": it is a perverse sexual act.

4. Contraception, then, is an act proceeding from a contralife will.
5. Contraception, then, is wrong.

We shall soon see that it is difficult to contest that it is wrong to have a contralife will if one accepts Grisez and associates' definition of a contralife will (though there is a weaker sense of a contralife will that often accompanies both contraception and also the use of methods of natural family planning [NFP] that seems perfectly moral). But, first, let us question whether every choice to use contraception entails a contralife will.

Let us return to their definition of contraception: "Contraception can be defined *only in terms of the beliefs, intentions, and choices* that render behavior contraceptive. To contracept one must think that (1) some behavior in which someone could engage is likely to cause a new life to begin, and (2) the bringing about of the new life might be impeded by some other behavior one could perform"[50] (my emphasis). And further they state:

> Since contraception must be defined by its intention that a prospective new life not begin, every contraceptive act is necessarily contralife. Those who choose such an act often also intend some further good—for example, not to procreate irresponsibly with bad consequences for already existing persons. But in choosing contraception as a means to this further good, they necessarily reject a new life. They imagine that a new person will come to be if that is not prevented, they want that possible person not to be, and they effectively will that he or she never be. That will is a contralife will. Therefore, each and every contraceptive act is necessarily contralife.[51]

Several claims here deserve examination. These authors state that contraception is always a contralife act. They also say that contraception always involves a contralife will. Are these two claims distinct or are they identical? I suspect that for them, they are identical claims. But I assert they are distinct claims. I claim that contraception is a contralife act (in a certain sense) but that many contraceptors do not have contralife wills. How one defines *contralife* is clearly of crucial importance; my understanding and their understanding of the meaning of *contralife* are very different.

Grisez and associates tell us precisely what they mean by a contralife will: "They [contraceptors] look ahead and think about the baby whose life they might initiate. Perhaps for some further good reason, perhaps not, they find the prospect repugnant: 'We do not want that possible baby to begin to live.' As the very definition of contraception makes clear, that will is contralife; it is a practical (though not necessarily an emotional)

50. Grisez, TOHV, 41.
51. Ibid., 43.

hatred of the possible baby they project and reject, just as the will to accept the coming to be of a baby is a practical love of that possible person."[52]

It seems possible to object to the description of all contraceptors as having a contralife will of the type described. Is it true that all contraceptors "look ahead and think about the baby whose life they might initiate" and then find the thought of this "possible baby" repugnant? Their language becomes even stronger: "In short, contraception is similar to deliberate homicide, despite their important differences, precisely inasmuch as both involve a contralife *will*. Our thesis is that the contralife will that contraception involves also is morally evil, although we do not claim that it usually is as evil as a homicidal will."[53] The likening of a contraceptive will to a homicidal will, no matter how qualified, still seems far-fetched. Those with homicidal wills will that a specific person cease to exist. Those using contraception will no evil to any specific person. These authors' talk of the "possible person" that contraceptors project and repudiate is talk of a nonexistent entity. They speak of the hatred that contraceptors have for a possible child, but it is not at all clear that there is any kind of hatred of possible persons inherently involved in contraception. Although they explain what they mean by emotional hatred, they do not explain what they mean by "practical hatred." The word *practical* suggests that it is something that the spouses *do* (not *will*) that is hateful. And that may be right, for the act of contraception seems to express some kind of hatred or at least dislike for fertility and fertility is ordained to life and in acting against one's fertility one is acting against life. But there is no evidence that this is what they mean. The fact that they speak of contraception as the choice of a couple who "project and reject" and who find the prospect of a child "repugnant" seems, again, to place the focus much more on the psychological state of the agents then on the nature of their acts.

Here it seems appropriate to explore further the possibility that couples, in fact, are not undergoing such a thought process. Is it not possible that some, and perhaps most, contraceptors reason in this way: "It would be best for us not to have a baby (or another baby) at this time. Let us find some way of rendering ourselves infertile (as we are periodically during a month anyway) and thus we can continue to engage in sexual intercourse responsibly"?

The most challenging counterexample to the position of Grisez, Boyle, Finnis, and May would be that of contraceptors who truly want another child and would welcome a child but who for some reason decide that it

52. Ibid., 46.
53. Ibid., 46.

would not be good to have another child at a certain time. Let us consider, for example, women in China who face the prospect of a forced abortion should they become pregnant with a second child. It may be that they actually desire another child and they would prefer not to use contraception. It seems wrong to speak of them as having a "practical hatred" of a possible child. It seems unfair to speak of them as projecting a future child and rejecting that child. Rather, they seem to be rejecting the death of that child through forced abortion and to be using contraception as a means of avoiding an abortion. (We could make the example even stronger: suppose these women know nothing of NFP and have been told by a Catholic priest, one who agrees with the revisionists, that contraception is morally licit.) They use contraception since they understand that they will be able to participate in acts of marital intercourse and not become pregnant, again, much as they are able to during the infertile periods. They do so, believing that what they do is moral. Is it fair to say that these women have "projected and rejected a possible child"? Do they have contralife wills? I am not suggesting that women in China are justified in using contraception, simply that many might do so in good faith and without a contralife will. I would insist that they have done wrong because their action violates right reason, because it is not duly measured to the end of regulating birth. Yet they are not culpable for the wrong that they have done because of their ignorance of the nature of their act. They do not, then, have a sinful will.

According to my view, it seems possible that many who contracept do not know the true nature of their acts; they do not know that it is wrong deliberately to render themselves infertile. I suspect that many contraceptors are not guilty of having contraceptive wills (let alone contralife wills). Nonetheless I doubt that they are altogether free from the guilt of wrongdoing. If they are choosing to be infertile because they value material goods, convenience, career, and so forth, above children, they may well be guilty of selfishness (but so are some who use NFP). Furthermore, if they are Catholics and disobeying their Church they may be guilty of the sin of disobedience and by extension of the sin of contracepting. Indeed, their ignorance may be culpable, for Catholics ought to respect and learn what the Church teaches and why.

Indeed, as has repeatedly been claimed, although some spouses may not be culpable for their acts of contraception, even with the best of wills they are still doing evil: they are still performing anti-procreative and contra–spousal-union acts. Evil acts generally have bad consequences, and thus those who contracept knowingly or unknowingly will likely experience some harmful effects. Contraception has many seriously evil consequences.

It does not take much imagination to see that much divorce, promiscuity, and abortion can be traced to both approval of and use of contraception. Even those who quite innocently use contraception, may, through their habitual use of it, come to be very selfish and even contralife, for they may come to prefer a life unencumbered by children. The constant dissociation of sexual intercourse from procreation may hinder them from appreciating the full meaning and grandeur of their fertility. Since contraception inhibits total self-giving, contraceptors will likely not experience the depth of intimacy that sexual intercourse fosters. Catholics who are being disobedient will find themselves somewhat estranged from their Church and perhaps thus from God as well. But to accuse all contraceptors of having contralife wills seems to distort what is happening in the minds, hearts, wills, and souls of many spouses who contracept.

Grisez and colleagues do grant that individuals can use contraception without sinning. They state, "We think that, while it is true that those who practice contraception in good faith—if they truly are in good faith—commit no sin. . . ."[54] They do not describe for us what might be the kind of reasoning engaged in by those who might practice contraception in good faith; one might think it would resemble that of the women from China, hypothesized earlier. The analysis there suggested that one could use contraception without having a contralife will, and this would be practicing contraception in good faith. But Grisez and his associates think that the choice to contracept always entails a contralife will: "The choice to contracept, even if it is made in conformity to a sincere conscience, is a contralife will."[55] It is difficult to understand how they could say that these individuals are not sinning, for one is responsible for the quality of one's will. On the other hand, if they are ignorant of what they are doing, they could not have a contralife (or evil) will, for ignorance can excuse the will (see *Summa Theologiae* I–II, q. 19, art. 6).

I would also argue that it is not always evil to have a contralife will as defined by Grisez and the others. The description of a contralife will given by them is very narrow: recall that they spoke of a couple's "look[ing] ahead and think[ing] about the baby whose life they might initiate" and of the contracepting couple's "projecting and rejecting that child." But could not any individual "look ahead and think about a baby whose life" might be initiated and decide not to initiate any process that would lead to such a life? Celibates might think of children they might have and think that it would not be good for such children to come to be since they are not in

54. Ibid., 108.
55. Ibid., 108.

a state of life suitable for raising children well. They choose to do something to ensure that such never happens. They may, for instance, choose to keep themselves out of the way of temptation. This is choosing to do something prior to a sexual act (a possible act!) to prevent the coming to be of a new life. I would say, good choice. But it would seem that according to Grisez, Boyle, Finnis, and May, they would be guilty of having a contralife will and of contracepting. Recall that May defines contraception in this way: "Contraception is not a sexual act, but is the choice (and in this sense an 'intent') to do something, prior to such a sexual act, during it, or subsequent to it, to prevent the coming-to-be of new human life."[56] This passage appears to be a paraphrase of a crucial passage in section 14 of *Humanae Vitae*: "There must be a rejection of all acts that attempt to impede procreation, both those chosen as means to an end and those chosen as ends. This includes acts that precede intercourse, acts that accompany intercourse, and acts that are directed to the natural consequences of intercourse." May rejects choices, whereas the encyclical rejects acts. May speaks of choices that "prevent" the coming to be of new life and the encyclical speaks of acts that "impede" procreation. The distinction is subtle but, I think, revealing. May's definition would place a dictator who puts sterility inducing drugs into the water and my celibate into the category of contraceptors, since they both seek to prevent new life from coming to be. The encyclical's definition would not classify them as contraceptors, for the word *impede* implies that an act—that is, an act of sexual intercourse—is being tampered with, is being made not to reach its natural end. It refers to a perverted sexual act, which neither the dictator nor my celibate performs.

This brings us to consider the acts of those who use natural methods of family planning. Some would want to argue that couples using NFP are going through the same reasoning process Grisez and the others attribute to contraceptors and would deduce that if it is what is chosen or willed that makes contraception wrong, NFP is equally wrong or contraception is equally as permissible as NFP. They would say that couples who use NFP are equally "look[ing] ahead and think[ing] about the baby whose life they might initiate" and "projecting and rejecting that child."

These writers allow that some couples using NFP may have contraceptive wills.[57] But they argue that most couples using NFP are engaging in a different reasoning process from those using contraception and that they make different choices. They allow that two couples might have equally

56. William May, letter to the editor in *Crisis* 8 (May 1990) 13.
57. Ibid., 82.

legitimate reasons for not having a baby. They distinguish their acts in this way:

> They differ not in the *reason* for the choices which are motivated, but in the *choices* which that reason motivates and in those choices' relationships to the benefits and burdens which such a reason represents. When contraception is chosen, the choice is *to impede the baby's coming to be* [my emphasis] in order that the goods represented by that reason be realized and/or the evils represented by it be avoided. When NFP is noncontraceptively chosen, the choice is *to abstain from intercourse* [my emphasis] that would be likely to result in both the baby's coming to be and the loss of goods and/or occurrence of evils represented by that same reason in order that the goods represented by that reason be realized or the evils represented by it be avoided.
>
> Even when based on good reason, the contraceptive choice by its very definition is contralife. It is a choice to prevent the beginning of the life of a possible person. It is a choice *to do something,* with the intent that the baby not be, as a means to a further end: that the good consequences of the baby's not-coming-to-be will be realized and the bad consequences of the baby's coming to be will be prevented. The noncontraceptive choice of NFP differs. It is a choice *not to do something*— namely, not to engage in possible fertile sexual intercourse—with the intent that the bad consequences of the baby's coming to be will be avoided, and with the *acceptance as side effects* of both the baby's not-coming-to-be and the bad consequences of his or her not-coming-to-be. In this choice and in the acceptance of its side effects, there need be no contralife will. The baby who might come into being need not be projected and rejected.[58]

I think this description is very hard to follow; I suspect it is so because it makes several careful distinctions that correspond closely to the true differences between the use of contraception and NFP but also creates distinctions where there are none. Compare the simplicity of *Humanae Vitae* 16: "The Church is not inconsistent when it teaches both that it is morally permissible for spouses to have recourse to infertile periods and also that all directly contraceptive practices are morally wrong, even if spouses seem to have good and serious reasons for using these. These two situations are essentially different. In the first, the spouses legitimately use a faculty that is given by nature; in the second case, the spouses impede the order of generation from completing its own natural processes." First, note that in *Humanae Vitae* the emphasis is on the differences between the cooperation with nature inherent in NFP and the contradiction of nature inherent in contraception. In the passage from Grisez and colleagues, however, the evil is always placed in the choice; there is no mention of nature. Since in the view of the authors morality is defined by choice, they must distinguish contraceptors from users of NFP by their choices. They

58. Ibid., 84.

argue that the couple using contraception are doing evil not because they are doing something that contradicts nature but because they intend that a child not come to be (this is their choice and what makes the act evil) and that leads them to do something contraceptive (either use a contraceptive or NFP in a contraceptive way). They argue that the couple morally using NFP are choosing not to engage in sexual intercourse (a moral choice) and as a side effect a child does not come to be.

But is this accurate? Are the choices of contraceptors and those who use NFP truly different? I do not believe that most couples using contraceptives are undertaking their act with the primary intent of seeing that a baby not come to be. I think they primarily intend to enjoy intercourse with their spouses and seek to prevent conception. I think Grisez and his colleagues characterize their decision in this way: (1) We wish to avoid the burdens of childbearing now (let us grant as they do that this may be for good reasons); (2) we wish to engage in sexual intercourse; (3) we might be fertile and thus might be bringing new life into existence; (4) we choose against this new life; we choose that it not come to be (it is at this point that Grisez and the others say that contraception takes place); (5) we now choose some action that will prevent that new life from coming to be; we use, for example, a condom, IUD, NFP.

They characterize the decision of couples using NFP in this way: (1) We wish to avoid the burdens of childbearing now (for good reasons); (2) thus we choose not to have intercourse during the fertile times; (3) a consequence of our acts is that we not have a child, and we accept the bad consequence of a child's not coming to be.[59]

But are these true portrayals? Do contracepting couples really project a child and repudiate that child? If they do, do couples who use NFP do so any less? I suspect that few contraceptors or users of NFP project and repudiate a child. Many simply judge that having a child at a given time would not be a responsible thing to do. They then take measures not to have a child: some may abstain completely; some may abstain periodically; some may contracept; some may have abortions. The distinction among them is the acts they choose as a means to that end. Couples using NFP make legitimate use of an infertile period; couples using contraception wrongly render themselves infertile.

To distinguish their acts, let me use the traditional terminology of means and ends. I would argue that two couples might have the same end: that is, they both may legitimately not desire to have a child (my "ends" are Grisez and associates' "reasons"). The couple contracepting have chosen

59. Ibid., cf. 84.

an evil means (for they have chosen a means that prevents the sexual act from achieving its natural *telos*) and the couples using NFP have chosen a moral means (for neither abstaining nor engaging in the sexual act during the fertile period prevents an act of sexual intercourse from achieving its natural *telos*; it may not achieve this *telos* but not as the result of any tampering with the act by the spouses). Grisez and colleagues argue that the couple contracepting has made an evil choice, whereas the couple using NFP has made a moral choice. And this is true, if it means the couple using contraception have chosen *to do* something evil and the couple using NFP have chosen *to do* something moral. But, again, I think they mean something different. They think the couple using contraceptives are doing wrong because they project a child and repudiate it (an immoral choice) and the couple using NFP have not done so; they have simply chosen not to have intercourse (a moral choice).

The fact that couples using contraception frequently express great anger should they become pregnant and that those who use NFP seem to accept a "surprise" pregnancy more calmly may suggest that contraceptors do have greater hostility to new life than do those using NFP. Yet, I wonder whether this is true. Is their anger a result of their hatred of their future child? Or is it not that contraceptors become angry because they do not have the control over their lives that they want; they are angry when they discover that the acts they engage in have a nature different from that which they intend them to have? They do not want the burdens of a child and do not think they "deserve" these burdens since they were taking precautions. Those who use NFP are less angry at a pregnancy since they recognize more clearly the nature of their acts; they more explicitly have in mind that, when engaging in sexual intercourse, they may become pregnant.

Another important distinction has emerged from the preceding analysis. Many in the natural family planning movement have argued that couples using NFP may be guilty of having contraceptive wills if they are using it without a sufficiently good reason for wanting to limit their family size. I think this is not an entirely precise claim. If they refuse to use contraception to achieve their end of preventing pregnancy and choose to use NFP precisely because it is not contraceptive, I do not think they can be accused of having contraceptive wills; they manifest no intention of tampering with the natural *telos* of the sexual act. Rather it would seem more precise to say that those using NFP so that they may avoid a pregnancy for selfish reasons have selfish wills.

Ultimately Grisez and colleagues and I are in complete agreement that couples ought never to contracept. Our differences lie in the way we describe what they are doing. Perhaps in most instances it would make very little differences in how we evaluate any given action. But then again it might. I suspect that many who contracept (let us say those who have legitimate reasons for limiting their family size) simply will not be able to see themselves in Grisez and associates' portrayal of conceptors. They will argue (and I suspect rightly) that they do not have contralife wills (any more so than do those who use NFP). And thus they will say that if what is wrong with using contraception is that it means the agent has a contralife will, they are not committing the evil of contraception since they do not have such a will. My position accepts their claim that all they wish to do is to render themselves infertile. My task then will be to demonstrate to them that it is evil deliberately to render themselves infertile. My argument will take the lines of demonstrating that they are engaging in acts that violate nature (whereas NFP does not); that they are thwarting acts from achieving their natural *telos* (whereas NFP does not); and that they are not fully giving of themselves (whereas those who use NFP are).

This appendix has attempted to show that Grisez and associates' arguments against contraception depart from the traditional ones in several disquieting ways. In doing so they lose a certain strength that those arguments have, a strength that lies in giving primacy of place to the natural *telos* of an action as the criterion for judging its rightness and wrongness. They also acquire some weaknesses that the traditional arguments do not have, such as a somewhat implausible description of the kind of willing that is involved in the decision to contracept.

Notes

CHAPTER ONE

1. Church tradition has not made extensive use of Scripture explicitly and directly in its condemnation of contraception, although certainly the Christian understanding of marriage, and of nature and the importance of children, is molded by Scripture and in turn shapes the Church's teaching on such matters as contraception. Throughout the Old Testament sexuality, marriage, and fecundity are considered to be great goods. Noonan argues that these emphases have been much more influential on the Church teaching than has been the text about Onan's spilling his seed (John T. Noonan, *Contraception* [1965] reprint Cambridge, Mass.: Belknap Press, 1986; 33ff.). Most biblical exegetes argue that Onan is condemned not for his contraceptive behavior but for his refusal to raise up progeny by his brother's wife.

The New Testament treats not only marriage but sexuality as holy (Noonan, *Contraception*, 40). Yet little is said about procreation in this context. The most influential passages are most likely those in Paul where he lists various unnatural sexual acts. The Christian community used these texts and others to construct its teaching against contraception. (And, certainly, it drew extensively on the wisdom of the philosophical community as well.) Vatican II echoed Pius XII's desire (expressed in *Humani Generis*) that Catholic moral theology work to show what support there is for Catholic moral teaching in Scripture. John Paul II in his commentaries on *Humanae Vitae* has himself undertaken this endeavor. See Chapter 5 for a fuller discussion of the scriptural basis for the condemnation of contraception.

2. John T. Noonan's *Contraception* shows the constancy of the Church's teaching but suggests that differing historical conditions could influence the teaching. For critiques of Noonan's interpretation, see Germain Grisez, "Marriage: Reflections Based on St. Thomas and Vatican Council II," *Catholic Mind* 64 (June 1966) 4–19; Fabian Parmisano, "Love and Marriage in the Middle Ages—I," *New Blackfriars* 50 (1969) 599–608, and "Love and Marriage in the Middle Ages—II," *New Blackfriars* 50 (1969) 649–60.

3. Noonan, *Contraception*, 6.

4. Certainly Noonan became an ardent advocate for change in the Church's teaching. See his "Authority, Usury, and Contraception," *Cross Currents* 16 (Winter 1966) 71–75; *The Church and Contraception: The Issues at Stake* (New York: Paulist Press, 1967); "The Pope's Conscience," *Commonweal* 85 (1967) 559–60; "Natural Law, the Teaching of the Church, and the Regulation of the Rhythm of Human Fecundity," *American Journal of Jurisprudence* 25 (1980) 16–37. See Joseph Boyle's response, "Human Action, Natural Rhythms, and Contraception: A Response to Noonan," *American Journal of Jurisprudence* 26 (1981) 32–47, and Noo-

nan's reply, "A Prohibition without a Purpose? Laws That Are Not Norms?: A Rejoinder to Professor Boyle," *American Journal of Jurisprudence* 27 (1982) 14–17. William E. May also critiqued Noonan's 1980 article in "Church Teaching and the Immorality of Contraception," *Homiletic and Pastoral Review* (Jan. 1982) 9–18. See also the entry on contraception by Noonan in *The Westminster Dictionary of Christian Ethics*, ed. James F. Childress and John MacQuarrie (Philadelphia: Westminster Press, 1986) 124–26.

5. Noonan, *Contraception*, 81–106, particularly 91.

6. There is much controversy over Augustine's understanding of sex; one disputed question is whether he thought it was moral for spouses to have sex if they were not specifically intending to have children. Noonan maintains, "Augustine requires both the objective possibility of procreation and the subjective intent to procreate" (*Contraception*, 130). For an opposing interpretation, see John J. Hugo, *St. Augustine on Nature, Sex, and Marriage* (Chicago: Scepter, 1968). Many portray the Catholic Church as having, or having had, a view that sexual intercourse is "dirty," and many fault Augustine for this view. Hugo's book also contests this understanding of Augustine.

7. Noonan, *Contraception*, 124.

8. From *Marriage and Concupiscence* 1.15.17, cited in Noonan, *Contraception*, 136.

9. Noonan, *Contraception*, 149.

10. Ibid., 162–67.

11. Ibid., 168.

12. Ibid., 169.

13. Ibid., 91, and see 232–37.

14. For a modern version of this argument see Germain Grisez, John C. Ford, S.J., Joseph Boyle, John Finnis, and William E. May, *The Teaching of Humanae Vitae: A Defense* (San Francisco: Ignatius Press, 1988). Their position is discussed in Chapter 4 and Appendix 4.

15. Noonan, *Contraception*, 238–39.

16. Ibid., 358–59.

17. Some have said that *finally* with *Casti Connubii*, the Church permitted use of the sterile period; this is a false construal of affairs: sexual intercourse had always been permitted between spouses who were sterile for such reasons as age or necessary medical sterilizations. It was not until the mid-nineteenth century that the timing of fertility began to be known. Questions put to the Penitentiary about having intercourse during the sterile period seemed to indicate approval (Noonan, *Contraception*, 439).

18. Pius XI, *Casti Connubii: Encyclical Letter of Pope Pius XI on Christian Marriage* (Boston: St. Paul Editions, n.d.) 7. (Hereafter DSP followed by page number.)

19. Ibid., 8.

20. Ibid., 27–28.

21. See in particular, Pius XII, "Speech to the Italian Catholic Union of Midwives," Oct. 29, 1951, AAS 43 (1951) 835–54, and "Speech to the Seventh Congress of the International Society of Hematology," Sept. 12, 1958, AAS 50 (1958) 446–47. A collection of his addresses on marriage and all the major addresses of popes from Benedict XIV to Pope John XXIII can be found in *Matrimony*, ed. Benedictine Monks of Solesmes, trans. Michael J. Byrnes (Boston: St. Paul Editions, 1963).

22. John J. Lynch, "Current Theology: Notes on Moral Theology," *Theological Studies* 23 (1962) 239.

23. Sept. 12, 1958, AAS 50 (1958) 735.

24. John Rock, M.D., *The Time Has Come: A Catholic Doctor's Proposals to End the Battle over Birth Control* (New York: Alfred A. Knopf, 1963). Rock was also a pioneer of in vitro fertilization. For a report of his highly unethical practices in obtaining eggs and embryos and for a good accounting of his influence in the promotion of the pill, see his biography by Loretta McLaughlin, *The Pill, John Rock, and the Church* (Boston: Little, Brown and Co., 1982).

25. Lynch, "Current Theology," 242.

26. Lynch, *Theological Studies* 26 (1965) 253.

27. Ibid., 255.

28. L. Janssens, "Morale conjugale et progestogènes," *Ephemerides Theologicae Lovanienses* 39 (1963) 787–826; W. van der Marck, O. P., "Vruchtbaarheidsregeling: poging tot antwoord op een nog open vraag," *Tijdshrift voor theologie* 3 (1963) 378–413; J. M. Reuss, "Eheliche Hingave und Zeugung," *Tübinger theologische Quartalschrift* 143 (1963) 454–76. A review of these articles can be found in Noonan's *Contraception*, 468–75, and Franz Boeckle, "Birth Control: A Survey of German, French and Dutch Literature on the Question of Birth Control," *Concilium* 5 (1965) 97–129.

29. Gerald Kelly, S.J., "Confusion: Contraception and 'The Pill,' " *Theology Digest* 12 (Summer 1964) 123–30. Lynch himself had written a critique of these views in the previous year's "Notes on Moral Theology," *Theological Studies* 25 (1964) 238–49.

30. Lynch, *Theological Studies* 26 (1965) 255.

31. The amount of literature on contraception and related problems is enormous. For a very thorough survey of the literature before *Humanae Vitae*, see Ambrogio Valsecchi, *Controversy: The Birth Control Debate 1958–1968*, trans. Dorothy White (Washington, D.C.: Corpus Books, 1968). A handy way of following the debate is to read the biyearly "Notes on Moral Theology" in *Theological Studies*. Richard A. McCormick, S.J., who has written nearly all of these notes since 1965, has reprinted his contributions in *Notes on Moral Theology: 1965–1980* (Lanham, Md.: University Press of America, 1981) and *Notes on Moral Theology: 1981–1984* (Lanham, Md.: University Press of America, 1984). Of interest as well are several collections of essays including statements both scholarly and anecdotal by theologians and laypersons; for essays written before *Humanae Vitae*, see Michael Novak, ed., *The Experience of Marriage* (New York: Macmillan Co., 1964); William Birmingham, *What Modern Catholics Think about Birth Control* (New York: New American Library, 1964); Archbishop Thomas D. Roberts, S.J., *Contraception and Holiness* (New York: Herder and Herder, 1964); Leo Pyle, *The Pill and Birth Regulation* (Baltimore: Helican Press, 1964). For essays written later, see Daniel Callahan, *The Catholic Case for Contraception* (London: Macmillan Co., 1969); Raymond Dennehy, *Christian Married Love* (San Francisco: Ignatius Press, 1981). The journal *International Review of Natural Family Planning* (now the *International Review*) quite regularly prints articles in defense of the teaching of *Humanae Vitae*. Also see Franz Boekle, "Birth Control: A Survey of German, French, and Dutch Literature," *Concilium* 5 (1965) 97–129, and Enda McDonagh, "Recent English Literature on the Moral Theology of Marriage," *Concilium* 5 (1965) 130–54.

32. Lynch, *Theological Studies*, 26 (1965) 255, citing Paul VI, July 31, 1964, *AAS* 56 (1964) 588–89.

33. Paul VI, "The Year Behind and the Year Ahead," *The Pope Speaks* 9:4 (1964) 355.

34. See *Third Session: Council Speeches of Vatican II*, ed. William K. Leahy and Anthony T. Massimini (Glen Rock, N.J.: Paulist Press, 1966) 215–33.

35. Richard McCormick, S.J., "Current Theology: Notes on Moral Theology," *Theological Studies* 26 (1965), reprinted in *Notes on Moral Theology 1965–1980* (Lanham, Md.: University Press of America, 1981) 38.

36. Ibid., 164.

37. Ibid., 41–42.

38. Ibid., 168; McCormick and others had an exchange on this subject in the pages of *America* in 1966 with particular reference to how the teaching of *Gaudium et Spes* related to the question of the status of the Church's condemnation of contraception; see Richard A. McCormick, S.J., "The Council on Contraception," *America* 114 (Jan. 8, 1966) 47–48; John C. Ford, S.J., "Footnote on Contraception" (letter to the editor), *America* 114 (Jan. 22, 1966) 103–7, reply by McCormick; John L. Thomas, S.J., "What Did the Council Say on Contraception?" *America* 114 (Feb. 26, 1966) 294–96; John C. Ford, S.J., "More on the Council and Contraception," *America* 114 (Apr. 16, 1966) 553–57. These articles and others are evaluated in John C. Ford, S.J., and John J. Lynch, S.J., "Contraception: A Matter of Practical Doubt?" *Homiletic and Pastoral Review* 68 (1968) 563–74. After *Humanae Vitae* was issued, McCormick continued to hold that the question was still in doubt; see "Notes on Moral Theology," *Theological Studies* 29 (Dec. 1968) 373. His position is challenged by David Fitch, S.J., "Humanae Vitae and Reasonable Doubt," *Homiletic and Pastoral Review* 69 (Apr. 1969) 516–23.

39. See Francis J. Connell, C.SS.R., "Answers to Questions: Delaying Ovulation," *American Ecclesiastical Review* 151 (1964) 408.

40. The kinds of questions that were initially asked about the pill can be seen in the following articles: William J. Gibbons, S.J., "Antifertility Drugs and Morality," *America* 98 (Dec. 14, 1957) 346–48; John L. Lynch, "Moral Aspects of Pharmaceutical Fertility Control," *Proceedings of the Catholic Theological Society of America* 13 (1958) 127–38; Louis Janssens, "L'inhibition de l'ovulation est-elle moralement licite?" *Ephemerides Theologicae Lovanienses* 34 (1958) 357–60, and Warren Reich, M.S.SS.T., "The Pill after Childbirth," *Homiletic and Pastoral Review* 66:8 (May 1966) 661–68, who takes up not only the question of the use of the pill during lactation but that of its proper use by women who fear rape. His notes provide references to both theological and medical literature. Further references are available in Ambrogio Valsecchi, *Controversy*.

41. The distinction made here between differences in application of principle and in fundamental beliefs corresponds with the distinction made between "evolutionary" and "revolutionary" changes in Edward MacKinnon, S.J., "*Humanae Vitae* and Doctrinal Development," *Continuum* 6 (1968) 269–75.

42. The story of this commission and *Humanae Vitae* has been told several times. See William H. Shannon, *The Lively Debate: Response to Humanae Vitae* (New York: Sheed and Ward, 1970); Robert G. Hoyt, ed., *The Birth Control Debate* (Kansas City, Mo.: *National Catholic Reporter*, 1968); Msgr. George A. Kelly, *The Battle for the American Church* (Garden City, N.Y.: Image Books, 1980); and Robert Blair Kaiser, *The Politics of Sex and Religion* (Kansas City, Mo.: Leaven Press, 1985). Michel Rouche offers explanations about the makeup of the commission and tries to explain its radical shift as the majority of the early days of the commission, which was altogether opposed to contraception, was replaced by one that later approved contraception, "La Préparation de l'encyclique 'Humanae Vitae,' " *Paul*

VI et la modernité dans l'église (Rome: Palais Farnese, 1984) 361–83. In the same volume Jan Gootaers attempts to explain what took place between the issuance of the reports of the Papal Commission and the writing of Humanae Vitae; "Quelques données concernant la rédaction de l'encyclique 'Humanae Vitae,' " 585–97.

All the documents that were leaked are available in Hoyt, Birth Control Debate. For citations from the Schema and Minority Report I will be citing Callahan, The Catholic Case. For citations from the Majority Rebuttal I will be citing Tablet, May 6, 1967. For the "Pastoral Approaches" I will be citing Kaiser's The Politics of Sex and Religion.

43. "Les fondements de la doctrine de l'église concernant les principes de la vie conjugale," Analecta Cracoviensia 1 (1969) 194–230. One author claims that Karol Wojtyla, along with Gustave Martelet, specially advised Paul VI in his writing of Humanae Vitae: Jan Grootaers, "Quelques données," 390. Paul Johnson, Pope John Paul II and the Catholic Restoration (New York: St. Martin's Press, 1981), reports that Paul VI was reading Wojtyla's Love and Responsibility as he awaited the reports of the Papal Commission (32–33).

44. The information about who voted for what is taken from The Tablet, Sept. 21, 1968, 949.

45. See Appendix 2 for information on Paul VI's views on contraception before Humanae Vitae.

46. Kaiser, Politics of Sex, 38–39, reports on what his sources thought were the purposes of the commission under both John XXIII and Paul VI.

47. Paul VI, "Continuing Study of Population Problems," The Pope Speaks 10:3 (1965) 225–27. See also "The Council's View of Marriage and the Family," The Pope Speaks 11:1 (1966) 5–12.

48. Bernard Haering, "The Encyclical Crisis," Commonweal 88:20 (Sept. 6, 1968) 588–94.

49. Kaiser, Politics of Sex, 83–92.

50. Paul VI worked with several other consultative bodies before writing Humanae Vitae. Jan Grootaers attempts to explain what took place between the issuance of the reports of the Papal Commission and the writing of Humanae Vitae; "Quelques données," 585–97.

51. Michal Rouche laments the lack of poetic or mystical vision in the Minority Report; he suggests that it might have been otherwise had Karol Wojtyla and Gustave Martelet had a hand in writing the report, "La Préparation," 374.

52. Callahan, Catholic Case, 179.

53. "The Birth Control Report," The Tablet, May 6, 1967, 511.

54. A version of this argument was advanced by Michael Novak (who has since accepted the teaching of Humanae Vitae): "In theological terms, his [Pope Paul VI's] decision is of the utmost importance because it provides a very clear test of the source of doctrinal authority within the Catholic church. There are several sources of this authority. One of them is the Pope, and another is the evangelical sense of the Catholic people, the sensus fidelium. It has often been true in the past that popes have been wrong and the people right, and it seems that now we have a clear case to this same effect in our own generation, after so many years of false adulation of the papacy" (Hoyt, Birth Control Debate, 201).

55. For a penetrating discussion of these matters, see Germain Grisez, The Way of the Lord Jesus (Chicago: Franciscan Herald Press, 1983) chap. 35. See Chapter 5, below, for a discussion of the infallibility of the teaching of Humanae Vitae.

56. Callahan, *Catholic Case*, 187. 57. "Birth Control Report," 510.
58. Ibid., 511. 59. Ibid.
60. Charles Curran, "Ten Years Later," *Commonweal* 195 (1978) 426.
61. See Grisez, *Contraception and the Natural Law* (Milwaukee: Bruce Publishing Co., 1964), and his (along with John C. Ford, S.J., Joseph Boyle, John Finnis, and William E. May) more recent *The Teaching of Humanae Vitae: A Defense* (San Francisco: Ignatius Press, 1988).
62. Callahan, *Catholic Case*, 182–83.
63. Ibid., 183. 64. Ibid., 183–84.
65. Ibid., 184.
66. These and other arguments against contraception are developed more fully in Chapter 4.
67. Callahan, *Catholic Case*, 184.
68. Joseph V. Dolan in "*Humanae Vitae* and Nature," *Thought* 44:174 (Autumn 1969) 358–76, although most supportive of the arguments of *Humanae Vitae*, notes that this is precisely the point where more work must be done. Since this is the point at which some of those who support *Humanae Vitae* find a weakness in their own argument, his demurral deserves some attention.
69. Ibid., 185–86.
70. The work of Grisez is more closely examined in Chapter 4 and Appendix 4.
71. Callahan, *Catholic Case*, 186. 72. "Birth Control Report," 510.
73. Ibid., 511. 74. Ibid., 511.
75. Ibid. 76. Ibid., 512.
77. Ibid. 78. Ibid., 513.
79. Ibid., 512. 80. Ibid.
81. Ibid. 82. Ibid.
83. Ibid., 513. 84. Ibid.
85. I have not been able to determine who introduced the argument justifying contraception on the basis of the principle of totality. A possible author of this argument is Louis Dupré; he uses it in several early articles; see, for instance, "Toward a Re-examination of the Catholic Position on Birth Control," *Crosscurrents* 14 (Winter 1964) 63–84; *Contraception and Catholics* (Baltimore, Md.: Helicon, 1964); "Natural Law and Birth Control," *Philosophy Today* 9 (1965) 94–100; and "Philosophical Analysis of the Catholic Moral Problem of Contraception," *Insight* (Fall 1967) 57–59. Another possible candidate is Bernard Haering, who served on the Papal Commission; he certainly used this argument in his rejection of *Humanae Vitae*; Chapter 6 examines his arguments in behalf of contraception.
86. Michael Dummett in "The Documents in the Papal Commission on Birth Control," *New Blackfriars* 50 (1969) 241–50, argues that the majority theologians on the commission greatly erred in not realizing the seriousness of this charge by the minority. He allows, though, that the argument that "if contraception were admitted as permissible, practically no sin concerning either sex or pregnancy could logically be prohibited . . . is the argument of the minority most likely to strike sympathizers with the reformist position as strained and specious" (247). Nonetheless, he maintains that the minority's argument is a strong one and that it would require a radical revision of Church teaching on sex to find reasons to allow contraception and retain condemnation of other acts traditionally condemned. Still, he finds that too much of the burden of the traditionalist arguments against

these acts rests on the claim that they violate the connection between sex and procreation; he calls for a better account of what chastity is. This better account may, perhaps, be found in the arguments in behalf of *Humanae Vitae* by John Paul II (see Chapter 8).

87. Callahan, *Catholic Case*, 204–9.   88. Ibid., 208.

89. "Birth Control Report," 513.

90. An attempt to define conjugal love is made in Chapter 2.

91. Charles Curran, *New Perspectives in Moral Theology* (Notre Dame, Ind.: University of Notre Dame Press, 1976) 20.

92. Kaiser, *Politics of Sex*, 261.   93. Callahan, *Catholic Case*, 153.

94. Ibid., 154.   95. Ibid., 156.

96. Ibid., 157–58.   97. Ibid., 158.

98. Ibid., 159.   99. Ibid., 160.

100. Ibid., 160–61.   101. Ibid., 161.

102. Ibid.   103. Ibid., 165.

104. Ibid., 165–66.   105. Ibid., 166.

106. Ibid.

107. See Chapter 7 for an examination of the claim that contraception involves only premoral evils.

108. Ibid., 166.

109. Several excellent articles have evaluated the reports of the commission. See Dummet, "Documents of the Papal Commission," and John Finnis, "*Humanae Vitae*: Its Background and Aftermath," *International Review of Natural Family Planning* 4:2 (Summer 1980) 141–53.

A very worthy critique of the report is to be found in Norbert Rigali, S.J., "The Historical Meaning of the *Humanae Vitae* Controversy," *Chicago Studies* 15 (1976) 127–138. He speculates about how history will evaluate *Humanae Vitae* as a response to the arguments of the time. Noting that the burden of proof was inarguably on those who advocated change, he observes of the document referred to here as the Majority Rebuttal: "While a position paper, obviously, differs from a final report, one would not expect to find simplistic thought in a position paper produced by members of a papal commission favoring radical change in Church teaching. It seems that historical theology will hardly be impressed to find in this paper such platitudes as argumentation against 'an unconditional respect for nature as it is in itself' and against the notion that 'all things be left untouchable just as they are.' From the stuff of straw men, epoch-making documents are not expected to be built" (130–31). Of the final report, he says, "if the way in which the report handled the question of what is natural left its own conception of the natural quite questionable, the same must be said about the way in which the question of the supernatural is treated by the report. It is difficult to imagine that historical theology will fault the magisterium for not having radically reversed Church teaching on the basis of this theology" (134). Indeed, he claims that it would have been a "moral disaster" for the Church to have endorsed the theology of the commission report, that it would have " 'canonized' the perennial minimalistic tendency of moral theology to be content with mediocrity in its quest for the minimum" (137). The thrust of his article is that the theologians advocating change had not then, and as of the writing of his article, had not yet, found satisfactory or convincing reasons for the change. He, himself, argues in the vein of those who hold that *Humanae Vitae* proposes a

Christian ideal for conjugal relationships, that contraceptive sex is "incompatible with Christian perfection," but that it may not be incompatible with certain stages of striving for that perfection (136).

CHAPTER TWO

1. There are a wide variety of books on Christian marriage. Among the classics in English are George Hayward Joyce, S.J., *Christian Marriage: An Historical and Doctrinal Study* (New York: Sheed and Ward, 1933) and E. Schillebeeckx, O.P., *Marriage: Human Reality and Saving Mystery*, vols. 1 and 2 (New York: Sheed and Ward, 1965); and, John C. Ford, S.J., and Gerald Kelly, S.J., *Contemporary Moral Theology*, vol. 2 (Westminster, Md.: Newman Press, 1964). For a more contemporary treatment see Walter Kasper, *Theology of Christian Marriage* (New York: Seabury Press, 1980). A recent and useful work is *Contemporary Perspectives on Christian Marriage*, ed. Richard Malone, S.J., and John R. Connery, S.J. (Chicago: Loyola University Press, 1984). See also Pontifical Council for the Family, *Marriage and the Family* (San Francisco: Ignatius Press, 1989), and Bernard A. Siegle, T.O.R., *Marriage According to the New Code of Canon Law* (New York: Alba House, 1986).

2. The translations for *Casti Connubii* are from *On Christian Marriage* (Boston: St. Paul Editions, 1930), 7. Hereafter references to page numbers in this edition are given in the text after the citation.

3. Translations for the documents of Vatican II are from *Vatican II: The Conciliar and Post Conciliar Documents*, ed. Austin Flannery, O.P. (Northport, N.Y.: Costello Publishing Co., 1975). References to the section number are given in the text after the citation. See a letter to the editor by Marc Calegari, S.J., in *America* 117 (Sept. 23, 1967) 316–17, where he explains some of the deficiencies of Abbott's translation.

4. Translations of *Humanae Vitae* are my own; a full text of this translation is to be found in Appendix 1. Section numbers are given in the text.

5. Joyce, *Christian Marriage*, Chapter 1, gives a rather extensive explanation of marriage and natural law. But perhaps the best discussion of the difference between natural and sacramental marriage is to be found in *The Roman Catechism*, trans. Robert I. Bradley, S.J., and Eugene Kevane (Boston: St. Paul Editions, 1985), 331ff.

6. *Denz.* 1198; in 1679 a series of propositions were condemned by Innocent XI; one of them claimed that fornication involved no intrinsic evil.

7. For instance, see Leo XIII, *Arcanum*, ASS 12 (1879) 388.

8. Pius XI, *Casti Connubii*, 18, citing Pius VI, *Rescript. ad Episc. Agriens.*, July 11, 1789.

9. My translation; the Latin is "*Ex valido matrimonio enascitur inter coniuges vinculum natura sua perpetuum et exclusivum; in matrimonio praeterea christiano coniuges ad sui status officia et dignitatem peculiari sacramento roborantur et veluti consecrantur.*"

10. An excellent discussion of the various terms used to describe marriage can be found in John C. Ford, S.J., "Marriage: Its Meaning and Purposes" in *Theological Studies* 3 (1942) 333–74 (see particularly 340). I accept his argument that *bond* is the term that most perfectly defines the essence of marriage. See also John MacQuarrie, "The Nature of the Marriage Bond," *Theology* 78:659 (May 1975), 230–36.

11. See particularly the work of Theodore Mackin, S.J., "Conjugal Love and

the Magisterium," *Jurist* 36 (1976) 263–301. He lists a number of other relevant articles in his first footnote.

12. These ends are also on occasion said to be "offspring, remedy for concupiscence, and mutual help," with fidelity and sacrament labeled the "blessings" of marriage (see n. 18). Since our intention here is to determine the primacy of procreation in relation to any of the other goods of marriage, it is not necessary to unravel this knot here.

13. *Casti Connubii* is here citing Saint Augustine, *De bono coniugium*, cap. 24, n. 32.

14. See for instance, Anthony Koznik et al., *Human Sexuality: New Directions in American Thought* (New York: Paulist Press, 1977).

15. This fact was not unknown to Aquinas and other scholastic philosophers, as is sometimes suggested (see the Majority Report or Schema).

16. For a comparison of animal and human sex along these lines, see Jean Guitton, "Eros and Agape" in *Christian Married Love,* ed. Raymond Dennehy (San Francisco: Ignatius Press, 1981), 77–80.

17. William May has written powerfully about this distinction. See his " 'Begotten, Not Made': Further Reflections on the Laboratory Generation of Human Life," *International Review of Natural Family Planning* 10:1 (Spring 1986) 1–22; and his "Catholic Moral Teaching on In Vitro Fertilization," in *Reproductive Technologies, Marriage and the Church* (Braintree, Mass.: Pope John Center, 1988), 107–21. See, also, Joseph Cardinal Ratzinger, "Man between Reproduction and Creation: Theological Questions on the Origin of Human Life," *Communio* (Summer 1989) 197–211.

18. AAS 36 (1944) 103. This decree was issued in response to the work of Herbert Doms, *The Meaning of Marriage,* Eng. trans. (New York: Sheed and Ward, 1939). For an analysis of Doms's work with a defense of the traditional understanding, see Ford, "Marriage: Its Meaning and Purposes."

19. AAS 43 (1951) 835–54.

20. See, for instance, Theodore Mackin, "Conjugal Love and the Magisterium," 270.

21. Note 14 in the Flannery edition of the documents of Vatican II.

22. *Acta Synodalia Sacrosancti Concilii Vaticani II,* vol. 4, pt. 7 (Rome: Typis Polyglottis Vaticanis, 1978) 477–79.

23. *Roman Catechism,* 332–33.

24. Ford, "Marriage: Its Meaning and Purposes," 332–73, and Germain Grisez, "Marriage: Reflections Based on St. Thomas and Vatican Council II," *Catholic Mind* 64 (June 1966) 4–19. See also B. J. F. Lonergan, "Finality, Love, Marriage," *Theological Studies* 4 (1943) 477–510; and John Haas, "The Inseparability of the Two Meanings of the Marriage Act," in *Reproductive Technologies, Marriage and the Church* (Braintree, Mass.: Pope John Center, 1988) 89–106. See Haas's first footnote for a more extensive listing of the literature on the subject.

25. Ford, "Marriage: Its Meaning and Purpose," 347–48.

26. Ibid., 370.

27. Grisez, "Marriage: Reflections Based on St. Thomas and Vatican Council II," 7.

28. Ibid.   29. Ibid.

30. Ibid., 7–8.

31. See, for instance, John Noonan, *Contraception,* rev. ed. (Cambridge, Mass.:

Belknap Press, 1986), and John Giles Milhaven, "Conjugal Sexual Love and Contemporary Moral Theology," *Theological Studies* 35:4 (Dec. 1974) 692–710, and further references in his footnote 6.

32. All of those who argue in behalf of contraception mention personalist values and increased appreciation of the importance of conjugal love and responsible parenthood, but few attempt to define what these values are and why it is that they justify the use of contraception. There have, of course, been some such efforts. See, for instance, Louis Janssens, "Considerations on 'Humanae Vitae,' " *Louvain Studies* 2 (Spring 1969) 231–53. An article published before *Humanae Vitae* provides perhaps the best defense of contraception in terms of serving the values of "responsible parenthood"; see Robert O. Johann, S.J., "Responsible Parenthood: A Philosophical View" *Proceedings of the Catholic Theological Society of America* 20 (1965) 115–28. For pre–*Humanae Vitae* arguments that personalist values do not legitimize contraception, see, too, the pre–*Humanae Vitae* article by Paul Quay, S.J., "Contraception and Conjugal Love," *Theological Studies* 22 (Mar. 1961) 18–40, and his later book, *The Christian Meaning of Human Sexuality* (Evanston, Ill.: Credo House, 1985) (now available through Ignatius Press).

33. See, for instance, John J. Hugo, *St. Augustine on Nature, Sex, and Marriage* (Chicago: Scepter, 1969) and W. H. M. Van der Marck, O. P., "Toward a Renewal of the Theology of Marriage," *Thomist*, 30:4 (Oct. 1966) 307–42.

34. Much of the modern interest in personalist values and conjugal love is attributed to the work of Dietrich Von Hildebrand, *In Defense of Purity* (London: Sheed and Ward, 1931), and Doms, *Meaning of Marriage*. A critique of Doms's work in the light of the traditional teaching of the ends of marriage can be found in Ford and Kelly, *Contemporary Moral Theology*, 20–25.

35. John Paul II (Karol Wojtyla) distinguishes the various kinds of feeling often confused with love in his *Love and Responsibility* (New York: Farrar Straus Giroux, 1981), 101–4 (first published in Poland in 1960).

36. AAS 22 (1930), 548; this passage is omitted from the translation printed in some of the St. Paul Editions; the translation used here is found in Kelly and Ford, *Contemporary Moral Theology*, 17.

37. The text by Ronald Lawler, Joseph M. Boyle, Jr., and William E. May, *Catholic Sexual Ethics* (Huntington, Ind.: Our Sunday Visitor, 1985), explains Catholic teaching on human sexuality while showing that there need be no incompatibility between personalist values and natural law principles.

38. Pius XII seems to have been one of the pioneers in the use of "personalist language," if you will. In 1940 in an address to newlyweds he spoke of making a "total, exclusive, irrevocable" gift of oneself and spoke of the "mutual gift" of marriage, in *Matrimony*, ed. Benedictine Monks of Solesmes, trans. Michael J. Byrnes (Boston: St. Paul Editions, 1963), 315; see also 427 and 431.

39. *Ad Uxorem*, 2, 9. I have taken this passage from the fine article by Cahal B. Daly, "Natural Law Morality Today," *American Ecclesiastical Review* 153 (1965) 384.

40. John R. Connery, S.J., "The Role of Love in Christian Marriage: A Historical Overview," *Communio* 11:3 (Fall 1984) 244–57, especially 247.

41. Fabian Parmisano, O.P., "Love and Marriage in the Middle Ages," pts. 1 and 2, *New Blackfriars* 50 (1969) 599–608, 649–60.

42. Ibid., 603.

43. Noonan, *Contraception*, 299–311.

44. Parmisano, "Love and Marriage," pt. 2, 649.

45. Connery, "Role of Love in Christian Marriage," 248.

46. Lonergan, for instance, finds that his "more excellent" vertical finality of marriage—or personal development—"corresponds at least roughly with the traditional secondary ends of *mutuum auxilium* and *honestum remedium concupiscentiae*" ("Finality, Love, Marriage," 49). John C. Ford for the most part also supports this view ("Marriage: Its Meaning and Purpose"). John Connery, however, cites Karol Wojtyla as rejecting it; he tells us that Wojtyla "cautioned against identifying this [*mutuum adiutorium*] with conjugal love. Such an identification might lead one to believe that love was secondary in marriage" ("Role of Love," 252, citing *Love and Responsibility*, 68).

47. The authors of *Gaudium et Spes* did not intend to provide a significant presentation on this subject. Paul VI was employing the services of a papal commission to advise him on dealing with this question and had indicated that he wished to make a complete statement himself.

48. The story of the intervention can be found in Xavier Rynne, *The Fourth Session* (London: Faber and Faber, 1966), 210–25, and in Robert Blair Kaiser, *The Politics of Sex and Religion* (Kansas City, Mo.: Leaven Press, 1985), 115–21. See Appendix 3 for a discussion of these interventions.

49. For a helpful selection of speeches and statements made about marriage by popes from Benedict XIV to John XXIII, see *Matrimony*.

CHAPTER THREE

1. *Humanae Vitae* is presented as an encyclical letter *de propagatione humanae prolis recte ordinanda*. The Latin very literally translated is "on the right ordering of the propagation of human offspring"; more loosely, but still precisely, it could be rendered "on the proper regulation of offspring." The Latin is not easily rendered into English; the translation of the Italian *sulla regolazione della natalità* as "on the regulation of birth" predominates. This translation, though, may cause some problems for it suggests that the encyclical is about birth control or even contraception. Certainly the chief concern of the encyclical is to define what are the principles for determining the moral means for limiting family size, but to say that the encyclical is *about* contraception may cause many to lose sight of its larger context. It might be truer to say that the encyclical is about the *munus* of transmitting human life or that it is about "responsible parenthood" (*paternitas conscia*). See footnotes to HV 5 and HV 6 to the translation included in Appendix 1.

2. Joseph Fuchs, S.J., *Natural Law*, trans. Helmut Reckter, S.J., and John A. Dowling (New York: Sheed and Ward, 1965), remains a standard treatment of natural law and revelation. Briefer and more updated introductions can be found in John Finnis, "The Natural Law, Objective Morality, and Vatican II" and William E. May, "The Natural Law and Objective Morality: A Thomistic Perspective" in *Principles of Catholic Moral Life*, ed. William E. May (Chicago: Franciscan Herald Press, 1980) 113–49, 151–90.

3. Translations of *Humanae Vitae* are mine. The full translation is printed as Appendix 1.

4. For an excellent introduction to Thomas's natural law theory, see Ralph McInerny, *Ethica Thomistica* (Washington, D.C.: Catholic University of America Press, 1982).

5. See Robert Sokolowski, "Knowing Natural Law," *Tijdschrift voor filosofie* 43 (1981) 625–41.

6. See three articles by Joseph Costanzo, S.J.: "Papal Magisterium and 'Humanae Vitae,' " *Thought* 44:174 (Autumn 1969) 377–412; "Academic Dissent: An Original Ecclesiology," *Thomist* 34:4 (Oct. 1970) 636–53; "Papal Magisterium, Natural Law, and Humanae Vitae," *American Journal of Jurisprudence* 16 (1971) 259–89, all reprinted in *The Historical Credibility of Hans Kung* (North Quincy, Mass.: Christopher Publishing House, 1979). See also Cahal B. Daly, "Natural Law Morality Today," *American Ecclesiastical Review* 153 (1965) 361–98.

7. This discussion draws on the following: Joseph V. Dolan, " 'Humanae Vitae' and Nature," *Thought* 44:174 (Autumn 1969) 358–76, Richard J. Connell, "A Defense of Humanae Vitae," *Laval Théologique et Philosophique* 26 (1970) 57–85 (a response to Connell was made by William Albury, "Discussion: Humanae Vitae and the Ecological Argument," *Laval Théologique et Philosophique* 27 [1971] 135–41, which is followed by a reply by Connell).

There was an interesting exchange on this matter before the issuance of *Humanae Vitae* between Herbert McCabe, O.P., "Contraception and Natural Law," *New Blackfriars* 46 (Nov. 1964) 89–95, and G. E. M. Anscombe, "Contraception and Natural Law," *New Blackfriars* 46 (June 1965) 517–21, and McCabe, "Contraceptives and Holiness," *New Blackfriars* 46 (Feb. 1965) 294–99. Germain Grisez laid out an early version of his position in *Contraception and the Natural Law* (Milwaukee: Bruce Publishing Co., 1964). This has been superseded by John C. Ford, S.J., Germain Grisez, Joseph Boyle, John Finnis, and William E. May, *The Teaching of Humanae Vitae: A Defense* (San Francisco: Ignatius Press, 1988).

8. *Discorsi e Radiomessaggi di Pio XII* 6, 191–92; the translations are in *Linacre Quarterly* 23 (Nov. 1956) 109–116, especially 110.

9. All the preceding passages are found in ibid., 114.

10. More is said about this in Chapter 6.

11. Leon R. Kass, M.D., *Toward a More Natural Science: Biology and Human Affairs* (New York: Free Press, 1985).

12. Both passages are in Kass, 254.

13. See *Birth Control: Why Are They Lying to Women?* by J. C. Espinosa, M.D. (New York: Vantage Press, 1980).

14. Some would argue that these methods do not qualify as early term abortions, since it is not clear when the human soul is infused or when personhood begins. Indeed, the Church has never ruled precisely when the human soul comes to be, and the condemnation of abortion does not depend on ensoulment at the moment of conception. When sperm meets and penetrates egg, conception of something that either is or will soon be a human person has taken place, and thus whatever destroys this new being cannot be rightly considered contraceptive ("against conception") for conception has taken place. Most forms of the pill on occasion work to destroy the life of an entity that has the genetic makeup of human beings, and thus it would seem proper to classify them more with abortifacients than with contraceptives.

15. Much of this section was published as part of an article, Janet E. Smith, "The *Munus* of Transmitting Human Life: A New Approach to *Humanae Vitae*," *Thomist* 54 (July 1990): 385–427. See also Janet E. Smith, "The Importance of the Concept of 'Munus' to Understanding 'Humanae Vitae,' " *Humanae Vitae: 20 Anni Dopo* (Milan: Edizioni Ares, 1989) 677–90.

16. *Familiaris Consortio* (1980) refers to a declaration made by the Synod Fathers wherein *Humanae Vitae* is cited; the Latin text is cited but *apertus* rather than *per se destinatus* appears (see paragraph 29).

17. *The Regulation of Birth*, trans. Alan C. Clark and Geoffrey Crawfurd (London: Catholic Truth Society, 1968) 13.

18. *Humanae Vitae*, trans. Alan C. Clark and Geoffrey Crawfurd (London: Catholic Truth Society, 1970) 13.

19. G. E. M. Anscombe, *Contraception and Chastity* (London: Catholic Truth Society, 1975) 18. Recall the passage cited in Chapter 3 from Charles Curran, *New Perspectives in Moral Theology* (Notre Dame, Ind.: University of Notre Dame Press, 1976) 20:

> Catholic theologians frequently deny the existing teaching of the hierarchical magisterium on such issues as contraception, sterilization, artificial insemination, masturbation, the generic gravity of sexual sins. Newer approaches have recently been taken to the question of homosexuality. . . . All these questions in the area of medical and sexual morality are being questioned today because some theologians believe that the absolute prohibitions define the forbidden action in terms of the physical structure of the act seen in itself apart from the context, the existing relationships or the consequences.

20. For an early statement (one much earlier than *Humanae Vitae*) of the recognition that arguments against contraception needed more than simply a description of the physiological ends of sexual organs and acts and for an article that remains one of the best explanations of the reasons for the Church's condemnation against contraception see Paul Quay, S.J., "Contraception and Conjugal Love," *Theological Studies* 22 (1961) 18–40. See also Mary Rosera Joyce, *The Meaning of Contraception* (New York: Alba House, 1969); her work was substantially completed before *Humanae Vitae*. Both Quay and Joyce offer excellent explanations of the role of the biological and physiological ends of the sexual organs in determining the morality of contraception and of why arguments solely dependent on this recognition are not adequate to demonstrate the immorality of contraception. Their work has been, it seems, ignored by revisionists.

21. *Casti Connubii* AAS 22 (1930) 560; the translation here is by the Daughters of Saint Paul, *Casti Connubii: Encyclical Letter of Pope Pius XI on Christian Marriage* (Boston: St. Paul Editions, n.d.) 29.

22. AAS 43 (1951) 843.

23. Some put such stress on the claim that it must be a conjugal act of intercourse that is tampered with that they hold that the use of contraception by those having sexual intercourse outside marriage does not compound the immorality of the act and that it can, in fact, diminish the immorality of the act. An argument against this position is made by Grisez et al., *Teaching of Humanae Vitae*, 36, who point out that the early condemnations of contraception by the Church (cf. the canon law before 1917) referred to any use of contraception, by the unmarried as well as the married.

24. Anscombe, *Contraception and Chastity*, 21.

25. Aquinas notes that there are narrow and broad senses to the term *unnatural*: "By human nature we may mean either that which is proper to man, and in this sense all sins, as being against reason, are also against nature, as Damascene states; or we may mean that nature which is common to man and other animals, and in

this sense, certain special sins are said to be against nature: e.g., contrary to sexual intercourse, which is natural to all animals, is unisexual lust, which has received the special name of the unnatural crime" (*Summa Theologiae*, q. 94, art. 3, reply to obj. 1, from *Introduction to St. Thomas Aquinas*, ed. Anton Pegis [New York: Modern Library Edition, 1945], 639). Here I am using it in the broad sense, though arguably the second and more narrow sense is suitable as well.

26. For an explanation of the connection of right reason and morality, see Vernon J. Bourke, *Ethics: A Textbook in Moral Philosophy* (New York: Macmillan Co., 1951).

27. Michael Novak comes perilously close to attributing this argument to the Church in "Frequent, Even Daily, Communion," in *The Catholic Case for Contraception*, ed. Daniel Callahan (London: Macmillan Co., 1969), 94–95.

28. Congregation for the Doctrine of the Faith, *Instruction on Bioethics: Respect for Human Life* (Boston: St. Paul Editions, 1987), 9.

29. Paul Quay, "Contraception and Conjugal Love," provides in note 10 a list of authors who he believes made such an argument. So, too, does Germain Grisez, *Contraception and the Natural Law*, 42, n. 1.

30. A series of articles about this matter appeared in the *American Ecclesiastical Review*. See E. J. Mahoney, "The 'Perverted Faculty' Argument against Birth Prevention," 79 (Aug. 1928) 133–45; John A. Ryan, "The Immorality of Contraception," 79 (Oct. 1928) 408–11; John M. Cooper, "Birth Control and the 'Perverted Faculty' Argument," 79 (Oct. 1928) 527–33; Henry Davis, S.J., "Birth Control: The Perverted Faculty Argument," 82 (July 1929) 54–69, with comments by Tyran and Cooper; and E. J. Mahoney, "The Immorality of Contraception," 81 (July 1929) 90–92.

31. Connell, "A Defense of Humanae Vitae," 77. Connell, in his reply to Albury, "Discussion: *Humanae Vitae*," gives this syllogistic presentation of his argument (142–43):

> Major premiss: Every action which applies medications (or surgery) to healthy organs in order to disrupt the normal operation is immoral.
> Minor premiss: Every use of pills for contraceptive effects is an action which applies a medication to healthy organs in order to disrupt the operation; therefore
> Conclusion: Every use of contraceptive pills for contraceptive effects is immoral.

32. Charles Curran, *Transition and Tradition in Moral Theology* (Notre Dame, Ind.: University of Notre Dame Press, 1979), 31.

33. Charles Curran, *Directions in Fundamental Moral Theology* (Notre Dame, Ind.: University of Notre Dame Press, 1985), 157.

34. See Barbara Seaman, *The Doctors' Case against the Pill* (Garden City, N.Y.: Doubleday, 1980); Dr. Ellen Grant, *The Bitter Pill* (London: Corgi Books, 1985); Kevin Hume, "The Pill and Cancer," *Linacre Quarterly* 52 (Nov. 1985) 297–320.

35. There have been many refutations of the use of the principle of totality to justify the use of contraception. See, for instance, Kevin T. Kelly, "Moral Theology Forum: A Positive Approach to *Humanae Vitae*," *Clergy Review* 57 (1972) 108–20, 174–86, 263–75, 330–48, especially 261–73; John F. Kippley, *Birth Control and the Marriage Covenant* (Collegeville, Minn.: Liturgical Press, 1976), 73–82; and

Ralph McInerny, "*Humanae Vitae* and the Judgement of Conscience" in *"Humanae Vitae"*: 20 Anni Dopo (Milan: Edizioni Ares, 1989), 199–209.

36. Louis Dupré may have been one of the originators of this argument: "Natural Law and Birth Control," *Philosophy Today* 9 (1965) 94–100. See also W. Van Der Marck, *Love and Fertility* (New York: Sheed and Ward, 1965), and Louis Janssens, "Considerations on 'Humanae Vitae'," *Louvain Studies* 2 (Spring 1969) 231–53.

37. AAS 45 (1953) 674, my translation. For a commentary on Pius XII's understanding of this principle, see Gerald Kelly, S.J., "Pope Pius XII and the Principle of Totality," *Theological Studies* 16 (1955) 373–96, and "The Morality of Mutilation: Towards a Revision of the Treatise," *Theological Studies* 17 (1956) 322–44.

38. May 14, 1956, AAS 48 (1956) 461–62; the translations cited here are from *The Pope Speaks* 3 (1959) 198–207.

39. Ibid., 200.

40. Ibid.

41. See my article " 'The Many Faces of AIDS' and the Toleration of the Lesser Evil," *International Review of Natural Family Planning* 12:1 (Spring 1988) 1–15.

42. Dec. 6, 1953, AAS 45 (1953) 798–99.

43. The translations are from "International Community and Religious Tolerance," *The Pope Speaks* 1 (1954) 68.

44. For a good explanation of the principle of double effect, see Joseph T. Mangan, S.J., "Making Moral Choices in Conflict Situations," in *Principles of Catholic Moral Life*, ed. William E. May (Chicago: Franciscan Herald Press, 1980), 329–58.

CHAPTER FOUR

1. Jan Grootaers attributes the basing of *Humanae Vitae* on natural law to Karol Wojtyla, "Quelques données concernant la rédaction de l'encyclique 'Humanae Vitae,' " *Paul VI et la Modernité dans l'Église* (Rome: Palais Farnese, 1984) 395.

2. A recent article by Martin Rhonheimer, "Contraception, Sexual Behavior, and Natural Law," *Linacre Quarterly* (May 1989) 20–57, categorizes the current natural law arguments against contraception very much along the lines followed in this chapter. William E. May, " 'Humanae Vitae,' Natural Law, and Catholic Moral Thought," *Linacre Quarterly* 56 (Nov. 1989) 61–87, provides another excellent explanation of natural law arguments and a response to their critics.

3. John Finnis, "Natural Law and Unnatural Acts," *Heythrop Journal* 11 (1970) 365–87, faults the encyclical for "its evident desire to avoid saying anything that would close the debate between three main schools of thought about the proper way of explaining the Christian doctrine on anti-procreative choices." In a note to this sentence (p. 356) he identifies these three schools: (i) a faculty ought not to be perverted (he cites Joseph Fuchs, *De Castitate et de Ordine Sexuali*, 3d ed. [Rome, n.p., 1963] 53, 79): (ii) the language of love ought to be true (he cites Gustave Martelet, "Morale conjugale et vie chrétienne," *Nouvelle Revue Théologique* 87 (1965) 245); (iii) the basic value of procreation ought not to be attacked (he cites Germain Grisez, "Methods of Ethical Inquiry," *Proceedings of the American Catholic Philosophical Association* 41 (1967) and "The First Principle of Practical Reason: A Commentary on the *Summa Theologiae*, 1–2, Question 94, Article 2," *Natural Law Forum* 10 (1965), and G. de Broglie, "Malice intrinsèque du péché et péchés heureux

par leurs conséquences," RSR 24 (1934); 25 (1935); 26 (1936); 27 (1937). Although I agree with Finnis that several different kinds of argument can be found in *Humanae Vitae*, I think the openness of the encyclical is a strength, not a weakness, for I believe sound arguments can be made by several schools with the proper refinements.

4. Cahal Daly, "Natural Law Morality Today," *American Ecclesiastical Review* 153 (1965) 379.

5. For early versions of this argument, see John Noonan, *Contraception* (1965; reprint Cambridge, Mass.: Belknap Press, 1986) 88–91.

6. A recent defense of this position has been made by Carlo Caffarra, "*Humanae Vitae: Venti Anni Dopo*," in *Humanae Vitae: 20 Anni Dopo* (Milan: Edizioni Ares, 1988) 183–95. He argues:

As was recently underlined, in the corpus of law that was in force until 1917, the Church used a very strong expression with regard to whoever—married or not—had recourse to contraception: "*tamquam homicida habeatur*" [let him be considered one guilty of homicide]. The equivalence, or better, the analogy that canon law established for centuries between homicide and contraception, no longer surprises us if we do not look exclusively at the material nature of the behaviour in the two cases, but rather at the intention or movement of the will that has recourse to contraception. Ultimately, in fact, the decision is rationalized and motivated by the judgement: "it is not good that a new human person should exist." . . . The anti-love inherent in contraception is identically antilife, since there is always implicit in it the refusal of the goodness of being, the refusal to exclaim: "How beautiful, how good it is that you should exist."

7. Thomas Aquinas, *Summa Theologiae*, I–II, q. 94, art. 2, in *Basic Writings of Saint Thomas Aquinas*, ed. Anton C. Pegis (New York: Random House, 1945) vol. 1, 866.

8. Even Plato had an intimation of this. In the *Phaedrus*, Diotima says, "Conception, we know, takes place when man and woman come together, but there's a divinity in human propagation, an immortal something in the midst of man's mortality which is incompatible with any kind of discord" (206c); *Plato's Collected Dialogues*, ed. Edith Hamilton (Princeton, N.J.: Princeton University Press, 1961).

9. *Summa Theologiae*, I–II, q. 50, art. 5.

10. Caffarra, "*Humanae Vitae.*" His statement aroused the ire of many theologians who accused him of equating contraception with homicide. The Declaration of Cologne was provoked by his speech.

11. This argument is made by John C. Ford, S.J., Germain Grisez, Joseph Boyle, John Finnis, and William E. May, *The Teaching of Humanae Vitae: A Defense* (San Francisco: Ignatius Press, 1988). See Appendix 4 for a consideration of Grisez's critique of earlier arguments against contraception made in *Contraception and the Natural Law* (Milwaukee: Bruce Publishing Co., 1964). This appendix also presents my critique of Grisez's arguments against contraception, both his earlier ones and the more recent arguments presented in this section.

These ethicists have a distinguished history of writing in defense of *Humanae Vitae*. The following is the list of their writings on contraception and related questions given in footnote 4 in their text (39): Germain Grisez, *Contraception and the Natural Law* (Milwaukee: Bruce Publishing Co., 1964); "Marriage: Reflections Based on St. Thomas and Vatican Council II," *Catholic Mind* 64 (June 1966) 4–

19; "Contraception and Reality," *Triumph,* in 3 parts: (Feb. 1968) 21–24; (Mar. 1968) 18–21; (Apr. 1968) 27–30; *The Way of the Lord Jesus,* vol. 1, *Christian Moral Principles* (Chicago: Franciscan Herald Press, 1983), chaps. 35 and 36; Joseph M. Boyle, Jr., "Human Action, Natural Rhythms, and Contraception: A Response to Noonan," *American Journal of Jurisprudence,* 26 (1981) 32–46; John Finnis, "Natural Law and Unnatural Acts," *Heythrop Journal* 2 (1970) 365–87; "Humanae Vitae: Its Background and Aftermath," *International Review of Natural Family Planning* 4:2 (1980) 141–53; "Personal Integrity, Sexual Morality and Responsible Parenthood," *Rivista di Studi sulla Persona e la Famiglia: Anthropos* 1 (1985) 43–55; William E. May, *Sex, Marriage, and Chastity: Reflections of a Catholic Layman, Spouse, and Parent* (Chicago: Franciscan Herald Press, 1981); *Contraception and Catholicism* Common Faith Tract No. 5 (Front Royal, Va.: Christendom Publications, 1983); *Contraception, "Humanae Vitae," and Catholic Moral Thought* (Chicago: Franciscan Herald Press, 1984); Ronald Lawler, O.F.M. Cap., Joseph M. Boyle, Jr., William E. May, *Catholic Sexual Ethics: A Summary, Explanation, and Defense* (Huntington, Ind.: Our Sunday Visitor, 1985).

See, also, William E. May, "The Sanctity of Human Life, Marriage and the Family in the Thought of Pope John Paul II," *Annales Theologici* 2:1 (1988) 83–97, and "The Moral Methodology of Vatican Council II and the Teaching of *Humanae Vitae* and *Persona Humana,*" *Anthropotes* 5:1 (1989) 29–45.

12. Grisez, *The Teaching of Humanae Vitae,* 36.

13. Ibid., 46.   14. Ibid.

15. Ibid., 62.

16. Grisez and other ethicists acknowledge that although recent Church teaching does not follow their line of argumentation, it does recognize the "antilife" character of contraception. They cite Paul VI's "Homily on the Feast of Saints Peter and Paul," June 29, 1978, AAS 70 (1978) 397, and John Paul II's "Homily at the Mass for Youth," Nairobi, Kenya, Aug. 17, 1985; *Insegnamenti di Giovanni Paolo II,* vol. 8, pt. 2 (Rome: Libreria Editrice Vaticana, 1985); see Grisez, *Teaching of Humanae Vitae,* n. 3.

17. John Finnis in "Natural Law in *Humanae Vitae,*" *Law Quarterly Review* 84 (1968) 467–71, lays out the lines of an argument similar to the latest Grisez, Boyle, Finnis, and May argument and states that this argument "itself obviously has nothing to do with respect for biological processes *qua* biological" (470).

18. The systematic presentation of the principles undergirding their thought have been published widely over the years and have undergone some refinement. See particularly Germain Grisez, "The First Principle of Practical Reason: A Commentary on the *Summa Theologiae* 1–2, Question 94, Article 2," *Natural Law Forum* 10 (1965) 168–201, and Germain Grisez, *The Way of the Lord Jesus,* vol. 1 *Christian Moral Principles* (Chicago: Franciscan Herald Press, 1983). A recent statement of their views can be found in Germain Grisez, Joseph Boyle, and John Finnis, "Practical Principles, Moral Truth, and Ultimate Ends," *American Journal of Jurisprudence* 32 (1987) 99–151. Russell Hittinger has offered a critique of their understanding of natural law and Thomism in his *A Critique of the New Natural Law Theory* (Notre Dame, Ind.: University of Notre Dame Press, 1987). A response to Hittinger (and a counterresponse) can be found in Germain Grisez, "A Critique of Russell Hittinger's Book, *A Critique of the New Natural Law Theory,*" *New Scholasticism* 62:4 (Autumn 1988) 438–66.

19. The foremost defender of this view is John Paul II, whose arguments are

discussed in this chapter and again more fully in Chapter 8. A text that incorporates the teachings of John Paul and provides a response to many of the current procontraceptive arguments is William E. May's *Sex, Marriage, and Chastity* (Chicago: Franciscan Herald Press, 1981). Some consider Gustave Martelet, S.J., one who did much to advance the personalist values of marriage, to be among the theologians highly influential in the writing of *Humanae Vitae*. Indeed, Paul VI recommended a text by Martelet, *Amour Conjugal et Renouveau Conciliare* (Lyon: Éditions Xavier Mappus, 1967), in a speech delivered shortly after the encyclical was promulgated, "The Genesis of 'Humanae Vitae,' " *The Pope Speaks* 13 (1968) 209. Also see Lawrence Porter, "The Theologian of Humanae Vitae," *Thomist* 42:3 (July 1978) 464–509; Jan Grootaers reports that Martelet and Carlo Colombo were the theologians who most closely advised Paul VI: "Quelques données concernant la rédaction de l'encyclique 'Humanae Vitae,' " *Paul VI et la Modernité dans l'Église* (École Française de Rome: Palais Farnèse, 1984) 390. Among the relevant works by Martelet are "Mariage, amour, sacrement," *Nouvelle Théologique* 85 (1963) 577–97; "Morale conjugale et vie chrétienne," *Nouvelle Théologique* 87 (1965) 245–66; "Pour mieux comprendre l'encyclique 'Humanae Vitae' I and II," *Nouvelle Revue Théologique* 9 and 10 (Nov. and Dec. 1968) 897–917, 1009–63; "Dix ans après *Humanae Vitae*," *Nouvelle Revue Théologique* 101 (1979) 246–59; and "Essai sur La Signification de l'Encyclique 'Humanae Vitae,' " *Paul VI et la Modernité*, 399–415. The work of Dietrich Von Hildebrand is also key, particularly *The Encyclical Humanae Vitae: A Sign of Contradiction* (Chicago: Franciscan Herald Press, 1969). See, too, the pre-*Humanae Vitae* article by Paul Quay, "Contraception and Conjugal Love," *Theological Studies* 22 (Mar. 1961) 18–40, and his later book, *The Christian Meaning of Human Sexuality* (Evanston, Ill.: Credo House, 1985). See also Mary Rosera Joyce, *The Meaning of Contraception* (New York: Alba House, 1969). The text by Ronald Lawler, Joseph M. Boyle, Jr., and William E. May, *Catholic Sexual Ethics* (Huntington, Ind.: Our Sunday Visitor, 1985), explains Catholic teaching on human sexuality while showing that there need be no incompatibility between personalist values and natural law principles. Lawler's text also provides a strong "anticonsequentialist" argument.

 20. The translations for passages from *Gaudium et Spes* are from *Vatican II: The Conciliar and Postconciliar Documents*, ed. Austin Flannery; hereafter the section number is given in the text.

 21. For a defense of the connection between *Humanae Vitae* and the personalist values of *Gaudium et Spes* see Karol Wojtyla, *Fruitful and Responsible Love* (New York: Seabury Press, 1979). In his article, "La visione antropologica dell' 'Humanae Vitae,' " *Lateranum* 44 (1978) 124–45, he maintains that *Humanae Vitae* signals progression in the Church's teaching as stated in *Gaudium et Spes* in its consideration of the subjective meaning of conjugal love. A historical note on *Humanae Vitae* supports an interpretation that would see *Humanae Vitae* closely connected with *Gaudium et Spes*; Lawrence Porter in "The Theologian of *Humanae Vitae*," *Thomist* 42:3 (July 1978) 464–509, argues that Gustave Martelet was the theologian "behind" *Humanae Vitae*. A central argument in this regard is the incorporation of personalist values of *Gaudium et Spes* into *Humanae Vitae*, an enterprise that Porter claims was a concern of Martelet's. Dissenters tend to claim that *Humanae Vitae* failed to incorporate the advances of *Gaudium et Spes*; see, for example, Leonhard M. Weber, "Excursus on *Humanae Vitae*," in *Commentary on the Documents of Vatican*

II, ed. Herbert Vorgrimler, vol. 5 (New York: Herder and Herder, 1969) 397–402; Louis Janssens, "Considerations on *Humanae Vitae*," *Louvain Studies* 2 (Spring 1969) 231–52; Philippe Delhaye, "The Encyclical and the Council," *Tablet*, Nov. 16, 1968, 1132–34; "L'Encyclique *Humanae Vitae* et l'Enseignement de Vatican II sur le Mariage et la Famille (*Gaudium et Spes*)," *Bijdragen* 29 (1968) 350–68; Michael Callahan, "The Changing Face of Catholic Moral Theology: From the Constitution De Ordine to Gaudium et Spes," *Louvain Studies* 3 (1970/71) 41–50.

22. DSP, 36.

23. Some critics of John Paul claim that he has an excessively romantic notion of love. This charge will be examined in Chapter 8.

24. John Paul II, *Reflections on Humanae Vitae* (Boston: St. Paul Editions, 1984); hereafter ROHV. Much of the material in this section is adapted from my article, "Pope John Paul II and *Humanae Vitae*," *International Review of Natural Family Planning* 10:2 (Summer 1986) 95–112.

25. Cormac Burke, "Marriage and Contraception," in *Creative Love: The Ethics of Human Reproduction*, ed. John Boyle (Front Royal, Va.: Christendom Press, 1989) 151–67. This essay has also been printed in *Linacre Quarterly* 55 (Feb. 1988) 44–45; see also Bartholomew Kiely, S.J., "Contraception, In Vitro Fertilization and the Principle of Inseparability," *Linacre Quarterly* 56 (May 1989) 68–75. The article by Paul Quay S.J., "Contraception and Conjugal Love," written several years before *Humanae Vitae*, remains a superb defense of the claim that contraception violates the value of conjugal love as well as the value of procreation and even anticipates John Paul's claims that contraceptive sexual intercourse is a lie. He also seems to be one of the forerunners in speaking of sexual intercourse as a kind of language and of contracepted sex as a lie (30 ff.). Mary Rosera Joyce, *Meaning of Contraception*, before *Humanae Vitae*, offered a powerful argument against contraception as analogous with lying.

26. John Kippley makes a similar argument, which he bases on what he calls "the theology of the covenant." He provides a sketch of it in his book *Birth Control and the Marriage Covenant* (Collegeville, Minn.: Liturgical Press, 1976). A new and revised edition of this text is being prepared for publication.

27. In commenting on the claim of Paul VI in HV 12 that modern Men are capable of understanding the reasonableness of the condemnation of contraception, John Paul states:

That "reasonable character" concerns not only the truth of the ontological dimension, namely, that which corresponds to the fundamental structure of the marital act, but it concerns also the same truth in the subjective and psychological dimension, that is to say, the correct understanding of the intimate structure of the marital act, that is, the adequate rereading of the significances corresponding to this structure and of their inseparable connection, in view of a morally right behavior. Herein lies precisely the moral norm and the corresponding regulation of the human acts in the sphere of sexuality. In this sense we say that the moral norm is identified with the rereading, in truth, of the "language of the body" (ROHV, 8).

28. John Paul II, *The Role of the Family in the Modern World* (Boston: St. Paul Editions, 1981) sec. 32.

29. See also, Quay, "Contraception and Conjugal Love," 30 ff.

30. ROHV, 33–34.

31. For a rich interpretation of the kind of lie that is being spoken through contracepted sexual intercourse, see Burke, "Marriage and Contraception," 160.

32. Ibid., 154.

33. Ibid., 155.

34. Catholics may take as a powerful sign of the inseparability of the meanings of conjugal love the fact that a marriage is not considered consummated until the spouses engage in a *noncontracepted* act of intercourse. That is, until they engage in such an act they have not engaged in a marital or conjugal act; thus for sexual intercourse to express and mean *spousal* love it must also express and mean an ordination to the creation of new life.

35. For a fuller statement of the good that children are to a marriage, see Cormac Burke, "Children and Values," *International Review of Natural Family Planning* 12:3 (Fall 1988) 181–92.

36. William E. May, " 'Begotten, Not Made': Reflections on the Laboratory Generation of Human Life," *Perspectives in Bioethics*, ed. Ronald D. Lawler and William E. May, vol. 1 (New Britain, Conn.: Mariel Publications, 1983).

37. Many fine articles explaining the difference between contraception and natural methods of family planning have been written. See the early efforts of Mary Rosera Joyce, *Meaning of Contraception*, chap. 8; Brian Shanley, O.P., "The Moral Difference between Natural Family Planning and Contraception," *Linacre Quarterly* 54:1 (Feb. 1987) 48–60; Elzbieta Wojcik, "Natural Regulation of Conception and Contraception," *International Review of Natural Family Planning* 9:4 (Winter 1985) 306–26; Joseph Boyle, "Contraception and Natural Family Planning," *International Review of Natural Family Planning* 4:4 (Winter 1980) 309–15; G.E.M. Anscombe, *Contraception and Chastity* (London: Catholic Truth Society, 1975); and Donald DeMarco, "Perspective: The Chief Obstacle in Teaching NFP," *International Review of Natural Family Planning*, 10:1 (Spring 1986) 65–68.

38. Useful texts for an introduction to these methods are John and Sheila Kippley, *The Art of Natural Family Planning*, 3d ed. (Cincinnati, Ohio: Couple to Couple League International 1985), and Nona Aguilar, *No-Pill, No-Risk Birth Control* (New York: Rawson Associates, 1986).

39. Michel Rouche, "La préparation de l'encyclique 'Humanae Vitae,' " *Paul VI et la Modernité, dans l'Église* (École Française de Rome: Palais Farnese, 1984), 370–71; he cites the report written on these programs: François et Michèle Guy, *Ile Maurice: Régulation des Naissances et Action Familiale* (Lyon: Éditions Xavier Mappus, 1968).

40. Complete infertility or reduced infertility in certain age groups is, of course, unhealthy and unnatural, and it is therefore permissible to make use of practices that restore individuals to a state of fertility.

41. G. E. M. Anscombe, *Contraception and Chastity*, 19.

42. Joyce, *Meaning of Contraception*, 42.

43. Anscombe, *Contraception and Chastity*, 20. This analogy bears some relationship to the argument given in Chapter 5 based on the concept *munus*.

44. Sidney and Daniel Callahan, *Understanding the Differences* (Hastings, N.Y.: Hastings Center Series in Ethics, 1984), and Kristan Luker, *Abortion and the Politics of Motherhood* (Berkeley: University of California Press, 1984), contend that the opposing sides in the abortion debate have very different understandings of the

world and our place within it; these very much parallel the differences between users of contraception and users of NFP.

45. This letter was published in the "Repartee" section of the *National Catholic Reporter* on October 11, 1987.

46. I know of no formal studies on this question; an informal study is in Aguilar, *No-Pill, No-Risk*, 195. See also Wojcik, "Natural Regulation," who reports that Josef Rotzer, an Austrian doctor, reports that his records kept over thirty years of fourteen hundred practitioners of NFP, reported no incidence of divorce (315). Pat Homan of the Couple to Couple League has informed me that of their eight hundred and fifty five couples certified to teach NFP, nine have divorced.

47. Robert T. Michael, "Why Did the U.S. Divorce Rate Double within a Decade?" *Research in Population* 6 (Greenwich, Conn.: JAI Press, 1988) 361–99; see also his "Determinants of Divorce," *Sociological Economics*, ed. Louis Levy-Garboua (London: SAGE Publications, 1979) 233–54, and his "The Rise in Divorce Rates, 1960–1974: Age-Specific Components," *Demography* 15:2 (May 1978) 177–82.

48. For a review of studies on the effectiveness of natural methods, see Kippley and Kippley, *Art of Natural Family Planning*, 14 ff.

CHAPTER FIVE

1. This section has been greatly assisted by the unpublished work of James Lehrberger, O.Cist.

2. In early Church condemnations of contraception, Genesis 38:1–9, the story of Onan, is often cited as a scriptural condemnation of contraception. More recent biblical scholarship identifies Onan's sin not as one of "spilling seed" but of refusing to do his duty by his brothers' wife. A recent study by Charles D. Provan, *The Bible and Birth Control* (Monongahela, Pa.: Zimmer Printing, 1989), makes the case for the immorality of contraception from the Bible; Provan argues for a traditional understanding of the Onan incident.

3. Translations for Scripture are taken from *The New American Bible* (Camden, N.J.: Thomas Nelson, 1971).

4. *Humanae Vitae* cites Scripture six times, in sections 8, 18, 25 (three times), and 28; there are nine additional scriptural references in the footnotes.

5. See footnotes 31, 33, 34, 35, 36, and 37 to HV 25.

6. Much of this section is taken from my article, "The *Munus* of Transmitting Human Life: A New Approach to *Humanae Vitae*," *The Thomist* 54:3 (July 3, 1990) 385–427.

7. The translations for passages from the conciliar documents are from *Vatican II: The Conciliar and Postconciliar Documents*, ed. Austin Flannery, O.P.; hereafter the section number is given in the text.

8. See the introduction to the translation of *Humanae Vitae* in Appendix 1.

9. Charlton T. Lewis and Charles Short, *A Latin Dictionary* (Oxford: Clarendon Press, 1975), lists *officium* (duty), *ministerium* (function), and *honos* (honor) as synonyms for *munus* but also notes that it is a *munus* that confers or entails *officia* ("Munus significat officium, cum dicitur quis munere fungi. Item donum quod officii causa datur" ["*munus* means 'duty' when someone is said to perform a *munus*. Also,

it is a gift that is given for the sake of a duty"]). Cicero uses the phrase *munus officii*, which clearly signals a difference between the two words.

10. Austin Flannery, O.P., ed., *Vatican Council II* (Northport, N.Y.: Costello Publishing Co., 1975).

11. Walter M. Abbott, S.J., ed., *The Documents of Vatican II* (Chicago: Follett Publishing Co., 1966).

12. Roy J. Deferrari, *A Latin-English Dictionary of St. Thomas Aquinas* (Boston: St. Paul Editions, 1960) lists only "gift" as a suitable translation for *munus*.

13. The abbreviations for the texts of Vatican II are standard. The translation given here is my own.

14. Translations for *Familiaris Consortio* are from *The Role of the Christian Family in the Modern World* (Boston: St. Paul Editions, 1981).

15. Karol Wojtyla, *Sources of Renewal*, trans. P. S. Falla (San Francisco: Harper & Row, 1980); 219, originally published in Poland in 1972.

16. Ibid., 220.

17. See the statement issued by a number of Catholic theologians under the leadership of Charles Curran, in *The Birth Control Debate*, ed. Robert G. Hoyt (Kansas City, Mo.: National Catholic Reporter, 1968) 180.

18. John Giles Milhaven, "The Grounds of the Opposition to 'Humanae Vitae,' " *Thought* 44 (1969) 343–57. Perhaps the most famous justification for the legitimacy of dissent and one of the most influential is that by Karl Rahner, S.J., "On the Encyclical 'Humanae Vitae,' " *Catholic Mind* 66 (Nov. 1968) 28–45, which also appeared in *National Catholic Reporter* Sept. 18, 1968. For a sampling of the argumentation made in behalf of conscientious dissent, see *Conscience: Its Freedom and Limitations*, ed. William C. Bier, S.J. (New York: Fordham University Press, 1971).

19. John Horgan, *Humanae Vitae and the Bishops* (Shannon: Irish University Press, 1972) 364.

20. See Chapter 3 for a discussion of this principle.

21. Hoyt, *Birth Control Debate*, 169–70.

22. Ibid., 172.

23. Horgan, *Humanae Vitae and the Bishops*, 360.

24. The document in its entirety can be found in *The Pope Speaks* 13:4 (1969) 377–94.

25. *Verordnungsblatt der Erzdiozese Salzburg* 4 (Apr. 1988) 54–58.

26. The bishops of Manitoba in April 1989 issued a pastoral letter, "Responsible Parenthood," which expressed strong support for *Humanae Vitae*.

27. The *locus classicus* for this is Thomas Aquinas, *Summa Theologiae*, I–II, q. 19, art. 5, 6.

28. Ibid., q. 6, art. 8.

29. See the statement of the U.S. bishops, *Pope Speaks*, 385.

30. See Carlo Caffarra, "Conscience, Truth, and Magisterium in Conjugal Morality" in *Marriage and Family* (San Francisco: Ignatius Press, 1989) 21–36.

31. Flannery, *Vatican II*, 379.

32. The U.S. bishops ("Human Life in Our Days," *The Pope Speaks* 13 [1969] 377–95) are quoting *A Letter to the Duke of Norfolk* (384). Bishop (now Cardinal) Bernardin issued a clarifying statement after the release of the bishops' statement, in which he stated, "The bishops in no way intended to imply that there is any divergence between their statement and the teaching of the Holy Father. It is true

that people must form their consciences, but it is equally true that they have the responsibility to form a correct conscience." He then cited *Lumen Gentium* 25 ("Statements on the Birth Control Encyclical," *Catholic Mind* 66 [Sept. 1968] 2).

The Irish bishops have also issued a statement on conscience, and their commentary on this passage from Newman is much to the point:

> The type of case Newman has in mind is where the Pope gives an injunction or precept in some matter of conduct to a member of the Church. But what he has to say applies with even greater force to the person who appeals to conscience against a declaration by the Pope on what the moral law requires in a particular matter. This is all the more true if (as happened, for example with the Encyclical *Humanae Vitae* of Paul VI, from which many claimed the right to dissent) the Pope, after long consideration, speaks formally and deliberately to settle a matter of public controversy in the Church, and in doing so confirms a doctrine traditionally held. Even a person with the necessary theological competence to judge such an issue, before claiming the right to dissent, would still have to ask himself whether his personal judgment, however reliable and well-founded he believed it to be, could possibly take precedence over such a decision of the Pope. For it is the Pope's divinely appointed task to give direction to the Church in these matters, and in so doing he is assured of the special assistance of the Spirit of Christ. (*Conscience and Morality* [Boston: St. Paul Editions, 1980] 19)

33. "Statement Accompanying Encyclical *Humanae Vitae,*" *Catholic Mind* 52.

34. As reported by Brian Harrison, "Appendix III: *Humanae Vitae e Infallibilitá,*" in *Religious Liberty and Contraception* (Melbourne: John XXIII Fellowship Co-op. Ltd., 1988) 175. Appendix III is a book review of Ermenegildo Lio's book, *Humanae Vitae e Infallibilitá: il Concilio, Paolo VI e Giovanni Paolo II* (Vatican City: Libreria Editrice Vaticana, 1986).

35. See, for instance, Karl Rahner, "On the Encyclical *Humanae Vitae*"; Gerard P. Kirk, S.J., "*Humanae Vitae* and the Assent Due It," *Continuum* 6 (1968) 288–94; John McHugh, "The Doctrinal Authority of the Encyclical 'Humanae Vitae,' " *Clergy Review* 54 (1969) 586–96; 680–93, 791–802; Sabbas J. Kilian, "The Question of Authority in 'Humanae Vitae,' " and John Giles Milhaven, "The Grounds of Opposition to 'Humanae Vitae,' " both in *Thought* 44:174 (Autumn 1969) 327–42 and 343–57; Peter Harris, "The Church and Moral Decision," *New Blackfriars* 51 (1970) 518–27; Gregory Baum, "The New Encyclical on Contraception," *Homiletic and Pastoral Review* 68 (Sept. 1968) 1001–4; Charles E. Curran and Robert E. Hunt, *Dissent In and For the Church: Theologians and Humanae Vitae* (New York: Sheed and Ward, 1969), and *The Responsibility of Dissent: The Church and Academic Freedom* (New York: Sheed and Ward, 1969); *Contraception: Authority and Dissent*, ed. Charles Curran (New York: Herder and Herder, 1969); Joseph A. Komonchak, "*Humanae Vitae* and Its Reception: Ecclesiological Reflections," *Theological Studies* 39 (1978) 221–57. All the above are by dissenters. Robert J. Dionne, who holds the teaching of *Humanae Vitae* to be true, argues that its proper theological note seems to be "*doctrina catholica,* not *de fide catholica,*": " 'Humanae Vitae' Reexamined: A Response," *Homiletic and Pastoral Review* (July 1973) 57–64.

36. Joseph F. Costanzo in "Papal Magisterium and 'Humanae Vitae,' " *Thought* 44:174 (Autumn 1969) 377–412, does not argue precisely that the teaching of the document is infallible but observes:

There is more impression than substance in pointing to the distinction between the infallibility of a solem *ex cathedra* definition and the authentic and authoritative teaching of the Roman pontiff. The insinuating argument is that what is not formally infallible is fallible. It supposes that infallibility may not derive from another source than a solemn *ex cathedra* definition. Church documents and the "theologians" themselves have traditionally acknowledged an infallibility *ex ordinario magisterio*. This means more than mere longevity but a continuing active and constant witness of the teaching authority of the Church to the general moral principle that opposes all contraceptive practices, the novelty being only its authoritative application to specific problems as they emerged in time. Further, who could honestly question the gravity and solemnity of the historical occasion for *Humanae Vitae?* The world-wide expectation of the papal pronouncement by the faithful and non-faithful alike, the critical nature of the controversy, the largely predictable divisive consequences—all these attest to the awesome responsibility with which Pope Paul has spoken. (396–97)

He concludes: "There was no need for the formality of an *ex cathedra* definition" (397). Nicholas Halligan, O.P., "The Church as Teacher," *Thomist* 33 (1969) 675–717, argues: "Every authentic or official teaching of pope (or local bishop) binds in conscience by virtue of its authority and not (by supposition) of its infallibility. Authority determines the obligation to give assent or obedience, infallibility only determines the kind of assent or adherence. As a matter of fact, infallibility is not of itself precluded from every non–*ex cathedra* pronouncement simply because it is in a non–*ex cathedra* mode, e.g., from the Council's teaching on episcopal collegiality; it merely cannot be verified" (705).

37. Harrison's review ("Appendix III") provides a good summary of Lio's work (*Humanae Vitae e Infallibilità*).

38. "Contraception and the Infallibility of the Ordinary Magisterium," originally published in *Theological Studies* 39:2 (June 1978) 258–312, and reprinted in *The Teaching of Humanae Vitae: A Defense* (San Francisco: Ignatius Press, 1988). References here are to the reprint. Russell Shaw summarized this argument in "Contraception, Infallibility and the Ordinary Magisterium," *Homiletic and Pastoral Review* 78 (July 1978) 9–19. Garth Hallett, S.J., responded to the Ford-Grisez argument in "Contraception and Prescriptive Infallibility," *Theological Studies* 43 (1982) 629–50, and Francis A. Sullivan, S.J., critiqued the Ford-Grisez argument in *Magisterium: Teaching Authority in the Catholic Church* (New York: Paulist Press, 1983) 119–52. Grisez replied to Hallett in "Infallibility and Contraception: A Reply to Garth Hallett," *Theological Studies* 47 (1986) 134–45, and to Sullivan in "Infallibility and Specific Moral Norms: A Review Discussion," *Thomist* 49 (1985) 248–87. Robert J. Dionne has two lengthy footnotes commenting on the Grisez-Sullivan debate in *The Papacy and the Church* (New York: Philosophical Library, 1987) 468–69.

39. Grisez, "Infallibility and Specific Moral Norms: A Review Discussion," *The Thomist*, 268.

40. Grisez and Ford, *The Teaching of Humanae Vitae: A Defense*, 145.

41. Ibid., 171.

42. Sullivan, *Magisterium*, 144.

43. Brian Harrison also replied to Sullivan in appendix II of *Religious Liberty*.

44. Grisez, "Infallibility and Specific Moral Norms: A Review Discussion," *Thomist*, 285, citing John Paul II, "General Audience of 18 July," *L'Osservatore Romano* (Eng. ed.) (July 23, 1984) 1.

45. *Catholic Mind* 66 (Sept. 1968) 2.

46. See, for instance, Joseph Costanzo, "Academic Dissent: An Original Ecclesiology," *Thomist* 34:4 (Oct. 1970) 636–53; see particularly 648–53.

47. See, for instance, Harrison, *Religious Liberty*; William H. Marshner, "*Dignitatis Humanae* and Traditional Teaching on Church and State," *Faith & Reason* 9:3 (Fall 1983) 222–48; William G. Most, "Religious Liberty: What the Texts Demand," *Faith & Reason* 9:3 (Fall 1983) 196–209.

48. Grisez and Ford offer such an argument, *The Teachings of Humanae Vitae*, 190ff.

49. See Chapter 2 and many of the sources cited therein.

CHAPTER SIX

1. The literature that has been generated on *Humanae Vitae* has been immense. For collections of essays written against *Humanae Vitae* shortly after its release, see Andrew Bauer, ed., *The Debate on Birth Control* (New York: Hawthorne Books, 1969); Daniel J. Callahan, S.J., ed., *The Catholic Case for Contraception* (New York: Macmillan Co., 1969); and Charles E. Curran, ed., *Contraception: Authority and Dissent* (New York: Herder and Herder, 1969). A few representative articles are James Tunstead Burtchaell, " 'Human Life' and Humane Love: The Birth Control Encyclical Was Disappointingly Inadequate and Largely Fallacious," *Commonweal* 89 (1968/69) 245–52; Joseph Coppens, "A Symposium on 'Humanae Vitae,' " *Louvain Studies* 2 (Spring 1969) 211–30; Louis Janssens, "Considerations on 'Humanae Vitae,' " *Louvain Studies* 2 (Spring 1969) 231–53. Denis F. O'Callaghan, "After the Encyclical," *Furrow* 19 (1968) 633–41; Timothy C. Potts, "The Arguments of *Humanae Vitae*," *Month* 227 (1969) 144–55. A fairly exhaustive listing of relevant articles can be found in the biyearly "Notes on Moral Theology" in *Theological Studies*. Richard A. McCormick, S.J., who has written nearly all of these notes since 1965, has reprinted his contributions in *Notes on Moral Theology: 1965–1980* (Lanham, Md.: University Press of America, 1981) and *Notes on Moral Theology: 1981–1984* (Lanham, Md.: University Press of America, 1984).

2. Bernard Haering, "The Encyclical Crisis," *Commonweal* 88:20 (Sept. 6, 1968) 588–94, 588. Ten years after *Humanae Vitae* the situation had not changed; as Joseph A. Komonchak, "*Humanae Vitae* and Its Reception: Ecclesiological Reflections," *Theological Studies* 39 (1978) 221–57, stated: "Almost since the day it was issued, *Humanae Vitae* (HV) has been the *signum cui contradicetur* which Pope Paul VI anticipated it might become. The encyclical met with an opposition and dissent stronger and more public than any papal statement within memory, and the controversy that ensued quickly excited profound and even violent emotions and reactions. If emotions are somewhat calmer today and a certain peace, or at least truce, now rules over the Church's pastoral practice, opinions have not ceased to be divided on the subject and authority of the encyclical" (221).

3. A translation of this speech is available in *Catholic Mind* 66 (Sept. 1968) 49–57; this passage is found on 54.

4. Ibid., 55.

5. Ibid.

6. A copy of this statement can be found in Callahan, *The Catholic Case for Contraception*, 67–70. A list of those who signed the statement can be found in *National Catholic Reporter*, Aug. 14, 1968, 8.

7. See the Sept. 18, 1968, issue of *National Catholic Reporter*, 6–7. The same article has been reprinted in *Catholic Mind* 66 (Nov. 1968) 28–45.

8. Karl Rahner, S.J., "On the Encyclical *Humanae Vitae*," *Catholic Mind* 66 (Nov. 1968) 2–4. Reports on many of the responses to *Humanae Vitae* can be found in the Aug. 7, 1968, issue of *National Catholic Reporter*; these responses and samples of other relevant documents have been reprinted in *The Birth Control Debate*, ed. Robert G. Hoyt (Kansas City, Mo.: National Catholic Reporter, 1968).

9. See "Curia Controlled Pope's Decision," *National Catholic Reporter*, Aug. 21, 1968, 6.

10. *National Catholic Reporter*, Aug. 7, 1968, 9.

11. Ibid., Sept. 18, 1968, 7.

12. A collection of a large number of these statements is to be found in John Horgan, *Humanae Vitae and the Bishops* (Shannon: Irish University Press, 1972).

13. *National Catholic Reporter*, Aug. 14, 1968, 8.

14. See the article "American Theologians Critical," *National Catholic Reporter*, Aug. 7, 1968, 1; John Noonan immediately issued a statement declaring the document fallible, "Historical Precedents for Fallible Statements," *National Catholic Reporter*, Aug. 7, 1968, 9; see also a statement by Mr. and Mrs. Patrick Crowley, leaders of the Christian family movement and members of the commission, in *National Catholic Reporter*, Aug. 7, 1968, 6; twenty years later, Mrs. Crowley remarked, "I'm afraid I've never forgiven the church for *Humanae Vitae*," *National Catholic Reporter*, Aug. 12, 1988, 5.

15. *National Catholic Reporter*, Aug. 7, 1968, 11.

16. Both polls are reported in *National Catholic Reporter*, Sept. 11, 1968, 9.

17. Jean Guitton, *The Pope Speaks: Dialogues of Paul VI with Jean Guitton*, trans. Anne and Christopher Fremantle (New York: Meredith Press, 1968), 270.

18. Ibid., 276.

19. Ibid.

20. These talks "The Genesis of 'Humanae Vitae,' " given to a general audience on July 31, 1968; "What the Encyclical Is and Is Not," remarks before Angelus recitation, Aug. 4, 1968; and "Prayers Sought for the Encyclical," remarks before Angelus recitation Aug. 11, 1968) are printed in Andrew Bauer, ed., *The Debate on Birth Control* (New York: Hawthorne Books, 1969) 30–41.

21. Bauer, *Debate on Birth Control*, 30.

22. Ibid., 34. 23. Ibid., 35.

24. Ibid. 25. Ibid., 38.

26. Ibid., 40–41.

27. Paul VI, "Speech to the Teams of Our Lady," May 4, 1970, trans. Marc Calegari from an unpublished manuscript.

28. A further defense of *Humanae Vitae* by Paul VI can be found in Jean Guitton, *Oeuvres Complètes* (Paris: Desclée de Brouwer, 1986) 944–49.

29. See, for instance, Edward V. Vacek, S.J., "Proportionalism: One View of the Debate," *Theological Studies* 46 (1985) 287–314, who observes: "The advocates of P [proportionalism] not only do not think it is opposed to a natural-law theory, but usually count it as one of the leading forms of natural law. The problem is that 'natural law' has many meanings. If it means an objective ethic, or an experience-

based ethic, or an ethic that pays special attention to the structures of human existence, P certainly strives to be just that" (288). See Chapter 7, n. 4.

30. See John O'Brien, "Father Haering Speaks on Marriage and Family Planning," *Homiletics and Pastoral Review* 69 (July 64) 831–41, and Charles Curran, *Christian Morality Today* (Notre Dame, Ind.: Fides Publishing, 1966).

31. The documentation and history for this case have been published in Charles E. Curran, *Faithful Dissent* (Kansas City, Mo.: Sheed and Ward, 1986). For various evaluations of the event, see "The Curran Case and Its Aftermath," pt. 5, in *Readings in Moral Theology*, ed. Charles E. Curran and Richard A. McCormick, S.J. (New York: Paulist Press, 1988) 357–539. See, also, Charles E. Curran, "My Theological Dissent: The Issues," in *Tensions in Moral Theology* (Notre Dame, Ind.: University of Notre Dame Press, 1988) chap. 1, 7–31.

32. For a report of this statement see Tommaso Ricci, "The 163 Rebels of Cologne," *Thirty Days* 2 (Mar. 1989) 20–21.

33. Richard McCormick, S.J., "Notes on Moral Theology," *Theological Studies* 47 (1986) 77, dates the beginning of this debate to the publication of Peter Knauer's "The Hermeneutic Function of the Principle of Double Effect," *Natural Law Forum* 12 (1967), reprinted in *Readings in Moral Theology*, vol. 1, ed. Charles E. Curran and Richard A. McCormick, S.J. (New York: Paulist Press, 1979), vol. 1. Many of the most significant articles written on this matter before 1977 have been reprinted in this volume.

34. Curran has written extensively on this subject, though many of his treatments are republications of what is essentially the same essay. For the sake of ease in citation, the primary source for his position is the most recent reprinting of his critique of natural law and *Humanae Vitae* in the chapter "Natural Law" in his text *Directions in Fundamental Moral Theology* (Notre Dame, Ind.: University of Notre Dame Press, 1985) (hereafter DIFMT); this passage appears on 128. But see also the chapter "Natural Law" in *Themes in Fundamental Moral Theology* (Notre Dame, Ind.: University of Notre Dame Press, 1977) 27–69; Charles E. Curran and Robert E. Hunt *Dissent In and For the Church: Theologians and Humanae Vitae* (New York: Sheed and Ward, 1969) 155–69 (hereafter DIFC); Charles E. Curran, *Contraception, Authority, and Dissent* (New York: Herder and Herder, 1969) 151–75 (hereafter CAD).

It is Curran's trademark to establish polarized categories for differing perspectives; for instance, he speaks of "both/and" understandings of nature and of "absolutized" versus "relativized" understandings of nature, of "primitive" versus "technological" attitudes, of "classicist" versus "historically conscious" worldviews. These serve to compartmentalize his objections and to simplify complex views, but at the same time this practice obscures some important nuances of sophisticated theories and has a way of forcing the discussion to adopt terms most likely not acceptable to all participants.

35. Curran, DIFM, 120.
36. Ibid., 121.
37. Ibid.
38. Ibid.
39. Ibid., 122.
40. Ibid., 122–23.
41. Ibid., 123.
42. Ibid.

43. Pius XI, *Casti Connubii*, Dec. 31, 1930, AAS 22 (1930) 580; translation from *Casti Connubii: Encyclical Letter of Pius XI n Christian Marriage* (Boston: St. Paul Editions, n.d.) 54–55.

44. Curran, DIFMT, 99.
45. Ibid., 126.

46. Ibid.

47. Ibid., 127.

48. Ibid.

49. Ibid., 126–27.

50. Curran, DIFC, 162.

51. Curran, DIFMT, 127.

52. Ibid., 130.

53. Ibid., 129.

54. Ibid., 130.

55. Ibid., 131.

56. Ibid., 134.

57. Curran, DIFC, 162.

58. Curran, DIFMT, 157.

59. Ibid., 131.

60. Charles E. Curran, *Moral Theology: A Continuing Journey* (Notre Dame, Ind.: University of Notre Dame Press, 1982) 163 ff (hereafter MTACJ). And see his *Transition and Tradition in Moral Theology* (Notre Dame, Ind.: University of Notre Dame Press, 1979) 37ff. (hereafter TTMT).

61. Curran, DIFMT, 138.

62. Ibid., 139.

63. Ibid.

64. Ibid., 140.

65. See Cahal B. Daly, "Natural Law Morality Today," *American Ecclesiastical Review* 153 (1965) 361–98; see 364ff. for some trenchant observations in this regard.

66. Curran, DIFC, 163.

67. Ibid., 164.

68. Ibid.

69. Ibid.

70. Ibid.

71. Bernard Haering, *Medical Ethics* (Notre Dame, Ind.: Fides Publishers, 1973) (hereafter ME). For critiques of Haering's position, see Felix Bak, "Bernard Haering and 'Humanae Vitae,' " *Antonianum* 69 (1974) 198–238, and Joseph Omoregbe, "Evolution in Bernard Haering's Ethical Thinking," *Louvain Studies* 7 (Spring 1978) 45–54.

72. Haering is citing Curran here: "Moral Theology and Genetics," *Cross Currents* 20 (Winter 1970) 73.

73. Haering, ME, 45–46.

74. Ibid., 54.

75. Ibid., 56.

76. Ibid., 61.

77. Ibid., 62.

78. For a critique of this expansion of meaning, see Gerald Kelly, S.J., "The Morality of Mutilation: Towards a Revision of the Treatise," *Theological Studies* 17 (1956) 322–44, and his earlier article "Pope Pius XII and the Principle of Totality," *Theological Studies* 16 (1955) 373–96.

79. Haering, ME, 54.

80. Ibid., 88.

81. Ibid., 86.

82. Bernard Haering, "The Inseparability of the Unitive-Procreative Functions of the Marital Act" in Curran, CAD, 181.

83. Ibid., 182.

84. In several public expressions of dissent from *Humanae Vitae*, Haering remarks, "Over the years I have received at least 50 letters which present cases in which the unsuccessful use of rhythm has led to psychoses for these women [the poor and uneducated] and required treatment for them in mental institutions." (This statement appeared in "The Encyclical Crisis," *Commonweal* 88 [Sept. 6, 1968] 593). This experience clearly touched him deeply and his concern should not be dismissed. It must be asked, however, whether the pill really is the answer. He does not mention this kind of case in his later treatment of sexuality and *Humanae Vitae* in *Free and Faithful in Christ* vol. 2 (New York: Seabury Press, 1979).

85. Haering in Curran, CAD, 184.

86. Haering, ME, 61.

87. Charles E. Curran, *Critical Concerns in Moral Theology* (Notre Dame, Ind.: University of Notre Dame Press, 1984), 12.

88. Ibid., 13.   89. Ibid.

90. Ibid., 15.   91. Curran, DIFMT, 158–61.

92. Curran, "Moral Theology in the Light of Reactions to *Humanae Vitae*," TTMT, 55.

93. Curran, MTACJ, 163.   94. Ibid., 149–50.

95. Bernard Haering, *Free and Faithful in Christ*, 516–30.

96. Ibid., 516, citing HV 10, see also 526–29.

97. Ibid., 519.   98. Ibid.

99. Ibid., 522.

100. Ibid., 527; and see n. 104, which refers to G. Martelet, *Amour Conugal et Renouveau* (Lyon; n.p., 1967) 17. Haering also speaks highly of the work of K. Wojtyla, *Fruitful and Responsible Love* (Slough/New York/Sydney: n.p., 1978).

101. Ibid., 527.   102. Ibid., 528.

103. For a copy of the Cologne statement and the Vatican response, see "The Moral Norms of 'Humanae Vitae,' " *Origins* 18:38 (Mar. 2, 1989) 631–34.

CHAPTER SEVEN

1. The bibliography on this topic is immense, and no attempt is made here to be exhaustive. A fairly thorough list of articles is given in note 3 of Bartholomew Kiely, S.J., "The Impracticality of Proportionalism," *Gregorianum* 66 (1985) 656–85.

Richard McCormick's "Notes on Moral Theology" in *Theological Studies* collected in 2 vols. (*Notes on Moral Theology: 1965–1968* [Lanham, Md.: University Press of America, 1981] and *Notes on Moral Theology: 1981–1984* [Lanham, Md.: University Press of America, 1984] [hereafter NMT]) has to some extent kept up-to-date on this issue.

Charles E. Curran and Richard McCormick, S.J., have provided a useful anthology of many of the most influential articles: *Readings in Moral Theology, No. 1: Moral Norms and Catholic Tradition* (New York: Paulist Press, 1979) (hereafter RMT). Many of the responses to some of the influential pieces included in this volume appeared after it was printed. It is extremely instructive to read these point/counterpoint exchanges. William E. May, "Aquinas and Janssens on the Moral Meaning of Human Acts," *Thomist* 48 (1984) 566–606, responds to Louis Janssens's attempts to prove that Thomas Aquinas endorsed the view known as proportionalism in "Ontic Evil and Moral Evil," *Louvain Studies* 4:2 (Fall 1972) 115–56, reprinted in RMT, 40–93, and his "Norms and Priorities in a Love Ethic" *Louvain Studies* 6:3 (Spring 1977) 207–38. Germain Grisez, "Moral Absolutes: A Critique of the View of Josef Fuchs, S.J.," *Anthropos* 1:2 (Oct. 1985) 155–201, responds to Joseph Fuchs, S.J., "The Absoluteness of Moral Terms," *Gregorianum* 52 (1971), 415–57, reprinted in RMT, 94–137. See also Grisez's "Against Consequentialism," *American Journal of Jurisprudence* 23 (1978) 21–72, and his *The Way of the Lord Jesus* vol. 1 (Chicago: Franciscan Herald Press, 1983) and John Finnis, *Fundamentals of Ethics* (Washington, D.C.: Georgetown University Press, 1983). The text by Rev. Ronald Lawler, O.F.M. Cap., Joseph Boyle, Jr., and William E. May, *Catholic Sexual Ethics* (Huntington, Ind.: Our Sunday Visitor, 1985), also offers a good critique of proportionalism and its fidelity to traditional Catholic teaching on sexual morality.

John R. Connery, S.J., has provided several critiques of these various challenges to traditional moral theology and, in turn, has received a steady response to his criticisms. His "Morality of Consequences: A Critical Appraisal," *Theological Studies* 34, (1973), 396–414, was reprinted in RMT, 244–66; Richard McCormick's response, which originally appeared in his biannual "Notes on Moral Theology," Apr.–Sept. 1974, in *Theological Studies* 36 (Mar. 1975) 93–100 was reprinted as "Reflections on the Literature" in RMT, 294–340. Connery next published "Catholic Ethics: Has the Norm for Rule-Making Changed?" *Theological Studies* 42 (1981) 223–50, to which Richard McCormick responded in "Notes on Moral Theology," 1981, in *Theological Studies*, 43 (Mar. 1981), 82–91, reprinted in NMT (1981–1984), 62–71. McCormick and Connery have another round: John R. Connery, S.J., "The Teleology of Proportionate Reason," *Theological Studies* 44 (1983) 489–96, with response by McCormick in his "Notes on Moral Theology," 1983, *Theological Studies* 45 (Mar. 1984) 88–94, reprinted in NMT 1981–84, 166–71.

Paul M. Quay, S.J., and Richard McCormick have also gone several rounds together. One of Quay's essays, "Morality of Consequences," appeared in RMT, 267–93; McCormick's response to this piece appears in the same volume, 309–15. Quay's "The Disvalue of Ontic Evil" appeared in *Theological Studies* 46 (1985) 262–86; McCormick's response appears in his "Notes on Moral Theology," *Theological Studies* 47 (1986) 85–86. Of interest as well are Quay's "The Unity and Structure of the Human Act," *Listening* 18:3 (Fall 1983) 245–59, and "The Theological Position and the Role of Ethics," 260–74, in the same volume.

See also Kevin T. McMahon, S.T.D., *Sexuality: Theological Voices* (Braintree, Mass.: Pope John Center, 1987), and Brian V. Johnstone, C.SS.R., "The Meaning of Proportionate Reason in Contemporary Theology," *Thomist* 49 (Apr. 1985) 223–47.

2. Often, as the two sides square off against each other, the line of battle is characterized as those who have a moral methodology based on "single *act*" analysis accompanied by the claim that some acts are intrinsically wrong over against those who focus on the totality of the goods of the human *person*, who claim that the preponderant good is to be sought. A recent consideration of the starkness of the conflict between these two groups is available in Norbert Rigali, "Artificial Birth Control: An Impasse Revisited," *Theological Studies* 47 (1986) 681–90. As representative "incommensurabilists" he names Germain Grisez and William May (my "traditionalists"); as representative "proportionalists" (my "revisionists"), he names Joseph Fuchs and Richard McCormick. Rigali's analysis argues that ultimately the debate is between those who have fundamentally different "consciousnesses," between those who are "historically conscious" and those who have a "classicist consciousness." (It is important to note that Rigali uses *historical consciousness* differently from the way it is used by Charles Curran and others; Rigali speaks of an act's being "a part of a larger, continuing temporal human process" [688–89], whereas Curran speaks of an awareness that nature is evolving, too, as history marches on [see Chapter 6]).

3. Richard McCormick, S.J., "Notes on Moral Theology" from *Theological Studies* reprinted in NMT 1981–84, 15–16. Knauer's article "The Hermeneutic of the Principle of Double Effect," is available in RMT, 1–39.

4. Richard McCormick, S.J., states, "Paul McKeever is correct, I believe, when he notes that 'defending proportionalism is not directly contrary to the explicit teaching of the Church. There is no such explicit teaching.' Indeed, there is the

contrary practice, if not the full-blown theory. So, rather than 'going against the tradition,' recent efforts are much more a dialogue with certain aspects of that tradition by adherents of the tradition" (NMT 1981–84, 71).

Lisa Sowle Cahill assesses the situation in this way:

> Revisionist moral theologians such [as] Richard McCormick, Charles Curran, Josef Fuchs, Bruno Schüller, and Louis Janssens share certain fundamental presuppositions with the tradition of Thomistic ethics, including those fellow members of the tradition who disagree with the conclusions regarding the norms. All are committed to an objective moral order, to nature as the norm of human action, to the knowability of nature by reasonable reflection, and to the responsibility of the Church (the *Magisterium*) to clarify the natural law and give moral guidance. What is distinctive about the revisionist approaches (to take the liberty of generalization about theories which are not actually identical) is their recognition of the historicity of human persons and communities, and thus of the development of human nature itself; of epistemological limits and the partial and progressive character of human knowing, which has implications for the *formulation* of norms which express what nature is and demands; and of the responsibility of each person to consider how the values protected by norms best can be realized in concrete situations. "Contemporary Challenges to Exceptionless Moral Norms" in *Moral Theology Today: Certitudes and Doubts* (St. Louis, Mo.: Pope John Center, 1984) 121–35; especially 125.

This chapter strives to show that the resemblances are more superficial than Cahill allows and that the divergence of the revisionists from the tradition is not a matter of "formulation" of norms; rather there is fundamental disagreement about the proper criteria for assessing the morality of human acts. Reading the point/counterpoint articles listed in note 1 may also serve to demonstrate how great is the disagreement between traditionalists and revisionists.

5. Edward V. Vacek, S.J., "Proportionalism: One View of the Debate," *Theological Studies* 46 (1985) 288–314, observes: "An argument could be made that *Humanae Vitae* has fueled the development of P [proportionalism] in Catholic thought, and that the birth-control debate has been so drawn-out and intense precisely because it is really a debate over a style of moral reasoning and a vision of what it means to be human, not to mention over what God is doing in the world—therefore over much larger matters than the use of a pill" (293).

6. Pius XI, *Casti Connubii*, AAS 559, DSP 28.

7. McCormick, NMT 1981–84, 64.

8. These terms are regularly linked and used synonymously by the revisionists (see McCormick, NMT 1965–80, 534 and 541, and Cahill, "Contemporary Challenges," 124). For a more thorough analysis of the precision and meaning of the terms than that offered in this chapter see Paul Quay's "The Disvalue of Ontic Evil," see also Norbert Rigali, S.J., "Dialogue with Richard McCormick," *Chicago Studies* 16 (1977) 299–308.

9. A useful study of the different positions is Brian Thomas Mullady, O.P., *The Meaning of the Term "Moral" in St. Thomas Aquinas* (Vatican City: Libreria Editrice Vaticana, 1986).

10. Grisez, "Against Consequentialism."

11. Cahill, "Contemporary Challenges," 133.

12. McCormick, NMT 1980–84, 110.

13. Peter Knauer, "The Hermeneutic Function of the Principle of Double Effect" in Curran, RMT, 2.

14. Richard McCormick repeatedly makes this point (e.g., NMT 1981–84, 64–65). We do, though, find Charles Curran saying, "One might argue that in individual cases the values of human sexuality would not be jeopardized or threatened by adultery. In theory this would always remain a possibility" (*Transition and Tradition in Moral Theology* [Notre Dame, Ind.: University of Notre Dame Press, 1979], 42). Curran does think there should be an absolute norm against adultery because of the social consequences of adultery, but this is a practical judgment, not a moral one. Joseph Fuchs, in Curran, RMT, 125, states: "*Theoretically*, no other answer seems possible: Probably there can be no universal norms of *behavior* in the strict sense of 'intrinsece malum.' *Practically*, however, norms properly formulated as universals have their worth, and indeed on several counts."

15. Vacek, "Proportionalism: One View of the Debate," 294.

16. Fuchs, RMT, 124.

17. Cahill, "Contemporary Challenges," 122.

18. Ibid., 123.

19. Richard McCormick, "Notes on Moral Theology," *Theological Studies* 47 (1986) 87, commenting on Sanford S. Levy's "Richard McCormick and Proportionate Reason," *Journal of Religious Studies* 13 (1985) 258–78.

20. I am not certain that McCormick is correct to attribute this position to Levy; as I read Levy, he is simply saying that an intelligible understanding of *McCormick's own principles* leads to this conclusion, not that this is the argument that he, Levy, would make.

21. Louis Janssens, "Norms and Priorities in a Love Ethics," speaks of "practically or virtuously [sic] exceptionless norms" and gives the prohibition against rape as an example (217).

22. Probably the most influential study by a revisionist on this subject is Peter Knauer's article, "Hermeneutic Function." A response to his analysis can be found in Germain Grisez's "Toward a Consistent Natural Law Ethics of Killing," *American Journal of Jurisprudence* 15 (1970) 79–83. Joseph Boyle has also provided a survey of the argument in "Toward Understanding the Principle of Double Effect," *Ethics* 90 (July 1980) 527–38. See also the articles by Janssens and May listed in note 1.

23. Some traditionalists hold that all direct killing is wrong; see, for instance, Germain Grisez, "Toward a Consistent Natural Law Ethics of Killing."

24. Translation by John A. Oesterle, *Treatise on Happiness* (Notre Dame, Ind.: University of Notre Dame Press, 1983), 165. All translations are from this text.

25. Cahill, "Contemporary Challenges," 124.

26. McCormick, NMT 1965–80, 775.

27. Cahill, "Contemporary Challenges," 131.

28. Ibid., 126–27.

29. Curran seems to be the exception. He registers his hesitation to attribute premoral evil to contraception in his chapter "Moral Theology in the Light of Reactions to *Humanae Vitae*" in *Transition and Tradition*, 37 ff.

30. Knauer, "Hermeneutic Function," 30. Traditionalists would agree with Knauer's statement for they too agree that unless "further content" is known, there is not necessarily any moral evil involved in the loss of procreative power. Indeed, as has been repeatedly noted, traditionalists allow the therapeutic taking of drugs that may cure an ailment of the woman but may also cause her reproductive organs

to lose their procreative power. In their view, reasoning in accord with the principle of the double effect permits the taking of drugs with this effect. They reason that the evil of the loss of the procreative power was not directly intended and that the well-being of the mother is a proportionate good to the loss of procreative power. Traditionalists do not consider the taking of such drugs properly speaking a "contraceptive act" for the intent of the act was not to rob the reproductive organs of their procreative power; this was an unavoidable and justifiable "double effect" of one's use of certain drugs. A woman taking such drugs is not acting directly against the good of procreation.

31. Paul M. Quay, S.J., "The Unity and Structure of the Human Act," 247.

32. Joseph Boyle, "The Principle of Double Effect: Good Actions Entangled in Evil," in *Moral Theology Today*, 250. Boyle notes that the best analysis of the "self-constituting character of a person's free choices" is in Karol Wojtyla's *The Acting Person* (Boston: D. Reidel Publishing Co., 1979).

CHAPTER EIGHT

1. These talks have been published by the Daughters of Saint Paul in four volumes: *The Original Unity of Man and Woman: Catechesis on the Book of Genesis* (Boston, Mass.: St. Paul Editions, 1981) (hereafter (OU); *Blessed Are the Pure of Heart* (Boston, Mass.: St. Paul Editions, 1983) (hereafter BPH); *The Theology of Marriage and Celibacy* (Boston, Mass.: St. Paul Editions, 1986) (hereafter TMC); and *Reflections on Humanae Vitae* (Boston, Mass.: St. Paul Editions, 1984) (hereafter ROHV). One talk was omitted from the final series, "Living According to the Spirit," Nov. 14, 1984.

2. Karol Wojtyla, *Love and Responsibility* trans. by H. T. Willetts (New York: Farrar Straus Giroux, 1981) (hereafter LR); *The Acting Person* trans. by Andrzej Potocki, *Analecta Husserliana*, vol. 10 (Boston, Mass.: D. Reidel Publishing Co., 1979) (hereafter AP), and *Familiaris Consortio: The Role of the Christian Family in the Modern World* (Boston, Mass.: St. Paul Editions, 1981) (hereafter FC).

3. FC, 50.

4. John Paul II occasionally cites this passage from *Optatam Totius*, 16. This citation is taken from a speech given to moral theologians, *L'Osservatore Romano*, Apr. 28, 1986, 12. The translations for passages from the conciliar documents are from *Vatican II: The Conciliar and Postconciliar Documents* ed. by Austin Flannery. O.P., (Northport, N.Y.: Costello Publishing Co., 1975); hereafter the section number is given in the text. This passage is occasionally cited by John Paul II; see, for instance his speech, "Rediscover the relationship of truth, goodness and freedom," *L'Osservatore Romano*, April 28, 1986; 12.

5. ROHV, 32–33.

6. Few scholars have done any extensive work on the pope's teachings on sexuality. Perhaps the most useful brief summary is to be found in Richard Hogan, "A Theology of the Body," *International Review of Natural Family Planning*, 6:3 (Fall 1982), 227–312 (rpt. from *Fidelity* 1 [Dec. 1981]), 10–15, 24–27. Useful, too, is Daryl J. Glick, "Recovering Morality: Personalism and Theology of the Body of John Paul II," *Faith and Reason* 12:1 (1986) 7–25. Although his book, *Sex, Marriage, and Chastity* (Chicago: Franciscan Herald Press, 1981), is not explicitly about John Paul II's teachings, William May nonetheless worked to integrate the pope's teaching into his book. See also A. Mattheeuws, S.J., "De la Bible à 'Humanae

vitae': Les catéchèses de Jean-Paul II," *Nouvelle Revue Théologique* 111:2 (Mar.–Apr. 1989) 228–48.

7. ROHV, 29.   8. AP, 108.

9. See note 4.

10. See John Finnis, "The Fundamental Themes of *Laborem Exercens*," *Catholic Social Thought and the Teaching of John Paul II* (Scranton, Pa.: Northeast Books, 1982) 19–31.

11. See, e.g., AP, 98–99 and 151.

12. See, e.g., LR, 115, and AP, 156.

13. ROHV, 46.   14. ROHV, 63.

15. ROHV, 62.   16. ROHV, 64.

17. ROHV, 64.   18. LR, 115.

19. LR, 116.

20. John F. Crosby, "The Personalism of John Paul II as the Basis of His Approach to the Teaching of 'Humanae Vitae,' " *Anthropotes* 5:1 (May 1989) 47–69; 48.

21. *Love and Responsibility* was written by John Paul II when he was Karol Wojtyla. For ease of reference, that distinction is not observed in the following exposition.

22. LR, 41.   23. LR, 18.

24. LR, 54–55.   25. LR, 56.

26. This argument is very reminiscent of the argument labeled version D in Chapter 4: (1) It is wrong to thwart actions whereby God might perform His creative act that brings forth a new human life; (2) contraception thwarts actions, whereby God might perform His creative act that brings forth new human life; (3) therefore, contraception is wrong.

27. LR, 52–53.   28. LR, 53.

29. LR, 53 and 248; cf. BOHV, 51 and 57.

30. LR, 229–30.   31. LR, 230.

32. ROHV, 39–40.   33. LR, 246.

34. LR, 239.

35. Much is said about the language of the body in Chapter 4.

36. See John F. Crosby, "Personalism of John Paul II." Crosby informs us that John Paul II understands *Humanae Vitae* (unlike *Gaudium et Spes*) to deal more with "subjective realities" than with "objective ones" (here the realities external to the human person), (53).

37. OU, 16.

38. John Paul takes the story of Adam and Eve so seriously that some might ask whether he understands it to be based on historical fact. Others might be disturbed by his referring to the "myth" of Adam and Eve as though this word suggests that he thinks it is a "made-up" story. Although John Paul does not disclose his assessment of the historicity of the story, he provides a lengthy footnote (OU, 32–33, n. 1) on the meaning of the word *myth*. He cites there the interpretations of several modern thinkers and concludes, "In short, the myth tends to know what is unknowable." John Paul turns to the "myth" of Adam and Eve since he believes that it reveals essential anthropological truths or truths about the very nature of man and of his existence: "The important thing, therefore, is not that these experiences belong to man's prehistory (to his 'theological prehistory'), but that they are always at the root of every human experience. That is true, even if, in the evolution of ordinary human existence, not much attention is paid to these essential experiences. They are, in

fact, so intermingled with the ordinary things of life that we do not generally notice their extraordinary character" (OU, 85).

39. OU, 36–37.

40. OU, 38.

41. OU, 52.

42. OU, 66.

43. OU, 79.

44. OU, 83.

45. Leslie Dewart, "*Casti Connubii* and the Development of Dogma," *Contraception and Holiness* (New York: Herder and Herder, 1964), 205–6.

46. OU, 114–15.

47. The topic of "self as gift" is considered in Chapter 4.

48. BPH, 19.

49. BPH, 50–51.

50. BPH, 133.

51. BPH, 172.

52. BPH, 185–86.

53. BPH, 194–95.

54. BPH, 249.

55. BPH, 260.

56. On the tenth anniversary of *Humanae Vitae*, John Paul (then Karol Wojtyla) highlighted some of its connections with *Gaudium et Spes*. This talk has been published in a volume entitled *Fruitful and Responsible Love* (New York: Seabury Press, 1979). See also his "La visione antropologica dell' 'Humanae Vitae,' " *Lateranum* 44 (1978) 125–45.

57. OU, 102.

58. OU, 103.

59. OU, 103.

60. OU, 109.

61. OU, 110.

62. OU, 107.

63. OU, 107–8.

64. OU, 75.

65. OU, 164.

66. OU, 114.

67. OU, 116–17.

68. OU, 74.

69. OU, 111.

70. BPH, 63.

71. OU, 83.

72. FC, 51–52.

73. ROHV, 84–85.

74. Lisa Sowle Cahill, "Catholic Sexual Ethics and the Dignity of the Person: A Double Message," *Theological Studies* 50:1 (Mar. 1989) 120–50. Quote from p. 146.

75. Ibid., 146.

76. *L'Osservatore Romano*, Apr. 16, 1984, 12.

77. *L'Osservatore Romano*, Dec. 3, 1979, 3.

78. John Paul, II, "Marriage and the Family," *The Pope Speaks* 28:4 (1983) 360–65, 362.

79. *L'Osservatore Romano*, Oct. 24, 1983, 3.

80. *L'Osservatore Romano*, Oct. 10, 1983, 7.

81. *L'Osservatore Romano*, Dec. 3, 1979, 15.

82. *L'Osservatore Romano*, Apr. 28, 1986, 12.

83. Ibid., 12.

84. *L'Osservatore Romano*, April 11, 1988, 6.

85. John Paul II, "The Magisterium and Infallibility," *The Pope Speaks* 34:1 (1989) 58.

86. John Paul II, *Building Up the Body of Christ* (San Francisco: Ignatius Press, 1987), 186.

87. *L'Osservatore Romano*, Dec. 19–26, 1988, 7.

88. Ibid., 7.

89. *L'Osservatore Romano*, May 11, 1981, 2.

90. *L'Osservatore Romano*, July 12, 1982, 4.

Select Bibliography

Abbo, John A., and Jerome D. Hannan. *The Sacred Canons: A Concise Presentation of the Current Disciplinary Norms of the Church.* Canons 870–2414. 2d rev. St. Louis: B. Herder Book Co., 1960.

Abbot, Walter M., ed. *The Documents of Vatican II.* Chicago: Follett Publishing Company, 1966.

Aguilar, Nona. *No-Pill, No-Risk Birth Control.* New York: Rawson Associates, 1986.

Albury, William. "Discussion: *Humanae Vitae* and the Ecological Argument." *Laval Théologique et Philosophique* 27 (1971): 135–41.

Anscombe, G. E. M. "Contraception and Natural Law." *New Blackfriars* 46 (June 1965): 517–21.

———. *Contraception and Chastity.* London: Catholic Truth Society, 1975.

Arraj, James. *Is There a Solution to the Catholic Debate on Contraception.* Chiloquin: Inner Growth Press, 1989.

Bak, Felix. "Bernard Haering and 'Humanae Vitae'." *Autonianum* 69 (1974): 198–238.

Bauer, Andrew. *The Debate on Birth Control.* New York: Hawthorne Books, 1969.

Baum, Gregory. "The New Encyclical on Contraception." *Homiletic and Pastoral Review* 68 (September 1968): 1001–4.

Benedictine Monks of Solesmes, eds. *Matrimony.* Translated by Michael J. Byrnes. Boston: St. Paul Editions, 1963.

The New American Bible. Camden: Thomas Nelson Inc., 1971.

Bier, William C., ed. *Conscience: Its Freedom and Limitations.* New York: Fordham University Press, 1971.

Birmingham, William. *What Modern Catholics Think about Birth Control.* New York: New American Library, 1964.

Boeckle, Franz. "Birth Control: A Survey of German, French and Dutch Literature on the Question of Birth Control." *Concilium* 5 (1965): 97–129.

Bourke, Vernon J. *Ethics: A Textbook in Moral Philosophy.* New York: Macmillan Co., 1951.

Boyle Jr., Joseph M. "Toward Understanding the Principle of Double Effect." *Ethics* 90 (July 1980): 527–38.

———. "Contraception and Natural Family Planning." *International Review of Natural Family Planning* 4:4 (Winter 1980): 309–15.

———. "Human Action, Natural Rhythms, and Contraception: A Response to Noonan." *American Journal of Jurisprudence* 26 (1981): 32–46.

———. "The Principle of Double Effect: Good Actions Entangled in Evil." In *Moral Theology Today: Certitudes and Doubts,* 243–60. St. Louis: Pope John Center, 1984.

————. "Personal Integrity, Sexual Morality and Responsible Parenthood." *Rivista di Studi Sulla Persona e la Famiglia: Anthropos* 1 (1985): 43–55.

Bradley, Robert I., and Msgr. Eugene Kevane, trans. *The Roman Catechism*. Boston: St. Paul Editions, 1985.

Brunelli, Lucio. "The Pill That Divided the Church." *Thirty Days* 4 (July–August 1988).

Burke, Cormac. "Children and Values." *International Review of Natural Family Planning* 12:3 (Fall 1988): 181–92.

————. "Marriage and Contraception." In *Creative Love: The Ethics of Human Reproduction*, edited by John Boyle, 151–67. Front Royal: Christendom Press, 1989.

Burtchaell, James Tunstead. " 'Human Life' and Humane Love: The Birth Control Encyclical Was Disappointingly Inadequate and Largely Fallacious." *Commonweal* 89 (1968/69): 245–52.

Caffarra, Carlo. "Humanae Vitae: Venti Anni Dopo." In *Humanae Vitae: 20 Anni Dopo*, 183–95. Milan: Edizioni Ares, 1988.

————. "Conscience, Truth and Magisterium in Conjugal Morality." In *Marriage and Family*, 21–36. San Francisco: Ignatius Press, 1989.

Cahill, Lisa Sowle. "Contemporary Challenges to Exceptionless Moral Norms." In *Moral Theology Today: Certitudes and Doubts*, 125–35. St. Louis: Pope John Center, 1984.

————. "Catholic Sexual Ethics and the Dignity of the Person: A Double Message." *Theological Studies* 50:1 (March 1989): 120–50.

Calegari, Marc, trans. *Humanae Vitae*. San Francisco: Ignatius Press, 1978.

Callahan, Daniel. *The Catholic Case for Contraception*. London: Macmillan Co., 1969.

Callahan, Michael. "The Changing Face of Catholic Moral Theology: From the Constitution *De Ordine* to *Gaudium et Spes*." *Louvain Studies* 3 (1970/71): 41–50.

Callahan, Sidney and Daniel. *Understanding the Differences*. Hastings: Hastings Center Series in Ethics, 1984.

Cavanagh, John R. *The Popes, the Pill, and People*. Milwaukee: The Bruce Publishing, Co., 1965.

Clark, Alan C., and Geoffrey Crawfurd, trans. *The Regulation of Birth*. London: Catholic Truth Society, 1968.

————. *Humanae Vitae*. London: Catholic Truth Society, 1970.

Congregation for the Doctrine of the Faith. *Instruction on Bioethics: Respect for Human Life*. Boston: St. Paul Editions, 1987.

Connell, Francis J. "Answers to Questions: Delaying Ovulation." *American Ecclesiastical Review* 151 (1964): 408.

Connell, Richard J. "A Defense of *Humanae Vitae*." *Laval Théologique et Philosophique* 26 (1970): 57–85.

Connery, John R. "Morality of Consequences: A Critical Appraisal." *Theological Studies* 34 (1973): 396–414.

————. "Catholic Ethics: Has the Norm for Rule-Making Changed?" *Theological Studies* 42 (1981): 223–50.

————. "The Teleology of Proportionate Reason." *Theological Studies* 44 (1983): 489–96.

―――. "The Role of Love in Christian Marriage: A Historical Overview." *Communio* 11:3 (Fall 1984): 244–57.

Cooper, John M. "Birth Control and the 'Perverted Faculty' Argument." *American Ecclesiastical Review* 79 (October 1928): 527–33.

Coppens, Joseph. "A Symposium on 'Humanae Vitae'." *Louvain Studies* 2 (Spring 1969): 211–30.

Costanzo, Joseph. "Papal Magisterium and *Humanae Vitae*." *Thought* 44:174 (Autumn 1969): 377–412.

―――. "Academic Dissent: An Original Ecclesiology." *Thomist* 34:4 (October 1970): 636–53.

―――. "Papal Magisterium, Natural Law and *Humanae Vitae*." *American Journal of Jurisprudence* 16 (1971): 259–89.

―――. *The Historical Credibility of Hans Kung*. North Quincy, Mass.: Christopher Publishing House, 1979.

Crosby, John F. "The Personalism of John Paul II as the Basis of His Approach to the Teaching of 'Humanae Vitae'." *Anthropotes* 5:1 (May 1989): 47–69.

Curran, Charles E. *Christian Morality Today*. Notre Dame: Fides Publishing, 1966.

―――. *Contraception, Authority, and Dissent*. New York: Herder and Herder, 1969.

―――. *The Responsibility of Dissent: The Church and Academic Freedom*. New York: Sheed and Ward, 1969.

―――. *New Perspectives in Moral Theology*. Notre Dame: University of Notre Dame Press, 1976.

―――. "Natural Law." In *Themes in Fundamental Moral Theology*, 27–69. Notre Dame: University of Notre Dame Press, 1977.

―――. "Ten Years Later." *Commonweal* 195 (1978): 426.

―――. *Transition and Tradition in Moral Theology*. Notre Dame: University of Notre Dame Press, 1979.

―――. *Moral Theology: A Continuing Journey*. Notre Dame: University of Notre Dame Press, 1982.

―――. *Critical Concerns in Moral Theology*. Notre Dame: University of Notre Dame Press, 1984.

―――. *Directions in Fundamental Moral Theology*. Notre Dame: University of Notre Dame Press, 1985.

―――. *Faithful Dissent*. Kansas City: Sheed and Ward, 1986.

―――. "My Theological Dissent: The Issues." In *Tensions in Moral Theology*, 7–31. Notre Dame: University of Notre Dame Press, 1988.

Curran, Charles E., and Robert E. Hunt. *Dissent In and For the Church: Theologians and Humanae Vitae*. New York: Sheed and Ward, 1969.

Curran, Charles E., and Richard McCormick. *Readings in Moral Theology, No. 1: Moral Norms and Catholic Tradition*. New York: Paulist Press, 1979.

Daly, Cahal B. "Natural Law and Morality Today." *American Ecclesiastical Review* 153 (1965): 361–98.

Davis, Henry. "Birth Control: The Perverted Faculty Argument." *American Ecclesiastical Review* 82 (July 1929): 54–69.

Deferrari, Roy J. *A Latin-English Dictionary of St. Thomas Aquinas*. Boston: St. Paul Editions, 1960.

Delhaye, Philippe. "The Encyclical and the Council." *Tablet*, November 16, 1968, 1132–34.

———. "L'Encyclique *Humanae Vitae* et l'Enseignement de Vatican II sur le Mariage et la Famille (Gaudium et Spes)." *Bijdragen* 29 (1968): 350–68.

DeMarco, Donald. "Perspective: The Chief Obstacle in Teaching NFP." *International Review of Natural Family Planning* 10:1 (Spring 1986): 65–68.

Dennehy, Raymond. *Christian Married Love.* San Francisco: Ignatius Press, 1981.

Dewart, Leslie. "*Casti Connubii* and the Development of Dogma." In *Contraception and Holiness.* New York: Herder and Herder, 1964.

Dionne, Robert J. " 'Humanae Vitae' Re-examined: A Response." *Homiletic and Pastoral Review*, July 1973, 57–64.

———. *The Papacy and the Church.* New York: Philosophical Library, 1987.

Djerassi, Carl. *The Politics of Contraception.* New York: W. W. Norton Company, 1979.

Dolan, Joseph V. "*Humanae Vitae* and Nature." *Thought* 44:174 (Autumn 1969): 358–76.

Doms, Herbert. *The Meaning of Marriage.* New York: Sheed and Ward, 1939.

Dummett, Michael. "The Documents of the Papal Commission on Birth Control." *New Blackfriars* 50 (1969): 241–50.

Dupré, Louis. *Contraception and Catholics: A New Appraisal.* Baltimore: Helicon Press, Inc., 1964.

———. "Toward a Re-examination of the Catholic Position on Birth Control." *Crosscurrents* 14 (Winter 1964): 63–84.

———. "Natural Law and Birth Control." *Philosophy Today* 9 (1965): 94–100.

———. "Philosophical Analysis of the Catholic Moral Problem of Contraception." *Insight*, Fall 1967, 57–59.

Durand, A. " 'The Encyclical'—A Fresh Translation." *Homiletic and Pastoral Review* 69:11 (August 1969): 851–64.

Egner, G. *Contraception vs. Tradition: A Catholic Critique.* New York: Herder and Herder, 1967.

Espinosa, J. C. *Birth Control: Why Are They Lying to Women?* New York: Vantage Press, 1980.

Finnis, John. "Natural Law in *Humanae Vitae*." *Law Quarterly Review* 84 (1968): 467–71.

———. "Natural Law and Unnatural Acts." *Heythrop Journal* 11 (1970): 365–87.

———. *Natural Law and Natural Rights.* Oxford: Clarendon Press, 1980.

———. "*Humanae Vitae*: Its Background and Aftermath." *International Review of Natural Family Planning* 4:2 (Summer 1980): 141–53.

———. "The Natural Law, Objective Morality and Vatican II." In *Principles of Catholic Moral Life*, edited by William E. May, 113–49. Chicago: Franciscan Herald Press, 1980.

———. "The Fundamental Themes of *Laborem Exercens*." In *Catholic Social Thought and the Teaching of John Paul II*, 19–31. Scranton: Northeast Books, 1982.

———. *Fundamentals of Ethics.* Washington, D.C.: Georgetown University Press, 1983.

———. Personal Integrity, Sexual Morality and Responsible Parenthood." *Rivista di Studi sulla Personal e la Famiglia: Anthropos* 1 (1985): 43–45.

Finnis, John, and Germain Grisez. "The Basic Principles of Natural Law: A Reply to Ralph McInerny." *American Journal of Jurisprudence* 26 (1981): 21–32.

Fitch, David. "*Humanae Vitae* and Reasonable Doubt." *Homiletic and Pastoral Review* 69 (April 1969): 516–23.

Flannery, Austin, ed. *Vatican Council II*. Northport: Costello Publishing Co., 1975.

Ford, John C. "Marriage: Its Meaning and Purposes." *Theological Studies* 3 (1942): 333–74.

———. "Footnote on Contraception." *America* 114 (January 22, 1966): 103–7.

———. "More on Council and Contraception." *America* 114 (April 16, 1966): 553–57.

Ford, John C. and Gerald Kelly. *Contemporary Moral Theology*. Vol. 2. Westminster: The Newman Press, 1964.

Ford, John C., and John J. Lynch. "Contraception: A Matter of Practical Doubt." *Homiletic and Pastoral Review* 68 (1968): 563–74.

Fuchs, Joseph. *De Castitate et de Ordine Sexuali*. Rome, 1963.

———. *Natural Law*. Trans. Helmut Reckter and John A. Dowling. New York: Sheed and Ward, 1965.

———. "The Absoluteness of Moral Terms." *Gregorianum* 52 (1971): 415–57.

Gibbons, William J. "Antifertility Drugs and Morality." *America* 98 (December 14, 1957): 346–48.

Glick, Daryl J. "Recovering Morality: Personalism and Theology of the Body of John Paul II." *Faith and Reason* 12:1 (1986): 7–25.

Grant, Ellen. *The Bitter Pill*. London: Corgi Books, 1985.

Grant, George. *Grand Illusions: The Legacy of Planned Parenthood*. Brentwood, Tennessee: Wolgemuth and Hyatt, 1988.

Greer, Germaine. *Sex and Destiny: The Politics of Human Fertility*. New York: Harper & Row, 1984.

Grisez, Germain. *Contraception and the Natural Law*. Milwaukee, The Bruce Publishing Company, 1964.

———. "The First Principle of Practical Reason: A Commentary on the *Summa Theologiae* I–II, Question 94, Article 2." *Natural Law Forum* 10 (1965): 168–201.

———. "A New Formulation of a Natural Law Argument Against Contraception." *Thomist* 30 (1966): 343–61.

———. "Marriage: Reflections Based on St. Thomas and Vatican Council II." *Catholic Mind* 64 (June 1966): 4–19.

———. "Methods of Ethical Inquiry." *Proceedings of the American Catholic Philosophical Association* 41 (1967).

———. "Contraception and Reality." *Triumph*. In three parts: February 1968, 21–24; March 1968, 18–21; April 1968, 27–30.

———. "Toward a Consistent Natural Law Ethics of Killing." *American Journal of Jurisprudence* 15 (1970): 64–96.

———. "Against Consequentialism." *American Journal of Jurisprudence* 23 (1978): 21–72.

———. *The Way of the Lord Jesus*. Chicago: Franciscan Herald Press, 1983.

———. "Infallibility and Specific Moral Norms: A Review Discussion." *Thomist* 49 (1985): 248–87.

————. "Moral Absolutes: A Critique of the View of Josef Fuchs, S.J.." *Anthropos* 1:2 (October 1985): 155–201.

————. "Infallibility and Contraception: A Reply to Garth Hallett." *Theological Studies* 47 (1986): 134–45.

————. "A Critique of Russell Hittinger's Book, A *Critique of the New Natural Law Theory*." *New Scholasticism* 62:4 (Autumn 1988): 438–66.

Grisez, Germain, Joseph Boyle, Jr., and John Finnis. "Practical Principles, Moral Truth, and Ultimate Ends." *American Journal of Jurisprudence* 32 (1987): 99–151.

Grisez, Germain, John C. Ford, Joseph Boyle, Jr., John Finnis, and William E. May. *The Teaching of Humanae Vitae: A Defense*. San Francisco: Ignatius Press, 1988.

Grootaers, Jan. "Quelques données concernant la rédaction de l'encyclique 'Humanae Vitae'." In *Paul VI et la Modernité dans l'Eglise*, 395. Rome: Palais Farnese, 1984.

Guitton, Jean. *The Pope Speaks: Dialogues of Paul VI with Jean Guitton*. Translated by Anne and Christopher Fremantle. New York: Meredith Press, 1968.

————. "Eros and Agape." In *Christian Married Love*, edited by Raymond Denney, 77–80. San Francisco: Ignatius Press, 1981.

————. *Oeuvres Complètes*. Paris: Desclée de Brouwer, 1986.

Guy, François and Michèle. *Ile Maurice: Régulation des Naissances et Action Familiale*. Lyon: Editions Xavier Mappus, 1968.

Haas, John. "The Inseparability of the Two Meanings of the Marriage Act." In *Reproductive Technologies, Marriage and the Church*, 89–106. Braintree: The Pope John Center, 1988.

Haering, Bernard. "The Encyclical Crisis." *Commonweal* 88:20 (September 6, 1968): 588–94.

————. "The Inseparability of the Unitive-Procreative Functions of the Marital Act." In *Contraception, Authority and Dissent*, edited by Charles E. Curran. New York: Herder and Herder, 1969.

————. *Medical Ethics*. Notre Dame: Fides Publishers, Inc., 1973.

————. *Free and Faithful in Christ*. New York: Seabury Press, 1979.

Hallett, Garth. "Contraception and Prescriptive Infallibility." *Theological Studies* 43 (1982): 629–50.

Hallgan, Nicholas. "The Church as Teacher." *Thomist* 33 (1969): 675–717.

Harris, Peter. "The Church and Moral Decision." *New Blackfriars* 51 (1970): 518–27.

Harrison, Brian. "Appendix III: *Humanae Vitae* e Infallibilitía." In *Religious Liberty and Contraception*. Melbourne: John XXIII Fellowship Co-op, Ltd., 1988.

Hartmann, Betsy. *Reproductive Rights and Wrongs*. New York: Harper and Row, Publishers, 1987.

Hittinger, Russell. *A Critique of the New Natural Law Theory*. Notre Dame: University of Notre Dame Press, 1987.

Hogan, Richard. "A Theology of the Body." *The International Review of Natural Family Planning* 6:3 (Fall 1982): 227–312.

Horgan, John. *Humanae Vitae and the Bishops*. Shannon: Irish University Press, 1972.

Hoyt, Robert G., ed. *The Birth Control Debate*. Kansas City: National Catholic Reporter, 1968.

Hugo, John J. *St. Augustine on Nature, Sex and Marriage.* Chicago: Scepter, 1968.

Hume, Kevin. "The Pill and Cancer." *Linacre Quarterly* 52 (November 1985): 297–320.

Ihm, Claudia Carla, ed. *The Papal Encyclicals, 1878–1903, 29–40.* Raleigh: McGrath Publishing Co., 1981.

Janssens, Louis. "L'inhibition de l'ovulation est-elle moralement licite?" *Ephemerides Theologicae Iovaniensis* 34 (1958): 357–60.

———. "Morale Conjugale et Progestogènes." *Ephemerides Theologicae Lovanienses* 39 (1963): 787–826.

———. "Considerations on 'Humanae Vitae'." *Louvain Studies* 2, Spring (1969): 231–53.

———. "Ontic Evil and Moral Evil." *Louvain Studies* 4:2 (Fall 1972): 115–56.

———. "Norms and Priorities in a Love Ethics." *Louvain Studies* 6:3 (Spring 1977): 207–38.

Johann, Robert O. "Responsible Parenthood: A Philosophical View." *Proceedings of the Catholic Theological Society of America* 20 (1965): 115–28.

John XXIII, Pope. "Mater et Magistra." *AAS* 53 (1961).

John Paul II, Pope. *Familiaris Consortio: The Role of the Christian Family in the Modern World.* Boston: St. Paul Editions, 1981.

———. *Love and Responsibility.* New York: Farrar, Straus, Giroux, 1981.

———. *The Original Unity of Man and Woman: Catechesis on the Book of Genesis.* Boston: St. Paul Editions, 1981.

———. *Blessed Are the Pure of Heart.* Boston: St. Paul Editions, 1983.

———. "Marriage and the Family." *The Pope Speaks* 28:4 (1983): 360–65.

———. "General Audience of 18 July." *L'Osservatore Romano,* July 1984, 1.

———. *Reflections on Humanae Vitae.* Boston: St. Paul Editions, 1984.

———. *Theology of Marriage and Celibacy.* Boston: St. Paul Editions, 1986.

———. *Building Up the Body of Christ.* San Francisco: Ignatius Press, 1987.

———. "The Magisterium and Infallibility." *The Pope Speaks* 34:1 (1989): 58.

Johnson, Paul. *Pope John Paul II and the Catholic Restoration.* New York: St. Martin's Press, 1981.

Johnstone, Brian V. "The Meaning of Proportionate Reason in Contemporary Theology." *Thomist* 49 (April 1985): 223–47.

Joyce, George Hayward. *Christian Marriage: An Historical and Doctrinal Study.* New York: Sheed and Ward, 1933.

Joyce, Mary Rosera. *The Meaning of Contraception.* New York: Alba House, 1969.

Kaiser, Robert Blair. *The Politics of Sex and Religion.* Kansas City: Leaven Press, 1985.

Kasper, Walter. *Theology of Christian Marriage.* New York: Seabury Press, 1980.

Kass, Leon R. *Toward a More Natural Science: Biology and Human Affairs.* New York: The Free Press, 1985.

Kasun, Jacqueline. *The War Against Population.* San Francisco: Ignatius Press, 1988.

Kelly, George A. *Birth Control and Catholics.* Garden City: Doubleday and Company, 1963.

———. *The Battle for the American Church.* Garden City: Image Books, 1980.

Kelly, Gerald. "Pope Pius XII and the Principle of Totality." *Theological Studies* 16 (1955): 373–96.

———. "The Morality of Mutilation: Towards a Revision of the Treatise." *Theological Studies* 17 (1956): 322–44.

————. "Confusion: Contraception and 'The Pill'." *Theology Digest* 12 (Summer 1964): 123–30.

Kelly, Kevin T. "Moral Theology Forum: A Positive Approach to *Humanae Vitae.*" *The Clergy Review* 57 (1972): 108–20, 174–86, 263–75, 330–48, and especially 261–73.

Kiely, Bartholomew. "The Impracticality of Proportionalism." *Gregorianum* 66 (1985): 656–85.

————. "Contraception, In Vitro Fertilization and the Principle of Inseparability." *Linacre Quarterly* 55 (February 1989): 68–75.

Kilian, Sabbas J. "The Question of Authority in 'Humanae Vitae'." *Thought* 44:174 (Autumn 1969): 327–42.

Kippley, John F. *Birth Control and the Marriage Covenant.* Collegeville: The Liturgical Press, 1976.

Kippley, Sheila, and John. *The Art of Natural Family Planning.* 3d ed. Cincinnati: The Couple to Couple League, 1985.

Kirk, Gerard P. "*Humanae Vitae* and the Assent Due It." *Continuum* 6 (1968): 288–94.

Knauer, Peter. "The Hermeneutic Function of the Principle of Double Effect." *Natural Law Forum* 12 (1967).

Komonchak, Joseph A. "*Humanae Vitae* and Its Reception: Ecclesiological Reflections." *Theological Studies* 39 (1978): 221–57.

Koznik, Anthony, et al. *Human Sexuality: New Directions in American Thought.* New York: Paulist Press, 1977.

Lawler, Ronald, Joseph M. Boyle Jr., and William E. May. *Catholic Sexual Ethics: A Summary, Explanation and Defense.* Huntington: Our Sunday Visitor, 1985.

Leahy, William K., and Anthony T. Massimini, eds. *Third Session: Council Speeches of Vatican II.* New Jersey: Paulist Press, 1966.

Leo XIII, Pope. "Arcanum." *ASS* 12 (1879): 388.

Levy, Sanford S. "Richard McCormick and Proportionate Reason." *Journal of Religious Studies* 13 (1985): 258–78.

Lewis, Charlton T., and Charles Short. *A Latin Dictionary.* Oxford: Clarendon Press, 1975.

Lio, Ermenegildo. *Humanae Vitae e Infallibilitá: il Concilio, Paolo VI e Giovanni Paolo II.* Vatican City: Libreria Editrice Vaticana, 1986.

Lonergan, B. J. F. "Finality, Love, Marriage." *Theological Studies* 4 (1943): 477–510.

Luker, Kristan. *Abortion and the Politics of Motherhood.* Berkeley: University of California Press, 1984.

Lynch, John J. "Moral Aspects of Pharmaceutical Fertility Control." *Proceedings of the Catholic Theological Society of America* 13 (1958): 127–38.

————. "Current Theology: Notes on Moral Theology." *Theological Studies* 23 (1962): 239.

————. "Current Theology: Notes on Moral Theology." *Theological Studies* 25 (1964): 238–249.

————. "Current Theology: Notes on Moral Theology." *Theological Studies* 26 (1965): 253.

————. "Contraception: A Matter of Practical Doubt." *Homiletic and Pastoral Review* 68 (1968) 563–74.

Mackin, Theodore. "Conjugal Love and the Magisterium." *The Jurist* 36 (1976): 263–301.

MacQuarrie, John. "The Nature of the Marriage Bond." *Theology* 78: 659 (May 1975): 230–36.

Mahony, E. J. "The 'Perverted Faculty' Argument Against Birth Prevention." *American Ecclesiastical Review* 79 (August 1928): 133–45.

———. "The Immorality of Contraception." *American Ecclesiastical Review* 81 (July 1929): 90–2.

Malone, Richard, and John R. Connery *Contemporary Perspectives on Christian Marriage.* Chicago: Loyola University Press, 1984.

Mangan, Joseph T. "Making Moral Choices in Conflict Situations." In *Principles of Catholic Moral Life,* edited by William E. May, 329–58. Chicago: Franciscan Herald Press, 1980.

Marshner, William H. "*Dignitatis Humanae* and Traditional Teaching on Church and State." *Faith & Reason* 9:3 (Fall 1983): 222–48.

Martelet, Gustave. "Mariage, amour, sacrement." *Nouvelle Revue Théologique* 85 (1963): 577–97.

———. "Morale conjugale et vie chrétienne." *Nouvelle Revue Théologique* 87 (1965): 245.

———. *Amour Conjugal et Renouveau Conciliare.* Lyon: Editions Xavier Mayppus, 1967.

———. "*Pour mieux comprendre l'encyclique 'Humanae Vitae'.*" *Nouvelle Revue Théologique* 90 (November 1968): 897–917; (December 1968): 1009–63.

———. "Dix ans après *Humanae Vitae.*" *Nouvelle Revue Théologique* 101 (1979): 246–59.

———. "Essai sur la signification de l'encyclique 'Humanae Vitae'." In *Paul VI et la Modernité dans l'Eglise,* 399–415. Rome: Ecole Française de Rome, 1984.

Mattheeuws, A. "De la Bible à 'Humanae Vitae': Les catéchèses de Jean-Paul II." *Nouvelle Revue Théologique* 111:2 (March/April 1989): 228–48.

May, William E. "The Natural Law and Objective Morality: A Thomistic Perspective." In *Principles of Catholic Moral Life,* 151–90, edited by William E. May. Chicago: Franciscan Herald Press, 1980.

———. *Sex, Marriage, and Chastity: Reflections of a Catholic Layman, Spouse, and Parent.* Chicago: Franciscan Herald Press, 1981.

———. "Church Teaching and the Immorality of Contraception." *Homiletic and Pastoral Review,* January 1982, 9–18.

———. *Contraception and Catholicism.* Common Faith Tract No. 5. Front Royal: Christendom Publications, 1983.

———. " 'Begotten, Not Made': Reflections on the Laboratory Generation of Human Life." In *Perspectives in Bioethics,* edited by Ronald D. Lawler and William E. May. New Britain: Mariel Publications, 1983.

———. *Contraception, "Humanae Vitae," and Catholic Moral Thought.* Chicago: Franciscan Herald Press, 1984.

———. "Aquinas and Janssens on the Moral Meaning of Human Acts." *Thomist* 48 (1984): 566–606.

———. " 'Begotten, Not Made': Further Reflections on the Laboratory Generation of Human Life." *International Review of Natural Family Planning* 10: 1 (Spring 1986): 1–22.

———. "The Sanctity of Human Life, Marriage and the Family in the Thought of Pope John Paul II." *Annales Theologici* 2:1 (1988): 83–97.

———. "Catholic Moral Teaching on In Vitro Fertilization." In *Reproductive*

Technologies, Marriage and the Church, 107–21. Braintree: The Pope John Center, 1988.

———. "The Moral Methodology of Vatican Council II and the Teaching of *Humanae Vitae* and *Persona Humana*." *Anthropotes* 5:1 (1989): 29–45.

———. *Moral Absolutes: Catholic Tradition, Current Trends, and the Truth*. Milwaukee; Marquette University Press, 1989.

———. " 'Humanae Vitae,' Natural Law and Catholic Moral Thought." *Linacre Quarterly* 56 (November 1989): 61–87.

McCabe, Herbert. "Contraceptives and Natural Law." *New Blackfriars* 46 (November 1964): 89–95.

———. "Contraception and Holiness." *New Blackfriars* 46 (February 1965): 294–99.

McCormick, Richard A. "The Council on Contraception." *America* 114 (January 8, 1966): 47–48.

———. "Notes on Moral Theology." *Theological Studies* 29 (December 1968): 373.

———. *Notes on Moral Theology: 1965–1980*. Lanham: University Press of America, 1981.

———. *Notes on Moral Theology 1981–1984*. Lanham: University Press of America, 1984.

———. "Notes on Moral Theology." *Theological Studies* 47 (1986): 85–86.

McDonagh, Enda. "Recent English Literature on the Moral Theology of Marriage." *Concilium* 5 (1965): 130–54.

McHugh, John. "The Doctrinal Authority of the Encyclical 'Humanae Vitae'." *Clergy Review* 54 (1969): 586–96, 680–93, 791–802.

McInerny, Ralph. "Naturalism and Thomistic Ethics." *Thomist* 40:2 (April 1976): 222–42.

———. "The Principles of Natural Law." *American Journal of Jurisprudence* 25 (1980): 1–15.

———. *Ethica Thomistica*. Washington, D.C.: The Catholic University of America Press, 1982.

———. "*Humanae Vitae* and the Judgement of Conscience." In *"Humanae Vitae": 20 Anni Dopo*, 199–209. Milan: Edizioni Ares, 1989.

MacKinnon, Edward. "*Humanae Vitae* and Doctrinal Development." *Continuum* 6 (1968): 269–75.

McLaughlin, Loretta. *The Pill, John Rock, and the Church*. Boston: Little, Brown and Co., 1982.

McMahon, Kevin T. *Sexuality: Theological Voices*. Braintree: The Pope John Center, 1987.

Michael, Robert T. "The Rise in Divorce Rates, 1960–1974: Age Specific Components." *Demography* 15:2 (May 1978): 177–82.

———. "Determinants of Divorce." In *Sociological Economics*, edited by Louis Levy-Garboua, 223–54. London: SAGE Publications, 1979.

———. "Why Did the U.S. Divorce Rate Double Within a Decade." In *Research in Population*, 361–99. Greenwich: JAI Press, 1988.

Milhaven, John Giles. "The Grounds of the Opposition to 'Humanae Vitae'." *Thought* 44:174 (Autumn 1969): 343–57.

———. "Conjugal Sexual Love and Contemporary Moral Theology." *Theological Studies* 35:4 (December 1974): 692–710.

Mosher, Steven W. *Broken Earth: The Rural Chinese.* New York: The Free Press, 1983.

Most, William G. "Religious Liberty: What the Texts Demand." *Faith & Reason* 9:3 (Fall 1983): 196–209.

Mullady, Brian Thomas. *The Meaning of the Term 'Moral' in St. Thomas Aquinas.* Vatican City: Libreria Editrice Vaticana, 1986.

Noonan, John T. "Authority, Usury, and Contraception." *Cross Currents* 16 (Winter 1966): 71–75.

———. *The Church and Contraception: The Issues at Stake.* New York: Paulist Press, 1967.

———. "The Pope's Conscience." *Commonweal* 85 (1967): 559–60.

———. "Natural Law, the Teaching of the Church, and the Regulation of the Rhythm of Human Fecundity." *American Journal of Jurisprudence* 25 (1980): 16–37.

———. "A Prohibition Without a Purpose? Laws That Are Not Norms?: A Rejoinder to Professor Boyle." *American Journal of Jurisprudence* 27 (1982): 14–17.

———. *Contraception.* 1965. Reprint. Cambridge: Belknap, 1986.

———. "Contraception": *Westminster Dictionary of Christian Ethics,* 124–26. Edited by James F. Childress and John MacQuarrie. Philadelphia: Westminster Press, 1986.

Novak, Michael. "Frequent, Even Daily, Communion." In *The Catholic Case for Contraception,* edited by Daniel Callahan, 94–5. London: Macmillan Co., 1969.

———, ed. *The Experience of Marriage.* New York: Macmillan Co., 1964.

O'Brien, John. "Father Haering Speaks on Marriage and Family Planning." *Homiletic and Pastoral Review* 69 (July 1964): 831–41.

O'Callaghan, Denis F. "After the Encyclical." *The Furrow* 19 (1968): 633–41.

Oesterle, John A. *Treatise on Happiness.* Notre Dame: University of Notre Dame Press, 1983.

Omoregbe, Joseph. "Evolution in Bernard Haering's Ethical Thinking." *Louvain Studies* 7 (1978): 45–54.

Parisella, Innocentius. "Latinae Quaedam Voces Locutionesque in Encyclicis Litteris Humanae Vitae Occurentes cum Sermone Italico Comparatae." *Ephemerides Iuris Canonici* 24 (1968): 115–20.

Parmisano, Fabian. "Love and Marriage in the Middle Ages, parts 1 and 2." *New Blackfriars* 50 (1969): 599–608, 649–660.

Paul VI, Pope. "The Year Behind and the Year Ahead." *The Pope Speaks* 9:4 (1964): 355.

———. "Continuing Study of Population Problems." *The Pope Speaks* 10:3 (1965): 225–27.

———. "The Council's View of Marriage and the Family." *The Pope Speaks* 11:1 (1966): 5–12.

———. "Populorum Progressio." *AAS* 59 (1967).

———. "The Genesis of 'Humanae Vitae'." *The Pope Speaks* 13 (1968): 209.

Pius XI, Pope. *Casti Connubii: Encyclical Letter of Pope Pius XI on Christian Marriage.* Boston: St. Paul Editions, 1931.

Pius XII, Pope. "Address to the Congress of the Family Front and of the Association of Large Families." *AAS* 43 (1951).

———. "Speech to the Catholic Union of Midwives." *AAS* 43 (1951): 835–54.

————. "Address to the Twenty-Sixth Congress of the Italian Association of Urology." AAS 45 (1953): 674–75.

————. "International Community and Religious Tolerance." *The Pope Speaks* 1 (1954): 68.

————. "Address to the Leaders and Members of the Italian Association of Cornea Donors and Italian Association for the Blind." AAS (1956).

————. "Speech to the Seventh Congress of the International Society of Hematology." AAS 50 (1958): 446–47.

————. "Address to the Seventh Congress of the International Society of Hematology." AAS 50 (1958): 734–35.

————. *The Major Addresses of Pope Pius XII*, 160–76. St. Paul: The Worth Central Publishing Co., 1961.

Pontifical Council for the Family. *Marriage and the Family*. San Francisco: Ignatius Press, 1989.

Porter, Lawrence. "The Theologian of *Humanae Vitae*." *Thomist* 42:3 (July 1978): 464–509.

————. "Intimacy and Human Sexuality: A Challenge to the Consensus on Contraception." *Communio* 7:3 (Fall 1980): 269–77.

Potts, Timothy C. "The Arguments of *Humanae Vitae*." *Month* 227 (1969): 144–55.

Provan, Charles D. *The Bible and Birth Control*. Monongahela: Zimmer Printing, 1989.

Pyle, Leo. *The Pill and Birth Regulation*. Baltimore: Helicon Press, 1964.

Quay, Paul M. "Contraception and Conjugal Love." *Theological Studies* 22 (March 1961): 18–40.

————. "Morality of Consequences." In *Readings on Moral Theology, No. 1: Moral Norms and Catholic Tradition*, edited by Charles E. Curran and Richard McCormick, 267–93. New York: Paulist Press, 1979.

————. "The Theological Position and the Role of Ethics." *Listening* 18:3 (Fall 1983): 260–74.

————. "The Unity and Structure of the Human Act." *Listening* 18:3 (Fall 1983): 145–59.

————. *The Christian Meaning of Human Sexuality*. Evanston: Credo House, 1985.

————. "The Disvalue of Ontic Evil." *Theological Studies* 46 (1985): 262–86.

Rahner, Karl. "On the Encyclical 'Humanae Vitae'." *Catholic Mind* 66 (November 1968): 28–45.

Ratzinger, Joseph. "Man Between Reproduction and Creation: Theological Questions on the Origin of Human Life." *Communio* (Summer 1989): 197–211.

Reich, Warren. "The Pill after Childbirth." *Homiletic and Pastoral Review* 66:8 (May 1966): 661–68.

Reuss, J. M. "Eheliche Hingave und Zeugung." *Tubinger theologische Quartalschrift* 143 (1963): 454–76.

Rhonheimer, Martin. "Contraception, Sexual Behavior, and Natural Law." *Linacre Quarterly*, May 1989, 20–57.

Ricci, Tommaso. "The 163 Rebels of Cologne." *Thirty Days* 2 (March 1989): 20–21.

Rigali, Norbert. "The Historical Meaning of the *Humanae Vitae* Controversy." *Chicago Studies* 15 (1976): 127–38.

———. "Dialogue with Richard McCormick." *Chicago Studies* 16 (1977) 299–308.

———. "Artificial Birth Control: An Impasse Revisited." *Theological Studies* 47 (1986): 681–90.

Roberts, Thomas D. *Contraception and Holiness.* New York: Herder and Herder, 1964.

Rock, John. *The Time Has Come: A Catholic Doctor's Proposal to End the Battle over Birth Control.* New York: Alfred A.Knopf, 1963.

Rouche, Michel. "La préparation de l'encyclique 'Humanae Vitae'." In *Paul VI et la Modernité dans l'Eglise,* 361–83. Rome: Palais Farnese, 1984.

Ryan, John A. "The Immorality of Contraception." *American Ecclesiastical Review* 79 (October 1928): 408–11.

Rynne, Xavier. *The Fourth Session.* London: Faber and Faber, 1966.

Schillebeeckx, E. *Marriage: Human Reality and Saving Mystery.* New York: Sheed and Ward, 1965.

Seaman, Barbara. *The Doctors' Case Against the Pill.* New York: Doubleday, 1980.

Shanley, Brian. "The Moral Difference Between Natural Family Planning and Contraception." *Linacre Quarterly* 54:1 (1987): 48–60.

Shannon, William H. *The Lively Debate: Response to Humanae Vitae.* New York: Sheed and Ward, 1970.

Shaw, Russell. "Contraception, Infallibility and the Ordinary Magisterium." *Homiletic and Pastoral Review* 78 (1978): 9–19.

Siegle, Bernard A. *Marriage According to the New Code of Canon Law.* New York: Alba House, 1986.

Simon, Julian. *The Ultimate Resource.* Princeton: Princeton University Press, 1981.

Smith, Janet E. "Pope John Paul II and *Humanae Vitae*." *International Review of Natural Family Planning* 10:2 (Summer 1986): 95–112.

———. " 'The Many Faces of AIDS' and the Toleration of the Lesser Evil." *The International Review of Natural Family Planning* 12:1 (Spring 1988): 1–15.

———. "Humanae Vitae at 20." *Crisis* 6:6 (June 1988): 14–21.

———. "Humanae Vitae: A Prophetic Document." *Crisis* 6:8 (September 1988): 30–35.

———. "The Importance of the Concept of 'Munus' to Understanding 'Humanae Vitae'." In *Humanae Vitae: 20 Anni Dopo,* 677–90. Milan: Edizioni Ares, 1989.

———. "The *Munus* of Transmitting Human Life: A New Approach to *Humanae Vitae.*" *Thomist* 54 (July 1990): 385–427.

Sokolowski, Robert. "Knowing Natural Law." *Tijdschrift voor filosofie* 43 (1981): 625–41.

Suenens, Leon Joseph. *Love and Control: The Contemporary Problem.* Translated by George J. Robinson. Westminster: The Newman Press, 1961.

Sullivan, Francis A. *Magisterium: Teaching Authority in the Catholic Church,* 119–52. New York: Paulist Press, 1983.

Thomas Aquinas. "*Summa Theologiae* I-II, 94, article 2." In *Basic Writings of Saint Thomas Aquinas,* edited by Anton Pegis. New York: Random House, 1945.

Thomas, John L. "What Did the Council Say on Contraception?" *America* 114 (February 26, 1966): 294–96.

Uricchio, William A., ed. *Proceedings of a Research Conference on Natural Family Planning.* Washington, D.C.: Human Life Foundation, 1973.

Vacek, Edward V. "Proportionalism: One View of the Debate." *Theological Studies* 46 (1985): 287–314.

Valsecchi, Ambrogio. *Controversy: The Birth Control Debate 1958–1968.* Translated by Dorothy White. Washington, D.C.: Corpus Books, 1968.

van der Marck, W. H. M. "Vruchtbaarheidsregeling: poging tot antwoord op een nog open vraag." *Tijdshrift voor theologie* 3 (1963): 378–413.

———. *Love and Fertility.* New York: Sheed and Ward, 1965.

———. "Toward a Renewal of the Theology of Marriage." *Thomist* 30:4 (October 1966): 307–42.

———. *In Defense of Purity.* London: Sheed and Ward, 1931.

von Hildebrand, Dietrich. *The Encyclical Humanae Vitae: A Sign of Contradiction.* Chicago: Franciscan Herald Press, 1969.

Wattenburg, Ben. *The Birth Dearth.* New York: Pharos Books, 1987.

Weber, Leonhard. "Excursus on *Humanae Vitae.*" In *Commentary on the Documents of Vatican II*, vol. 5, edited by Herbert Vorgrimler, 397–402. New York: Herder and Herder, 1969.

Wenisch, Ernst. *Elternschaft und Menschenwuerde.* Vallendar-Schoenstatt: Patris Verlag, 1984.

Wiltgen, Ralph M. *The Rhine Flows into the Tiber.* Rockford: Tan Books, 1967.

Wojcik, Elzbieta. "Natural Regulation of Conception and Contraception." *International Review of Natural Family Planning* 9:4 (Winter 1985): 306–26.

Wojtyla, Karol. "Les fondements de la doctrine de l'église concernant les principes de la vie conjugale." *Analecta Cracoviensia* 1 (1969): 194–230.

———. "La visione antropologica dell' 'Humanae Vitae'." *Lateranum* 44 (1978): 125–45.

———. *The Acting Person.* Translated by Andrzej Potocki. Boston: Reidel, 1979.

———. *Fruitful and Responsible Love.* New York: Seabury Press, 1979.

———. *Sources of Renewal.* Translated by P. S. Falla. San Francisco: Harper and Row, 1980.

Yzermans, Vincent A. *The Major Addresses of Pope Pius XII.* St. Paul: Worth Central, 1961.

Index

abortion, 321, 328, 382n14; and China, 364; mentioned in *Humanae Vitae*, 285
abstinence, 308–9, 319
Anglican position on contraception, 5
anovulant pills: truly contraceptive? 9, 374n40
Anscombe, Elizabeth, 82, 122, 125, 382n7
Apostolicam Actuositatem, 334
Aquinas, 195–98, 357; analysis of moral action, 215–21; and natural law, 70, 173, 318; and the creation of the human soul, 102; contraception against nature, 4; ends of marriage, 51; moral character, 226–27; on conjugal love, 60
Aristotle: meaning of "primary," 49
Arrupe, Pedro, 163
Augustine, 372n6; conjugal love, 54, 56; ends of marriage, 4, 42

biologism, 88; *see* physicalism
Boyle, Joseph, 227, 340; contraception is contralife, 105; list of articles, 387n11; *see* Appendix 4
Burke, Cormac, 110, 115

Cafarra, Carlo, 104, 386nn6,10
Cahill, Lisa, 199, 208, 209, 221–23, 400n4; on John Paul II, 258
canon law, 47, 310–11; canon 1134, 39
Casti Connubii, 5, 14; cited, 6, 38, 39, 42, 44, 46, 47, 56, 66, 83, 84, 109, 171, 195, 300, 304, 307, 322, 324, 354; Majority Rebuttal, 23, 32; use of infertile period, 6, 372n17
Catechism of the Council of Trent, 48, 322; and HV 4, 302
Catholic Church: as teacher, 287–88, 330; authority of, 16–18; the people are the Church, 16
chastity, 235, 289, 331
children: a gift, 36, 42, 319; as bond in marriage, 117; proper number to have,

64, 320; *see* procreation as primary end of marriage
Church teaching against contraception: changeable, 16; constancy of, 15, 32; history of, 3; Majority Rebuttal, 17; Minority Report, 17
conjugal love, 54–57, 107–8; and *Gaudium et Spes*, 62, 64, 66; and HV12, 109; and HV9, 108, 314–16; and mutual perfection, 56; and mutual self-giving, 108–16; and romantic love, 55, 61; definition of, 55; history of Church teaching, 59; not sufficiently recognized by church, 37, 59–60
Connell, Richard, 87, 384n31
conscience, 148–55; Austrian bishops, 149–50; Canadian bishops, 148–49, 150, 153; Church teaching, 151–53; French bishops, 148; *Gaudium et Spes*, 152; *Humanae Vitae*, 148; Irish bishops, 155; John Henry Newman, 154–55, 393n32; U.S. bishops, 149, 154, 392n32
contraception as artificial argument, 86–87
contraception as contralife argument, 105–7; *see* Appendix 4
contraception: a matter of practical doubt, 9; and perverse sexual acts, 27; and the principle of probabilism, 311; as abortifacient, 77, 321, 383n14; as artificial, 86; as homicide, 4, 101–2, 105, 386n6; as intrinsic evil, 83–85, 358; as unnatural, 85; Church's condemnation of, 307–11; consequences of, 285–87, 328–29; definition of, xiii, 77, 276nj, 381n1; difference from natural family planning, 118–28; and divorce, 127; history of Christian condemnation of, 3–7; licitness of use of infertile period, 7; literature on, 373n31; natural law and *Humanae Vitae*, 77; natural law arguments against, 98 (*see* natural law); perverted faculty argument (*see* perverted faculty